On the Wo

Alice Hart-Davis was born in Wales and grew up on a farm in the Chilterns. She studied history at Oxford University, and went on to work at *Vogue*. In 1987, she joined the *Telegraph* Magazine, where she edited the Shop Front section for two years before moving on to more diverse projects. She now works for the *Sunday Telegraph*.

Fontana Non-Fiction

Fontana is a leading paperback publisher of non-fiction. Below are some recent titles.

One Summer's Grace

A Family Voyage Round Britain

Libby Purves

In the summer of 1988 Libby Purves and her husband Paul Heiney set sail in their cutter *Grace O'Malley* with their children Nicholas, aged five, and Rose, three. They sailed the 1,700 miles around Britain, from the offshore labyrinths of the sandy south-east to the towering stacks of Cape Wrath and back home through the North Sea. Her account of the voyage is a new classic of the sea.

'It is that rarest of all books on the yachting shelf – a work of acerbic realism. Libby Purves is wonderfully sharp on the woes of containing a marriage and a family inside their pressure-cooker of a small boat. Her portrait of coastal Britain in the 1980s is wise, affectionate and sceptical; her pleasure in our scary seas rings true because there is not a word of cant or overstatement in her story. This is how it is – and Miss Purves tells it beautifully'

Jonathan Raban

'A delightful book, warm, wise and candid'   *Sunday Telegraph*

Fontana

On the Waterfront 1993

Edited by
Alice Hart-Davis

Researchers: Andrew Baker, Michèle Batcabe,
Sarah Bradnock, Emilia Bulman, Penelope Gibbs,
Guy Hart-Davis, Vanessa Horne, Rachel Perkins,
David Prout, Elizabeth Sackville-West, Jane Schofield,
Nicci Selby, Mark Swallow, Kate Valentine,
Gareth Williams and Rupert Winchester

With new contributions from: Paddy Burt,
Gill Charlton, Mike Gerrard, Penny Lewis,
John Morgan, Peter Orr, Erik Russell
and Martin Symington

Fontana
An Imprint of HarperCollins*Publishers*

Fontana
An Imprint of HarperCollins*Publishers*
77–85 Fulham Palace Road,
Hammersmith, London W6 8JB

A Fontana Original 1991
Third edition with revisions 1993
9 8 7 6 5 4 3 2 1

A catalogue record for this book
is available from the British Library

ISBN 0 00 673937 0

Printed and bound in Great Britain by
HarperCollinsManufacturing Glasgow

Grateful acknowledgement is made to the following for
permission to reproduce their photographs:
Tom Dobbie: The Waterfront Wine Bar, Portmeirion Hotel,
New Hall Hotel; John Higginson: The River House Restaurant,
The Butt and Oyster Pub, Waterton Park Hotel, Kirkby
Fleetham Hall; Erik Russell: Eddrachilles Hotel, Green Park
Hotel, Altnaharrie Inn; Jeremy Young: Warehouse Oyster Bar,
The Royal Oak, St Michael's Manor House, The Trout Inn,
Black Jack's Mill, The Old Manse Hotel, The Pump House,
Watermill Coffee Shop

Contents

Notes for Readers

Booking is advisable for all hotels and restaurants. You should specify water-view rooms when booking – some hotels add a small surcharge for these. Many hotels and guest houses offer special rates for weekend breaks. Many places have disabled access, but few have full disabled facilities: telephone before you visit to check on specific points. Unless stated otherwise, hotels and pubs with accommodation have dining facilities for residents. Non-resident diners are welcome at many hotels. All establishments can cater for vegetarians, though smaller hotels may need advance notice. You are advised to check when booking. Pub hours given are for summer opening; winter opening hours may be shorter. All establishments have been visited to ensure that their situation is memorable. Readers are advised that this is a selective guide. The researchers did not eat or stay at the establishments mentioned, nor did they accept free hospitality. All information and prices correct at time of going to press.

Symbols

- 🏨 Hotel
- 🍴 Restaurant
- 🍺 Public house
- **inn** Inn (a pub with accommodation)
- $\frac{5/10}{\approx}$ Five out of 10 bedrooms have a view of the water
- Children welcome
- No children
- $_5$ Only children aged five and over welcome
- Dogs/pets welcome
- No dogs/pets
- One or more of the major credit cards are accepted
- No credit cards accepted
- Disabled access
- No access for the disabled

The South-west

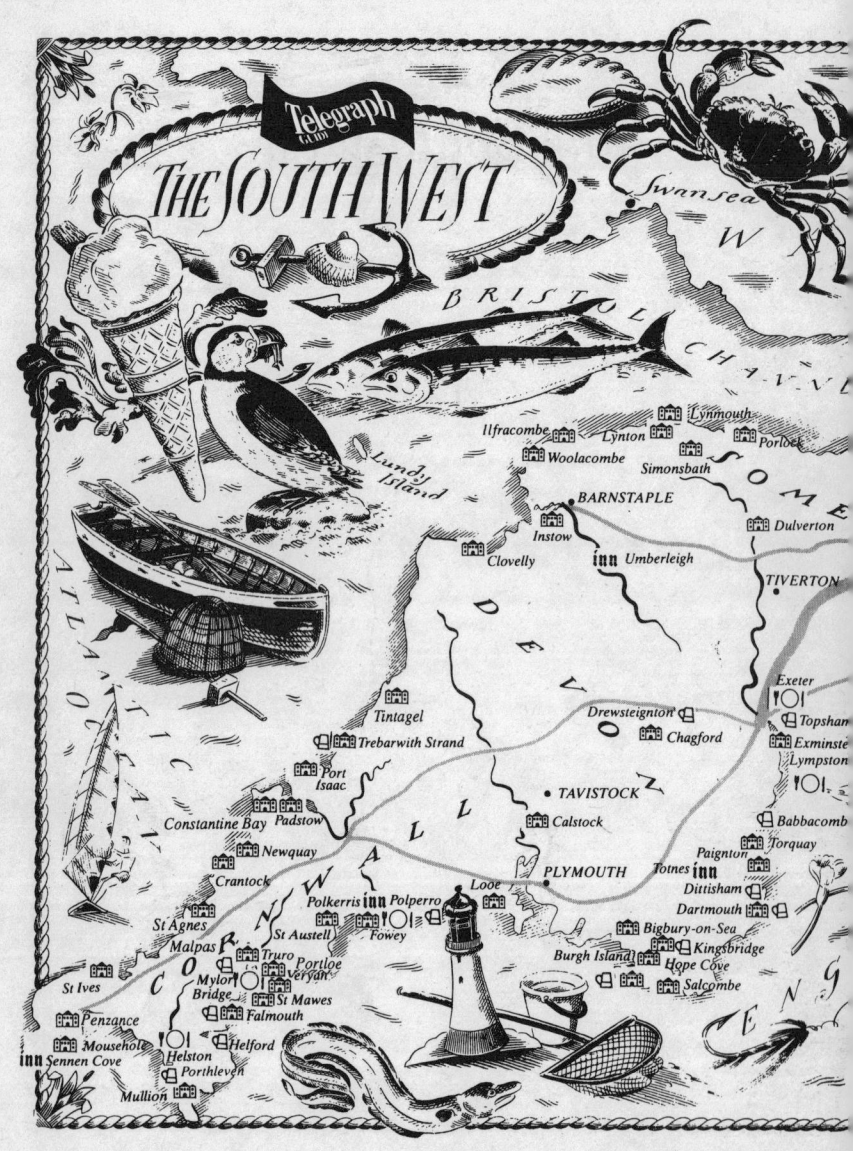

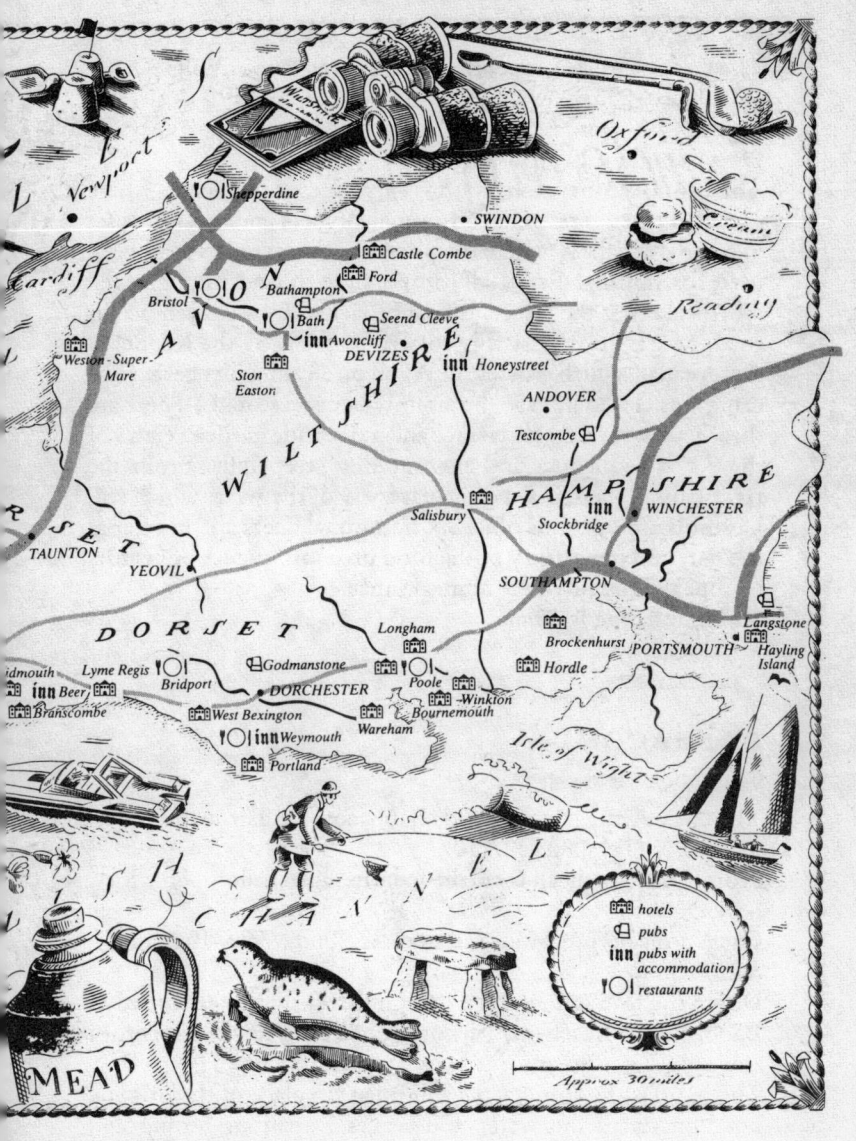

Newport
Shepperdine
SWINDON
Cardiff
Castle Combe
Bristol
AVON
Bathampton
Ford
Reading
Bath
Seend Cleeve
Avoncliff
Weston-Super-Mare
DEVIZES
Honeystreet
Ston Easton
WILTSHIRE
ANDOVER
Testcombe
HAMPSHIRE
Salisbury
WINCHESTER
TAUNTON
Stockbridge
YEOVIL
SOUTHAMPTON
DORSET
Longham
Langstone
Brockenhurst
PORTSMOUTH
Hayling Island
idmouth
Lyme Regis
Godmanstone
Hordle
Beer
Bridport
Poole
Branscombe
DORCHESTER
Winkton
West Bexington
Bournemouth
Weymouth
Wareham
Portland
Isle of Wight

CHANNEL

MEAD

hotels
pubs
inn pubs with accommodation
restaurants

Approx 30 miles

AVONCLIFF

inn ≋³/³ 🏠 🚭 ⌁ 💳

The Cross Guns, Avoncliff, Bradford-on-Avon, Wilts
(Tel. 02216 2335)
Open 11am–3pm, 6.30pm–11pm all week
£16 pp single, £20 pp double b&b
This 16th-century inn is the only one in England where
a road, a river, a railway and a canal all meet and cross; it is set
in a narrow valley, where the power of the river has long been
used for milling. Practically impossible to find, though well
worth making the effort, it is approached by a perpendicular
road. Much the easiest way to arrive here is by the Kennet &
Avon canal, which crosses the Avon on an aqueduct here. (The
canal was closed in 1956, but is now being restored.) There are
three levels of riverside terrace and a riverside garden, views of
the Avon, aqueduct and surrounding steep hills. From the
river banks, there is a spectacular view of the weir, which still
has mills at both ends of it. Six traditional beers are on offer at
the bar, and the quality of the food prompts queues of visitors
to appear from nowhere at meal times.
Walks; watersports; fishing

BABBACOMBE

🍺 ≋⁴/⁴ 🏠 🚭 ⌁ 🛏

The Cary Arms, Beach Road, Babbacombe, Torquay
TQ1 3LX (Tel. 0803 327110)
From Torquay, head for Babbacombe, then follow signs for
beach
Open noon–11pm Mon–Sat; noon–2.30pm, 7pm–10.30pm
Sun
Down the fearsomely steep (one in three) single-track road to
Babbacombe Beach (car park at the bottom), this 18th-century
smuggling house has a fine view over the beach and Lyme Bay.
The bar has the stone walls and open fireplace of the original
building, faces the water and serves Dartmoor Strong and
Dartmoor Best. Extensive terraced garden overlooks beach

and bay. Bar meals are available at lunchtime, and can be eaten out at the seaside tables.
Beach a few yards away; fishing, pedal-boats and motorboats all nearby

BATH

IOI 🏠 ✂ ◁ ▱

Bath Puppet Theatre, Riverside Walk, Pulteney Bridge,
Bath (Tel. 0225 312 173)
Open 9.30am–6pm, later in summer
This excellent puppet-theatre-cum-coffee-shop looks directly on to the Avon and the weir beneath Pulteney Bridge, right in the centre of Bath. Puppet shows are held at 3.30pm on Saturdays and daily during school holidays (it is advisable to telephone in advance to check when the shows are on). The coffee shop has room for up to 40 people and serves tea, cakes and wholesome snacks. Most of the inside tables have a view of the water; in summer, go for two tables outside. A delightful and unusual place.
Small maze nearby (a favourite attraction with children); canal; boat trips; car park five minutes away

BATHAMPTON

▱ 🏠 ✂ ◁ ▱

The George Inn, Mill Lane, Bathampton, Bath BA2 6TR
(Tel. 0225 425 079)
Off A36 Warminster Road in village of Bathampton; or over tollbridge
Open 11am–2.30pm, 6pm–11pm Mon–Sat; noon–3pm, 7pm–10.30pm Sun
An attractive, creeper-clad 15th-century inn by the Kennet & Avon canal. There are two gardens, one enclosed and one looking on to the water and towpath. A charming place, and genuinely 'olde worlde'. Inside is beamed and cosy, with views of water from first floor and family room. The menu of snacks

includes four or five daily specials, but no chips. No bookings taken.
Walks along towpaths to Bath and Devizes

BEER
inn 6/8

The Anchor Inn, Fore Street, Beer, East Devon
(Tel. 0297 20386)
Open 11am–11pm
£24–£32 pp b&b
A traditional small inn, situated at the top of the slipway down to the beach in a quaint seaside village. The accommodation is comfortable and unpretentious, with fitted furniture and floral fabrics. Most of the rooms have good sea views, and you can watch the fishing boats in the harbour from the pub garden. The bar serves a range of traditional ales; bar meals are available, and there is a full menu on offer in the restaurant, with seafood a speciality.
Beer beach is small and primarily a working beach, but motorboats, deck chairs and beach huts can be hired, and fishing trips can be arranged. Cliff walks recommended for the energetic; golf, riding, squash and scuba diving can all be found nearby

BIGBURY-ON-SEA
6/8

Henley Hotel, Folly Hill, Bigbury-on-Sea, Devon TQ7 4AR
(Tel. 0548 810240)
At the coast end of the B3392
£20.95–£23 pp b&b
The hotel looks out from its cliff top across the mouth of the Avon estuary. The view is very spectacular, and Turner is said to have painted it; certainly the Long Stone, a high landmark at the end of the beach, can be found in one of his works. The dining room is open to non-residents and seats up to 20; two window tables look out to sea. A non-smoking establishment.

Fishing off the steps at high tide; watersports at the beach; diving (mostly professional) nearby; coastal path walks. Private cliff path of 127 steps leads down to the beach (the road offers a gentler descent)

BOURNEMOUTH

🏨 ⁸⁰/¹³¹ 🛏 🍷 🚫 💳

Royal Bath Hotel, Bath Road, Bournemouth BH1 2EW
(Tel. 0202 555 555)
£91.50–£280 per room
Situated in the town centre near the pier, this large, five-star Victorian hotel owes some architectural debt to the Brighton Pavilion, especially on the inside. There is a first-rate leisure club, 'The Leisure Pavilion', in the grounds, which is open to residents from 7.30 am–10.30 pm. The hotel's five-star rating is evident in the high-quality decor, and the staff's willingness to arrange activities and excursions for visitors. Separated from the sea by three acres of gardens, the hotel has good, but not spectacular, views over Poole Bay. Oscar's Restaurant (à la carte, and inside the hotel) seats 65–70 people; a set lunch costs £14.50, a three-course dinner £24. Teas are served in the main lounge (£5.50). Full conference and banqueting facilities are available. The hotel has some ground-floor bedrooms but no special facilities for the disabled.
Nearby theatres, sailing, fishing, three golf clubs, cinemas, water-skiing, horse riding, ice skating

BRANSCOMBE

🏨 ⁶/⁶ 🛏 🍷 ⟨⟩ 💳

The Look Out, Branscombe (near Lyme Regis), Devon EX12 3DP   (Tel. 029780 262)
From Branscombe, approach through the shallow ford between two 'Private: Access Only' signs, then follow the cliff-side drive to the hotel.
£50 single, £80–£82 double
The perfect, 'away-from-it-all' location; rugged, beautiful and highly photogenic. Six coastguards' cottages perched on the

side of a cliff have been converted into a small private hotel with superb unspoilt views over Lyme Bay. Branscombe is picturesque and popular, and the beach is packed in summer, though guests, up on their private terrace, are well away from all of this. The conversion has managed to retain much of the cottages' original charm and provides personal and intimate surroundings among good antique and period furniture. The restaurant seats 24 people – with no water views, and open for dinner only – non-residents are welcome.

Coastal path walks; beach; windsurfing; fishing; boats for hire

BRIDPORT

IOI 🏠 👌 ⬦ ▭

Riverside Café and Restaurant, West Bay, Bridport, Dorset DT6 4EZ   (Tel. 0308 22011)
On island across footbridge in centre of village
Open 10.30am–3.30pm; 6.30pm–8.30pm; closed Monday, and generally closed from November to March (Telephone to check first)

Popular eating place specializing in ultra-fresh seafood, located on a small island where the River Brit meets the harbour. West Bay may not appear to embody the best aspects of the Great British seaside, but this restaurant is well worth a detour if you happen to be in the area: the Watsons' cooking and service merits an enthusiastic entry in *The Good Food Guide*. The restaurant seats 80, nearly all tables look out at the water. Tables can be booked (at a small charge) in the restaurant; the café is self-service. Pets are welcome as long as they have not just been for a swim in the sea or the river. There are ramps to all areas for disabled visitors.

Beach nearby; walks; watersports; fishing

BRISTOL

IOI 🏠 ♿ ✍ 💳

Arnolfini Café Restaurant, 16 Narrow Quay, Bristol
BS1 4QA   (Tel. 0272 279330)
Next door to the Bristol Tourist Information Centre
Open 10am–11pm Mon–Sat; noon–10.30pm Sun
This sleek and popular café, with its etched glass and steel interior, has established itself in an arts complex converted from dockside warehouse. The late-eighties designer atmosphere is enhanced by the 180 different spirits on offer at the bar. There is seating for up to 60 people, and tables provide good views of Narrow Quay. There are also four picnic tables outside by the quay. Creative light meals include soups, salads and cakes. Beside the spot where the Kennet & Avon canal joins the sea, there are moorings for those arriving by canal boat or yacht. A new section of the canal has opened recently, joining Bristol to Bath and London. The bar and a small dining area are on the ground floor, but there are no special facilities for the disabled.
Walks; 15-minute walk to watersports

BRISTOL

IOI 🏠 ♿ ✍ 💳

The Glass Boat Restaurant, Welsh Back, Bristol BS1 4SS
(Tel. 0272 290 704)
At the Bristol Bridge end of Welsh Back and Baldwin Street
Open 7.30am–10am, noon–2.30pm, 6.30pm–10.30pm Mon–Fri; 6.30pm–11pm Sat; noon–2.30pm, 6.30pm–10pm Sun
A converted boat resting at the dockside in the heart of Bristol. Most of the 70 seats in upper-deck restaurant command fine water views. (There is a wine bar on the lower deck, though this is now only used for functions.) The cuisine is French/ Continental. High chairs can be provided for children.
Walks; watersports; fishing; boat trips 100 yards along quay

BROCKENHURST

🏨 ⁴/₂₃ 🚣 ♿ ⌖ 💳

Master Builder's House Hotel, Buckler's Hard, Beaulieu,
Brockenhurst, Hants   (Tel. 0590 616253)
From Beaulieu, follow signs to Brockenhurst Maritime
Museum
£55 single, £75 double, £95 four poster
Attractive hotel gardens slope down to the wide curve of the
River Beaulieu and an exclusive marina where many yachts are
moored. The hotel was once a master ship-builder's home –
hence the name. There are tasteful rooms in the Old Wing,
with views of the river and film-set-pretty village: some have
four-poster beds. Avoid rooms in the new wing which mostly
have views of the car park. Almost all of the tables in the smart
restaurant have a view of the river, and there is also a restaurant
terrace which overlooks the water (the table d'hôte dinner
costs £12). Watch out, when approaching, for the New Forest
ponies that wander freely across the roads. There are some
ground-floor rooms, and ramps, though no specific facilities
for the disabled.

BURGH ISLAND

🏨 ¹⁶/₁₆ 🚣 ♿ 🚫 💳

Burgh Island Hotel, Burgh Island, Bigbury-on-Sea,
South Devon TQ7 4AU   (Tel. 0548 810 514)
Open all year
Suites £65–£90 pp for dinner and b&b
This unique Art Deco hotel was famous in the twenties and
thirties, and has recently been restored to its former, full-
blown glory by Tony and Beatrice Porter. Telephone from the
mainland, and you can be fetched across to the island by Land
Rover at low tide, or by the giant sea-tractor at high tide. All of
the accommodation is in suites of rooms with sea views (the
finest suites have sea views on two sides), and there is a helipad
for high-flying arrivals. The chef and pastry chef are Roux
brothers trained; their classic French cuisine features fresh local
produce, and in summer island-caught shellfish. Jackets and

ties are required at dinner. Some suites are served by a lift, but there are no special facilities for the disabled.
Watersports; windsurfers and diving boats for hire nearby; indoor exercise machines; bird sanctuary; tennis on the island; golf on the mainland

BURGH ISLAND

Pilchard Inn, Burgh Island, Bigbury-on-Sea, South Devon
TQ7 4AU   (Tel. 0548 810 344)
Open in spring and summer 11am–11pm Mon–Sat; noon–3pm, 7pm–10pm Sun. In autumn and winter 11am–3pm, 6.30pm–11pm Mon–Sat; noon–3pm, 7pm–10pm Sun
If you want to make a day trip to Burgh Island, you can visit the Pilchard Inn. This pub dates from 1336, and is run by the Burgh Island hotel: it is the only other building on the island. The pub has two bars overlooking the water, and a waterside garden; Ruddles, Ushers Best, and draught cider are on offer. Bar snacks are available at lunch and in the evenings.
Walks on the island or around the coast; watersports; fishing; beaches on mainland

CALSTOCK

Danescombe Valley Hotel, Lower Kelly, Calstock, Cornwall
PL18 9RY   (Tel. 0822 832414)
Half mile west of Calstock Village, along River Road
Open Easter to end October
£79.50 pp per night (inc. four-course dinner and breakfast)
Set on a sweeping bend of the River Tamar, this beautiful, Grade II listed house was built for Lord Ashburton in 1850. An extremely tranquil place to stay, thanks to the absence of televisions and small children. A slate-floored bar leads out to a terrace with panoramic river views. Even more impressive than the setting and the rooms is the food, cooked by Anna

Smith and widely praised. Guests present themselves for dinner each evening at 7.30 for 8pm, and are served four-course 'West Country' dinners. Four of the tables in the dining room look on to the river. (Only two non-residents can be accommodated for dinner each evening.)

Canoeing nearby; riverboat rides from Calstock village; National Maritime Museum nearby; Cotehele House (National Trust property) is a 15-minute walk away

CASTLE COMBE

25/36

The Manor House, Castle Combe, Chippenham, Wilts
(Tel. 0249 782206)
Off B3049
£95–£250 per room b&b

Situated in the beautiful village of Castle Combe, this hotel is a splendid 17th-century manor house, festooned with creepers. The public rooms are large, light, tastefully decorated, and most have lovely views of the lawns, the valley and the river Bybrook – the bedrooms are even better. There is also a cottage in the grounds for guests. Though the river is not the focal point of the place, it is always there in the background. The dining room seats 110. Non-residents can savour the atmosphere and the surroundings by dropping in for tea in the panelled lounge or, in fine weather, out on the lawn. There are some ground-floor rooms, though no specific facilities for the disabled.

Fly fishing (hotel provides rods); riverside walks; riding; croquet; tennis; heated outdoor swimming pool; helipad

CHAGFORD

9/14

Gidleigh Park, Chagford, Devon TQ13 8HH
(Tel. 0647 432367)
Two miles from village of Chagford; telephone for directions
£205–£350 double occupancy, dinner and b&b; cottage, £425 for two guests; £510 for four

An extremely luxurious and relaxing country-house hotel (Relais et Chateaux member), set in 40 acres of secluded grounds inside the Dartmoor National Park. The River Teign has been landscaped and re-routed directly in front of the house: a pleasant but not dramatic water view. Great attention is paid to all those small details that make the visitor feel at home, but not overwhelmed. Gidleigh Park was decreed Egon Ronay Hotel of the Year 1990, and in 1989 received the César award for the most sumptuous traditional country-house hotel. The highly praised restaurant seats 40 (three tables have a water view). Pets are allowed, though only in owners' bedrooms. Children are welcome, but only if they behave themselves.

Three croquet lawns; all-weather tennis court; bowling green. Plenty of scope for walking; fishing and riding can be arranged

CHAGFORD

Mill End Hotel, Sandy Park, Chagford, Devon TQ13 8JN
(Tel. 0647 432282)
Exeter–Okehampton Road (A30) to Whiddon Down, then A382 to hotel
£45–£72 per room
Log fires, comfortable public rooms, and lots of nooks and crannies make the Mill End a peaceful spot with an olde worlde feel. A former flour mill, the hotel rests on the bank of the River Teign at the head of Fingle Gorge. All bedrooms have fine views of the river valley, though only two look directly over the water. The courtyard and working water-wheel form a pleasant tableau for diners in the 40-seat restaurant; three tables have a river view. The hotel runs special wine and food weekends (gourmet menus and accommodation for two people for two nights costs £275), and is also very strong on fishing: rods can be hired, and a ghillie is on call for guidance on the river. The bar, dining room and some bedrooms are on the ground floor, but there are no special facilities for the disabled.

Six miles of salmon and seatrout fishing on River Teign; trout fishing on reservoir and golf nearby; swimming; tennis; shooting; riding; Castle Drogo and other National Trust properties nearby

CLOVELLY

Red Lion Hotel, Clovelly, Devon EX39 5TS
(Tel. 0237 431237)
Off the A39 between Bude and Bideford
£27.50 b&b
The hotel sits on the very steep hill that descends through the picturesque village to the pebble beach and quay. Small, old, traditional, unassuming, and a good place to eat if visiting Clovelly: the dining room seats 40, and four tables overlook the water. A pleasant place to stay. Recent refurbishment has left all bedrooms more comfortable and with *en suite* bathrooms (there is one *en suite* family room).
Good walks; sea fishing; riding, surfing, golf and safe beach nearby

CONSTANTINE BAY

Treglos Hotel, Constantine Bay, near Padstow, Cornwall
PL28 8HJ   (Tel. 0841 520727)
Open mid–March–end October
Half–board only; £52–£67 per person depending on season
Guests return year after year to this comfortable whitewashed hotel which stands in its own grounds facing the sea. The bedrooms and suites are wonderfully light and airy and tastefully decorated in peaches and greens. A few have seaview balconies. There is an attractive heated indoor pool and Jacuzzi, and the patio overlooking the bay is a popular place for tea or an early evening drink. The restaurant offers good English and French cooking with an extensive hors d'oeuvre buffet followed by soup, roasts and fresh fish. Jacket and tie is required for dinner. Non–residents should make reservations. The seven–course table d'hôte dinner costs £18; last orders at 9pm. There is wheelchair access to several rooms in the hotel, and a lift.
One of Cornwall's finest beaches, good for surfing and sandy rock pools for children, is a five-minute stroll away; Constantine Bay golf course

CRANTOCK

Crantock Bay Hotel, Crantock, Newquay, Cornwall
TR8 5SE   (Tel. 0637 830229)
From A3075, head for Crantock, then West Pentire
Open March–November
£38.50–£50 pp dinner and b&b
Traditional seaside hotel, with gardens that run down to the western end of the beautiful, sandy Crantock Beach. The setting is tranquil, and the views across the bay are fabulous. Most tables in the dining room look out to sea, and so does the bar. Visible in the bay is the Goose (a rocky island, and a target for intrepid swimmers). The hotel boasts a new extension complete with a games room, indoor pool (free to non-residents if they have a meal), sauna, sun terrace and croquet lawn.
Outdoor tennis court; hotel boat available for water skiing; windsurfing at Newquay (3 miles); rock fishing, freshwater fishing on inland waterways and reservoir; walks on (ubiquitous) coastal path; exercise room and putting green at hotel

DARTMOUTH

Carved Angel, 2 South Embankment, Dartmouth, Devon
TQ6 9BH   (Tel. 0803 83 2465)
In the middle of town, opposite the passenger ferry
Open for lunch 12.30pm–1.45pm Tues–Sun, and for dinner 7.30pm–9.30pm Tues–Sat
Closed in January and the first two weeks of February
This highly rated restaurant looks across the road and a broad promenade to the River Dart. There is seating for 55 people; five of the tables have a direct view of the river; six more look on to the quayside scene of boats, ferry and promenade. There are wide picture windows on the ground floor; the outlook is better from upstairs, from where there are splendid views down to the mouth of the river. One room upstairs can be booked for private parties. The cooking is described as 'modern English' – fish,

shellfish, poultry, meat and game all find their way on to the menu, and the emphasis is on using local produce, depending on the season. The set menu at lunch costs £21–£25; set dinner is £34–£39 for three courses, plus sorbet, cheese, petits fours, and coffee. Sunday lunch £28. The ground-floor dining room is up two steps, and the lavatories are on the first floor.

Fishing, rowing and sailing can be found in the vicinity; there is a yacht club nearby, a marina ten minutes' walk up the road, and boat trips leave from the promenade

DARTMOUTH

🏨 10/24 ♿ ⚡ 🐾 ▭

Royal Castle Hotel, The Quay, Dartmouth, Devon TQ6 9PS (Tel. 0803 83 3033)
£37–£49 pp b&b

Dating from the 16th century, this listed building on the quay is bursting with character. The façade is Regency and crenellated but the core of the hotel is an old coaching inn, popular as a location for films and television drama. There are open log fires, antique furnishings and several four-poster beds (three with a water view). The two bars just overlook the water and have a good atmosphere (locals, lots of dogs) and serve local beers. The Galleon lounge serves lunch, cream teas, and bar snacks. The first-floor restaurant specializes in seafood, and has the same view (slightly better because of the elevation); it seats 60, and five tables look on to the river.

Sailing; fishing; hotel can arrange watersports; walks to Castle and on coastal path; riding and golf nearby

DARTMOUTH

🏨 3/3 ♿10 ⚡ 🐾 ▭

Wavenden House, Compass Cove, Dartmouth, Devon TQ6 0JN   (Tel. 0803 83 3979)
Off the A379, Dartmouth–Kingsbridge
£17 pp b&b (four-course dinner £12)

A gem of a hideaway, set in an isolated position on the clifftop, on the site of a gun emplacement (to ward off the Spaniards, French, Germans, etc.) and so with a marvellous view of the Dart Estuary and the bay. Wavenden House does not pretend to be a hotel or guest house; the owners, the highly hospitable Mr and Mrs Gardener, simply take in paying guests (there are only three rooms, all of which have a sea view) and cook them delicious dinners on most nights. The large dining table seats 10 (residents only) and looks out across the estuary to Kingswear Castle. The surrounding countryside is National Trust owned, and Wavenden House is the only building in the vicinity. The house is on a precipitous hill, so it is unsuitable for young children and the disabled.

Lots of walks (the coastal path runs right by the gate); sailing can be arranged; sailing courses in Dartmouth; fishing off rocks below; Sugary Cove beach (five-minute walk)

DITTISHAM

The Ferry Boat Inn, Dittisham, Dartmouth, South Devon
(Tel. 080422 368)
Follow Ferry sign from Dartmouth; access also by boat
(and ferry)
Open 11am–3pm, 6pm–11pm Mon–Sat; noon–3pm, 7pm–
10.30pm Sun
A white-painted inn at bottom of steep hill, right by the water's edge at high tide and popular with yachtsmen. At low tide, the riverbank finds itself providing additional parking spaces. The one bar overlooks the water, and serves real ales and snacks.

Windsurfing at the Ham; boating; walks

DREWSTEIGNTON

The Anglers Rest, Fingle Bridge, Drewsteignton, Exeter
EX6 6PW   (Tel. 0647 21287)
Signposted from Drewsteignton

Open in summer 11am–3pm, 6pm–11pm Mon–Sat; noon–3pm, 7pm–10.30pm Sun. In winter 11 am–2.30pm Mon–Fri
This 94–year-old pub is set beside an Elizabethan bridge in a quiet wooded valley. It has always been run by the same family, and boasts a fine collection of antique fishing tackle. The one bar overlooks the river; outside, the terraced garden, with seating for 60 people, reaches down to the water. Beers on offer include Wadworth 6X, Cotleigh Tawny, and Dorset IPA. In the summer, the restaurant is open from 10.30am, for morning coffee, to 5.30pm for cream teas, and serves roast lunches on Sundays. Children are welcome in the restaurant or the garden, but not in the pub.
Trout, salmon, and seatrout fishing (pub hires out rods and sells flies); miles of woodland walks, including one to Castle Drogo (about 45 minutes on foot for the average walker), Hunters' Path and Fishermen's Path

DULVERTON

🏚 6/14 🏠 🍴 🌂 💳

Tarr Steps Hotel, Hawkridge, Dulverton, Somerset TA22 9PY (Tel. 064 385293)
West of Dulverton–Exford road
£36 pp b&b
A remote sporting hotel, once a Georgian rectory, set in eight acres of grounds on Exmoor, with lovely views of the River Barle and its valley. Two hundred yards from the house, there is a hewn-stone bridge, Tarr Steps, which is believed to date from the Bronze Age. Inside, the hotel is welcoming, comfortable and homely, with open fires, sporting pictures and the blissful tranquillity engendered by the absence of televisions and telephones. Some of the rooms have splendid river views. Traditional English cooking served in Georgian dining room. Set lunch £16, dinner £16. There is a ground-floor bedroom available for disabled guests.
Three miles of trout and salmon fishing (fishing tuition available); rough shooting; clay pigeon shooting; driven pheasant shooting can be arranged, as can riding and hunting

EXETER

The Captain's Table, The Basin, Haven Road, Exeter
(Tel. 0392 413678)
Open 11am–2pm, 7pm–10pm Mon–Sat
Strategically positioned in the heart of Exeter's old docks at the entrance to the Maritime Museum, this is Exeter's only floating restaurant. It seats 20 (the seven tables by the portholes have the best views of the quay) and is housed in an unusual and attractively converted tug that worked on the Thames during the Second World War, and made no less than three trips across to Dunkirk. Tony Gulliver aims to keep the cooking crustacean-oriented; at lunchtime, the menu is based on galettes, and in the evenings, prawns, crayfish, lobster and steaks are likely to be on the menu.
Haven Banks canoe club has its HQ a few yards away; fishing up and down the canal; windsurfing

EXMINSTER

Turf Hotel, Exminster, Exeter EX6 8EE   (Tel. 0392 833128)
Call for directions
Closed in January and first two weeks of February
£17.50 b&b
This small hotel enjoys a unique position at the point where the Exeter canal emerges into the Exe estuary. There is no road access, so it is a silent haven and a walker's paradise; once there, you are well away from the distractions of the modern world. Wading birds and avocets also find the area attractive, and are evident in numbers: the spot is well known to, and popular with, bird watchers. The dining room seats 30 people; food is home cooked, and all tables have a view of the water. Bar meals are available, and there are 'cook-your-own-barbecue' evenings in the summer. The hotel has recently been recommended by the *Good Pub Guide*. Because of its solitary, watery situation, the area can look a little bleak in winter, though the landlords deny this strenuously. It is certainly an

unusual location, and very different from everywhere else on the visiting list. Disabled visitors are made welcome, though there are no special facilities.

Hotel served by its own canal boat, The Water Mongoose, *for trips up the river; sailing, waterskiing, fishing*

FALMOUTH

The Chainlocker, Customs House Quay, Quay Hill, Falmouth, Cornwall TR11 3HG   (Tel. 0326 311085)
Turn left 200 yards past the church in the town centre
Open 11am–11pm Mon–Sat; noon–2.30pm, 7pm–10.30pm Sun
This 250-year-old pub has a great deal of atmosphere and much in the way of ships' paraphernalia (wheels, barometers and such). It is situated next to the lifeboat station and the customs house on a busy working harbour; take your drinks to the tables outside the pub, and watch the comings and goings on the quay. There is a good variety of Steam beers and lagers on offer at the bar, and bar meals are now available at lunchtimes and in the evenings all year round. The Marine Restaurant has recently been converted into two new bars, both of which overlook the harbour. No disabled facilities, though access is not difficult for anyone in a wheelchair.

Sailing and shark-fishing trips from harbour; river trips; beach (other side of Falmouth); coastal walks, also walks at Flushing, reached by ferry

FALMOUTH

The Greenbank Hotel, Harbourside, Falmouth, Cornwall TR11 2SR   (Tel. 0326 312440)
Signposted from main roundabout outside town
£47–£67 pp b&b, set dinner £16.50
A 17th-century building with a comfortable atmosphere, airy public rooms, and bedrooms named after ships: lots of

maritime bits and pieces (old etchings, brass fittings). In 1640, the building was a ferryman's house – the ferry to Flushing leaves from opposite the hotel. The hotel has its own private quay and fine views of the Penryn river and harbour. The downstairs bar has tables on the quay in summer. There is seating for 70 people in the dining room, and both lunch and dinner are served. Nearly all tables have a water view. Additional facilities include a beauty salon and solarium. The hotel has recently spent £1 million on an extension; there are 20 new bedrooms, an underground car park, a gymnasium, and conference facilities, but no facilities for the disabled are being considered.

Watersports at Marina, 10 minutes' walk away; motorboats, yachts; windsurfing at Custom House Quay; waterskiing at Swanpool Beach, and on Helford River (five miles away); diving from dockyard; rock fishing nearby; hotel can arrange sea fishing; beach (five minutes' drive); five-minute walk to ferry to Flushing, where there are walks round headland

FORD

White Hart at Ford, nr Chippenham, Wilts SN14 8RP
(Tel. 0249 782213)
Off main A420 towards Bristol from Chippenham. Take first left in the village of Ford
£59 double b&b

This 16th-century inn is a good combination of country pub and small hotel, with timbered bar and log fire, and honest portions of pub grub on offer. The bedrooms are civilized and characterful, if not enormous, and the restaurant is pleasant, though it does not have a view of the river. Outside, there is a river terrace, with tables, beside a bona fide babbling trout stream, all set in beautiful grounds. Don't expect to go fishing, however: the trout are to be fed, not caught. The à la carte restaurant over the river seats 70, all tables with water view. There are no specific facilities for the disabled, though access is 'no problem', and four of the bedrooms are only up one step.

Swimming pool; walks along footpaths through grounds; fishing nearby

FOWEY

Food for Thought, The Quay, Fowey, Cornwall PL23 1AT
(Tel. 0726 83 2221)
Closed Sunday (open bank holidays)
Dinner only, set menu £16
This renowned restaurant is set in a 500-year-old, Grade II listed building almost on the water's edge on the quay in Fowey. The town is delightful, and not congested with traffic thanks to the draconian restrictions on vehicles, banishing them to the car parks on the edge of the town. Food for Thought boasts the distinction of having held a Michelin 'red M' for the last six years. Cooking is classic and French, with much use of fish and shellfish. There is seating for 38 people, and six tables have a good view of the quay. Advance booking is essential.
Nearby walks on National Trust land; windsurfing and sailing at harbour; beach at harbour mouth

FOWEY

Marina Hotel, Esplanade, Fowey, Cornwall PL23 1HY
(Tel. 0726 83 3315)
Open March to October
£25–£38 pp b&b
Perched on the harbour with fine views over the river and sea, this charming hotel has three private moorings, and a small quayside garden with steps down to the beach. If you are planning on driving down the steep hill to the hotel to deliver your luggage (you have to leave your car outside the town, see above), warn the proprietor: when you stop in front of the hotel you will be blocking the whole street. Seven of the 11 rooms have a splendid view of the water, and big windows. Four rooms have balconies which give access to the garden. All 12 tables in the dining room share the panoramic view. The set menu at dinner costs £16; bar meals are available at lunchtime.
Beach at end of hotel garden; sailing, windsurfing, fishing and riding nearby; walks

GODMANSTONE

Smiths Arms, Godmanstone, nr Dorchester, Dorset
(Tel. 0300 341 236)
Open 11am–3pm, 6pm–11pm
The Smiths Arms is the smallest pub in England, and that's official: it features in the *Guinness Book of Records*, with its external dimensions checking in at 39ft 6in by 11ft by 12ft. The pub can seat 28 customers on old church pews, and there is a stretch of a suitably diminutive River Frome running past, to provide a waterside garden. The building dates from the 15th century. Originally it was a blacksmith's shop, and the story goes that King Charles II once stopped here to have his horse shod, wanted a drink and granted the place a licence. The horse-racing memorabilia in the bar was collected by one landlord who was an ex-jockey. Good home cooking, especially ham and bread pudding. No children under 14 in bar.
Interesting walks (for example to Cerne Abbas Giant; ask staff for details)

HAYLING ISLAND

Cockle Warren Cottage Hotel, 36 Seafront, Hayling Island, Hants PO11 9HL (Tel. 0705 464961)
£35–£45 single, £56–£68 double room
A marvellous, tiny hotel, which won the AA Best New-comer of the Year Award for 1990, with a small dining room set in a conservatory overlooking the outdoor swimming pool. Two of the bedrooms, both with four-posters, overlook the Solent, with lovely views across to the Isle of Wight. A good-looking, home-cooked menu includes regional French country dishes (residents' friends are welcome at dinner). American tourists go into raptures over the hotel; British visitors take its charm in their stride. The surroundings, although seaside, are not particularly picturesque.
Six-and-a-half-mile sandy beach; sailing; windsurfing; deep-sea fishing; golf; tennis; squash; badminton; riding

HELFORD

🏠 ⚓ 🔥 🏷 🚏

Shipwright's Arms, Helford Village, nr Helston, Cornwall
(Tel. 0326 23 235)
On the road through Helford
Open 11am–2.30pm, 6pm–10.30pm Mon–Sat; noon–2.30pm,
7pm–10.30pm Sun
An ancient and highly picturesque thatched pub on Helford
Passage Creek, with about 15 tables on a terraced patio going
right down to sea wall. Bar food available from noon to 2pm
and 7pm to 9pm (on Sundays in winter, only from noon to
1.30pm). Barbecue dinners are served out on the patio in
summer. Very attractive when the tide is in. Beers include
Cornish Original, Newquay Steam beers, and draught
Guinness.
*Boats for hire in Helford (and St Anthony, two miles away); walks
on coastal path; fishing from rocks, or fishing trips from Manaccan
(one mile away); beach (10 minutes' walk)*

HELSTON

🍽 🚲 🏠 🔥 🏷 🚏

Riverside Restaurant with Rooms, Helford Village, nr
Helston, Cornwall TR12 6JU   (Tel. 0326 23 443)
Open 7.30pm–9.30pm daily, mid-February to
mid-November; also open for lunch on Fri–Sun, May to
September
£75–£95 per double, including a substantial continental
breakfast. Full English breakfast available, £3–£4
Situated 10 yards from the water on a tidal creek in the quiet
Cornish village of Helford, the Riverside Restaurant is housed
in a Grade II listed building, and describes its cuisine as 'French
provincial'. The emphasis in the menu is on fresh produce;
herbs and vegetables come from the garden, the fish is local,
and the croissants and marmalade served at breakfast are home
made. Gourmet oils and vinegars are also made on the
premises; these are for sale by the bottle so guests can
experiment with them at home. There is seating for 40 in the

dining room, and five of the tables have a view out over the creek. The set menu for dinner – four or five courses – costs £28. Dogs can be accommodated by prior arrangement. No special disabled facilities, but the dining room is on the ground floor.

Sailing and windsurfing at St Anthony; golf near Mullion (six miles away); deep-sea fishing can be arranged; National Trust gardens; walks along the coast; bird watching

HONEYSTREET

inn ~~ 4/4 ⚐ ⚒ ⬦ ▭

The Barge Inn, Honeystreet, nr Pewsey, Wiltshire SN9 5PS (Tel. 0672 851238)
Cross the bridge at Honeystreet on to the south bank of the canal, turn immediately right and continue for about 200 yards
Open all day during summer; opening hours may vary in winter
Single b&b, £22; double, £40

A beautifully located pub in an Area of Outstanding Natural Beauty on the Kennet and Avon canal in the Vale of Pewsey. There are wonderful views up and down a peaceful stretch of water, and across the valley to the Marlborough Downs presided over by a fine white horse cut into the chalk. It's principally a place to go in summer in order to sit by the water and watch the barges chug gently by or toss a crust of sandwich to the flotillas of expectant wildfowl. The interior doesn't match the delights of the beer garden, but there is a large main bar serving good hand-pumped Ushers' ales and standard pub food. There is also a restaurant serving fresh trout and salmon among other fish and meat dishes, and a reasonably priced wine list.

Walking on the Marlborough Downs and along the canal; fishing

HOPE COVE

🏠 ≈ 26/35 🏘 🔥 ⬦ 🚳

The Cottage Hotel, Hope Cove, nr Kingsbridge, South
Devon TQ7 3HJ   (Tel. 0548 561 555)
From A381 (Kingsbridge to Salcombe), head for Hope Cove,
then Inner Hope
£27.50–£58 dinner and b&b

Originally a small cottage built in 1880, the hotel has been
developed in stages since 1927, and stands in two acres of
grounds. The beautiful gardens lead down to the beach. The
hotel is surrounded by National Trust land, so there is plenty
of scope for walks in glorious surroundings. The restaurant
seats 80 (the 14 window tables have the best sea view), and
serves bar/snack lunches, and dinner; non-residents are
welcome. Devonshire cream teas and after-dinner coffee are
served on the sun terrace, which has superb views overlooking
Bolt Tail and Bigbury Bay. Two of the ground-floor rooms
are suitable for the disabled.

*Coastal walks; watersports nearby (bring equipment) or at
Thurlestone Sands; fishing (trips in season, or off breakwater), or at
Bolt Head; two beaches; favourable rates with nearby golf course;
Bigbury golf course 20 minutes by car*

HORDLE

🏠 ≈ 3/7 🏘 7 🔥 🚳 🚳

Gordleton Mill and Restaurant Gastronomique Français,
Silver Street, Hordle, nr Lymington, Hampshire SO41 6DJ
(Tel. 0590 682219)
Open seven days a week in summer; closed on Tuesdays, and
Sunday evenings from November to March
Double rooms, from £85 b&b

Gordleton Mill is special. Unusually, it is run by its chef – Jean
Christophe Novelli – whose culinary flair has earned him a
reputation in foodie circles. Driving into the car park, you
glimpse sluices, streams, lawns, ducks and exotic white-
painted tree trunks. The entrance to the Mill is across a little
wooden plank bridge. Inside, floors are expensively carpeted

or tiled, or both. The staircase has a brass baluster rail. Bedrooms are luxuriously kitted out. The refurbishment is very stylish indeed. In the downstairs no-smoking sitting-room you sip drinks to the sounds of rushing mill water. Dinner in the tiled Restaurant Gastronomique (open to non-residents) is an *experience* – and costs £17.50 for three courses Monday to Friday and £28.50 for two courses on Saturday. The staff are all young and exceptionally professional. This hotel is not cheap but, if you've got it, then Gordleton Mill has too. Restaurant has wheelchair access and a lavatory for disabled visitors.

The New Forest Stonehenge, Winchester and Salisbury are all nearby; sailing at Lymington

ILFRACOMBE

🏨 22/37 🛁 🐕 ⚓ 💳

Cliffe Hydro Hotel, Hillsborough Road, Ilfracombe, North Devon EX34 9NP   (Tel. 0271 863606)
From town centre, follow Hillsborough Road
£30–£70 per room b&b

The location is fabulous; views sweep across the harbour and coastline to Wales. The hotel itself is not quite so impressive: its saving grace is a very smart health complex, equipped with a swimming pool, sauna, steam room, whirlpool spa and weight training machines. The restaurant seats 75; half the room overlooks the sea (seven tables have a direct water view). Non-residents are welcome for meals. There is an à la carte dinner menu; a four-course dinner costs £9.95. Main courses at lunch are about £5. The hotel gardens reach down to the quay.

Raparee beach (five minutes' walk); fishing nearby; coastal path walks

INSTOW

The Commodore Hotel, Marine Parade, Instow, North
Devon EX39 4JN   (Tel. 0271 860347)
Off the A39 Barnstaple–Bideford road
£51.50–£95 double b&b

A long, low, white, villa-style building in an excellent position
right on the sea front, with spectacular views of the Taw/
Torridge estuary. The gardens are highly manicured, and the
bar opens straight on to the patio terrace, which overlooks the
estuary. The glass-fronted restaurant seats 80; everyone has a
water view, though few tables are actually in the window. The
table d'hôte menu is £18; the à la carte menu features
seafood and game. Children are allowed into the restaurant, as
long as they can sit on their own chairs. Saturday night dinner
dances are held during the winter. There are no specific
facilities for the disabled, though non-resident visitors in
wheelchairs will be able to find their way into the restaurant
without trouble, as it is all on one level.

Wonderful long sandy beach; coastal path walks; sailing, waterskiing,
windsurfing, paragliding; fishing

KINGSBRIDGE

Thurlestone Hotel, Thurlestone, nr Kingsbridge, South
Devon TQ7 3NN   (Tel. 0548 560382)
From A379, drive through Churchstow and turn left at
roundabout. Then take first right, signposted Thurlestone
From £61, dinner and b&b

In 1897, William John Grose moved into a twelve-room
farmhouse in Thurlestone village and put up a sign: 'Golfers
accommodated. Picnic parties catered for. Terms moderate'.
The Grose family has been running the hotel, now with 68
bedrooms, ever since, and it still accommodates golfers, now
attracted both to the clifftop Thurlestone Golf Club and to the
9-hole course in its own grounds. The original 16th-century
farmhouse is now a part of the AA/RAC 4-star hotel, which

also offers tennis, squash and badminton, as well as a beauty parlour, multi-gym, snooker and indoor and outdoor pools. The Egon Ronay recommended sea-view restaurant caters for special diets (vegetarians are spoilt for choice), and the cellar boasts 160 bins. Families are welcome: there are plenty of facilities for children, those sharing their parents' room stay free, and children's suppers mean mum and dad can dine later in peace. The hotel overlooks Thurlestone Bay, one of several sandy coves in the area, and National Trust Coastal Walks, trips up the River Dart and sailing in Salcombe are within easy reach. Wheelchair access to rooms.

Half-a-mile from the beach, either via the village or through the hotel's palm- and banana-tree-studded grounds

KINGSBRIDGE

Start Bay Inn, Torcross, Kingsbridge, South Devon TQ7 2TQ (Tel. 0548 580553)
On the A379 between Dartmouth and Kingsbridge
Open 11am–3pm, 6pm–11pm Mon–Sat; noon–2pm, 7pm–10.30pm Sun
The pub is a 14th-century thatched cottage right on the beach, opposite a freshwater ley (an inland lake, about a mile long). The bar and patio look directly out to sea. The bar menu, served at lunch and dinner, is strong on seafood; the landlord dives for as much fish as possible (such as lobster, crabs, scallops) and has won an award for serving the freshest fish in Britain. Beers include Marston's and Flowers IPA. Pets should be kept on leads. There is a ramp to facilitate wheelchair access to the pub, but no specific disabled facilities.

Watersports at Blackpool Sands (two or three miles away); fishing on beach and on ley; coastal path walks; Slapton Sands beach, long, sandy and straight, where many American soldiers died in the war practising for D-Day (a recovered Sherman tank stands in the beach car park near the inn)

LANGSTONE

The Royal Oak, High Street, Langstone, Hants
(Tel. 0705 483125)
From A3M–A27 Chichester Road, follow signs to Hayling
Island
Open 11am–11pm Mon–Sat; noon–3pm, 7pm–10.30pm Sun
A pretty, bona fide old inn situated right on the harbour (on an
inlet, rather than sea), with flag floors, heavy beams, real ales
and (alas) Muzak. The bar overlooks the water, and there are
waterside seats outside, though the view can be uninspiring at
low tide. There is a strong 'local' feeling to the pub, plenty of
seagulls, and always two great ales and bar food available.
Though busy in summer, it is rarely congested. At the back of
the pub there is a pets' corner (featuring rabbits and ducks),
which is popular with children.

LONGHAM

The Bridge House Hotel, Longham, Dorset BH22 9AN
(Tel. 0202 578828)
Off A348 between Poole and Fransham
£52 pp single, £75 double b&b
A Mediterranean-style hotel sitting, rather incongruously,
right on the river bank in the Stour Valley. Verandas, terraces
and balconies add considerably to the atmosphere. The
grounds enclose an island, which is linked to the hotel by a
bridge. There is a large bar, and the carvery restaurant, which
overlooks the river, seats 45–50 people. The rooms which have
a view of the river are very comfortable, but ground-floor
rooms look on to car park and road (some of the rooms are for
non-smokers only). Greek food and music evenings are held
on the last Sunday of the month, if the Greek owners are
not hosting a wedding. There are conference facilities, and
some ground-floor rooms which are suitable for disabled
visitors.

Fishing (the hotel has rights on the Stour river; bring equipment); golf at local courses (golf weekends can be organized); walks; beach (six miles away); watersports

LOOE

Talland Bay Hotel, nr Looe, Cornwall PL13 2JB
(Tel. 0503 72667)
Take the Polperro road from Looe. After one mile ignore a signpost pointing left to Talland. Continue on the Polperro road for another mile, then follow the 'Talland Bay Hotel' sign at the crossroads
Closed in January
£44–£88 pp dinner and b&b
Parts of this fine Cornish house date back to the 16th century. It is set in beautiful gardens 150 feet above sea level, with magnificent views over the bay, so it is a five-minute walk to descend to the beach, which is sandy at low tide. Bedrooms are spacious (there are two four-posters), individually furnished and fully equipped. The dining room seats 60, with five tables overlooking the bay. Lunch is served between 12.30pm and 2pm; dinner between 7.30pm and 9pm (set dinner, £18). In the summer there are occasional evening barbecues under the pine trees in the garden. Dogs can be accommodated by arrangement (£4 per night). Children are welcome, though no under-fives are allowed in the dining room – they are provided with high tea, and packed off to bed at a sensible hour. The hotel is strong on special interest holidays, including landscape painting, geology, archaeology, murder-mystery, Scrabble and bridge. The dining room and one bedroom are on the ground floor, and a ramp is available for wheelchair access to the garden; otherwise there are no special facilities for the disabled.
Swimming pool (heated May to November); sauna; solarium; the hotel has its own boat for waterskiing, and a yacht; beach; golf, tennis, riding, watersports and fishing nearby; walks along cliff path (the hotel can provide a booklet of local walks)

LYME REGIS

17/26

Alexandra Hotel, Pound Street, Lyme Regis, Dorset
(Tel. 029744 2010)
Closed in January
£45–£60 pp dinner and b&b
Built in 1735, this house has been a hotel since the beginning of the century. It is very pleasant, and medium-sized, with fine gardens and excellent views of the Cobb and Lyme Bay. The bedrooms and public rooms are comfortable and tastefully furnished. Altogether, a very civilized place, though not a family hotel. The restaurant seats 65 people, and most tables have a view out to sea. Dorset cream teas served. They have no disabled facilities, and there are a lot of steps, which makes wheelchair access difficult.
Inland and coastal walks; boat hire; sea angling; charter boats; sandy beach

LYME REGIS

2/3

The Red House, Sidmouth Road, Lyme Regis, Dorset
DT7 3ES   (Tel. 029744 2055)
Open March–November
£38–£46 per room b&b
Another very friendly guest house with prime southerly views of Lyme Bay, though not right beside the sea. It is situated at the top of the hill out of town, and thus a good 15-minute walk uphill from the town and the beach. An excellent spot for walkers – the house is close to the path that leads through the Undercliff (which should strike a chord with readers of John Fowles's *The French Lieutenant's Woman*). Large, comfortable rooms. Weather permitting, breakfast is served on the balcony overlooking the bay. Pets are accepted by prior arrangement only.
Trout fishing can be arranged; walks; beach; watersports; visits to National Trust properties and famous gardens

LYMPSTONE

IOI ⚓6 ⚒ ⊘ ▭

The River House, The Strand, Lympstone, Exmouth, Devon
EX8 5EY   (Tel. 0395 265 147)
Six miles from Exeter on A376 Exmouth road
Closed Sunday dinner, all Monday
All tables water-view, 34 covers
In the heart of the picturesque village of Lympstone on Exe,
the River House provides a friendly welcome for serious diners
in congenial surroundings. The first-floor restaurant has a glass
wall, which gives a magnificent view of Powderham Castle
and the Exe estuary. The cooking is European: a three-course
meal costs about £32.50 (the three-course vegetarian menu
costs £25), and the restaurant is famous for its vegetable (as
opposed to vegetarian) cookery. Cookery demonstrations and
full tasting lunches are held at least four times a year. There are
two rooms available for diners who wish to go no further: £52
single, £69 double, with a light breakfast included.
*Walks, sailing, windsurfing; watersports, fishing and beach two miles
away, at Exmouth*

LYMNOUTH

🏠 12/16 ⚓5 ⚒ ◁ ▭

The Rising Sun Hotel, Harbourside, Lynmouth, North
Devon EX35 6EQ   (Tel. 0598 53223)
Closed for the first three weeks of December
£35–£45 pp b&b, Shelley's honeymoon suite, £55 pp b&b
An immaculate 14th-century smugglers' inn right on the
quayside in Lynmouth, with a terraced garden and very
comfortable cottage-style rooms. R. D. Blackmore wrote
Lorna Doone here, and there is the added bonus of the garden
cottage, where Shelley spent his honeymoon (the cottage has a
four-poster, sitting room, and private garden with spectacular
views). The inn overlooks the small picturesque harbour and
the East Lyn salmon river. The oak-panelled dining room and
bar have crooked ceilings, thick walls and uneven oak floors.
Thirty-two people can be seated for lunch and dinner (six

tables have a water view); the chef specializes in local Exmoor game and seafood. The set dinner costs £18.50. Pets can be accommodated, but only by prior arrangement.

The hotel has private fishing; superb walks; hunting nearby; swimming; 10 minutes' walk to beach

LYNTON

Hewitts Hotel and Restaurant, North Walk, Lynton, Devon EX35 6HJ   (Tel. 0598 52293)
Closed in January
£38–£46 pp b&b, lunch £13.50, dinner £19.75
A rambling, late 19th-century house in a wonderfully dramatic location, with tremendous views from the 150-foot terrace overlooking Lynmouth Bay and the Bristol Channel. The panelled two-storey hall with gallery would make a perfect Agatha Christie set: the whole place has a strong country-house feel. Great character throughout, and very secluded, with 27 acres of wooded grounds stretching down to Lynmouth. The restaurant seats 26, all tables have a water view (set lunch £12.50, set dinner £16.50). Children under 12 are allowed in the dining room only between 7pm and 8pm.

Walks (the coastal path leads into the Exmoor National Park); watersports, fishing, beach; riding

LYNTON

The Lynton Cottage Hotel, North Walk Hill, Lynton, Devon EX35 6ED   (Tel. 0598 52 342)
Closed in January
£98–£115 dinner and b&b
Once the residence of a Knight of the Realm, the hotel is set on the cliffs 500 feet above the bay. The views have the extra dimension of the inland aspect up the Lyn valley, so there is a breathtaking panorama of the coastal boundaries of Exmoor, the East Lyn valley, and Lynmouth Bay. The restaurant seats

65, and 10 of the tables have a water view. Cuisine features modern French dishes. The restaurant is open to non-residents in the evening, serving four-course dinners for £17–£25. Murder and mystery weekends are occasionally arranged, as well as gastronomic house parties.
Walks on coastal path and to Exmoor; coarse and sea fishing; rocky beach; riding, clay pigeon shooting and tennis can be arranged by the staff at the hotel

MALPAS

The Heron Inn, Malpas, Truro, Cornwall   (Tel. 0872 727 73)
Two miles south of Truro
Open noon–3pm, 6.30–11pm Mon–Sat; noon–3pm,
6pm–10.30pm Sun
Situated at the confluence of the Fal, Truro and Tresillian rivers, this waterside inn is a lovely place for lunch or dinner, expecially in summer when you can sit out on the terrace and admire the view over this tranquil wooded area. The food is simple and tasty: marinated chicken wings, liver and bacon kebab, ham and prawn mornay and steak casserole are menu regulars, served with chips or jacket potato. Parking is limited so arrive early in high season, or take a boat from Truro. Last orders: lunch 2pm; dinner 9pm. There are steps up to the pub, so disabled access is difficult.

MOUSEHOLE

The Ship Inn, Mousehole, Cornwall TR19 6QX
(Tel. 0736 731234)
Open 10.30am–11pm Mon–Sat; noon–2.30pm,
7pm–10.30pm Sun
£40 double b&b
Parts of this charming pub are 300 years old. There is nowhere to sit outside, as the road runs right past, but you can stand on the road with your drinks and admire the harbour. Both bars

look out on to the water, and serve St Austell beers (including HSD, Bosuns, and Mild). Bar snacks are available, but not on Sunday. The bedrooms (summer only) are cheerful. The hotel has recently undergone a major refit: new kitchens and cellars have been added and all bedrooms have now *en suite* bathrooms.

Harbour beach right in front of pub; sea fishing trips from harbour, or fishing from quay; yacht club at Penzance; coastal path walks

MULLION

25/40

Polurrian Hotel, Mullion, Helston, Cornwall TR12 7EN
(Tel. 0326 240421)
From Mullion, follow signs to Mullion Cove then Polurrian Cove.
Closed November to March
£50–£86 pp b&b
This imposing Edwardian building occupies a wonderful location overlooking Polurrian Cove, on the Lizard Peninsula. There are 12 acres of terraced lawns descending to the sea and a sandy beach. The spring storms in 1989 took a vast bite out of the roof, so there has been extensive rebuilding and redecorating to restore the hotel to its former glory. The restaurant seats 100 and has 15 sea-view tables. A five-course dinner costs £15.80; bar snacks are served at lunchtime. Indoor pool, spa bath, sauna, solarium, squash. Positively welcoming to, and geared up for, children, with play areas inside and out. All public rooms and some bedrooms are on the ground floor, but there are no special facilities for the disabled.

Outdoor pool, tennis, croquet, putting; coastal path walks (walk to The Lizard and the hotel will collect you); watersports (on reservoir, 20 miles away); fishing·from cove, or on bigger boats (also from Helford); sandy beach below hotel garden; riding and golf can be arranged (both 3 miles away)

MYLOR BRIDGE

🍴 🏠 🚫 🖊️ 💳

The Pandora Inn, Restronguet Creek, Mylor Bridge,
Falmouth, Cornwall TR11 5ST   (Tel. 0326 372678)
For Mylor Bridge, turn off the A39 at Penryn
Restaurant open 7pm–10pm. Bars open in the summer 11am–
11pm Mon–Sat (for food, noon–10pm); noon–3pm, 7pm–
10.30pm Sun
An immensely charming building, with thatched roof and
whitewashed walls, low ceilings, heavy beams and many
nautical souvenirs, by Restronguet Creek. One of the lower
rooms floods at (very) high tide, frustrating all attempts to stop
it. The restaurant seats 50 (including the semi-private Captain
Edwardes Room, suitably furnished with portholes). The
menu is strong on seafood, the dish of the day depending on
the local catch (main courses £10–£15). There is space for 60 in
the bars, outside seating for 80 on the floating pontoon patio
and an extensive bar menu. Most tables have views of the
water. Children are allowed in limited areas. Dogs must be on
leads. Local beers include Bowsons, Tinner, Bass, and HSD
(Hicks Special Draught, known to locals as High Speed
Death).
Sailing tuition nearby at Mylor Yacht Harbour; coastal path walks;
beach at Falmouth (four miles away); pontoon only accessible to
yachts for three hours either side of high water; shower for yachtsmen

NEWQUAY

🏨 25/50 🏠 🚫 🖊️ 💳

Hotel Riviera, Lusty Glaze Road, Newquay, Cornwall
TR7 3AA   (Tel. 0637 874251)
£33–£39.50 pp b&b
Large hotel with friendly staff situated next to Newquay's
Barrow Field. Bedrooms are slightly dated, but some have
excellent views over Barrow Field and the sea; others have
poor views, so specify when booking (there is a supplement of
£2.80 for sea-view rooms). The hotel is very popular for food
(set lunch, £8; set dinner, £12; bar snacks can be taken outside),

and with an older clientele. Babysitting can be arranged (with notice). Pets can be accommodated for a charge of £5 per day. No disabled facilities, and a considerable number of stairs.

Outdoor swimming pool; squash and racquetball courts; sauna; games room with full-sized snooker table; children's play area; Lusty Glaze beach two minutes' walk away; Newquay's speciality is surfing; there is some windsurfing and waterskiing; hotel can advise on sea and rock fishing; walks on coastal path

PADSTOW

🏨 5/7 🛶14 🔥 ⬨ 💳

The Old Mill Country House, Little Petherick (nr Padstow), Cornwall PL27 7QT (Tel. 0841 540388)
On A389 by bridge in Little Petherick
Open March to November
£18.50–£23 pp b&b
This converted 16th-century grist mill is now a Grade II listed building, set in its own gardens, next to a stream that dawdles into the Camel Estuary. A new water-wheel has been installed outside the dining-room window; one of the bedrooms looks down on to it (it is turned off at night, for the sake of tranquillity). All but one of the bedrooms are *en suite*. The dining room seats 16 and serves lunch by arrangement, and dinner at 7pm.

Sandy beaches on Camel Estuary; sailing, windsurfing and water-skiing nearby; walks around estuary and along National Trust coastline; freshwater (on lakes, six miles away) and sea fishing; pony trekking; golf

PAIGNTON

🏨 39/60 🛶 🔥 ⬨ 💳

Redcliffe Hotel, Marine Drive, Paignton, Devon TQ3 2NL (Tel. 0803 526397)
£34–£46 b&b
Built to the design of Colonel Robert Smith (he bought the tower in 1853 and added to it), the hotel is an unusual example

of Indo-European architecture, hyped as the jewel in Torbay's crown. The hotel meets the beach at the sea wall: the Colonel built the subterranean passage to the beach as a walkway to his plunge bath. Eight of the rooms have balconies overlooking the sea. The dining room seats 180; 20 tables overlook the water. As well as dinner (table d'hôte £12.50), there are bar meals available, and the restaurant serves Sunday lunch, from £6.95. The restaurant has recently been mirrored, to make it easier for diners to admire the sea. The ballroom and the residents' lounge have sea views. Additional attractions are a putting green and an outdoor swimming pool. NB: All rooms are the same price, though widely varying in size and view, so ask for the best.

Beach; watersports; fishing (through contacts, in Paignton harbour); walks to Brixham, Paignton, Torquay, and Dartmoor is not too far by car

PENZANCE

The Abbey Hotel, Abbey Street, Penzance, Cornwall
TR18 4AR   (Tel. 0736 66906)
From £75, for double b&b

All but one of The Abbey's rooms have a view of the sea, which is over the harbour wall just across the street. The hotel, painted a startling bright blue, stands on a steep hill and is run by Jean (Shrimpton) Cox and her husband. Mrs Cox's passion is antiques and the house is crammed with amusing objects: Victorian furniture, carvings, antique toys and books, hangings, old chests and so on. The elegant drawing room is painted a soft coral, one of the bedrooms a bright blue, while another has a huge pine-panelled bath and a set of antique weighing scales. Food veers towards the French, there's usually a fish, meat or vegetarian course to choose from and the menu is changed each day (£21.50 per person). For those who'd like to catch a little of Jean Cox's flair, the good news is that she has opened her own antique shop nearby.

POLKERRIS

inn 🏠 ♿ 🚫 💳

The Rashleigh Inn, Polkerris, Par, nr Fowey, Cornwall
PL24 2TL   (Tel. 0726 81 3991)
Signposted from A3082 (road from St Austell to Fowey)
Open 11am–2.30pm, 6pm–11pm Mon–Sat; noon–3pm, 7pm–
10.30pm Sun. Summer Saturdays, 11am–11pm; August,
11am–11pm Mon–Sat

You couldn't get much closer to the beach if you tried. The pub
has seating for 100 on the sea-wall terrace which looks directly
on to the beach, and is attractive inside. The restaurant, which
seats 24, serves an extensive buffet lunch, and à la carte dinners
Wednesday to Saturday. Prices range from £4 for bar snacks,
through about £6 for lunch buffet, to £12 for dinner main
courses. Local beers include St Austell HSD, Burtons, and
Bolsters Bitter. Live jazz piano entertainment on Friday and
Saturday evenings, all year round. Children are allowed in for
meals only, by prior arrangement. The bar and restaurant are
on the ground floor, but there are no special facilities for the
disabled.

*Right on the beach; fishing off sea wall; windsurfing equipment and
boats for hire on beach in summer; coastal path walks*

POLPERRO

🍺 🏠 ♿ 🍴 💳

The Blue Peter Inn, The Quay, Polperro, Cornwall
(Tel. 0503 72743/72467)
Past Looe, at the end of the A387
Open 11am–11pm Mon–Sat; noon–3pm, 7pm–10.30pm Sun

The 'smallest pub in Polperro' is an attractive whitewashed
building by the harbour, with views of the cliffs and open sea
from upstairs. There is water on two sides of the pub, and the
interior is cosy. Approach on foot through Polperro's tiny
streets (leave your car in the main car park outside the
exclusion zone and believe the signs that say there are no
parking spaces in the town). There are just four chairs outside
the pub, and seating for 32 inside. There is a variety of home-

cooked food at lunch and dinner; the blackboard menu changes daily: Jennie Craig-Hallam is Burmese, and prepares authentic curries and lots of seafood. Live jazz on Sunday lunchtimes. Local scrumpy; beers include St Austell HSD, Tinners, Wreckers (strong keg bitter) and a guest beer every week.

Safe beach nearby, with caves; boat cruises from Polperro; fishing from beach and harbour (bring own equipment); fishing trips from nearby towns; coastal path walks

POOLE

15/16

The Salterns Hotel, 38 Salterns Way, Lilliput, Poole, Dorset BH14 8JR (Tel. 0202 707 321)
From Poole, take B3369 to Sandbanks/Lilliput
£66–£110 single, £80–£120 double

The approach to this hotel does not reveal its best side: it is a marvellous quasi-Tudor pile, which used to house the Poole Harbour Yacht Club (the bar is still the PHYC Clubroom). A family-run hotel, it is situated in the middle of its own marina. Nearly all the rooms have excellent views of the boats in the marina, the sandbanks and Brownsea Island beyond. Decor is standardized, but of a high quality. The restaurant has been expanded, so that there are now 50 tables, all with a view of the water. The marina can take boats up to 59-foot, and has full back-up facilities. Visitors to the hotel pay the usual mooring fee, and moorings are subject to availability. Meeting room facilities; secretarial services can be arranged.

Games room with snooker table; charter motorboats available; sea fishing trips (from Poole); sailing; golf and riding can be arranged; tennis; squash; good walks; small private beach; Sandbanks beach (two miles away)

POOLE

IOI ⌂ 🏃 ⊘ ▭

The Warehouse Oyster Bar, Poole Quay, Poole, Dorset
BH15 1HJ   (Tel. 0202 677238)
Oyster bar open 11am–11pm; restaurant open
noon–2pm, 7pm–10pm (11pm Fri and Sat)
An old warehouse right on the quay has been converted to
form this restaurant and oyster bar. It is very comfortably
appointed and well-restored, and energetically run. The
well-stocked wine cellar, behind wrought-iron gates, is a
feature in the bar. The Oyster Bar serves light lunches
and snacks (choose your own crustaceans from the live
menagerie); the first-floor restaurant has a wider menu (lots
of local fish), and even better views of the quay from its 24
tables.
Walks; watersports; fishing; beach nearby

PORLOCK

🏠 15/24 ⌂ 🏃 ◁ ▭

Anchor Hotel & Ship Inn, Porlock Weir, nr Minehead,
Somerset   (Tel. 0643 862636)
A39 to Porlock
£30–£57 pp b&b
The Ship Inn, a thatched 16th-century converted cider barn,
combines with the 19th-century Anchor Hotel to offer both
modern comforts and old world charm. Half of the rooms
overlook Porlock Weir's picturesque harbour and the Severn
Estuary. The Ship opens out to a garden and terrace. Home-
made food is available from the bars, which also look out on to
the harbour.

PORTHLEVEN

The Ship Inn, Porthleven, Cornwall TR13 9JS
(Tel. 0326 572841)
West side of Porthleven harbour
Open 11.30am–11pm Mon–Sat; noon–3pm,7pm–10.30pm
Sun

A fine, 17th-century smugglers' pub, complete with original stone walls. Both bars overlook the water, as does the garden, which has tables that can seat 60–70 people. Curiosities include the statutory collection of portholes and sea-faring bric-a-brac, and old (from 1860s) British coins and foreign currency stuck to bar pillars (more coins always welcome). Children are only allowed into the family room. The inn is known for its good seafood (served both at lunchtime and in the evening), and the considerable efforts made by the landlord are reflected in the congeniality of the surroundings.

Coastal path goes right past the door; short surfing break off Porthleven, considered good; windsurfing (eight miles away); boat hire and beach nearby; rock and sea fishing

PORT ISAAC

Slipway Hotel, The Harbour Front, Port Isaac, Cornwall
PL29 3RH   (Tel. 0208 880264)
By the harbour in Port Isaac
Closed in February
£20–£25 pp b&b

A 16th-century, Grade II listed building, all funny little staircases, oddly shaped rooms, slanting ceilings at bang-your-head level and other manifestations of age, at the bottom of the narrow streets that wind down to the harbour. Since the hotel is small and overlooks the fishing port, the higher floors have the best views. Cosy bar, apparently the scene of many a sing-song. A small stream runs past the side of the hotel. The restaurant (no water view) seats 32, and is proud of its reputation for good, fresh food; fish, crabs and lobsters are landed daily. No children under nine years (because of the very steep stairs).

Coastal path walks; fishing trips; harbour beach right in front of hotel, though Gaverne beach (10 minutes' walk) is better; surfing at Polzeath (three miles away); other watersports on Camel Estuary; two championship golf courses within 10 miles

PORT ISAAC

The Castle Rock Hotel, 4 New Road, Port Isaac, Cornwall PL29 3SB   (Tel. 0208 880300)
Adjacent to main car park in Port Isaac Bay
Apart from splendid vistas, there is nothing grand about this modest, but agreeable, establishment. The licensed restaurant seats 36, and 16 tables enjoy sea views. A four-course meal costs £12, and there is an extensive menu. Local seafood is, of course, the speciality of the house, but dedicated carnivores may watch their steaks being cooked at the table. Bar snacks and cream teas are available, and in fine weather are served in the hotel's own garden overlooking the bay. There is Cornish Bitter in the bar, as well as other beers on draught and in bottle, and also alcohol-free drinks. The bedrooms are pleasant, though some are on the small side: a few have facilities for partially disabled visitors, and there is easy access into the hotel.

Sea-fishing (free). Watersports, bird-watching, golf, tennis and riding within a short distance. The coastal footpath runs in front of the hotel. Tintagel, Boscastle and Padstow are within easy reach, and there are festivals of music at Easter and in summer at nearby St Endellion

PORTLAND

Pennsylvania Castle Hotel, Pennsylvania Road, Portland,
Dorset DT5 1HZ   (Tel. 0305 820 561)
From Weymouth, take the A354, then the B3154 to end of the
Portland promontory
£24–£37 pp b&b
An unusual place: a castle with strongly built towers and
battlements designed by James Wyatt and completed by 1800,
and thought to be Sylvania Castle in Hardy's *The Well Beloved*.
George III suggested the building of the Castle, which was
later occupied by his daughter, Princess Elizabeth. One special
new feature here is the honeymoon suite, complete with
mahogany four-poster and spa bath in one of the castle towers,
with views over the Dorset coastline and Rufus Castle. The
chef's speciality is fresh seafood. The main restaurant has 12
tables, half with water views. The garden room restaurant has
passion flower creepers and 30 seats, all with a view. Bar meals
also available. The sub-tropical garden leads steeply down to a
cove.
Walks; bird-watching; watersports; fishing; windsurfing; beach

PORTLOE

The Lugger Hotel, Portloe, Truro, Cornwall TR2 5RD
(Tel. 0872 501 322)
Closed December and January
£49 per person b&b in sea-view room; £59 dinner, b&b
At the heart of a charming and unspoilt fishing hamlet stands
this rambling white-washed hotel, originally an inn dating
back to the 17th century. The public rooms, with their beamed
ceilings and comfortable seating, managed to be both bright
and cosy. Bedrooms are prettily decorated, sometimes with
antiques. Three rooms in the old wing have the best sea views;
those in the new wing are more spacious but less characterful.
The dining room overlooks a tiny beach on which the fishing
boats are pulled up, and in fine weather, bar lunches are served

on slate-flagged terraces above the bay. The restaurant has a good reputation, using fresh local produce where possible, especially fish and seafood. Non-residents should make reservations in advance. Last orders: bar lunches 2.15pm; dinner 8.30pm. There is wheelchair access to the restaurant and bar, but no special facilities for disabled visitors.

The hotel can arrange both freshwater and deep-sea fishing; nearby Veryan has indoor and outdoor bowling clubs, tennis courts and a riding stables; reduced green fees at ten local golf courses; coastal path walks

ST AGNES

Trevaunance Point Hotel, Trevaunance Cove, St Agnes, Cornwall TR5 0RZ   (Tel. 0872 553235)
Open all year
£32.50–£40 per person b&b

Perched on the cliffside above the bay, this small, ivy-covered hotel was once a store for fishing gear, with hammocks above for the weary fishermen. Now it has been converted into a comfortable small hotel set in a tiny cliff-edge garden. Bedrooms are decorated in a tasteful cottagey style to complement the beamed ceilings and antique country furniture. Downstairs, the bar and restaurant occupy another long, low-beamed room. Local seafood is a speciality and there's an imaginative and extensive vegetarian set menu. The wine list includes offerings from all over the world including China, Lebanon and Argentina. Last orders: lunch 2pm; dinner 9pm. A five-course table d'hôte lunch costs £10.95; a seven-course dinner, £17.95. It is possible, but not easy, to get wheelchairs into the restaurant.

Hotel can organize freshwater and sea angling, surfing, windsurfing and yachting; lovely coastal walks; sandy beach at low tide with lifeguard in season; the pretty mining village of St Agnes is a 20-minute walk up the valley

ST AUSTELL

🏨 43/73 🏡 ♿ 🚫 💳

Carlyon Bay Hotel, Carlyon Bay, St Austell, Cornwall
PL25 3RD   (Tel. 0726 81 2304)
£56–£83 pp b&b
This luxurious and peaceful 1920s hotel occupies 250 acres of
gardens overlooking the three-quarter-mile-long Crinnis
beach. The bedrooms are comfortable and airy, and many have
sea views. The dining room seats 150 people, and 20 tables
have a view out to sea. Non-residents are welcome for lunch
and dinner (set lunch £10.50; five-course dinner £17). Guests
should dress smartly in the evenings: jacket and tie required in
public rooms after 7pm. There is a playroom and 'play
paddock' for children; in summer the hotel organizes games
and entertainment. Some rooms are served by a lift, but there
are no special facilities for the disabled.
Hotel has its own 18-hole golf course, nine-hole approach and putting
lawn, indoor and outdoor pools, spa/solarium and sauna room, two
tennis courts; croquet lawn; nearby walks along coastal path or beach
and golf course; watersports; fishing in Fowey; beaches (five minutes'
walk); helipad

ST AUSTELL

🏨 17/24 🏡 ♿ 🚫 💳

Porth Avallen Hotel, Sea Road, Carlyon Bay, St Austell,
Cornwall PL25 3SG   (Tel. 0726 81 2802)
On sea road, call for directions
Closed for 10 days at Christmas
£53.50 single, £74 double, £85.50 luxury double
A private house built in 1930, the hotel enjoys excellent
unimpeded views of the sea. As the crow flies, the water is only
100 yards away, but for pedestrians it is a ten-minute walk.
Friendly staff and comfortable decor add to the relaxed
country-house atmosphere. Bedrooms are comfortable and
well furnished; two have four-poster beds. The dining room
seats 45, with the best views from four window tables. A set

lunch costs £7.50; a five-course dinner, £12.50. The bar and sunny conservatory also have excellent sea views.

Coastal path walks (the hotel can provide a ramblers' booklet); riding; windsurfing at Newquay, canoeing and jetskis at Pentewan (five miles away)

ST IVES

🏠 10/33 🏡 ♿ 🔖 💳

Carbis Bay Hotel, Carbis Bay, St Ives, Cornwall TR26 2NP
(Tel. 0736 795311)
Open 30 March to November
£30–£52 pp dinner and b&b

A large hotel set in grounds just above the sweeping curve of Carbis Bay. The hotel owns and manages the beach, and rents out deck chairs, windbreaks and so on. As well as the rooms in the hotel (two of which have four-poster beds as well as sea views), the hotel has some self-catering flats for rent. These tend to be booked up early, so move fast if you want one during high season. A kidney-shaped heated outdoor pool on a sun-trap terrace also looks out over the beach. The restaurant seats 100; 10 tables overlook the sea. Special diets catered for. High season entertainments here include Punch and Judy shows, magic shows, live Country and Western music evenings, and barbecues.

Outdoor pool; coastal path walks; waterskiing and surfing (bring own equipment); sea fishing off beach, or hotel can organize fishing trips from Penzance; golf nearby; trips to the Scilly Isles

ST IVES

🏠 36/36 🏡 ♿ 🔖 💳

Pedn-Olva Hotel, Porthminster Beach, St Ives, Cornwall
TR26 2EA   (Tel. 0736 796222)
£32–£40 per person b&b

The location of this family-run seaside hotel could not be more perfect. It stands on a rocky promontory just feet from the sea. From the bar there is a picture-postcard view of this classic

Cornish fishing village and its harbour; from the dining-room tables there is a knockout panorama of the pale sands of Porthminster Beach, reminiscent of the old French Riviera. All the bright, sunny rooms have lovely sea views and are decorated in a simple tasteful way. Some open on to sunbathing terraces, one with a small pool, built out over the rocks. Steps lead down to the beach. The restaurant specializes in fresh fish and seafood and home-made food, including curries and chilli, is available in the bar at lunchtimes. There is wheelchair access to the hotel, the bar and the restaurant, and two of the bedrooms are on the ground floor.

ST MAWES

Idle Rocks Hotel, Tredenham Road, St Mawes, Cornwall
TR2 5RD   (Tel. 0326 270771)
On A3078
£34–£69 pp dinner and b&b (b&b only £15 less)
This bright and cheerful hotel enjoys a fine situation, right on the sea wall. The rooms are full of character, and there is a cocktail bar and terrace that look out to the harbour and the sea, and make the perfect spot for a pre-dinner drink. There is seating for 80 people in the restaurant, and all of the tables have a sea view. The castle opposite the hotel was built for Henry VIII, and makes up a matching pair with Falmouth Castle. Pets can be accommodated by arrangement.
Beach (three minutes' walk); coastal path walks and marked trails along Percuil river (National Trust); sailing classes, fishing from quay and shark fishing nearby

SALCOMBE

Sunny Cliff Hotel, Cliff Road, Salcombe, Devon TQ8 8JX
(Tel. 054884 2207)
£25–£35 pp b&b
Open all year: November to April b&b; April to November half-board

Set on the side of the estuary, this friendly hotel, five minutes' walk from the town centre, has large, bright family rooms. From its vantage point 100 feet above the water, there are superb views straight across the estuary and out to sea; the gardens slope down to the water, where there are six moorings and a landing stage. There is a heated salt-water swimming pool by the sea wall. The dining room seats a maximum of 44 people (the five window tables have the best view of the water).

Beaches at North Sands (10 minutes' walk), South Sands (further), and across estuary by ferry; windsurfing and sailing nearby, but no waterskiing in the bay (8 mph speed limit); and, of course, plenty of coastal walks along the spectacular coastline

SALCOMBE

🏘️ 20/40 🏘️ 🏃 🔷 ▭

South Sands Hotel, South Sands, Salcombe, Devon TQ8 8LL (Tel. 054884 3741)
From Salcombe, follow signs to South Sands
Sea-view rooms £46–£65 pp dinner and b&b
Comfortable and friendly hotel in a small sandy cove: the water actually comes up to the hotel at high tide. There is an excellent view from sea-facing rooms and the dining room, where there is seating for 100 people, and all tables have a sea view. All bedrooms are well-equipped; half of them look out to sea, and cost a little more than the others. If you feel like a change from the dining room, you can choose to eat in the new bistro. There is a charge for dogs: £3 a day, food extra. One hundred yards from Tides Reach Hotel, and not much to choose between the two.

Pool; sauna and solarium; beach starts where hotel stops; ferry from beach to Salcombe (10 minutes away); watersports from boat house next door; coastal path walks; sea fishing nearby

SALCOMBE

🏨 37/41 ⛪ 🍷 ◁ 💳

Tides Reach Hotel, South Sands, Salcombe, Devon TQ8 9LJ
(Tel. 054884 3466)
From Salcombe, follow signs to South Sands
Closed November to February
£55–£90 pp dinner and b&b
An elegant, family-run hotel on a sandy cove and just across
the road from the beach. Some of the attractive bedrooms have
sea-view balconies, the staff are attentive, and there is a
sheltered water garden by the hotel. The sea aquarium in the
cocktail bar displays a number of locally caught fish. The
dining room seats 94 people, and the 15 window tables have
the best view of the sea. Non-residents are welcome for meals;
a four-course dinner costs £23.50. Snacks are available in the
bar at lunchtime. Within the hotel, there is an impressive
indoor leisure complex complete with heated pool, sauna,
squash court, multi-gym and hair salon. All floors are served
by a lift, and doorways are wide enough to accommodate
wheelchairs, but there are no special facilities for the disabled.
Coastal and country walks (the hotel can supply a booklet that gives
details of 15 walks); ferry from beach to Salcombe (10 minutes);
sailing; windsurfing; waterskiing; scuba diving, and sea or freshwater
fishing can be arranged; beach immediately across the road

SALCOMBE

🏨 19/28 ⛪ 🍷 ◁ 💳

Bolt Head Hotel, South Sands, Salcombe, Devon TQ8 8LL
(Tel. 054884 3751)
Call for directions
Closed November to end of March ·
£52–£75 pp per night dinner and b&b
Perched on a headland 140 feet above sea level, the hotel
overlooks the sea and the Salcombe Estuary. The hotel
grounds slope down a steep hill, and the beach is 50 yards
beyond. Bedrooms are modern and furnished with a good deal
of pine. The terrace, lounge and bar all have magnificent views

over Salcombe Estuary. Fifteen tables in the 60-cover dining room overlook the water. Non-residents are welcome for dinner; four courses cost £20. There are some ground-floor rooms but no special facilities for the disabled.

Cliff walks on National Trust property next to the hotel grounds; windsurfing from the beach (equipment for hire); fishing; heated swimming pool

SALCOMBE

Soar Mill Cove Hotel, Salcombe, Devon TQ7 3DS
(Tel. 0548 561566)
Off the A381; call for directions
Closed for five weeks in January and early February
£56–£90 pp dinner and b&b

A long, low one-storey building in an idyllic, remote setting high above the sea. Extensive grounds lead down to the sandy sun-trap beach. The bar is cosy, and the lounge has wonderful views: there are sliding glass doors that can be opened up for an even better impression of the bay on warm summer evenings. Bedrooms are soothing and airy, and all open on to private terraces and the garden. Most tables in the 50-cover dining room have sea views. Cuisine is 'modern English' and focuses on the fresh shellfish caught by the hotel's own lobster boat, though the owner warns that the crabs 'get a bit thin in mid-winter'. Local lamb is also a speciality. Light seafood meals are available at lunchtime. Set dinners cost £30, and lunches about £15. Dogs can be accommodated by prior arrangement. Rooms are on the ground floor, but there are no special facilities for the disabled.

Outdoor and indoor swimming pools (the indoor one is kept at 88°F all year); walking; sailing; windsurfing; waterskiing; fishing; putting; tennis

SALISBURY

The Mill House, Berwick St James, Salisbury, Wilts SP3 4TS
(Tel. 0722 790 331)
One mile from A36 at Stapleford; one mile from A303 at
Winterbourne Stoke
£18–£27 pp b&b (less for students)
In a word: priceless. Charming, traditional bed and breakfast
accommodation, in a small and picturesque village. The Mill
House was built in 1785, adjacent to the Old Mill; enlarge-
ments and modernizations 30 years ago have not detracted
from its character. The Mill still works, pumping water for the
farm. Surrounded by lovely gardens and the babbling river
Till, the house is virtually on an island, and is approached by
bridges from all sides. Inside, hunting pictures and family
portraits abound. The views are super; guests can admire the
river from the waterside terrace outside. Admittedly, the river
dried up in 1990, but that was due to the drought. The dining
room (for breakfast only) seats eight people, with one table
that looks out on to the river (there are several good pubs
nearby where guests can find an evening meal).
*Three golf courses within 10 miles; brown trout fishing; walks in the
12-acre nature reserve nearby; swimming in mill pool; riding*

SALISBURY

The Rose and Crown Hotel, Harnham Road, Harnham, Wilts
SP2 8JQ   (Tel. 0722 327908)
Approach on A354 Coombe Bissett Road, turn left on the
A3094 New Harnham Road, right on Harnham Road; Rose
and Crown is just before bridge, on the left
£92–£118 double b&b
A fine 13th-century inn, with original half-timbering, set in a
rose garden on the banks of the river Avon, with a modern
restaurant (set dinner, £13.50) and a new accommodation wing
attached. Pleasant gardens, with geese and ducks. All the
rooms – in the old wing as well as the new wing – have recently

been refurbished, and all are individually decorated; some have four-poster beds, and most have views of the river and of Salisbury Cathedral. The hotel is a trifle bland, but the views are lovely, and the outlook from the restaurant, across the river Avon to Salisbury Cathedral, is spectacular. In the 18th century a drinker tried to cut off a piece of ham while the landlady was out of the room, but his hand slipped: he cut off his finger by mistake and fled. The landlord still has the knife and finger as souvenirs. Beers on offer in the bars include Ushers and Ruddles; one of three bars overlooks the water. There are two bedrooms with facilities for the disabled, and a lavatory for the disabled in the foyer.
Walks, fishing

SALISBURY

🏨 11/11 🏡 🍴 🚫 ▭

Old Mill Hotel, Town Path, West Harnham, Salisbury, Wilts SP2 8EU   (Tel. 0722 327517)
Just off the A3094, from Salisbury to Wilton
£40–£75 pp b&b
This hotel was originally a warehouse; the cosy restaurant is housed in a 12th-century water mill, with plenty of rushing water and loads of ducks outside. As the restaurant has few windows, the views are not outstanding, but there are lovely views of the river from the rooms, which are all *en suite*. The restaurant seats up to 55 people, and is open all year. No special facilities for the disabled, although there is access to the restaurant and the gardens.
Good trout fishing; interesting walks; riding nearby; squash; nice walks and views of the Cathedral

SEEND CLEEVE

The Barge, Seend Cleeve, Wiltshire (Tel. 0380 828230)
Open 11am–2.30pm, 6pm–11pm Mon–Sat; noon–2.30pm,
7pm–10.30pm Sun
Off the A361, between Seend Village and signpost to Seend
Head
A nice, simple pub with good canalside views. There are
waterside tables in the eating area; amazing floral decoration
and barge-painting lends a gypsyish air to the bar, where
painted milk churns serve as bar stools. There are Wadworth
beers on offer, and good cheap bar food (fresh fish on Fridays,
and there are always two vegetarian items on the menu).
Outside, there is a terrace and a sizeable lawn, with 22 tables by
the canal, which is just as well, as the pub is popular and the bar
can become very crowded in summer. Moorings are available
on the canal. The pub has wheelchair access and a lavatory for
the disabled.
Walks along towpath; fishing (licence needed)

SENNEN COVE

Old Success Inn, Sennen Cove, Cornwall TR19 7DG
(Tel. 0736 871232)
Open 11am–2.30pm, 6.30pm–11pm Mon–Sat; noon–3pm,
7pm–10.30pm Sun; summer holidays, 11am–11pm Mon–Sat
£29–£34 pp dinner and b&b
A 17th-century fishermen's inn, in a fantastic location just
north of Land's End, overlooking Whitesand Bay. The
bedrooms include two honeymoon four-poster suites; some
views are much better than others, so be sure to ask exactly
what you're getting when you book. There is an extensive
menu available from the bar; dinner is for residents only, and
there is a set menu. Some tables in the restaurant have a view of
the sea. The bay is a blue flag beach (which means that there is
lots of sand and no dogs are allowed on it). There are two
family cottages available for rent (£330 a week in high

season), and two flats (£330 a week high season, both sleep four or five).
Coastal path walks; fishing off pier, or trips from Penzance; surfing, windsurfing and canoeing on beach (equipment for hire); two surfing schools nearby

SHEPPERDINE

IOI ⌂ ♦ ⌀ ▭

The Windbound Inn, Shepperdine, nr Oldbury-on-Severn, Avon BS12 1RW   (Tel. 0454 414 343)
From Thornbury town centre, follow signs towards Oldbury-on-Severn, Shepperdine and finally the river
Large and popular eating-house pub in an attractive spot on the Severn. Friendly and unpretentious, the Windbound Inn specializes in good home cooking, and there are daily specials for vegetarians. The spacious first-floor dining lounge has panoramic views over the estuary. Downstairs, there is another restaurant, and a bar which also serves food. There is seating outside in the large garden and by the estuary. Children are welcome in both restaurants (high chairs are available). One dining room and lavatory are on the ground floor, but there are no special facilities for the disabled.
Walks (start of 50-mile Severn Way Walk); salmon fishing on the Severn; skittle alley; children's play area in the garden

SIDMOUTH

▦ ²²/³⁴ ⌂ ♦ ⌀ ▭

Hotel Riviera, The Esplanade, Sidmouth, Devon EX10 8AY (Tel. 0395 515201)
£42–£63 pp b&b; with seven-course dinner from £48–£69
The most attractive of Sidmouth's seafront hotels, the Riviera retains much Georgian character and elegance without seeming pompous or pretentious. Set right on the esplanade, with views across Lyme Bay, it is a stone's throw from the beach, and the recently refurbished rooms are tastefully done and well appointed. The restaurant seats 85, and has an

impressive menu; most tables have a water view. The hotel has recently been placed, by the AA, in the top two per cent of hotels in the British Isles. There are some rooms for disabled visitors, and special bathrooms, that have been designed in conjunction with disabled organizations.

Walks; watersports can be arranged at nearby beaches; golf at Sidmouth Golf Club

SIDMOUTH

🏨 35/68 🏠 🏃 🐾 ▭

Royal York and Faulkner Hotel, The Esplanade, Sidmouth, Devon EX10 8AZ   (Tel. 0395 513043)

Closed in January

£25–£48.50 dinner and b&b

A fine Regency building at the centre of the Esplanade, dating from 1809, the Royal York and Faulkner was Sidmouth's first purpose-built hotel. King Edward VII stayed here in 1856 (when he was Prince of Wales). The hotel is a rabbit warren of rooms, and seems to be much larger than it appears from the outside. In a fine position, right opposite Sidmouth's main beach, some of the sea-view rooms have balconies. The restaurant seats 120; about 25 tables have a water view. Non-residents are welcome in the evening. An impressive (they have won an award for it) 'health complex' within the hotel comprises a sauna, spa bath, solarium, and exercise equipment. Other attractions inside the hotel include a short-mat bowls rink and a full-size snooker table. Dogs can be accommodated, for a charge of £3 per day, which includes their dinner.

Nearby sailing, tennis, cricket, golf, riding, bowls, squash, coastal walks, surfing, windsurfing, sea and some river fishing; beach opposite hotel

SIDMOUTH

🏨 50/61 ⛵ 🏌 👤 🚫 ▭

The Victoria Hotel, The Esplanade, Sidmouth, Devon
EX10 8RY   (Tel. 0395 512651)
£110–£196 per room b&b
One of Sidmouth's finest hotels, the Victoria has occupied a
commanding position at the end of the Esplanade since shortly
after the death of its namesake monarch. A Brend hotel, so
decor and service are to the standards one would expect, with
friendly staff and rooms that are comfortable, if a touch more
utilitarian than tasteful. The restaurant seats 120 people, and
most of the tables have a view of the sea. A six-course lunch
costs £11; bar snacks are available for those with less robust
appetites. The set dinner is also six courses and costs £18.
Added attractions inside the hotel include a swimming pool,
sauna, solarium, spa bath and snooker room. There are no
special facilities for the disabled, but a lift serves all rooms and
doorways are wide enough to accommodate wheelchairs.
Indoor and outdoor swimming pools; tennis courts; plenty of walks;
watersports (equipment for hire nearby); fishing; beach

SIMONSBATH

🏨 6/7 ⛵10 🏌 🚫 ▭

Simonsbath House Hotel, Simonsbath, Exmoor, Somerset
TA24 7SH   (Tel. 064 383 259)
Closed December and January
£42–£44 pp b&b
A fine 17th-century hunting lodge in the heart of Exmoor
Forest. Most rooms have good southerly views of River Barle,
and some have four-poster beds. Mike and Sue Barns aim to
create a home, not a hotel, atmosphere: there are plenty of fresh
flowers in evidence, a convivial library bar and log fires.
Bedrooms are characterful, and furnished to a high standard.
Generous portions served in the elegant dining room. Three
self-catering barn units and a bistro have recently been added to
the hotel.
Fishing; riding; many interesting walks

STOCKBRIDGE

inn ~~0/3~~ 🏠 🚫 ◁ ▭

The Vine, High Street, Stockbridge, Hants SO20 6HF
(Tel. 0264 810652)
Open 11am–3pm, 7pm–11pm Mon–Sat; noon–2.30pm, 7pm–
10.30pm Sun
£22.50 single, £40 double b&b
A cosy, 16th-century high street pub, with village trophies
displayed in cabinets around the bar. Ales on offer include
Wadworth's 6X, Marston's Pedigree and Flowers. There is a
willow tree and seven big tables in the garden, and a pretty
little stream with a tiny bridge and plenty of trout. Bar food is
available at lunchtimes and evenings (except on Sunday
evenings), and fish dishes are a speciality.
*Trout fishing on the River Test (permits available locally); pheasant
shooting (details from Winchester tourist information); pretty river
walks*

STON EASTON

🏢 ~~6/19~~ 🏠₁₂ 🚫 ◁ ▭

Ston Easton Park, Ston Easton, nr Bath, Avon BA3 4DF
(Tel. 0761 241 631)
On the A37 from Bristol to Shepton Mallet
£195–£320 per room b&b
The River Norr runs through the landscaped park grounds of
this magnificently restored, Grade I listed Palladian mansion.
Guests are pampered in luxurious period surroundings. Some
rooms have river views, and the master bedroom has antique
Chippendale furniture. The fine interiors were decorated by
Jean Monro in 18th-century style. For those who want total
seclusion, and a slightly less formal atmosphere, there is an
isolated riverside cottage that has two suites. The hotel dining
room, with four tables looking out on to the river, is open to
non-residents. The table d'hôte lunch costs £24; a jacket and tie
should be worn for dinner (set dinner £35). A Victorian kitchen
garden provides flowers, vegetables and herbs for the hotel.
Picnic lunches are a speciality, and can be ordered, at a cost of

£17.50 per person, by both residents and non-residents. You must give at least three hours' notice when ordering, and then you can take the wicker baskets and a blanket off into the park for as long as you fancy.

On-site croquet and hot-air ballooning; nearby golf and shooting (clay and game); walks; trout fishing; tennis court; riding can be arranged

TESTCOMBE

The Mayfly, Testcombe, Stockbridge, Hants
(Tel. 0264 860283)
Between the A303 and the A30, Stockbridge to Andover
Open 11am–11pm Mon–Sat; noon–2.30pm, 7pm–10.30pm
Sun
A delightful and peaceful place on the banks of the River Test. There are nine tables outside beside the road bridge (not too busy) and the small weir. A small clear stream runs past the other side of the pub and there are about 18 more tables along the river and stream banks. The Victorian-style lounge on the river bank would also be a fine place to pass a summer evening. A selection of guest ales are on offer at the bar, and the food – available from noon to 2pm, and 7pm to 9pm – merits a mention in Lord Lichfield's *Courvoisier's Book of the Best.*

Fishing (must have permit, £50–£80 a day per rod) and walking along Test Way (just over bridge)

TINTAGEL

Willapark Manor Hotel, Bossiney, Tintagel, Cornwall
PL34 0BA   (Tel. 0840 770782)
£22 per person, b&b
Tintagel is not blessed with appealing hotels, but this substantial 1930s house in the nearby hamlet of Bossiney is a good place to spend a night or two if you are touring. The decor is rather dated but the hotel's situation more than makes up for that. A gate leads from the carefully tended grounds on

the coastal path and there is a lovely walk around to the magical Rocky Valley. Five bedrooms have expansive views over this dramatic section of coast. Downstairs, there is a bar in the lounge and a handsome dining room where dinner is served. The four-course table d'hôte menu is based on fresh produce and main course choices may include duck in port and orange, fish of the day, steak, and a vegetarian dish. The restaurant is open to non-residents. (Set menu, £10.50.) There are two ground-floor bedrooms, but no special facilities for disabled visitors.

Steep paths lead down to two sandy coves, which are revealed at low tide, and where locals swim; lovely coastal walks around Tintagel with its castle, medieval Old Post Office and extraordinary King Arthur's Halls

TOPSHAM

The Bridge Inn, Topsham, Exeter, Devon
(Tel. 0392 87 38762)
Two and a half miles from M5 junction 30; take A376 for Exmouth from Topsham
Open noon–2pm, 6pm–10.30pm
A 16th-century maltings above the River Clyst, the inn is a fascinating and eccentric place to visit, and a must for real ale freaks. It has been scheduled as an historic and ancient monument. Two of the four bars overlook the river, and there is an area of grass by the water. There are 16 real ales on offer, basic bar food is available at lunchtime, and visitors are guaranteed a warm reception by the entire Cheffers clan. Winners of the *Consumer Guide* award 'National Cellarman of the Year' in 1989.

Walks; salmon fishing on River Exe (check ahead on licence requirements); sailing and sea fishing can be arranged at Exmouth, five miles away

TORQUAY

🏨 43/64 🏠 🚴 ⚓ 💳

Livermead Cliff Hotel, Seafront, Torquay, Devon TQ2 6RQ
(Tel. 0803 299 666)
From Torquay, head for Livermead; the hotel is hard to miss
£44–£52 pp b&b; £53–£60 dinner and b&b
A family-owned hotel right on the seafront, with direct access
to the shore and the sea wall. From the elongated terrace in
front of the hotel, there are excellent views of the bay. The
restaurant seats 120, and most of the tables have a sea view (set
lunch costs £8.50). Snacks are available in sea-facing lounge.
Small pets can be accommodated by arrangement, for a charge
(£6 a day). It is worth noting that this hotel often has rooms
available, even at short notice. According to the manager,
people seem to assume they'll always be full.
*Heated outdoor swimming pool; solarium; walks to Cockington and
into Torquay; waterskiing and windsurfing nearby (ask at hotel);
jetskis and paragliding; fishing from hotel garden and steps (bring
equipment); beach adjacent*

TORQUAY

🏨 13/23 🏠 🚴 ⚓ 💳

The Osborne Hotel, Meadfoot Beach, Torquay TQ1 2LL
(Tel. 0803 213 311)
East of Torquay harbour; call for detailed directions
£54–£67 pp b&b (Suites cost £12 extra per person)
The hotel is in a Grade II listed Regency-style crescent out of
sight of Torquay, with large, well-decorated suites and a
terrace overlooking the sea. The rest of the crescent comprises
46 timeshare apartments run by the hotel. Five and a half acres
of private gardens sweep down to Meadfoot Beach. There are
two restaurants which seat 45 people each; in each, seven tables
have a sea view. A four-course dinner costs £19.95. Sporty
guests will find plenty to keep them busy: there are heated
swimming pools indoors and out, a games room, a snooker
room, a health club, a putting green, and an all-weather tennis

RYAN

3/3 ⌂14 ♪ ⌔ ▭

om Parc, Camels, Veryan, Cornwall TR2 5PJ
. 0872 501803)
50 b&b; dinner £8.50

bay-fronted Edwardian house stands alone in a magnifi-
cliff-top position on an exceptionally unspoilt part of the
h coast. It was a major star in last year's television
matisation of Mary Wesley's novel, *The Camomile Lawn*.
friendly owners, Keith and Lindsay Righton, have kept a
tograph album of the filming, during which time the house
redecorated three times, and the wallpapers used in the
are still on the walls. There are three large double rooms,
ith attached shower rooms. Two look straight out to sea
it is not unusual to see seagulls flying past at window level.
sts share the comfortable family sitting room and good
e cooking – including home-grown vegetables – is served
equest in the handsome dining room.
stal walks; the pretty fishing hamlet of Portloe and its pub are a
minute walk away along the coastal path

REHAM

2/4 ⌂ ♪ ⌔ ▭

Old Granary, The Quay, Wareham, Dorset BH20 4LP
. 0929 552010)
the A351 from Poole to Swanage
£33 pp b&b

attractive converted grain warehouse which is at least 200
s old, in a picturesque setting on the banks of River Frome,
rlooking the Purbeck Hills. The rooms are comfortable
unpretentious, with cottagey decor, and local prints on the
s. There are two restaurants (open from 9am to 9pm)
ch seat 65 altogether: both are homely and relaxing, with
cious home-made food (set lunch £7.95, set dinner £11.95).
of the restaurant tables have views of the river. Weather
mitting, the riverside terrace serves food all day, from
ning coffee, via cream teas, to dinner. Private moorings

court. Some rooms are accessible by ramp and lift, but there
are no special facilities for the disabled.
Beach (two minutes' walk); cliff walks; waterskiing and jetskiing in
Torbay (ask at hotel); fishing can be arranged

TOTNES

inn 3/7 ⌂ ♪ ⌔ ▭

The Waterman's Arms, Bow Bridge, Totnes, Devon
TQ9 7EG   (Tel. 0803 732214)
On the Tuckenhay road from Totnes
Open 11am–3pm, 6pm–11pm Mon–Sat; noon–2.30pm, 7pm–
10.30pm Sun
From £23.50 pp b&b
A snug yet extensive inn, which has grown out of an old
smithy, in a beautiful setting by Bow Bridge (which dates back
to the Domesday Book). The inn itself was once a jail for
Napoleonic prisoners. The decor includes old guns, copper
ornaments and brasses, and there are new stained-glass panels
above the bar, which overlooks the road and the river. The
dining room seats 64, and there is an extra family room, which
seats 30 people. There is seating for another 80 people in the
waterside garden. Bar specialities include Palmers, Dartmoor,
Tetley and Burton bitters, and guest beers, and fish dishes.
Fishing (salmon and trout, bring equipment); beach five miles away

TREBARWITH STRAND

⌂ ♪ ⌔ ▭

The Port William, Trebarwith Strand, Tintagel, Cornwall
PL34 0HB   (Tel. 0840 770230)
Open 11am–11pm Mon–Sat Easter–November (and noon–
3pm, 6pm–11pm Mon–Sat November–Easter); noon–
2.30pm, 7pm–10.30pm Sun
The pub is cosy within, though not beautiful on the outside,
and in a marvellous setting, on cliffs overlooking the beach at
Trebarwith Strand. Formerly, the building was a harbourmaster's house, office and stables. There are good sea views

from the bar, and the main attraction is the splendid front terrace, on the clifftop. St Austell ales, guest beers, and the local cider (in summer) are worth noting. There is an extensive menu of bar snacks (£1.40–£4.50), and main meals are served in the evening (£6–£10). Well-behaved pets are allowed into the bar if they are on leads. Children are allowed in the family areas. There is one self-catering holiday flat available for rent, which has two bedrooms overlooking the sea. Book well in advance, as it is very popular.

Trebarwith Strand swimming beach is half a minute away (has lifeguards in summer); surfing on beach; fishing from end of the drive; sea fishing trips from Boscastle (ask landlords); coastal path walks

TREBARWITH STRAND

The Old Millfloor, Trebarwith Strand, Tintagel, Cornwall
PL34 0HA   (Tel. 0840 770234)
Open for dinner all year; accommodation closed late
November to late March
£15 pp b&b
A converted mill dating from the 16th century, half a mile before Trebarwith Strand, and down a steep hill. There are ten acres of grounds, with the millstream winding through the pretty garden and right past the house. The dining room – from which you can hear, but not see, the stream – seats 14 people. Non-residents are welcome for the three-course dinner (£10.50; no lunch). The dining room is not licensed, so bring your own wine.

Sandy beach at Trebarwith Strand (half a mile away); walks on coastal path (to Boscastle and St Juliet), and to beach on path through grounds; golf at Rock; riding (four miles away); surfing at Trebarwith Strand beach, where the Surf Shop hires out equipment

UMBERLEIGH

Rising Sun, Umberleigh, North Devon EX
(Tel. 0769 60447)
On the A377 Barnstaple to Exeter
Open 11am–2.30pm, 6pm–11pm Mon–Sat
10.30pm Sun
£24.95 single, £47.50 double
A pleasant and historic inn near the River T
and seatrout river). An ideal place for fish
room and three and a half miles of private
views are not particularly impressive, b
extremely comfortable. The residents' lo
with angling souvenirs, and the front patio
river. Dogs can be accommodated by prior
*Fishing, £17.50 per day, for residents only (sea
September); riverside walks*

VERYAN

The Nare Hotel, Carne Beach, Veryan, Tru
TR2 5PF   (Tel. 0872 501279)
£51–£75 pp b&b
A fine hotel in a very peaceful location,
tended gardens and a safe sandy beach. The r
decorated; the result is an elegant yet home-l
rooms have a balcony or a patio from which t
A courtesy car is provided to fetch guests fro
station 12 miles away. Men are advised that j
recommended attire in the evenings. The rest
tables have a sea view), and serves light lunch
dinner £22). Dogs, but no other pets, are acc
all-weather tennis court at the hotel, togethe
pool, paddling pool, games room, sauna, and
*Coastal path walks; watersports along beach; ho
and one sports boat for waterskiing; complimenta
miles away)*

are available for use by guests. There is wheelchair access to the ground floor and the lavatories, though no specific facilities for the disabled.

Walks; watersports in Poole Harbour; fishing; beaches (6 miles away); riding; swimming pool; squash; badminton; boat hire (100 yards away)

WAREHAM

The Priory Hotel, Church Green, Wareham, Dorset
BH20 4ND   (Tel. 0929 551666)
Open all year
From £37.50 per person b&b; suites £85 per person
This medieval cluster of buildings has been sensitively converted into a splendidly luxurious hotel whose four acres of gardens lead down to the River Frome, with views of the distant Purbeck Hills – it's not cheap, but what nicer place to celebrate an anniversary or a birthday. From the windows you can see fluttering doves, lawns, topiary, herbaceous borders, roses, shrubs and a few masts poking up through the trees. On the river bank itself, a boathouse has been converted into four elegant double rooms, with balconies, antique furniture and whirlpool baths. The main dining room – the Abbot's Cellar – is in the vaulted cellars, while the other – the Greenwood Room – is altogether a much lighter affair. Dinner in both costs a set £22.50 (Sunday to Friday) and £26.50 on Saturdays, plus coffee, and on offer are dishes such as broccoli and almond soup and halibut with a champagne cream sauce. In the drawing-room leading out to the terrace a pianist plays jazz on Saturday nights.

Corfe Castle, the last outpost of Royalist resistance to Cromwell, is close by

WEST BEXINGTON

🏨 ≈ 10/13 🏠 ⚓ 🚫 💳

The Manor Hotel, Beach Road, West Bexington, Dorset
DT2 9DF   (Tel. 0308 897 785)
On coast road between West Bay and Weymouth
£32 pp b&b, £47.95 dinner and b&b
A small and very comfortable hotel, with Jacobean oak
panelling in the hall, and two lounges for residents. The
original building was the Ancient Manor House of Bessington,
which merited a mention in the Domesday book. This has
been interestingly and thoughtfully developed: a pine conservatory extension of the bar fits in surprisingly well, and has
good sea views. The original stone-lined cellar is now a bar,
and there is an extensive bar menu, and the restaurant (no
water views) seats 64 people for more serious meals.
Boating; sea fishing; golf; riding; shooting; walks; beach

WESTON-SUPER-MARE

🏨 ≈ 24/40 🏠 ⚓ 🚫 💳

The Royal Pier Hotel, Birnbeck Road, Weston-super-Mare,
Avon BS23 2EJ   (Tel. 0934 626 644)
£49.50–£80 pp b&b
A ten-minute walk from the town centre, this large, seafront
hotel stands on a headland and enjoys good views across
Weston Bay to Wales. Public rooms and bedrooms have
recently been redecorated in comforting tones of peach, green
and brown. Over half the bedrooms overlook the water,
which recedes quite a distance at low tide. The lounge and two
bars look out to sea, as do all the tables in the 80-cover
restaurant. Five-course dinners cost £12.95, and full lunches
are available. Snacks and simple, hearty meals are served
in the bar. Conference facilities available. Rooms are accessible
by lift, but there are no special facilities for the disabled.
Walks; fishing trips can be arranged; beach; two golf courses in
Weston; nearby watersports, tennis courts and riding facilities

court. Some rooms are accessible by ramp and lift, but there are no special facilities for the disabled.
Beach (two minutes' walk); cliff walks; waterskiing and jetskiing in Torbay (ask at hotel); fishing can be arranged

TOTNES

inn ³/7

The Waterman's Arms, Bow Bridge, Totnes, Devon
TQ9 7EG   (Tel. 0803 732214)
On the Tuckenhay road from Totnes
Open 11am–3pm, 6pm–11pm Mon–Sat; noon–2.30pm, 7pm–10.30pm Sun
From £23.50 pp b&b
A snug yet extensive inn, which has grown out of an old smithy, in a beautiful setting by Bow Bridge (which dates back to the Domesday Book). The inn itself was once a jail for Napoleonic prisoners. The decor includes old guns, copper ornaments and brasses, and there are new stained-glass panels above the bar, which overlooks the road and the river. The dining room seats 64, and there is an extra family room, which seats 30 people. There is seating for another 80 people in the waterside garden. Bar specialities include Palmers, Dartmoor, Tetley and Burton bitters, and guest beers, and fish dishes.
Fishing (salmon and trout, bring equipment); beach five miles away

TREBARWITH STRAND

The Port William, Trebarwith Strand, Tintagel, Cornwall
PL34 0HB   (Tel. 0840 770230)
Open 11am–11pm Mon–Sat Easter–November (and noon–3pm, 6pm–11pm Mon–Sat November–Easter); noon–2.30pm, 7pm–10.30pm Sun
The pub is cosy within, though not beautiful on the outside, and in a marvellous setting, on cliffs overlooking the beach at Trebarwith Strand. Formerly, the building was a harbour-master's house, office and stables. There are good sea views

from the bar, and the main attraction is the splendid front terrace, on the clifftop. St Austell ales, guest beers, and the local cider (in summer) are worth noting. There is an extensive menu of bar snacks (£1.40–£4.50), and main meals are served in the evening (£6–£10). Well-behaved pets are allowed into the bar if they are on leads. Children are allowed in the family areas. There is one self-catering holiday flat available for rent, which has two bedrooms overlooking the sea. Book well in advance, as it is very popular.

Trebarwith Strand swimming beach is half a minute away (has lifeguards in summer); surfing on beach; fishing from end of the drive; sea fishing trips from Boscastle (ask landlords); coastal path walks

TREBARWITH STRAND

🏠 2/3 🛝 🚭 🐾 🚽

The Old Millfloor, Trebarwith Strand, Tintagel, Cornwall PL34 0HA   (Tel. 0840 770234)
Open for dinner all year; accommodation closed late November to late March
£15 pp b&b
A converted mill dating from the 16th century, half a mile before Trebarwith Strand, and down a steep hill. There are ten acres of grounds, with the millstream winding through the pretty garden and right past the house. The dining room – from which you can hear, but not see, the stream – seats 14 people. Non-residents are welcome for the three-course dinner (£10.50; no lunch). The dining room is not licensed, so bring your own wine.

Sandy beach at Trebarwith Strand (half a mile away); walks on coastal path (to Boscastle and St Juliet), and to beach on path through grounds; golf at Rock; riding (four miles away); surfing at Trebarwith Strand beach, where the Surf Shop hires out equipment

UMBERLEIGH

inn ³/₈ 🏠 🚴 🖉 💳

Rising Sun, Umberleigh, North Devon EX37 9DU
(Tel. 0769 60447)
On the A377 Barnstaple to Exeter
Open 11am–2.30pm, 6pm–11pm Mon–Sat; noon–3pm, 7pm–
10.30pm Sun
£24.95 single, £47.50 double
A pleasant and historic inn near the River Taw (a good salmon
and seatrout river). An ideal place for fishermen, with a rod
room and three and a half miles of private fishing. The river
views are not particularly impressive, but the rooms are
extremely comfortable. The residents' lounge is bedecked
with angling souvenirs, and the front patio area overlooks the
river. Dogs can be accommodated by prior arrangement.
*Fishing, £17.50 per day, for residents only (season is 1 March to 30
September); riverside walks*

VERYAN

🏘 ²⁶/₄₀ 🏠 🚴 🖉 💳

The Nare Hotel, Carne Beach, Veryan, Truro, Cornwall
TR2 5PF   (Tel. 0872 501279)
£51–£75 pp b&b
A fine hotel in a very peaceful location, overlooking well-
tended gardens and a safe sandy beach. The rooms are tastefully
decorated; the result is an elegant yet home-like interior; many
rooms have a balcony or a patio from which to enjoy the views.
A courtesy car is provided to fetch guests from Truro railway
station 12 miles away. Men are advised that jackets and ties are
recommended attire in the evenings. The restaurant seats 80 (all
tables have a sea view), and serves light lunches and dinner (set
dinner £22). Dogs, but no other pets, are accepted. There is an
all-weather tennis court at the hotel, together with swimming
pool, paddling pool, games room, sauna, and solarium.
*Coastal path walks; watersports along beach; hotel has windsurfers,
and one sports boat for waterskiing; complimentary golf at Truro (10
miles away)*

VERYAN

Broom Parc, Camels, Veryan, Cornwall TR2 5PJ
(Tel. 0872 501803)
£17.50 b&b; dinner £8.50
This bay-fronted Edwardian house stands alone in a magnificent cliff-top position on an exceptionally unspoilt part of the south coast. It was a major star in last year's television dramatisation of Mary Wesley's novel, *The Camomile Lawn*. The friendly owners, Keith and Lindsay Righton, have kept a photograph album of the filming, during which time the house was redecorated three times, and the wallpapers used in the film are still on the walls. There are three large double rooms, all with attached shower rooms. Two look straight out to sea and it is not unusual to see seagulls flying past at window level. Guests share the comfortable family sitting room and good home cooking – including home-grown vegetables – is served on request in the handsome dining room.
Coastal walks; the pretty fishing hamlet of Portloe and its pub are a 20-minute walk away along the coastal path

WAREHAM

The Old Granary, The Quay, Wareham, Dorset BH20 4LP
(Tel. 0929 552010)
On the A351 from Poole to Swanage
£19–£33 pp b&b
An attractive converted grain warehouse which is at least 200 years old, in a picturesque setting on the banks of River Frome, overlooking the Purbeck Hills. The rooms are comfortable and unpretentious, with cottagey decor, and local prints on the walls. There are two restaurants (open from 9am to 9pm) which seat 65 altogether: both are homely and relaxing, with delicious home-made food (set lunch £7.95, set dinner £11.95). Half of the restaurant tables have views of the river. Weather permitting, the riverside terrace serves food all day, from morning coffee, via cream teas, to dinner. Private moorings

are available for use by guests. There is wheelchair access to the
ground floor and the lavatories, though no specific facilities for
the disabled.

*Walks; watersports in Poole Harbour; fishing; beaches (6 miles
away); riding; swimming pool; squash; badminton; boat hire (100
yards away)*

WAREHAM

The Priory Hotel, Church Green, Wareham, Dorset
BH20 4ND   (Tel. 0929 551666)
Open all year
From £37.50 per person b&b; suites £85 per person
This medieval cluster of buildings has been sensitively
converted into a splendidly luxurious hotel whose four acres of
gardens lead down to the River Frome, with views of the
distant Purbeck Hills – it's not cheap, but what nicer place to
celebrate an anniversary or a birthday. From the windows you
can see fluttering doves, lawns, topiary, herbaceous borders,
roses, shrubs and a few masts poking up through the trees. On
the river bank itself, a boathouse has been converted into four
elegant double rooms, with balconies, antique furniture and
whirlpool baths. The main dining room – the Abbot's Cellar –
is in the vaulted cellars, while the other – the Greenwood
Room – is altogether a much lighter affair. Dinner in both costs
a set £22.50 (Sunday to Friday) and £26.50 on Saturdays, plus
coffee, and on offer are dishes such as broccoli and almond
soup and halibut with a champagne cream sauce. In the
drawing-room leading out to the terrace a pianist plays jazz on
Saturday nights.

*Corfe Castle, the last outpost of Royalist resistance to Cromwell, is
close by*

WEST BEXINGTON

🏠 10/13 🛶 ⚓ 🚫 💳

The Manor Hotel, Beach Road, West Bexington, Dorset
DT2 9DF   (Tel. 0308 897 785)
On coast road between West Bay and Weymouth
£32 pp b&b, £47.95 dinner and b&b
A small and very comfortable hotel, with Jacobean oak
panelling in the hall, and two lounges for residents. The
original building was the Ancient Manor House of Bessington,
which merited a mention in the Domesday book. This has
been interestingly and thoughtfully developed: a pine conservatory extension of the bar fits in surprisingly well, and has
good sea views. The original stone-lined cellar is now a bar,
and there is an extensive bar menu, and the restaurant (no
water views) seats 64 people for more serious meals.
Boating; sea fishing; golf; riding; shooting; walks; beach

WESTON-SUPER-MARE

🏠 24/40 🛶 ⚓ 🚫 💳

The Royal Pier Hotel, Birnbeck Road, Weston-super-Mare,
Avon BS23 2EJ   (Tel. 0934 626 644)
£49.50–£80 pp b&b
A ten-minute walk from the town centre, this large, seafront
hotel stands on a headland and enjoys good views across
Weston Bay to Wales. Public rooms and bedrooms have
recently been redecorated in comforting tones of peach, green
and brown. Over half the bedrooms overlook the water,
which recedes quite a distance at low tide. The lounge and two
bars look out to sea, as do all the tables in the 80-cover
restaurant. Five-course dinners cost £12.95, and full lunches
are available. Snacks and simple, hearty meals are served
in the bar. Conference facilities available. Rooms are accessible
by lift, but there are no special facilities for the disabled.
*Walks; fishing trips can be arranged; beach; two golf courses in
Weston; nearby watersports, tennis courts and riding facilities*

WEYMOUTH

inn ⁰/⁶ 🏠 ♿ 🚫 ▭

The Smugglers Inn, Osmington Mills, nr Weymouth,
Dorset DT3 6HF (Tel. 0305 833125)
One mile from the A353, clearly signposted
Open 11am–2.30pm, 6pm–11pm Mon–Sat (11am–11pm July
and August); noon–3pm, 7pm–10.30pm Sun
£20–£28 single, £40–£48 twin, £40–£50 double b&b
An attractive pub, set in a hollow on the Dorset coastal path,
with a bubbling stream and clifftop views, 50 yards from the
beach where Constable painted 'Weymouth Bay'. There has
been an inn here since the 13th century; four and a half acres of
grounds extend to the high-tide mark. Refurbishments a few
years ago have in no way detracted from the Smugglers'
immense character. Real ales are served at the bar. The
restaurant seats 80 (no water views), and provides the famous
Osmington Bay lobsters (£14–£24 for a whole one). The
restaurant is open from noon to 2pm and 7pm to 9.30pm; bar
snacks available from 11.30am to 2.30pm, and 6.30pm to
9.30pm. In summer, the barbecues here are very popular.
Coastal and inland walks; jetskiing, waterskiing, windsurfing (all at
Weymouth); yachting (in Kingstead); coarse, beach and sea angling;
Weymouth and Preston beaches, Ringstead Bay and Osmington Bay

WEYMOUTH

🍴 🏠 ♿ 🚫 ▭

The Sea Cow Restaurant, 7 Custom House Quay, Weymouth,
Dorset DT4 9BE (Tel. 0305 783524)
On the harbourside in Weymouth
Open noon–2pm, 7.30pm–10.15pm; closed Sunday evenings
September–June
On the harbourside, five minutes' walk from ferry terminal,
the restaurant is made up of four rooms, each with a different
character. Most of the tables have harbour views. The ground-
floor rooms offer evening meals and in summer (June to
September) one room is open from 10am for coffee and light
lunches. The first floor offers a cold-buffet-and-carvery lunch.

Much of the fish comes straight from the quay, and the menu also has varied and extensive vegetarian and meat dishes. The restaurant has held the Routiers Casserole Award for three years running, and the chef, Terry Woolcock, is a member of the British Team of Chefs. A very hospitable place. No specific facilities for the disabled, though the doorways are wide, the restaurant is all on one level, and the lavatories are large enough for wheelchair access.

Beach; coastal walks; watersports; fishing; Deep Sea Adventure Museum; History Museum in Brewers Quay; hydrofoil to the Channel Islands leaves from the harbour

WINKTON

Fisherman's Haunt Hotel, Salisbury Road, Winkton, Christchurch, Dorset BH23 7AS   (Tel. 0202 477283)
On the B3347
£48 pp b&b, £51 double b&b (four-posters £55)
An attractive 17th-century hotel with good gardens and extensive parking; very popular for its food, so be warned that the restaurant can get very busy. The restaurant and conservatory seat 80, and offer excellent traditional English fare and unspectacular water views. There are two four-poster beds, and the hotel is a popular place for weddings. Despite the name, the hotel is not particularly geared up for fishermen: the location is better suited to walkers, and guests who want to fish must make their arrangements in Christchurch. If you do happen to find fishermen staying, they have probably dropped by for the food. One room is designed to accommodate wheelchairs.

Walks; beach and watersports in Bournemouth and Christchurch (15 minutes by car)

WOOLACOMBE

🏨 7/10 ♨ ⚓₇ 🐕 ⟐ 💳

The Little Beach Hotel, The Esplanade, Woolacombe, Devon
EX34 7DJ   (Tel. 0271 870 398)
Open March to October
£31–£43 pp dinner and b&b
Small, family-run and on the seafront, the Little Beach is a
solid Edwardian house built of local slate and stone. Newly
refurbished, the rooms are comfortable and bright, with good
decor; the three seafront rooms share a balcony. The spacious
dining room seats 22 people, and all tables look out over the
beach. Non-residents can enjoy the 'imaginative home
cooking', but must book in advance. A five-course dinner
costs £11.50. Altogether, good value: you won't find hidden
extras working their way mysteriously on to your bill. The
hotel has a small antique shop, open to residents only. Popular
for spring mini-breaks (March to May).
*Three miles of golden-sand beach 500 yards from hotel; walks on
coastal path and in surrounding National Trust land – the hotel staff
are happy to provide maps and ideas for itineraries; clay pigeon
shooting can be arranged; surfing and windsurfing; fishing from beach
and surrounding rocks*

WOOLACOMBE

🏨 24/26 ♨ ⚓ 🐕 ⟐ 💳

The Watersmeet Hotel, Mortehoe, Woolacombe, North
Devon EX34 7EB   (Tel. 0271 870 333)
Closed December and January
£45–£75 pp dinner and b&b
A medium-sized hotel by a small cove on the headland at
Mortehoe, with fabulous views, especially from the new
octagonal Pavilion restaurant (50 places; all tables have an
excellent view of the sea). The food is particularly good; in
1989, the chefs won second and third places in Roux Brothers'
Chefs Scholarship. The rooms are very comfortable indeed –
each has individual designer decor – and the whole place is
peaceful and not ostentatious. Bridge and painting weekends

are a speciality. Pets can be accommodated by arrangement. There is one ground-floor suite, which is popular with disabled visitors.

Walks on Devon coastal path; windsurfing and surfing; river, lake, and sea fishing (boats from local harbour); secluded, semi-private beach in front of hotel; golf (championship course at Saunton), clay pigeon shooting; painting holidays

WOOLACOMBE

39/59

Woolacombe Bay Hotel, South Street, Woolacombe, Devon
EX34 7BN   (Tel. 0271 870 388)
Closed January
£44–£88 pp dinner and b&b

Oldest and grandest of Woolacombe's hotels: a rambling Victorian building standing in grounds that sweep down to the sea. There is a splendid air of fading grandeur to the place, and many original features give a pleasant feel to public rooms, though the bedrooms can be fairly utilitarian, and the views are not exceptional. The dining room seats 140 (non-residents are welcome), with about 20 tables overlooking the sea. The hotel is famous for its seven-course dinners; these and the full English breakfasts are included in the room price, and many guests find they cannot manage lunch as well. Those that can might visit Maxwell's bistro, within the hotel. Diversions for guests include a sauna, spa bath, squash courts, solarium, fitness room, tennis, croquet, swingball, short-mat bowling, a snooker room, and indoor and outdoor swimming pools. No facilities for the disabled, though there is a ramp that gives wheelchair access to the restaurant, and hotel has a lift to three floors.

Walks; golf; sea fishing from Ilfracombe can be arranged; the main three-mile beach, and other smaller beaches, are set between the National Trust headlands of Morte Point and Baggy Point; the Frolica, *the hotel boat (a 40-foot Swordsman), can take guests on day trips to Lundy Island (home to many puffins and seals, £44 pp), or up and down the coast. The crew are members of a sub-aqua club, and can take people diving in the protected area off Lundy*

Scotland

Telegraph
SCOTLAND

PENTLAND FIRTH

Stroma

THURSO

WICK

Helmsdale

Buckie

Bridge of Marnoch

Banff

Golspie

Lairg

Tain

Delnies

DINGWALL

INVERNESS

Kinlochbervie

Scourie

Lochinver

Achiltibuie

Ullapool

Dundonnell

Bunchrew

Whitebridge

Fort Augustus

Shieldaig

Plockton

ISLE OF LOCHALSH

Glenbhiel

THE MINCH

Skye

MORAY FIRTH

NORTH

HIGHLAND

CAIRN...PIAN

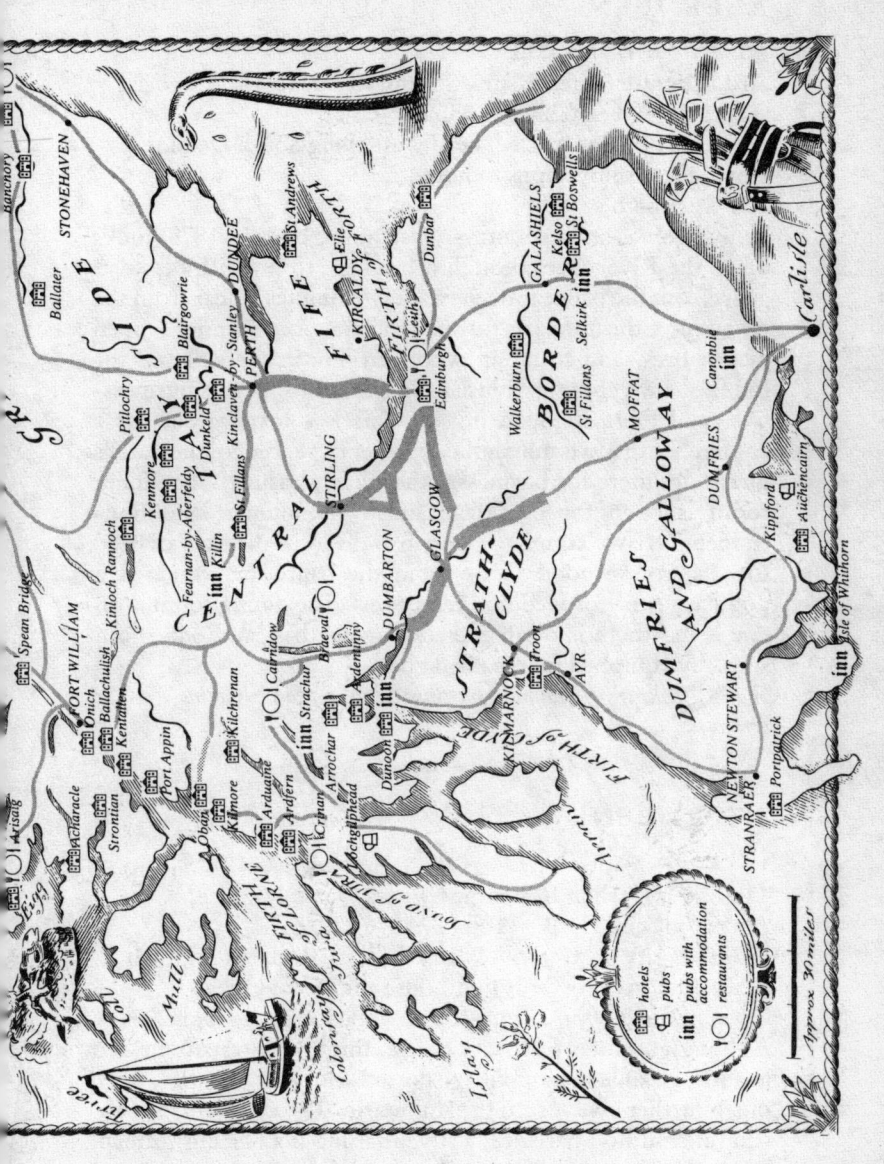

ABERDEEN

Ardoe House Hotel, Blairs, South Deeside Road, Aberdeen
AB1 5YP   (Tel. 0224 867 355)
From Old Bridge of Dee, head west along South Deeside
Road, then follow signs to hotel
£70–£125 b&b
This baronial-style country-house hotel, built in 1878, looks
on to the River Dee, though it has little to do with the river
apart from the panoramic views. Five minutes by car from the
city centre, the hotel has turrets and heraldic inscriptions; open
hearth fires, and stunning wood carving in the hall and the
lounge lend a country-house feel. The atmosphere is business-
like, and there is piped music. This is a better place for a
conference than a family holiday: seventy per cent of the hotel's
guests are there for business rather than pleasure. The dining
room is open for breakfast, lunch and dinner, and non-
residents are welcome; vegetarian and special diets are catered
for. There are good views from the ballroom, which is a
popular venue for wedding receptions. The dining room is on
one level, there is disabled access to the bar, and one room
specially equipped for disabled guests.
Walks; fishing; pétanque; putting; clay pigeon shooting can be
arranged

ABERDEEN

The Silver Darling Restaurant, Pocra Quay, Footdee,
Aberdeen AB2 1DQ   (Tel. 0224 576 229)
From the city centre, follow Beach Boulevard, turn right at
beach and drive towards lighthouse and Pocra Quay
Open noon–2.30pm, 7pm–10pm Mon–Sat; 7pm–10pm Sun
Although minutes from city centre, this lovely restaurant, set
in a picturesque fishing village dotted with tiny cottages, feels
much further away from the real world. The menu focuses on
fish (in common parlance, a silver darling is a herring), much
of it cooked on the wood barbecue, and the fresh pastries are

well worth sampling. There is seating for 30 people, and the three window tables offer the best sea views. The restaurant is an attractive shape, with pretty decor: the watercolours and Victorian prints on the walls are for sale (prices start at £17). There is a wide door, a ramp, and a lavatory for disabled visitors.
Walks; watersports; fishing; beach

ACHILTIBUIE

Summer Isles Hotel, Achiltibuie, by Ullapool, Ross–shire IV26 2YG   (Tel. 085 482 282)
Turn left off the A835 10 miles north of Ullapool; it's then 15 miles to Achiltibuie
Open April to October
£51–£75 per room b&b
Fifteen miles of single-track road lead to this remote hotel with spectacular views out over the Summer Isles. It is certainly well off the beaten track: Lucy Irvine, sister of the proprietor, wrote *Castaway* here. The interior is spacious, the decor warm and comfortable, and the large windows make the most of the views, though the Hydroponicum, an indoor garden building on the shore 200 yards from the house, is less than beautiful. There is a snug bar; the restaurant seats 26 people, with six sea-facing window tables – a five-course dinner costs £28. Vegetarians should give advance notice. All of the tables in the restaurant face the sea. Dogs can be accommodated by arrangement.
Mountain-range walks; fresh water and sea fishing (equipment not supplied); boating around islands; bird watching; sandy beaches

ACHARACLE

Glencripesdale House, Loch Sunart, Acharacle, Argyll PA36 4JH   (Tel. 096 785 263 – this is a radio telephone, so keep trying)

Detailed directions (which are crucial) are sent to guests when a booking is made

Open March to October, Christmas and New Year

£57.25 full board pp

A modernized 18th-century farmhouse 200 yards from the shores of Loch Sunart, in a remote spot at the end of a nine-mile track from the main road, which takes an hour to drive. No other buildings are visible from the house, and there is no mains electricity supply. The views across Loch Sunart, backed by the Ardnamurchan mountains, are magnificent. Inside, the hotel is neat and modern yet comfortable, with ornaments and the odd antique that add character. The general atmosphere tends to be formal, but this must vary, depending on your co-guests: you will escape the world here but not the other refugees. (The proprietors consider that any air of formality comes entirely from the visitors: they just want guests to enjoy themselves.) The food and wine are very fine: there are three puddings every night, and guests are encouraged to 'do the hat-trick'. Dogs are not allowed into the house. *Conducted trips around the loch in an inflatable boat; hotel fishing dinghy and two windsurfers (bring own wetsuit); scuba diving (limited equipment, e.g. cylinders available); walking*

ARDENTINNY

The Ardentinny Hotel, Loch Long, nr Dunoon, Argyll
PA23 8TR   (Tel. 036 981 209)

Twelve miles north of Dunoon on the A880

Accommodation closed November–March; food available all year

£30–£80 b&b

From its perch on a Loch Long promontory, this white 18th-century droving inn enjoys brilliant views up and down the loch. It is popular with Clyde yachtsmen, and there are private moorings for boats. The Argyll Forest Park surrounds the hotel. The bedrooms are straightforward and practical, and most of them have loch views. An unfussy and friendly place, where the waterside gardens are regularly full at lunchtime. The restaurant seats 65 people (set dinner £17.50). There is access for the disabled, and lavatory facilities, but no suitable bedrooms.

Fifty miles of forest walks; garden walks; fishing; sailing; boating; sandy beach (one mile away)

ARDFERN

🏨 2/9 🏠 🕯 ✐ 💳

The Galley of Lorne Hotel, Ardfern, by Lochgilphead, Argyll PA31 8QN   (Tel. 085 25 284)
On the B8002, signposted off the A816 Lochgilphead to Oban
£19–£27 pp b&b
An attractive, informal hotel, right on Loch Craignish. There are big navigation lamps in the panelled bar, where food is served up in generous portions. The bistro area has a piano and a dance floor, though apparently these are only called into action for Hogmanay. The restaurant, called Creels, offers two window tables; its specialities are Loch Craignish king prawns and Scottish cheeses: an à la carte dinner will set you back £14. Vegetarian dishes can be provided, given advance notice. The entire hotel – motel-style bedrooms and bathrooms included – is on one floor, and so should not present a problem for disabled visitors.

Waterskiing; windsurfing; trout and sea fishing; boat trips; clay pigeon shooting; riding

ARDUAINE

🏨 25/26 🏠 🕯 ✐ 💳

The Loch Melfort Hotel, Arduaine, by Oban, Argyll PA34 4XG   (Tel. 085 22 233)
Signposted off the A816, 19 miles south of Oban
Closed January and February
£42.75–£51.50 pp b&b
Set in 30 acres of rolling pasture and woodland, the hotel faces south across Asknish Bay, with magnificent views of Shuna, Scarba and Jura: it is no idle boast that they possess the finest

location on the West Coast. There are mooring facilities and showers for passing yachtsmen. The chartroom bar opens out on to a waterside terrace and has a pair of tremendous mounted marine glasses for spotting seals in the bay. All rooms but one look out to sea; the six rooms in the old part of the hotel are particularly attractive, but those in the modern extension are utilitarian, though saved by the splendid views. Fifteen tables enjoy views from the restaurant's huge windows; the set dinner costs from £19.95. The hotel is renowned for its shellfish, which are kept in their own pots at the end of the jetty. It also has a well-stocked library. There is a portable ramp and four ground-floor rooms for the disabled.

Riding; sailing; windsurfing; canoeing; waterskiing; fishing on hill lochs, river and sea; garden walks (Arduaine Gardens are next to the hotel); small sandy beach

ARISAIG

Arisaig House, Beasdale, by Arisaig, Inverness-shire
PH39 4NR   (Tel. 06875 622)
On the A830 at Beasdale, three miles south-east of Arisaig
Open from mid-March to early November
£84.50–£134 pp dinner and b&b

Giant Sequoia and Wellingtonia line the drive of this stone mansion overlooking Loch nan Uamh. Built in 1864 and completely refitted in the 1930s, the hotel has now been sensitively modernized, with fine wallpapers which run through the beautiful bedrooms: each room is named after a different loch, and nearly all of them look out over the loch. The atmosphere is one of spacious, solid luxury (the hotel is a Relais et Châteaux member, with attendant high standards), and the large windows make for a light interior. Four tables in the dining room look out to the loch. There are 20 acres of grounds. It is a 10-minute walk down to the sea, through private woods, so the views are long range, but excellent because the house is so well situated.

Croquet; golf; fishing; climbing; walks; sailing at Arisaig; beach

ARISAIG

‖◯‖ ⁴/₇ ⌂ 🚶 ◁ ▭

The Old Library Lodge and Restaurant, Arisaig, Inverness-
shire PH39 4NH   (Tel. 06875 651)
On the A830 in Arisaig village, 10 miles before Mallaig
Open from April to October
£28 pp b&b
This 200-year-old converted barn, in an area famous for its
links with the Jacobite Rebellion, has good views of Loch nan
Ceall and the Inner Hebrides. The village street – which is also
the main road to Skye – runs between the hotel and the sea. The
sea-view bedrooms are slightly cramped; the rooms in the
modern extension at the rear are larger, but have no view of
the water. The residents' lounge is homely; the highlight of the
hotel is its charming bistro-style restaurant. This seats 28
people: there is one table in the window, and several outside.
Cooking is modern and British, with a strong emphasis on
local fish; Alan Broadhurst, the chef, was a former navy diver,
who has now turned passionate cook. The set dinner menu
costs £16.50; light lunches are also available.
*Walks; visits to Skye, Rhum, Eigg and Muck; boat trips and fishing
on Loch Morar; spectacular beach three miles away was used as a*
Local Hero *location; golf (three miles away)*

ARISAIG

🏨 ⁹/₁₅ ⌂ 🚶 ◁ ▭

The Arisaig Hotel, Arisaig, Inverness-shire PH39 4NH
(Tel. 06875 210)
In Arisaig village, 10 miles before Mallaig on the A830
£34–£45 pp b&b
This comfortably old-fashioned hotel was an early Jacobite
inn. Now modernized, its rooms have recently been upgraded;
there are good open fires and fine views of the island of Eigg
across the road and the marina. The bar is cosy and has over 100
malt whiskies on offer as well as a wide range of bar food; a
two-course dinner at the bar costs from £5 to £12. The

restaurant offers good home cooking, with the emphasis on fresh local fish; a full dinner costs £21.50. One unusual attraction of the locality is a cave where Bonnie Prince Charlie once stayed.

Fishing and boating can be arranged; walks; sandy beach and golf (three miles away); cruising to the islands

ARROCHAR

38/83

Arrochar Hotel, Arrochar, Dunbartonshire G83 7AU
(Tel. 0301 2482)
At Tarbert (Loch Lomond) take A83 for Arrochar (2 miles)
Open March to November
From £18 pp, b&b

Here the visitor will find Scotland at its very best, an area of wild beauty, with many lochs and several peaks over 3,000 feet. No wonder that the Vikings came visiting in earlier times. It is said that at the turn of the century pubs outnumbered inhabitants in Arrochar, but the balance has since been redressed. Situated 50 yards from Loch Long, a sea-loch, this large hotel enjoys all the advantages of a magnificent position and glorious scenery, yet lies only an hour's drive from Glasgow. The restaurant seats 143, and 25 tables have a view of the water. Everything on the large varied menu is home-made, and a three-course meal costs £11.50. Bar meals are also available. Loch Lomond is virtually next door, with fresh-water fishing and frequent boat-trips during the season. For the disabled, the hotel has 12 ground-floor bedrooms. All public areas, including lavatories, are on one level on the ground floor, and there is a lift to upper floors.

Fishing (boat-hire necessary). Walking, climbing, birdwatching, hunting and swimming in the immediate vicinity. Golf, ice-skating, indoor bowls, curling, sauna and cinema within 20 miles

AUCHENCAIRN

🏨 7/13 🏕 🎿 🐦 ▭

The Balcary Bay Hotel, Auchencairn, nr Castle Douglas,
Kirkcudbrightshire DG7 1QZ (Tel. 055 664 217/311)
Village is on the A711 between Kirkcudbright and Dalbeattie.
Hotel is signposted on shore road, two miles out of village
Open from March to mid November
£38–£45 pp b&b, £55–£60 pp dinner and b&b
Originally built as a country house for a firm of smugglers in
1625, the hotel nestles in a secluded spot right on Balcary Bay.
The area is well off the main tourist trail to the Highlands.
There are three acres of gardens and super views across the bay
to Heston Island (which can be reached on foot at low tide).
Inside, the hotel has been discreetly modernized, with an open
fire in the reception on chilly evenings. The interior, with its
utility furniture, is not especially easy on the eye, but the
bedrooms are light and airy, and the public rooms comfortable. The restaurant seats 50 people; most tables have a water
view, and there is one table in a bay window (set dinner
£17).
*Walks; eight miles to golf; sailing and windsurfing (bring equipment);
rocky beaches; riding nearby*

BALLACHULISH

🏨 17/30 🏕 🎿 🐦 ▭

The Ballachulish Hotel, Ballachulish, Argyll PA39 4JY
(Tel. 085 52 606)
On the A828 Oban to Fort William road
£46.35–£52.60 pp b&b
This listed Scottish Baronial building on Loch Linnhe retains
its grand character despite modernizations; the site was
formerly a ferry port for crossing the loch. By night, it is
floodlit; inside, the reception rooms are gracious, with high
ceilings. Large gothic-arched windows look across the road on
to Loch Linnhe and up to the main road bridge. The cheery
bedrooms are furnished in country style, with pine furniture
and floral prints. The restaurant has room for 70, with seven

window tables that have the best views of the loch. Light lunches are served all day, and the set dinner costs £17.50.

Hotel can arrange mountain hikes; canoeing; sailing; windsurfing; fishing; cruising on the loch; walks

BALLATER

Monaltrie Lodge, 5 Bridge Square, Ballater, Grampian
(Tel. 03397 554417)
On A93, 42 miles from Aberdeen, or 70 miles from Perth
Open January to December
£65 per room

This place has real character. In a former incarnation, it was known as the Invercauld Arms, and was a rambling building of eccentric charms, most of whose customers came for the hunting, shooting and fishing. They seemed not to object to a diet of brown Windsor soup, overcooked cabbage and stodgy puddings. Times have changed, and in these more democratic days the hotel has been smartened up under new managment, catering standards have improved and members of the landed gentry are seen there less frequently. As well as the Scottish cuisine available at lunchtimes in the lounge bar, you can try the exotic specialities offered by the hotel's Thai Orchid restaurant. The setting is idyllic, just beside the River Dee, with its soothing sound of running water. There are pleasant walks alongside the river, and on the other side of the water, over the sturdy, granite bridge, towers the mass of Craig Coillich, bristling with conifers, its summit easily accessible by footpath. Little changed since the time of Queen Victoria, Ballater is one of the most charming of Scottish villages, several of its shops enjoying the patronage of royal visitors from nearby Balmoral.

Skiing; gliding; golf; pony trekking

BANCHORY

🏨 8/14 ⚓️₈ 🍴 🚫 💳

Invery House, Bridge of Feugh, Banchory, Kincardineshire
AB3 3NJ (Tel. 03302 4782)
Just past Bridge of Feugh, on the B974 (off the A93 at
Banchory)
£90–£140 pp b&b April to September; October to March
dinner and b&b for the same price
This attractive hotel sits at the end of a lovely drive, on the west
bank of the River Feugh in 47 acres of grounds. Carefully
restored in 1910, the decor pays meticulous attention to detail.
Everything matches, and the bedrooms are exceptionally
comfortable: even the pickiest perfectionist should be happy
here. Books, magazines, whisky, ice and glasses are provided
in the rooms, as well as fine bathrobes, towels and luxury bath
oils. The restaurant seats 34, and six of the tables overlook the
river: a five-course dinner costs £33.50, and the menu changes
daily. The wine cellar is well stocked, with over 500 wines.
There are kenneling facilities for dogs within the hotel
grounds. There are ground-floor facilities and a lavatory for
disabled visitors, but no specially adapted bedrooms.
*Billiard room; tennis; croquet; putting; one mile salmon and trout
fishing on the River Feugh in hotel grounds (free); fishing on the Dee
(£100 a day in season); walks; gliding; riding; pony trekking; 20 golf
courses within 20 miles (£6 winter, £15 summer)*

BANCHORY

🏨 14/23 ⚓️ 🚫 🖐 💳

Banchory Lodge Hotel, Banchory, Kincardineshire AB3 3HS
(Tel. 03302 2625)
On the A93, 18 miles west of Aberdeen
Closed 12 December to 25 January
£70.50 single, £99.90 double, £117.50 deluxe double dinner
and b&b. No charge for children if they are sharing parents'
room

Richly wooded grounds surround this secluded Georgian country house. The interior is comfortably furnished in period style, with open log fires in lounge and bar. Both lounges enjoy beautiful views over the River Dee. Altogether, the hotel is very comfortable, and completely unstuffy, and the staff are very friendly. Three of the bedrooms have four-poster beds. The restaurant has room for 80, and all tables overlook the water. Non-residents are welcome: a three-course lunch costs £11.50; a four-course dinner costs £23.50, and the menu is strong on local fish. There are facilities for holding private dinner parties at the hotel. Additional attractions inside the hotel include a pool table and sauna. At Bridge of Feugh, nearby, you can see salmon leaping upstream. The hotel was awarded an RAC Blue Ribbon in 1990 (the only one in Scotland).

Bowling; golf; tennis; pony trekking; gliding; salmon and sea trout fishing on a one-and-a-half-mile stretch of River Dee (five rods, book in advance); forest walks and nature trails

BANFF

7/8

Banff Links Hotel, Swordanes, Banff AB4 2JJ
(Tel. 02612 2414)
Signposted off the A98, between Banff and Portsoy
£25–£30 pp b&b

Close to the beach, the hotel looks out to sea across the Moray Firth. New owners offer friendly hospitality, which adds to the warm decor to create a 'country inn' atmosphere. All tables in the 50-seat restaurant have good sea views, if you ignore the caravan site to the left of the hotel. Lunches, afternoon teas, high teas, bar meals and à la carte dinners are served. Our researcher was impressed, though a subsequent visitor found service and food sub-standard. The bedrooms have been refurbished, so all have *en suite* bathrooms.

Children's playground; good coastal walks; 12 golf courses within a 20-minute drive (golfing packages available); windsurfing on beach; rod fishing

BLAIRGOWRIE

15/29

Kinloch House Hotel, by Blairgowrie, Perthshire PH10 6SG
(Tel. 025 084 237)
On the A923 between Blairgowrie and Dunkeld, about three
miles from Blairgowrie
Closed 15 December to 30 December
£69.75 single, £132 double, suite £165 dinner and b&b
A fine 19th-century hotel overlooking the water 400 yards
from the loch, set off by a rhododendron-lined drive and
grazing Highland cattle. Dunsinane Hill (of *Macbeth*) is also in
view. Indoors, features include splendid oak panelling, a
stained-glass skylight and a conservatory with ornamental
pool and tropical plants. Six of the bedrooms have four-poster
beds. Mr Shentall offers a choice of 130 malt whiskies at the bar
and serves dinner clad in a kilt. The restaurant seats 55, with a
view over the ornamental pool. Light and full lunches cost
from £2.50 to £12.50. Four-course dinner £20.75 (men are
advised to wear a jacket and tie). The menu is long and well
regarded, with game and seafood specialities. Guests can buy
jars of home-made bramble jelly, marmalade and jam as
souvenirs of their visit (£1.50–£2.75). There are four rooms on
the ground floor for disabled guests.
*Fishing nearby; golf (there are nearly 40 courses within a little more
than an hour's drive from the hotel, including the championship
courses of Carnoustie, St Andrews, and Rosemount); shooting (there
are arrangements with local estates for driven and rough shooting)*

BRAEVAL

101   12

Braeval Old Mill, Braeval, by Aberfoyle, Stirling FK8 3UY
(Tel. 087 72 711)
On the A81, one mile from Aberfoyle (ask for detailed
directions when booking)
Closed on Sunday evenings, Mondays, last two weeks of
February, one week in May, and first two weeks of November

This 18th-century flax and corn mill has been completely renovated, though its waterwheel still runs on a trickle, and the floor is flagged with grey stone. Creative seafood dishes and local game feature on a menu combining classic French and Scottish cuisine, cooked by Nick Nairn. The fixed-price three-course dinner, with four choices at each course, costs £29.50; the set lunch costs £17.50. Accolades include winning the *Scottish Field*/Bollinger 'Newcomers 87/88' award; *Scottish Field*/Carlton 'Best Restaurant' 1988/9, and a Michelin red 'M'. No cigar or pipe smoking in restaurant. Bed and breakfast accommodation is available locally (from £15 pp). Wide doorways allow wheelchair access, and there is a lavatory for disabled visitors.

Trout fishing at Lake Menteith, £20 per session

BRIDGE OF MARNOCH

The Old Manse of Marnoch, Bridge of Marnoch, Huntly, Aberdeenshire AB54 5RS   (Tel. 0466 780873)
On the B9117 less than a mile off the A97, hotel well signposted
£16.50–£36 pp b&b

With the River Deveron at its edge and Crombie Burn running through, the five-acre garden is a main feature of this spacious Georgian house. Most of the rooms enjoy the pretty view, and there are many antiquities that the Carters have collected from the Middle East. One of the lounges is non-smoking. The bedrooms, which are comfortable and cheery, are equipped with china teacups, pots, and fresh milk, and all sorts of items that might have been left out of a hastily packed sponge bag, such as cotton wool, razors, a sewing kit, aspirins and nail files. Even more impressive than the high degree of comfort is the friendliness of the owners. The dining room table overlooks the water and seats up to 12 guests, who all eat together. The bread is home made, the vegetables are organic, grown in a walled kitchen garden, and a four-course dinner costs £16.50. In the morning, the table groans with bountiful Scottish

breakfasts. Packed lunches can be made for guests for £6.50. The hotel has a herb nursery, with 80–90 aromatic and culinary varieties of herb for sale. The home-made jams are also for sale.
Walks; salmon and sea trout fishing (February to October), licence £15–£20 per day; pony trekking, £3 per hour; stalking and shooting arranged

BUCKIE
IOI 🏘8 🍴 🚫 ▭

The Old Monastery Restaurant, Drybridge, nr Buckie, Banffshire AB5 2JB   (Tel. 0542 32660)
Turn off the A98 at Buckie junction on to Drybridge road. Follow road for 2½ miles (do not turn right into Drybridge village)
Open noon–2.30pm, 6.45pm–11pm Tues to Sat (last orders at 1.45pm and 9.30pm)
Closed Sun, Mon; last three weeks of January; and first two weeks of November
The cloisters of the old monastery have been turned into a bar; the chapel has become the restaurant, with marvellous views over the mountains of Sutherland and the Moray Firth. The cooking is mainly Scottish and inspired by the fresh local supplies, with a little French influence: a hint of the Auld Alliance. The Grays are charming and friendly, very proud of their high standards, but keen to keep the atmosphere in the restaurant easy and relaxed – they say they take pleasure in continuing the tradition of hospitality for which monks were always known. There are beautiful original Benedictine stencils in the chapel. The restaurant can seat 45 people; three inside tables and two outside have good water views. If you are planning to visit on a Saturday night, you will be well advised to book three weeks in advance. Guide dogs are allowed into the restaurant.
Harbour and fishing tours available; walks; sailing; river (£15–£40 a day) and sea fishing (£10–20 a day); beach (three miles away); riding; skiing in winter (20 miles away)

BUNCHREW

Bunchrew House Hotel, Highland, Bunchrew, Inverness
IV3 6TA   (Tel. 0463 234 917)
£65–£85 single, £85–£110 double suite b&b
The Beauly Firth borders the lovely 15-acre landscaped
gardens of this 17th-century Baronial house. The house, with
its turrets and castellated front, was built by Simon Fraser, the
eighth Lord Lovat, and portraits of the Fraser family dating
back to 1655 adorn the dining room, the lounge and the
cocktail bar. Inside, it is spacious and peaceful, with dark oak
panelling, good sofas and the open fire in the lounge all adding
to the atmosphere of calm comfort. The owners, Alan and
Patsy Wilson, extend a warm welcome to guests, and
bedrooms are well equipped, from the four-posters right
down to the baskets of fruit and complimentary sherries.
There are two dining rooms, seating 120 people altogether,
with seven tables overlooking the water. A three-course
lunch costs £9.50; a four-course dinner costs £19.50. The
award-winning chef combines classic Scottish cuisine with
French influences. Conferences and business functions can
be accommodated in the Mackenzie Room. There are
lavatories for disabled visitors, but no specially adapted
rooms.
Walks in 18 acres of grounds; croquet; shooting (wild game, deer);
sailing; free salmon fishing on tidal firth; shingle beach; championship
golf, swimming, riding, ice-skating and tennis can all be arranged

CAIRNDOW

Loch Fyne Oyster Bar, Clachan Farm, Cairndow, Argyll
PA26 8BH   (Tel. 04996 217/264)
On the A83 10 miles out of Inveraray at the head of Loch Fyne
Open 9am–6pm; 9am–9pm on summer weekends
Converted from a cow shed, this bright and down-to-earth
restaurant, with white walls and larch-wood fittings, has

seating for 80 with five window tables overlooking Loch Fyne. Tables outside the restaurant can seat an additional 30 people. The menu features the same wide range of Loch Fyne produce which is being packed in the back rooms and sent worldwide. One aim here is to restore oysters to their 'affordable snack' status of last century: at present they are £7.40 a dozen. Champagne to accompany them is £25 per bottle; if you prefer wine, the house white is £5.95 a bottle, or there is an extensive choice of bottled beers. Smoke-house and seafood shop on premises. There is a ramp and lavatories for the disabled.

Sea fishing; hill walking; boating on loch; wildlife park and castle in Inveraray; Pinetum in Cairndow with the tallest tree in Britain

CANONBIE

inn

Riverside Inn, Canonbie DG14 0UX   (Tel. 03873 71295)
Just off the A7 between Langholm and Carlisle
Open 11am–2.30pm, 6.30pm–11pm; closed Sunday lunch, last two weeks of February, first two weeks of November, and Christmas Day
£35 pp b&b

A road separates this attractive inn from the nearby River Esk. The bar is furnished with a curious mixture of Singer sewing machine tables, old chairs and stuffed animals, which is nonetheless attractive. There is one bar, with Yates Bitter and real ale on offer. Bar lunches are available between noon and 2pm. The set dinner costs £20. The meals are highly praised – food is described as English with French influence, with puddings 'like Granny used to make' – and the breakfasts are said to be exceptional. The bar provides a charcoal grill selection from 7pm–9pm. Vegetarians can be catered for if advance notice is given. The bedrooms are especially bright and comfortable-looking, with little finishing touches that make guests feel at home. There are two rooms available in the cottage annexe, with a garden that runs down to the river.

Walks (Hadrian's Wall not far); hotel can arrange fishing; riding (five miles away); golf (four courses within 30 miles); shooting can be arranged

CRINAN

IOI ⚒ 🕯 ⌀ ▭

Lock 16 Restaurant, at the Crinan Hotel, Crinan, by
Lochgilphead, Argyll PA31 8SR   (Tel. 054683 261)
From Lochgilphead, take A816, then A841 to Crinan
Dinner promptly at 8pm; lunch by request only. Restaurant
closed Sunday and Monday

In a fine vantage point on the roof of the Crinan Hotel, this
popular restaurant has a prized reputation for fresh seafood,
which is off-loaded from the loch 50 yards from the hotel and
prepared by chef/proprietor Nicholas Ryan (dinner £35).
Decor is unfussy and spartan, and there is seating for 20 at the
large windows looking on to the loch. No pushchairs in the
restaurant. There are lifts and lavatories for disabled visitors.
The hotel has 22 rooms, all with good loch views (£50–£60 pp
b&b) and another restaurant on the ground floor serving dishes
other than seafood. Dogs can be accommodated in the hotel by
prior arrangement. Fifty yards away, on the quayside of the
Crinan Canal, is the renowned Crinan coffee shop: two low
rooms, formerly the stables for the barge horses, which are
separated from the water by a pathway. There are benches
outside, overlooking the boats and the lock apparatus, and
cakes, quiches and open sandwiches are served every day from
9am to 5pm.

Walks; waterskiing; windsurfing; fishing; beach (200 yards away)

DELNIES

🏛️ 7/14 🏠 🍴 🍷 💳

The Carnach House Hotel, Delnies, Nairn IV12 5NT
(Tel. 0667 52094)
Two miles west of Nairn on the A96
£31.50 b&b (£36.50 in July and August)
To be completely honest, Carnach House is not directly on the
water: the Moray Firth is half a mile away, but there is nothing
between it and the hotel apart from the A96: on a clear day, you
can see for 55 miles. The view across the sea, Ben Clibrek and
the Suters of Cromarty is splendid. This fine stone house, built
in 1914, is set in eight acres of lawns and woods; the bar has
tables overlooking the Firth, and a fine selection of malt
whiskies. Dinner for residents costs £14.50; for non-residents,
£16.50. Decor is simple but adequate; the rooms are well
equipped with alarm radios, sewing kits and shoe-cleaning
kits.
Beach; walks; historic castles nearby

DUNBAR

🏛️ 6/14 🏠 🍴 🍷 💳

The Bayswell Hotel, Bayswell Park, Dunbar EH42 1AE
(Tel. 0368 62225)
Off the A1 to Dunbar
£38 single pp b&b, £56 double b&b
A friendly and comfortable seafront hotel, where you are quite
likely to find local pensioners discussing politics in the bar at
11am. Built of red sandstone, and set high up on the cliff, the
hotel has private access to the beach; the public rooms have fine
views to the Bass Rock, May Island, Dunbar Harbour and the
ancient ruins of Dunbar Castle. Three sides of the bistro
restaurant have windows overlooking the rugged and exciting
beach. The main restaurant seats 60; six tables have a water
view. Lunch and dinner available; all main courses cost less
than £12, and food is described as British/Italian. Table d'hôte
menu, £12.50; carvery on Sunday from £5.50; dinner dances
are held every Saturday night. There are two downstairs

bedrooms with wide bathroom doors, and the bistro is on the ground floor.

Walks; watersports; fishing (trout £12 a day, equipment for hire); long sandy beach nearby; golf (there are 14 golf courses nearby, including Muirfield, the 1992 Championship course); pony trekking (£5 an hour); bowling; putting

DUNDONNELL

The Dundonnell Hotel, Dundonnell, by Garve, Ross-shire IV23 2QS   (Tel. 085 483 234)
On the A832 from Ullapool to Gairloch
£29.50–£37.50 pp b&b

An old coaching inn for travellers in Wester Ross, now modernized and family run, sheltering beneath the massive mountain range of An Teallach, with views down Little Loch Broom. The building is separated from the loch only by the main road and a small filling station. The interior is modern, the decor plush: all the rooms look very comfortable and well equipped. The restaurant seats 70, with 10 window tables (dinner costs £17.50). Vegetarians can be catered for if they give advance notice. There is a special flat for disabled guests.

Mountain walks; bird watching; fishing can be arranged (hill lochs only, bring equipment); beach (12 miles away); golf (25 miles away); Inverewe Gardens (25 miles away).

DUNKELD

The Taybank Hotel, Dunkeld, Perthshire PH8 0AQ
(Tel. 03502 340)
Twelve miles from Pitlochry on the A984
£30 for a double room

This small hotel, the best part of 200 years old, is set in beautiful surroundings: the pine-covered hills of what one might be tempted to call Macbeth Country (Burnham Wood is nearby). The accommodation is basic (no *en suite* bathrooms, no telephones or televisions in bedrooms) but excellent value. There is a good pub garden, with picnic tables on the bank of the River Tay, and views of the hills, the bridge and the pretty town of Dunkeld. Bar food available (scampi and burgers £2.20–£4.40); lunch noon–2pm; supper 6pm–8pm between Easter and October.

Tennis and golf nearby; Scottish horse museum, tea rooms and antique shops in Dunkeld; Highland games nearby in August

DUNOON

inn ³/³

The Coylet Inn, by Dunoon, Loch Eck, Argyll PA23 8SG
(Tel. 036984 426)
On the A815, east side of Loch Eck, north of Dunoon
Open 11am–2.30pm, 5pm–11pm weekdays; until midnight
Fri and Sat; noon–2.30pm, 6.30pm–11pm Sun
£17.50 pp b&b

Black and white, low-slung, 18th-century coaching inn on shores of Loch Eck, surrounded by Argyll Forest Park. The interior is very attractive and cosy, with open log fires; the downstairs rooms are pleasantly furnished in traditional inn style. Bedrooms are pretty, small, and simple, and all have a fine view of the tree-lined shores of the loch. The bar serves McEwans 80/-, and Youngers No. 3 and bar snacks (no children allowed in the bar). The restaurant seats 50–60 people, and there is room for 40 more at tables in the garden, looking over the loch. A three-course dinner costs £10–£15.

Walks; inn has six boats with motors for hire and fishing permits; loch cruises

DUNOON

🏨 5/12 🏘 ◇ ▭

The Enmore Hotel, Marine Parade, Dunoon, Argyll
PA23 8HH   (Tel. 0369 2230/2148)
On the A815 on the outskirts of Dunoon, half a mile from
Hunters Quay ferry terminal
Closed for second and third weeks of January
£29–£60 pp b&b
A Victorian building with a fair view of the Clyde estuary,
separated by the road from the seafront. There is always
something going on on the water; the passing craft vary from
cruisers to yachts. Decor is sumptuous, with gilt reproduction
furniture, soft lighting, and some startling colour schemes.
The bedrooms are luxuriously appointed, and the beds are
something of a speciality: there are three four-posters, one
canopied bed, and one queen-size heated water bed. The
bathrooms have similarly indulgent touches, with canopied
silk ceilings (two have whirlpool baths), and golden swan-
shaped tap fittings. The hotel restaurant seats 40 people,
with two window tables that have the best view of the
estuary: dinner costs £18, and the food is Scottish/French.
There are two international standard squash courts, and
the hotel grounds include a private shingle beach across the
road.
*Walks; hotel can arrange pony trekking and fishing; private shingle
beach; sandy beach (five miles away); three golf courses in Dunoon;
trips to the isles of Arran and Bute*

EDINBURGH

🏨 46/144 🏘 ⚲ ◇ ▭

The Hilton National, Bells Mills, Belford Road, Edinburgh
EH4 3DG   (Tel. 031 332 2545)
Off Queensferry Road, close to city centre
£70–£110 pp b&b
Built around a 19th-century grain mill, the hotel stands on the
edge of the Water of Leith and is within easy reach of all
Edinburgh's attractions. Only steps away, a pleasant walkway

follows the Water through the town centre; kingfishers and other waterfowl add to the scenery. The comfortable, functional bedrooms and public rooms have modern decor, though windows in river-facing bedrooms do not make the most of the view. A sociable pub occupies what was once the mill, and serves bar lunches and snacks all day. The 110-cover restaurant has 20 water-view tables; a three-course carvery dinner costs £15.75, lunch is £12. There is a self-contained meeting and conference centre. Pets are allowed in guests' rooms only. Public rooms and some bedrooms have wheel-chair access.

Walks; visits to the castle; theatres; shops; art galleries

ELIE

The Ship Inn, The Toft, Elie, Fife   (Tel. 0333 330 246)
Follow signs to harbour
Open 11am–midnight, Mon–Sat; 12.30pm–11pm, Sun; outside bar open 11am–11pm during July and August
In an old seaside village, this small, white 18th-century fishing pub has a strong nautical atmosphere. Heavy beams, wood panelling and high-backed leather seats give the bar a cosy, welcoming feel. On sunny days, the best spot for a drink is the beach-facing beer garden, where there are barbecues every lunchtime and evening in summer. The bar serves Belhaven real ale and basic food (rolls and soup). The new landlord is busy making improvements such as new kitchens and more seating areas. Children are allowed into some areas of the pub. Bed and breakfast accommodation available nearby.

Excellent walks along beach, cliffs and golf course; watersports; rod fishing; golf (£18 a day); tennis; putting green; nine-hole junior golf course

FEARNAN-BY-ABERFELDY

Tigh-an-Loan, Fearnan-by-Aberfeldy, Tayside PH15 2PF
(Tel. 08873 249)
£34 pp dinner and b&b

Across the road from the shores of Loch Tay, this solid stone
house is well run by friendly proprietors. The bedrooms are
comfortable and not over-modernized; some have fine loch
views. There are four tables overlooking the water in the 30-
cover restaurant, and non-residents are welcome. A four-
course traditional Scottish dinner costs £12. There is a fine
selection of malts on offer at the bar, and bar meals are available
at lunch and in the evenings and can be enjoyed at picnic tables
in the garden.

Hill and forest walks; watersports; beach; golf (three courses nearby);
fishing on Loch Tay (hotel has rights)

FORT AUGUSTUS

Inchnacardoch Lodge Hotel, by Fort Augustus, Inverness-
shire PH32 4BL   (Tel. 0320 6258)
On the A82 half a mile north of village
Open from April to December
£45–£75 b&b for two

With its rugged old architecture, beaming local faces and
distinct lack of rush, the area feels lost in time, especially in low
season. The hotel was once Lord Lovat's hunting lodge, and
retains its period flavour with antiques and generously proportioned rooms. The village is situated at the southern end of
Loch Ness, where it meets the Caledonian Canal. Most bedrooms have good views of Loch Ness; there is an old brass bed
in one, and the attic rooms are quite pretty. The restaurant
seats 40, with 12 tables overlooking the water. A three-course
dinner costs £17.50. The lounge and bar have loch views, and
snacks are served at lunchtime.

Golf (nine-hole course, £4 a day); walks; watersports can be arranged at waterpark (eight miles away); fishing (£3 a day); rowing and canoeing on loch

FORT AUGUSTUS

The Lock Inn, Canalside, Fort Augustus, Inverness-shire
PH32 4BL   (Tel. 0320 6302)
A friendly local pub, the Lock Inn is right on the Caledonian Locks and has delightful canal views. Loch Ness comes up to the edge of the village, so there is plenty of scope for thirst-building walks along the loch or towpath. McEwan's Export and Younger's Tartan Special round out the selection of beers, and for those after stiffer refreshment, there are no fewer than 30 whiskies on offer. Full cooked bar meals have an excellent reputation and feature fresh local haddock, salmon, and meat (from the butcher next door). These are served in summer only and cost from £3 to £7. The pub is on the ground floor, and doorways are wide enough to accommodate wheelchairs, but there are no special facilities for the disabled. Children are allowed in for meals only.
Forest, lochside and towpath walks; salmon and trout fishing (permits available locally); watersports at South Laggan Water Park (20 miles away)

GLENSHIEL

Kintail Lodge, Glenshiel, by Kyle of Lochalsh, Ross-shire
IV40 8HL   (Tel. 059 981 275)
On the A87, at the head of Loch Duich, near Kyle of Lochalsh
Closed over Christmas and New Year
£39.50 pp dinner and b&b
This former shooting lodge is right on the shores of Loch Duich, at the foot of the Five Sisters of Kintail. A large National Trust property borders the four acres of hotel grounds, and there are plenty of mountain and lowland walks nearby. Views across the loch and up to the Five Sisters

combine with the rough shooting lodge atmosphere to make this a fine Highland retreat. Bedrooms vary from classic old lodge-style to modern, and a new sun lounge affords wonderful loch views. There is seating for 30 in the restaurant; three window tables overlook the loch. Dinner costs £17.50 for non-residents. Lunches are served in the loch-view public bar. Well-behaved dogs can be accommodated by arrangement, but are not allowed into public rooms.

Mountain or lowland walks, advice centre nearby; hotel can arrange fishing with sufficient notice (bring equipment), and canoeing; four acres of walled garden; sandy beach and watersports (10 miles away)

GOLSPIE

The Golf Links Hotel, Golspie, Sutherland KW12 6TT
(Tel. 0408 633408)
£22–£26 pp b&b

Adjacent to the Golspie golf course, this small hotel looks out to Ben Baraggie at the rear and to Dornoch Firth at the front. The sunny residents' lounge has lively decor and good views of the sea, which is just across the road. Bedrooms and public rooms have a comfortable, relaxed feel; three self-catering chalets are open from April to the end of October. Lunches are available in the bar, and the 48–cover restaurant serves four-course dinners for £13.50. Nearby are the fairy-tale towers of Dunrobin Castle, seat of the earls and dukes of Sutherland since the 13th century. The Royal Dornoch golf course is within striking distance, as is the Loch Fleet Bird Sanctuary. Chalet rooms are accessible by wheelchair, but there are no special facilities for the disabled.

Good walks (beach, golf course); fishing (free to £12 a day); bird watching; beach; golf (£12–£17 a day)

HELMSDALE

12/16

Navidale House, Helmsdale, Sutherland KW8 6JS
(Tel. 04312 258)
Just after Helmsdale on the A9
£21–£32 pp b&b

This pretty house is perched right on the clifftop, with excellent sea views over Moray Firth and the Ord of Caithness. Built as a hunting lodge for the Duke of Sutherland in the 1830s, it is set in six acres of woodland and garden which ramble down to the foreshore; there is a path to the beach. The (non-smoking) restaurant seats 45 people and has 10 tables overlooking the water. A set dinner costs £18.00. There is a ground-floor annexe, but no special facilities for the disabled.

Walks; watersports; salmon fishing at £13–£18 a day (there are only 12 rods, so book well in advance and bring equipment); beach; golf (local £9 a day, Royal courses nearby); squash and tennis courts nearby; Dunrobin Castle also nearby; gold panning in Balle an Or, scene of 1869 Kildonan gold strike (11 miles away)

ISLE OF WHITHORN

inn 3/5

The Steam Packet, Isle of Whithorn, Dumfries and Galloway
DG8 8LL   (Tel. 09885 334)
At the end of the A747, on the Wigtown peninsula
Bar open: 11am–11pm Mon–Sat; noon–11pm Sun (January to March 11am–2.30pm, 5.30pm–11pm Mon–Sat; noon–2.30pm, 5.30pm–11pm Sun)
£22.50 pp b&b

The most southerly pub in Scotland, the Steam Packet is set on a lovely natural harbour bustling with fishermen, yachtsmen and a colourful variety of boats. The bar has a cosy feel with a picture window and wood-burning stove, and is popular with both visitors and locals. Reasonably priced snacks are available at lunch and in the evening; garden tables are the perfect spot for a meal if the weather is fair. The dining room seats 60, with 12 tables overlooking the water, and a big model steamship hangs from one of the walls. Cooking features fresh seafood (scallops and lobsters are landed at the harbour), and a full dinner costs £12.50. *En suite* bedrooms are simple but comfortable; three enjoy pretty harbour views, and two look out over the garden. Vast Scottish breakfasts, not for the faint hearted, include potato scones, haggis and kippers. The ground-floor bar and dining room are accessible to wheelchairs, but there are no special facilities for the disabled.

Inn can arrange fishing (even for shark); boat trips from harbour; St Ninian's Church behind the inn; golf (six miles away)

KELSO

Ednam House Hotel, Kelso, Roxburghshire
(Tel. 0573 24168)
£40 pp dinner and b&b

Built in 1761, and considered the finest Georgian building in Roxburghshire, the house overlooks the River Tweed and the Junction Pool with the River Teviot. The atmosphere is relaxed yet opulent, and guests generally feel surrounded by gracious country-house hospitality. Three acres of gardens and a generous stretch of river frontage offer plenty of scope for pleasant strolls. All lounges, both bars and the beautiful old function room overlook the Tweed. The restaurant serves bar lunches Monday to Saturday and a more elaborate spread on Sunday (the four-course Sunday lunch costs about £9.50); the river is in view from all tables. A treat for anyone, Ednam House is especially recommended for the serious fisherman.

Fishing: salmon and trout (£1.50 a day); tennis, golf, swimming and riding all nearby; many walks

KENMORE

The Kenmore Hotel, The Square, Kenmore, by Aberfeldy, Perthshire PH15 2NU   (Tel. 08873 205)
On the A827 and Loch Tay, six miles from Aberfeldy
£70–£82 per room b&b
This lovely hotel dates back to 1572 and claims to be the oldest inn in Scotland, and Robbie Burns once graced one of the walls with a graffiti'd poem. With a good position beside the River Tay, it is situated in a pretty village with a (private) castle. The hotel has a tennis court, and a par 69 18-hole golf course in the castle grounds. The bar-lounge is charmingly rustic, with an old stone-and-beam bar. The bedroom with a veranda over Loch Tay is particularly attractive; and all bedrooms have bathrooms *en suite*. The restaurant seats 80, with 12 tables overlooking the water. Fish and game feature prominently on the menu; a three-course dinner costs £19. Pets are allowed in the sportsman's lodge only. There is easy access to ground-floor rooms, but no special facilities for the disabled.
Walks; windsurfing; jetskiing nearby; two miles of private fishing (£10–£15 a day); beach on Loch Tay

KENTALLEN

Ardsheal House, Kentallen, Appin, Argyll   (Tel. 063174 227)
Off the A828 (Oban from Fort William); clearly signposted from road
Open April to November
£65–£90 pp dinner and b&b
An ancient pile of a hotel, found at the end of a one-mile-long private drive that winds along beside Loch Linnhe. From its superb elevated position in Stevenson's *Kidnapped* country, the hotel's view, especially from the tower, is unparalleled. Nine hundred acres of private woodland, gardens and shore front surround the stone and granite mansion, which was built in 1545, sacked in the 1745 uprisings, and rebuilt in 1760. The

estate does not belong to the hotel, but they have access through it, down to their own pebbled beach. The bedrooms are well furnished with antiques in an old-fashioned style with some boisterous wallpapers. There is an oak-panelled reception lounge, a cosy bar, and an open fire on an old stone hearth in the reception area. The dining room, which has a conservatory extension, seats 45 people; dinner costs £32.50.

Billiards room and tennis court at hotel; fishing can be arranged; riding; walks in Glencoe and surrounding area; private shore-front pebble beach; boating nearby

KENTALLEN

🏨 10/12 ⌂ 🍴 ✍ 💳

The Holly Tree Hotel, Kentallen, Appin, Argyll PA38 4BY
(Tel. 063174 292)
On the A828, 15 miles south of Fort William
Open early March to end of October; also Christmas and New Year (quite often, the hotel is actually open when it is meant to be closed, so it is worth ringing up to find out)
£44–£65 dinner and b&b
A former turn-of-the-century railway station overlooking Loch Linnhe and the mountains of Ardgour, this hotel has been cleverly converted, with close attention to Glasgow art nouveau detail. The Railway Bar, for instance, used to house the station's tea room. The dining room (no smoking in here) has picture windows and seating for 50 people, and has recently been revamped. It now has a split-level floor this season, which makes the most of the wonderful view over the floodlit garden, former railway pier and out over Loch Linnhe. The bedrooms are spacious, with solid modern furniture and stylish fabrics, and give a particularly strong impression of being on the water. There is a strong family atmosphere about the hotel, with the Robertsons' children and personal possessions everywhere. The hotel grounds run for a mile down the disused railway. Dogs can be accommodated by special arrangement only; they are not allowed into the public rooms.

Two of the ground-floor rooms have special bathrooms for disabled visitors.
Walks; hotel can arrange riding, fishing, sailing, boat trips and canoeing

KILCHRENAN

🏨 5/14 ♿8 🎻 🚳 💳

Ardanaiseig, Kilchrenan, by Taynuilt, Argyll PA35 1HE
(Tel. 08663 333)
Leave the A85 at Taynuilt, take the B845 to Kilchrenan, then follow signs to Ardanaiseig (three miles)
Open from Easter to October
£58–£105 dinner and b&b
A Scottish Baronial-style house, dating from 1834, set in 100 acres of woodland garden beside Loch Awe. The gardens are beautifully kept, and boast a collection of rare shrubs. Modernizations have, of course, been carried out, but these are most discreet, and do not in any way interfere with the civilized elegance of the place. There are plenty of large windows and log fires, and the bedrooms are stylish and individually furnished. The view down across the fine lawn and out over the loch is exceptionally good. The restaurant seats 30 people, with two window tables (five-course set dinner, £33.50). Vegetarians can be catered for, with advance notice. Diversions for guests inside the hotel include a billiard room. The hotel has recently changed hands, but no dramatic changes are planned. Dogs can be accommodated by prior arrangement only.
Three boats (engines for hire); fishing (rods supplied); tennis; croquet; clay pigeon shooting (guns supplied)

KILCHRENAN

🏨 11/15 ♿ 🎻 🚳 💳

Taychreggan Hotel, Kilchrenan, by Taynuilt, Argyll PA35
(Tel. 08663 211)
Signposted from the A85 just east of Taynuilt

Open March to October, weekends throughout the year,
Christmas and New Year
£55–£72 dinner and b&b
Situated right on waterfront, the Taychreggan hotel looks out
along Loch Awe – the longest fresh-water loch in Scotland – in
25 acres of its own grounds. Originally an old drovers' inn, it
now has modern extensions and an attractive suntrap of a
courtyard where guests can eat in the summer. Most of the
bedrooms are identical except for their pleasantly differing
colour schemes, and the whole place looks generally comfortable and relaxed. The bar is airy, and well populated with
stuffed birds and fish. There are three window tables by the
picture windows in the restaurant, and these have the best view
of the loch. Dinner costs £24. Vegetarians can be catered for,
with advance notice. Limited facilities for the disabled.
Hotel can arrange fishing, boats, shooting, riding, and croquet;
swimming from hotel lawn

KILLIN

inn 4/9 🏠 ♨ ◁ ▭

The Clachaig Hotel, Falls of Dochart, Gray Street, Killin,
Perthshire   (Tel. 05672 270)
On the A827
£17.50 pp b&b; self-catering chalet £180–£275 per week
A listed, rambling, 18th-century inn, which incorporates an
even older smithy, the Clachaig Hotel is also known as the
Salmon Lie because of its excellent angling location. There are
beautiful views of the Falls of Dochart and the bridge. This is
McNab country, so history positively drips from the walls.
The bar has a wide range of malt whiskies, and an original
fireplace with log fire, and a pool table. There is no residents'
lounge, so the hotel may not be suitable for people who like
somewhere other than their bedrooms where they can read in
peace and quiet. The dining room seats 32 people, with two
water-view tables. If you feel like a lighter meal, try the salad
restaurant. The hotel has won a 'bar meal of the year' award for
Scotland. Pets can be accommodated for a charge of £2 for the

first night, and £1 for subsequent nights. There is a lavatory for disabled visitors.

Walks, hiking, canoeing, waterskiing, sailing, private salmon and trout fishing on River Dochart, £35 per day for salmon fishing trips on Loch Tay (equipment can be hired); salmon fishing beat on Loch Tay; fishing packages can be arranged; nine-hole village golf course, £7 a day for two rounds

KILMORE

Glenfeochan House, Kilmore, by Oban, Argyll PA34 4QR
(Tel. 063177 273)
Five miles south of Oban on the A816
Open March to October
£112 per room b&b
A listed, turreted and recently restored Victorian sandstone building, with beautiful ornate plaster work on high ceilings, and a finely carved American-pine staircase. The hotel is situated half a mile from Loch Feochan, and is surrounded by 350 acres of land, which includes a stretch of shore. The five-acre garden is full of rare specimen trees, rhododendrons (they're on the Gulf Stream), and often, deer – it is open to the public. This is very much a private house with paying guests, all of whom eat together at the Babers' dining-room table (dinner costs £25–£50, and is for residents only). The bedrooms are large and decorated in a plain, sensible, old-fashioned style, and the views from them are splendid, with mountains and trees as well as the loch. Pets can be accommodated, but only by prior arrangement.

Hotel can arrange clay pigeon shooting, riding, sailing, windsurfing and fishing (salmon and sea trout on rivers and loch); golf (three miles away); walks; bird watching; loch-bathing; croquet

KINCLAVEN BY STANLEY

🏨 14/28 🏊 🍸 🐟 💳

Ballathie House, Kinclaven by Stanley, Perthshire PH1 4QN
(Tel. 025083 268)
Off the A9 two miles north of Perth
£36–£67 pp b&b
A Baronial mansion built in 1850, now comprehensively
refurbished and set in its own estate overlooking the River
Tay, up an impressive private drive. It is more like a private
house than a hotel, with log fires in original marble fireplaces in
the public rooms, and lovely grounds full of rhododendrons.
The decor is tasteful, with draped beds and turreted bathrooms, and there are fresh flowers and Victorian dressing table
sets in each room. The light and airy Sportsman's Lodge
annexe sleeps an additional 11 people (£26–£31 pp b&b) and is
separate from house so that guests can come and go at all hours
without disturbing the night porter. The dining room seats
70 people, and most of the tables have good views of the
river. Children and pets can be accommodated by prior
arrangement only. There are two rooms for disabled visitors
on the ground floor, with large bathrooms.
Walks; prime salmon fishing on River Tay (salmon fishing holiday
packages available for Ballathie Water, January–July, August–13
October, book well in advance); trout fishing on loch and river; clay
pigeon shooting; golf; Scone Palace and Glamis Castle nearby

KINCRAIG

🍽 🏊 🍸 🚫 💳

The Boathouse Restaurant, Kincraig, Inverness-shire
(Tel. 05404 272)
Once in Kincraig, follow signs to Loch Insh Watersports
Closed late October to 27 December
The restaurant is housed in a log cabin above a stone
boathouse, with seats on the balcony that give a grandstand
view of Loch Insh, and the windsurfers and waterskiers down
below. There is seating for 35; all tables share the view, and
meals cost from £2.95–£12. The restaurant serves pâté, ham

and soup at lunch; cakes and toasted sandwiches at high tea. Fondue nights, with *glühwein* on tap, are held every evening. In July and August, there are barbecues on the beach every lunchtime, and on Friday and Saturday nights. The restaurant doubles as a gift/craft shop, selling tempting jams and presents. Visitors can find accommodation at Insh Hall (also overlooking Loch Insh, and next to Aviemore; same telephone number). The Hall formerly the village hall, dates from 1899 and has two to six bunks per room and two self-catering kitchens, television room and keep-fit gym. The place has an alpine feel, and offers good value packages for skiing or watersports (telephone for further details). Log chalets are also available for rent, which might make a good base for a family (telephone restaurant for details). There is a ramp into the restaurant for visitors in wheelchairs, and one six-person chalet is suitable for the disabled.

Canoeing, sailing and windsurfing hire and instruction May to October; close to Aviemore (seven miles) and Cairngorms (15 miles) for skiing; artificial ski slope hire and instruction all year; downhill and cross-country hire and instruction December to April; walks; fishing; beach on site

KINLOCHBERVIE

Kinlochbervie Hotel, by Lairg, Sutherland IV27 4RP
(Tel. 097 182 275)
Closed (hotel but not the bar) December, January and February
£73–£95 twin/double b&b; garden annexe £23 pp
A modern family hotel overlooking Kinlochbervie harbour and Loch Clash, with unbeatable panoramic views from the lounge of sunsets over the Atlantic. The rooms have large windows with views of either the working harbour or the sea. The highlight of the day is going down to the fish market to watch the buyers arranging orders with Billingsgate on their portable telephones: a marvellous blend of the old and the new. From the lounge, you can watch the seals following the fishing

boats out to sea. Five miles up the road there is the most beautiful white sandy beach; wild and wonderful. The public bar has a choice of 180 malt whiskies and a pool table, and is used by local skippers and fishermen. Bar meals are available. Occasionally, you can find a travelling Ceilidh band playing there. The restaurant seats 40, and 12 tables have sea views. Fish is, obviously, a speciality; the menu changes daily and a four-course dinner costs £27. No specific disabled facilities, though the annexe has wheelchair access.

Walking; mountaineering; golf; sailing; river/loch/sea fishing (hotel offers fly fishing on lochs, £1–£15 a day); pony trekking; beach; trips by speedboat to Handa Island Bird Reserve, Cape Wrath lighthouse, etc.

KINLOCH RANNOCH

🏨 12/17 ⛰ 🔥 ◁ ▭

The Loch Rannoch Hotel, Kinloch Rannoch, by Pitlochry PH16 5PS   (Tel. 08822 201)
One mile from Kinloch Rannoch
£35–£50 pp dinner and b&b (also self-catering lodges, see below)

The hotel is a fine, late 19th-century building in a lochside setting, with a good atmosphere and friendly staff. The restaurant seats 65; all tables have a view of the loch, and the set dinner costs £13.95. Bar meals are available in the grill room, and guests can be provided with packed lunches. This is an excellent place for an active holiday in beautiful surroundings. There are full indoor leisure facilities (indoor swimming pool, multi-gym, sauna, solarium, spa bath, squash, snooker, exercise trail, games room), and windsurfers, bicycles, rowing boats, and an adventure playground outside. Eighty-five self-catering lodges, rented from time-share owners, are available for rent. These are large and airy, with big windows and balconies facing the water, sleep up to eight people, and cost from £250 a week. Three-quarters of the lodges have their own saunas. The scenery along the road between the motorway and the hotel (a 20-mile drive) is truly spectacular, though the road can become clogged with traffic in summer. Some of the lodges would be suitable for the disabled.

From forest walks to mountain climbs; on-site sailing, windsurfing, white-water rafting, canoeing (no motorized watersports, to preserve peace of the loch); loch (fly and spinner) and river fishing; beach; dry-slope skiing, mountain biking; ski trips to resorts; clay pigeon shooting; pony trekking; pottery classes; trips to distilleries; golf can be arranged

KIPPFORD

The Anchor Hotel, Kippford, Dalbeattie, Kirkcudbright
DG5 4LN   (Tel. 055662 205)
Off the A710 south of Dalbeattie
Open 10.30am–midnight from April to October; 10.30am–
2.30pm, 6pm–11pm October to March
Despite its name, the Anchor has no accommodation, but don't let that put you off. The pub, separated from the busy yacht harbour by the village street, has three bars; the lounge bar and the Anchor bar overlook the water, and the former, with Dalbeattie granite walls, is a little more formal than the latter. All the bars serve local beers, and are beautifully panelled, including the ceilings. There is an open fire, and interesting ornaments, pictures, and a collection of jugs in the main bar. Children can be despatched to the games room, to play pool or video games, or watch MTV. Excellent, home-cooked meals are served in the lounge bar from noon to 2.30pm, and 6pm to 9pm – main courses cost about £4. No specific facilities for the disabled, though there are no stairs into the bar, and the doorways are wide enough to admit wheelchairs.

Boat trips can be arranged; walks

LAIRG

🏨 〰️15/27 ⛺ 👤 🔷 ▭

The Sutherland Arms Hotel, Lairg, Sutherland IV27 4AT
(Tel. 0549 2291)
Open Easter to mid-October
£52 single, £86 double b&b
Originally a 17th-century coaching inn on the shores of Loch
Shin; the main part of the hotel was built in 1850. The
bedrooms have proper old windows, and there are good views
from all reception and dining rooms. There are two bars, one
of which overlooks the loch, and there is a waterside garden.
Bar meals are available at lunchtime, and a four-course dinner
in the restaurant costs £17.50. There are also six self-catering
cottages available for rent; each of these sleeps between two
and eight people and costs £170–£260 a week.
*Walks; golf; pony trekking; trout and salmon fishing (the hotel
arranges special fishing holiday packages); grouse shooting and
stalking can be arranged; watersports and windsurfing can be arranged*

LEITH

🍽️ ⛺5 👤 🚫 ▭

The Waterfront Wine Bar, 1c Dock Place, Leith EH6 6LU
(Tel. 031 554 7427)
At the back of Dock Place, off Commercial Street
Open noon–11pm, Mon–Thurs; noon–midnight, Fri and Sat;
12.30pm–4pm Sun. Closed 25 and 26 December; 1 and 2
January
The wine bar is housed in a 17th-century listed building which
used to be the lock keeper's office, on the historic dockside, by
a swingbridge. The bar and restaurant have been created out of
hatch covers off fishing boats, with old lamps and the original
panelled ceiling. There are excellent waterside seats in the
Victorian-style conservatory and on the floating platform
(book well in advance of your visit for these); altogether, they
can accommodate 190 people. The clientele ranges from
businessmen to students, via tourists and passers-by. Cuisine is

national and international; the menu changes twice daily, and a three-course meal costs from £12; vegetarians should give advance notice. Guide dogs are allowed in. They stock more than 80 wines, and won a Scottish wine bar of the year award in 1989. There is a lavatory for disabled visitors, and there are no steps into the restaurant.
Start/finish of Water of Leith river walkway through Edinburgh; beach (one and a half miles away)

LOCHGILPHEAD

The Tayvallich Inn, by Lochgilphead, Argyll PA31 8PR
(Tel. 05467 282)
On the B8025, off the A816, 10 miles south of Kilmartin
Open 11am–11pm; closed 2.30pm–5pm November to March
A low modern building in a picturesque village, separated from the waterfront by the village street. You'll need to make a lengthy detour from the main road to visit the inn, but it's worth it. The inn has lightwood furnishings and fittings inside, and opens on to a water-view beer garden, from which you can admire the boats gathered in the bay. The restaurant seats 36 people; there are three tables by the window inside, and five outside in the garden. The house speciality is seafood (including oysters, mussels and scallops), which is brought straight into the village from the sea. Bar meals cost from £5; a full dinner costs £15–£20. The landlord has recently added a conservatory/sun lounge on to the patio area. The inn is all on one level, but there are no special facilities for the disabled.
Walks; watersports; fishing; darts; sailing

LOCHINVER

Inver Lodge Hotel, Lochinver, Sutherland IV27 4LU
(Tel. 05714 496)
Drive down waterfront and take second left after village hall in Lochinver

Open 17 April to 17 October
£50–£77 pp b&b

A modern hotel, built two years ago, and set high above a small fishing village, looking over Loch Inver and across the Minches to the Isle of Lewis. The hotel is well designed, and all the bedrooms, decorated with pretty chintzes, have splendid views across the village to the loch, with a backdrop of wild, craggy mountains. The restaurant has the same view, and seats 60 people (the set dinner costs £25); bar meals are also available. There is a sauna, a solarium and a billiard room for when guests do not feel like venturing outside.

Walks (Ardvreck Castle and Inverpolly Nature Reserve nearby; Smoo Cave on north coast; Fas a Chual Aluinn Falls nearby; salmon and trout fishing (hotel has rights for 10 rods on nearby Inver, Oykel and Kirkaig rivers, and also 10 rods for loch fishing; bring equipment); beach

OBAN

The Manor House Hotel, Gallanach Road, Oban, Argyll
(Tel. 063162 087)
Half a mile from Oban town centre; follow signs to ferry terminal
£37–£70 dinner and b&b

On the outskirts of town, this small late-Georgian house has fine views over the harbour and Oban Bay. The bedrooms are beautiful; prettily decorated, and with fine views. The reception and bar areas are less easy on the eye, with flocked walls and patterned fitted carpets, but the dining room, with its dark green walls and fine panelling, and the lounge, with a log fire, help to achieve the private-house atmosphere. The dining room seats 30 people (no bay views), and the set five-course dinner costs £19.90. No pets in public rooms.

A wide range of activities can be arranged: ask at hotel; ferry to Mull (terminal 500 yards away)

OBAN

🏨 18/18 🏠 ♿ 🚫 💳

The Knipoch Hotel, Oban PA34 4QT (Tel. 08526 251)
On the A816, six miles south of Oban
£59.50 pp b&b
Once the local tax collector's residence, and since extended, this ochre-coloured Georgian house enjoys lovely views of Loch Feochan. A road separates the hotel from the water and a pebbly beach. Interior features include pine floors, Persian rugs and dark wood furniture. The bedrooms are functional yet comfortable, and all are identical save for their colour schemes: upstairs is done in 'old rose', while downstairs is mustard/ochre, and all have dark wood furniture and overlook the loch. The 44-seat restaurant occupies three separate rooms, with a total of four tables in the window. Home-smoked salmon and halibut (both wild) highlight the dinners, as does an endless wine list. Five courses cost £35. Mr Craig offers a selection of over 50 single malts, the oldest of which date back to before the Second World War. A measure of vintage 1938 runs to between £14 and £15.
Hotel can arrange waterskiing, windsurfing, riding, sailing and fishing; swimming from the beach; good walks

ONICH

🏨 19/21 🏠 ♿ 🔽 💳

The Allt-nan-Ros Hotel, Onich, by Fort William, Inverness-shire PH33 6RY (Tel. 08553 210)
Open April to November
On the A82, 10 miles south of Fort William
£53.50–£66.50 pp dinner and b&b
This attractive Victorian shooting lodge enjoys panoramic views of Loch Linnhe (across the main road), and the rooms are geared to make the most of these. A stream winds through its four acres of garden down to the water's edge. Guests can relax in front of an open fire in the lounge. The spacious bedrooms are comfortably furnished with dark wood, and several have bay windows. The restaurant seats 50 people (non-residents

are welcome), and thirteen of the tables have loch views. The set dinner costs £17.50–£20. On a fine summer's evening, you can enjoy the views from the hotel's terraced lawns. There is a ramp at the front door, and two ground-floor rooms are suitable for the disabled.

Hotel can arrange riding; golf; skiing; windsurfing (wetsuits and boards can be hired); yachting; scuba diving (equipment can be hired); speed boats; cruises; stalking; fishing (some rods available)

ONICH

🏨 16/20 ⚕ ⚬ ◁▷ ▭

The Lodge on the Loch, Onich, nr Fort William PH33 6RY
(Tel. 08553 237)
On the A82, five miles north of Glencoe and 10 miles south of Fort William
Open March to November, Christmas and New Year
£51.50–£67.50 pp dinner and b&b
From its five-acre gardens the lodge looks over the road and Loch Linnhe to Argyll and the Morvern mountains. A recently refurbished, modern interior sets it apart from most other Highland hotels. Sponged walls and pastel colours work well, and the bar, in tones of heather and soft blue with a tented silk ceiling, is certainly unique. Soft fabrics and more pastel colours highlight reception rooms and new-wing bedrooms, while bedrooms in the old wing retain their traditional flavour. The bay windows in the drawing rooms and dining room open out to striking loch views. The restaurant seats 50, with four window tables (non-residents welcome; set dinner £19.50). Guests can make use of the hotel's private moorings. There is a ground-floor room for disabled visitors, and a specially adapted lavatory.

Watersports and fishing nearby (ask for details); spring and autumn watercolour painting courses (details on request)

PITLOCHRY

🏨 30/37 🏠 🍷 ◁ 💳

The Green Park Hotel, Clunie Bridge Road, Pitlochry,
Perthshire PH16 5JY   (Tel. 0796 3248)
Off the A9, Pitlochry turning
Open 1 April to 28 October
£30–£38 pp b&b
The gardens of this 18th-century country-house hotel run
down to the banks of Loch Faskally. It is quiet and peaceful
inside, with original panelling and tapestries in public rooms;
the bedrooms are large and comfortable. There are spectacular
loch views from the sun lounge. The restaurant has seating for
100 people, and 28 of the tables overlook the water. A four-
course dinner costs £17.50. Bar meals are served at lunch and
dinner, and can be taken outside and eaten on the lawns during
the summer. The hotel would make a good base for touring, as
it is situated just off the main road to the Highlands and the
West Coast, and it is popular with visitors to the Pitlochry
Festival Theatre (this is daily rep, so you can see six plays in a
week, if you're up to it). Ground-floor rooms available which
are suitable for the disabled.
*Putting on hotel lawns; table tennis; bar billiards; children's play
area; walks; watersports; trout and salmon fishing on loch (free, bring
own equipment); Pitlochry Festival Theatre (3 May to early
October)*

PITLOCHRY

🏨 1/11 🏠 🍷 ◁ 💳

The Killiecrankie Hotel, by Pitlochry, Perthshire PH16 5LG
(Tel. 0796 3220)
Well signposted off the A9 between Pitlochry and Blair Atholl
Open March to Christmas (open for Christmas and New Year)
£42 pp b&b
Though not directly on the water, the hotel has exceptional
views over the River Garry, and stands in lovely surroundings,
overlooking the historic Pass of Killiecrankie and the RSPB
nature reserve opposite. A cheery sun room and the cosy, pine-

furnished bedrooms add to the charm of this rambling country house (the bedrooms have recently been revamped, so now all have *en suite* bathroom, television and direct-dial telephone). The dining room seats 34 people, and five tables have views over the garden. The hotel has a particularly good reputation for food; the cooking features fresh local fish and meats, and the five-course set dinner costs £23 (non-residents are welcome). Bar meals are available at lunch and supper. Four ground-floor bedrooms, and only two steps at the front of the hotel, though there are no specific facilities for disabled visitors.

RSPB reserve immediately across river; golf; shooting; Pitlochry Festival Theatre; walks; watersports on Loch Tay; trout and salmon fishing can be arranged

PLOCKTON

🏠 ²ᐟ⁴ 🏠 🏃 🐦 🛏

Plockton Hotel, 41 Harbour Street, Plockton, Ross-shire
IV52 8TN   (Tel. 059 984 274)
Off the A890
£17.50–£20 pp b&b

In a tiny village where the cows roam free, this pretty, low stone house looks out to Black Rock Island; by a quirk of geography, it is on the West Coast, but faces due east. Its waterside beer garden across the street has been known to disappear at high tide, and a solitary palm tree attests to the presence of the Gulf Stream. The atmosphere is outstandingly friendly and comfortable; the rooms are homely, and the large yet cosy bar is carpeted in tartan. The bar food is memorable – prawns are a speciality here – and there are plenty of games (such as shove ha'penny and dominoes) with which to while away an evening. Other attractions include the village sailing regatta, held in late July/early August.

Hotel has a canoe; motor boats and windsurfers for hire in the village; seal-spotting trips (money back if no seal spotted); coral beach within walking distance; swimming on nearby beaches

PORT APPIN

🏨 ⬇ 6/12 🏘6 🏂 🚫 🛏

The Airds Hotel, Port Appin, Appin, Argyll PA38 4DF
(Tel. 063 173 236)
Off the A828, south of Fort William, 25 miles north of Oban
Open 6 March to 6 January
£90–£106 pp dinner and b&b
This extended cottage, formerly a ferry inn, dates back 300
years and has views past a little lighthouse to Loch Linnhe. Its
gardens, across the village street, nearly touch the shore. The
bedrooms are superb: large and well decorated in an old-
fashioned style, with pretty wallpapers and plain, fitted
carpets. Useful extras include electric blankets. The public
rooms are comfortable, made cosy by the open fires, and the
tasteful paraphernalia of books and ornaments. The dining
room (for dinner only) seats 36 people; there are 15 tables, and
all have good views of the loch. The set dinner costs £37, and,
by all accounts, is something to write home about.
Walks; hotel can arrange windsurfing, jetskiing, boating and fishing;
shingle beach nearby

PORTPATRICK

🏨 ⬇ 5/12 🏘 🏂 🤿 🛏

The Crown Hotel, North Crescent, Portpatrick, Stranraer
DG9 8SX   (Tel. 077681 261)
On the A77, south of Stranraer
£30 single, £56 double b&b
Separated from the harbour by the village street, the hotel has
good views past a disused lighthouse and west across the
Irish Channel. Some of the comfortable bedrooms look across
to Northern Ireland. The bars are cosy and traditionally
furnished; two of the three have water views. The tile-floored
restaurant seats 60 people and opens out through a conservatory into the sheltered back garden. On summer
evenings, you can make the most of the waterside ambience
by taking your drinks out to the seats in front of the hotel.
Lunch and dinner cost from £6.95.

Hotel can arrange fishing, shooting and pony trekking; golf and tennis in Portpatrick

PORTPATRICK

🏚 5/10 ⚶ 🏃 ◁

Knockinaam Lodge, Portpatrick, Stranraer DT9 9AD
(Tel. 077681 471)
Off the A77 between Stranraer and Portpatrick, signposted from the main road
Open March to January
£76–£92.50 pp dinner and b&b
Once the site of a secret Churchill–Eisenhower meeting, this secluded Victorian house is bordered on two sides by cliffs and on one by sea. The fine lawns run down to a reasonably sandy beach. The decor pays close attention to detail and features antique clocks and rich wood panelling and beautiful wallpapers. There are log fires in the comfortable sitting rooms, and a good country-house atmosphere. Some of the bedrooms (inevitably, there is one dubbed 'Churchill') have views to Ireland. The restaurant seats 26 and has two window tables; the four-course dinners (£30) are renowned. Vegetarians should give the chef advance notice.
Hotel can arrange fishing; golf (three miles away); garden visiting; walking; croquet

ST ANDREWS

🏚 19/50 ⚶ 🏃

Rusacks Hotel, Pilmour Links, St Andrews, Fife KY16 9JQ.
(Tel. 0334 74321)
On the A91 towards Cupar
£80–£275 per room
This carefully refurbished Victorian hotel is in a superb position, overlooking the fairways of the famous Old Course, the Royal and Ancient club house, and beyond these, the curve of the beach and the sea. The reception rooms are large, with

fine high ceilings; decor is consistently smart, and the walls are adorned with Scottish paintings. The sun lounge has excellent views of the sea and hills; it is also a perfect spot for watching the golf Opens. There is a snug basement bar with a good deal of tartan in the furnishings, and a solarium and sauna. The restaurant seats 64 (no water views), and a three-course dinner will cost you between £21 and £30. All of the staff, whatever their level of responsibility, are quite astonishingly polite, efficient and helpful. Dogs can be accommodated by arrangement only. There is a lavatory for disabled visitors, but no specially adapted rooms.

Walks; watersports; sand yachting; riding (£4.50 an hour); fishing (sea trout, £10 a day); beach; golf; bird-watching weekends; historical buildings to visit

ST BOSWELL'S

Dryburgh Abbey Hotel, St Boswell's, Roxburghshire
TD6 0RQ   (Tel. 0835 22261)
From the A68, take the B6404 at St Boswell's for two miles.
Turn left on to the B6356, signposted to the hotel, for a further two miles
£45–£95 pp dinner and b&b
This established hotel, in the heart of Border country, was 'in need of some attention' when Thurlestone Estates bought it in 1991. They closed it for six months, spent £1 million on refurbishments and reopened it in April 1992 with a new management and staff. The men from the Scottish Tourist Board were impressed, and awarded it five crowns and Highly Commended status. Guests, too, will be impressed, not least by its location on the banks of a beautiful stretch of the River Tweed, next to the ruins of the 12th-century Dryburgh Abbey. The hotel was built 700 years later and has been extended three times: its 31 rooms lie beneath an assortment of turrets, spires and battlements that together present an imposing Scottish Baronial house. Inside, design rules: everything is brand new and colour co-ordinated, from the

menu folders to the tartan skirts worn by the female staff. The restaurant has a lovely view of the Tweed and offers a six course table d'hôte dinner menu for £21.50 per head, with 150-bin wine list and impeccable table service. Discounts and early suppers for children. Ramp and lift to rooms.

Trout (free) and salmon fishing, walks, trail-riding, golf and clay pigeon shooting. AA/RAC rating pending

ST FILLANS

The Four Seasons Hotel, St Fillans PH6 2NF
(Tel. 076 485 333)
Closed January and February
On the A85 towards Crianlarich
£26.50–£38.50 pp b&b

A pleasant hotel, in an idyllic lochside situation, with exceptionally good views from the terrace and picture windows. There is a warm family atmosphere to the place; the bedrooms are pretty, and the ones at the front of the house share the splendid views across Loch Earn to the mountains beyond. The restaurant seats 60 and specializes in fresh game and seafood; all tables overlook the loch. The public rooms are simply decorated, but comfortable, and there is a library to provide reading matter for a quiet afternoon inside. The bar and coffee shop enjoy good water views. Snacks are available all day in the bar; teas in the coffee shop; packed lunches can be made up for guests planning a day out. Service, provided by various members of the Scott family, is enthusiastic and welcoming. There are six chalets behind the hotel. There is disabled access to the hotel, but no specific facilities for the disabled.

Riding; watersports centre; private jetty; sailing club nearby; fishing; golf (there are five courses nearby); walks

SCOURIE

🏚 6/11 🏠3 ♨ ⌀ ▭

The Eddrachilles Hotel, Badcall Bay, Scourie, Sutherland
IV2 4TH   (Tel. 0971 2080)
Signposted from the A894
Open 1 March to 31 October
£29–£35 pp b&b

At the head of island-studded Badcall Bay, this 18th-century
church manse is surrounded by a 320-acre estate. It really is
miles from anywhere, and an extremely good hideaway. You
would be pushed to find a more peaceful location, and it is very
popular with bird watchers and fell walkers. Visitors can
admire the seals and dolphins in the bay, but there isn't an
immense amount for children to do, so it is not perhaps the best
place for a family holiday. A large sunny conservatory opens
out to lovely views of the loch and hills, and watercolours by
local artists decorate the walls. There are no fewer than 105
malt whiskies on offer in the bar, and snacks are available at
lunchtime. The restaurant has stone walls and flagstoned
floors, log fires and loch views. A three-course dinner costs
from £10; packed lunches cost £4. There are four ground-floor
rooms, but no specific facilities for disabled visitors.
Fell walks; fishing (£3 a day); bird watching; boat hire (£15 a day)

SELKIRK

inn 2/6 🏠 ♨ ⌀ ▭

Tibbie Shiel's Inn, St Mary's Loch, Selkirk TD7 5NE
(Tel. 0750 42231)
On the A74, 20 miles from Selkirk
Closed Mondays, and November to Easter
£16–£20 pp b&b

This isolated old inn enjoys a striking position on the isthmus
between St Mary's Loch and Loch of the Lowes. It was named
after Isabella Shiel, who after her husband's death in 1824
supported herself by taking in lodgers. The inn became a
popular place to stay among the rich and famous, as well as
among the shooting fraternity: there is an impressive roster of

famous guests, including Sir Walter Scott, Wordsworth, Carlyle and Gladstone. The cosy bar and the adjacent small dining room occupy the original late 18th-century cottage; the whole place is still tiny, and there are only six bedrooms. The dining room overlooks the loch and offers full Scottish high teas. The main courses at dinner cost between £6.95 and £9.50. Snacks are served in the bar from noon to 8.30pm. Backpackers can camp for a mere pound (per person, per night); a bolstering breakfast costs £3.50. There is one ground-floor room with a large bathroom available for disabled visitors.

Walks (Southern Upland Way passes the front door); sailing; windsurfing; loch fishing (£5 a day for non-residents, equipment not provided); stony beach

SHIELDAIG

Tigh an Eilean Hotel, Shieldaig, by Strathcarron, Ross-shire IV54 8XN   (Tel. 05205 251)
Off the A896, 17 miles from Kinlochewe, 43 miles from Garve
Open Easter to October
£27.35–£30.75 pp b&b
The hotel enjoys an extremely beautiful location, at the centre of a tiny unspoilt village, with only the village road separating it from Loch Shieldaig. The excellent views stretch over the water, past the Isle of Pines (which is less than a mile away), across Loch Torridon, to the Isle of Skye. The decor in both the original 17th-century building and the modern extension is charming, with pretty wallpapers and attractive chairs and prints. The restaurant is open for dinner and seats 26 people; there are three window tables, and the set dinner costs £15.50.

Hotel can arrange fishing (book in advance); golf (15 miles away); diving and windsurfing (no equipment supplied); boat hire in village; spectacular drive over Applecross peninsula, the 2000-foot pass of Bealach na Bo

SPEAN BRIDGE

The Letterfinlay Lodge Hotel, Spean Bridge, Inverness-shire
PH34 4DZ   (Tel. 039 781 622)
On the A82, seven miles north of Spean Bridge
Closed November to February
£20–£35 pp b&b
The grounds of this country house run down through
rhododendrons to a jetty and Loch Lochy. The bedrooms are
simply decorated and unfussy; each is named after the colour
of its walls, and the public rooms have wood panelling. The
whole aura of the place is practical, friendly and down-to-
earth. The hotel is a popular stop-off point for families and for
visitors cruising the lochs and the Caledonian Canal; there
are showers and toilet facilities for passing boat-people.
Banknotes 'gifted' by appreciative customers decorate the
walls, and one glass wall gives marvellous views of the loch.
Bar lunches are served in a sun lounge overlooking the loch.
The dining room seats 60 people and a four-course dinner will
cost you £16. There is a caravan area next to the hotel. Packed
lunches can be supplied.
Walks; waterskiing; fishing (salmon £100 a week, trout free);
shooting can be arranged

STRACHUR

The Creggans Inn, Strachur, Argyllshire PA27 8BX
(Tel. 036986 279)
Take the A83 or A815 from Dunoon car ferry to Strachur, near
Inveraray
£50–£60 pp b&b
An attractive, 17th-century Highland inn, set among magnificent scenery, and separated from Loch Fyne only by the main
road. There has been extensive modernization, but this has
been tastefully done. The bedrooms are beautifully decorated
in a traditional style. One of the two cosy bars overlooks the
loch; both have open log fires and serve the inn's own malt,

Old MacPhunn. The Victorian-style restaurant has a wide-ranging reputation, and the six window tables enjoy the best loch views; dinner from the à la carte menu costs about £20–£23. The hotel has its own beach on the loch, and there is an outstanding woodland walk devised for guests through the Macleans' own estate behind the hotel. There is one ground-floor room with large bathroom for disabled visitors.

Private beach; woodland walks on estate; hotel can arrange pony trekking, fishing, shooting and boating; golf (18 miles away)

STRONTIAN

Kilcamb Lodge Hotel, Strontian, Argyll PH36 4HY
(Tel. 0967 2257)
Open Easter to October
Village on the A884, driveway signposted at bridge
£50 dinner and b&b
Set apart from the village, this small hotel was formerly an 18th-century dower house, and has large stained-glass windows in the hall. The interior is pretty, and the lounge has huge windows that look across 100 yards of grass to Loch Sunart and the massive mountains beyond. The hotel has 30 acres on this beautiful Ardnamurchan peninsula and half a mile of loch front. All the bedrooms are prettily decorated; the comfortable if utilitarian furniture is gradually being replaced by owner John Bradbury, who makes his own. The restaurant seats 25; the one window table has the best view. The set dinner costs £20.

Walking; riding, fishing, boating and stalking can be arranged

TAIN

Morangie House, Morangie Road, Tain, Ross-shire IV19 1PY
(Tel. 0862 892281)
Follow Morangie Road from town centre
£35–£70 per room b&b

This fine Victorian mansion was built in 1903 and, although modernized, retains its period character. There is a good view of the Dornoch Firth from the bar and some of the bedrooms, despite the new supermarket and petrol station that have sprung up at the end of the drive. Fine Victorian stained-glass windows light the hallway and many of the public rooms. The bedrooms are spacious and individually decorated, and are thoughtfully supplied with sherry, mints and biscuits. One double room has a brass bed, and one has a four-poster. The restaurant seats 50 (no water view). The menu is built around salmon, venison and game in season, and the food is widely recommended (four-course dinner, £15.50). Service is excellent: in 1990 the hotel won second place in an Ashley Courtenay exceptional service competition, and an RAC award for hospitality and service.

Walks; fishing; beach; golf; sports centre 15 miles away

TROON

45/72

The Marine Highland Hotel, Troon, Ayrshire KA10 6HE
(Tel. 0292 314 444)
On the Royal Troon golf course on the outskirts of Troon, just north of Prestwick on the A77
£80–£125 pp b&b

This four-star hotel overlooks the 18th fairway of the Royal Troon Championship Golf Course, with breathtaking views across the Firth of Clyde to the Isle of Arran. The large picture windows and other traditional features of the house have been retained amid the trappings of first-class luxury. The stylish bedrooms are well appointed and will suit either the well-heeled tourist or the businessman. The dining room is splendid, and has a brasserie for lively, continental-style eating. There is seating for 150 and 10 tables in the window. A four-course dinner costs £19.95. Facilities include a conference and banqueting centre, heated pool, squash courts, gymnasium, solaria, spa bath, saunas, snooker room and beauty room. There is one bedroom designed for use by the disabled, and there are also disabled facilities in the conference and leisure centres.

Walks; boating and windsurfing at Troon Marina; beach; fishing 3 miles away

ULLAPOOL

The Altnaharrie Inn, Ullapool, Wester Ross IV26 2SS
(Tel. 085483 230)
Ring from Ullapool and wait for private ferry (no charge) for the one-mile crossing. Leave car in Ullapool
Closed November to March
From £110–£120 pp dinner and b&b
Guests are fetched by ferry across the water to the peaceful old drovers' inn and its extraordinary, perfectionist environment. The inn is positioned right on the water, looking back to Ullapool, and has a beautiful interior that combines antiques with modern art and traditional Scottish decor. The dining-room floor is of scrubbed red pine, and there are rugs and weavings everywhere. Dinner is a set, five-course meal cooked by Gunn Eriksen (the Norwegian wife of owner Fred Brown) who has acquired an international reputation for her cuisine. Her food (featured on television) and Fred's wine are both taken very seriously. The dining room seats up to 16 people; half the room has a water view; depending on how full the hotel is, non-residents can sometimes be brought across for dinner, which will cost them £40–£45 per person. Vegetarians should give advance notice. The Altnaharrie is a non-smoking hotel, and there is no mains electricity. Accommodation for pets can be arranged; children can only stay if they are old enough to appreciate, and sit through, dinner.

Fishing can be arranged; walking (the activities are far less important here than the food)

WALKERBURN

Tweed Valley Hotel, Walkerburn, Peeblesshire EH43 6AA
(Tel. 0896 87636)
Closed December 25 and 26
From £40 per person b&b; dinner and b&b, from £59

A fine Edwardian house on a hillside above the village of Walkerburn, overlooking the river Tweed, with sweeping views from its dining room, up and down the lush green valley. It has traditionally been a fishing hotel, attracting anglers from abroad as well as from all over Britain. They come for the trout in nearby private lochs, as well as the famous Tweed salmon which can be fished from just below the hotel. There is an unstuffy dining room and lounge themed on fishing with prize catches on display in glass cabinets. Appropriately, trout and salmon feature prominently on the menu, although carnivores can also get their teeth stuck into steaks and venison. A smoke-house is a recent addition to the hotel, providing home-smoked delicacies. Staff are friendly and informal amid a relaxed atmosphere and tales of the latest excitement from the river.

Fishing permits arranged by the hotel; golf courses at Innerleithen (2 miles) and Peebles (8 miles)

WHITEBRIDGE

Knockie Lodge, Whitebridge, Inverness-shire IV1 2UP
(Tel. 04563 276)
Off the B862, on the eastern shore of Loch Ness
Open late April to late October
£75 single, £120–£182 double dinner and b&b

Another of Lord Lovat's old hunting lodges, built in 1798 and set above Loch nan Lann. An immensely peaceful place: there are no signs of civilization in sight, and no televisions in the hotel, partly to maintain the peace and quiet, and partly to keep the conversation flowing. The hotel has been beautifully done up, and is perfect for people who want tranquillity, beautiful walks or a high–class touring base. Far more like a grand country house than a hotel, it was declared the best country-house hotel in Scotland in the Caithness Glass/Taste of Scotland Awards 1990. The hotel is particularly popular with Americans, who cannot believe that such a quiet and remote place exists. Given the high standards of the food, the service and the general atmosphere, the prices seem par for the course. An additional attraction is the full-size, three-ton billiard table in a room with panoramic views. The dining room (open for dinner only) seats 23 people, and half the tables have a view of the loch. Open bar – guests sign for what they drink. Teas and packed lunches available. Pets can be accommodated by special arrangement only.

Walks; sailing; fishing (free, hotel owns three boats); stalking £250 a stag (book in March for October)

London, the South-east and the Isle of Wight

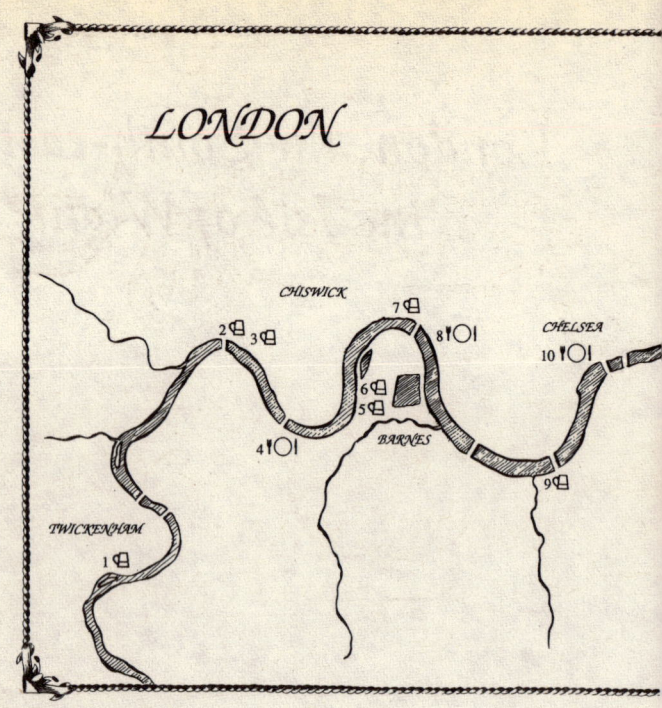

London Thames–side

1. THE WHITE SWAN

Riverside, Twickenham TW1   (Tel. 081–892 2166)
Summer drinkers at The White Swan in Twickenham sit out
on the balcony overlooking the Thames and Eel Pie Island, or
spill along the riverbank where wildfowl paddle about and
cruisers chug up and down. A good selection of pub food is
served including soup and several hot dishes. As well as the
popular Ruddles beer, there is a wide selection of trendy
bottled lagers, kept very cold. The interior is dominated by its
Rugby theme with club jerseys and ties, left by visiting teams,
adorning the walls. The manager, Steve Roy, is as devoted a

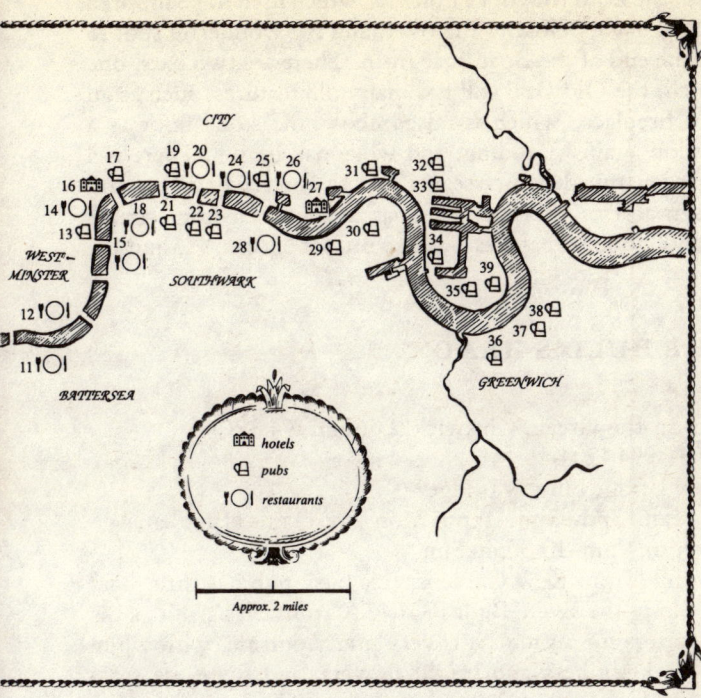

Rugby fan as any of the hundreds of supporters who descend on The White Swan on the days of England home internationals at the Twickenham ground ten minutes' walk away. At other times, the pub reflects its peaceful setting on a narrow riverside lane. Pets must be well behaved, and kept on a lead.
Walking along the riverside path; rugby

2. THE CITY BARGE

Strand-on-the-Green, Chiswick, London W4
(Tel. 081-994 2148)
Open 11am–11pm Mon–Sat; noon–3pm, 7pm–10.30pm Sun
This 15th-century riverside pub was named after the state

barge of the Lord Mayor of London, which used to be moored nearby. It is very close to the river, and is a wonderful spot to watch the end of the Boat Race from. There are two bars, one of which, the Old Bar, still has many old features, such as an ancient fireplace, which is raised above the stone floor as a protection against flooding, and worn oak beams. There is a beer garden outside which seats 120 with good river views, and a conservatory. The pub does bar meals, with home-made steak and kidney pie, pizzas, and so on, for between £3 and £5.

3. THE BULL'S HEAD

Strand-on-the-Green, Chiswick, London W4 3PQ
(Tel. 081-994 1204)
By Kew Bridge railway bridge
Open 11am–3pm, 5pm–11pm Mon–Fri; 11am–11pm Sat;
noon–3pm, 7pm–10.30pm Sun
Half a mile from Kew Gardens, this busy pub has three bars overlooking the river. Built in 1642 (Cromwell used it as his headquarters for a time), it is very pretty outside, with white walls, dark timbers and bright flowers, and there are seats along the towpath, and a conservatory. The beers on offer include Ruddles Best and County, Websters, Budweiser, and Holsten, and they do a good range of bar food. There are eight or ten hot dishes on offer, which cost from £4, and the pub is a particularly popular venue for Sunday lunch.

4. THE DEPOT

Tideway Yard, Mortlake High Street, Mortlake, London
SW14 8SN   (Tel. 081-878 9462)
Open from 10am; restaurant meals served from noon–2.45pm,
and 6–11pm
It's a café in the morning, a tea room all afternoon and a restaurant at lunch and dinner, when there is virtually never an

unreserved table. If you want to sit at one of the tables next to the wall of expansive plate-glass windows overlooking the Thames, you'll have to book several weeks in advance. The clientele is predominantly young, trendy and sophisticated; there is always a strong arty flavour to the place; intense conversations go on across the tables packed tightly together. With light streaming in from the river and open playing fields beyond, the large main room feels light and airy. Staff are young, informal and very effective; the food is basically Italian, and rather less exciting than the atmosphere. The wine list is well chosen, but on the pricey side.
Walks along the Thames towpath

5. THE BULL'S HEAD INN

373 Lonsdale Road, London SW13 9PY   (Tel. 081-876 5241)
Open 11am–11pm Mon–Sat; noon–3pm, 7pm–10.30pm Sun
This old pub, originally recorded in 1700 but rebuilt in 1845, stands close to Barnes Bridge, and its balconies provide a prime viewing position for the Boat Race. Unfortunately the Thames Flood Wall obscures the views from the bars, but most of the visitors are there for the jazz – for which the pub is famous – rather than the view. The Bull's Head has been playing host to jazz musicians for 31 years, and is one of the longest-serving jazz venues in Europe. There are top-class jazz acts every night, and lunchtime big band sessions (£2.50–£6 for admission). There is a carvery in the saloon bar, and another restaurant in the original stable buildings which is open in the evenings and Sunday lunchtimes, and specializes in steaks, fish and the like. Pre-music suppers are available, priced £8.95. The restaurant does not have a river view. The pub serves Young's beers.

6. THE SUN INN

7 Church Road, Barnes, London SW13 9HE
(Tel. 081-876 5893)

Barnes Pond, with its grassy banks overhung with drooping weeping willows, is at the heart of one of the most 'villagey' districts in London. Everybody seems to be a regular at The Sun Inn, which overlooks the water, reinforcing the atmosphere of a parochial hub: pre-Sunday lunch drinks are particularly jolly occasions. The interior is large with a rectangular bar in the middle of the room surrounded by enough space for a couple of hundred people. Salads, a few hot dishes and other pub fare are served (lunchtime only). There are several quiet little alcoves to which the less gregarious can escape. However, The Sun Inn really comes to its own on warm evenings when an almost carnival atmosphere prevails on the banks of Barnes Pond while trays of drinks are carried outside and down to the water's edge.

7. THE DOVE

19 Upper Mall, Hammersmith, London W6 9TA
(Tel. 081-748 5405)

Open 11am–11pm Mon–Sat; noon–3pm, 7pm–10.30pm Sun

This old-fashioned riverside pub, which dates back to 1796, is in the *Guinness Book of Records* for having the smallest bar in the world – only 4 feet 2 inches by 7 feet 10 inches (and they once got 27 rugby players in it at the same time!). It also has many historical connections; Nell Gwyn and King Charles II drank here, and *Rule Britannia* was written in an upstairs room. There are great river views from a small terrace, and from the beer garden. Bar food is available, prices from £2.50 to £5. There is a pleasant atmosphere in all the low-ceilinged bars, and there are no jukeboxes or fruit-machines to intrude upon the old-fashioned feel of the place.

8. THE RIVER CAFÉ

🍴 ⌂ & ◇ ▭

Thames Wharf Studios, Rainville Road, Hammersmith,
London W6 9HA   (Tel. 071-381 8824)
Open 12.30pm–3pm, 7.30pm–9.30pm Mon–Fri; closed Sat,
Sun, and two weeks in August

This restaurant, in a Thames-side studio converted by its
owner, architect Richard Rogers, has swiftly become one of
the most fashionable places to eat in London. While Rogers'
idiosyncratic and controversial style is doubtless part of the
attraction here, the main draw for visitors is the cooking, done
by Rose Grey and Rogers' wife Ruth. The food is regional
Italian – the recipes are chiefly from Tuscany – and revolves
around ingredients high in flavour, such as mozzarella, plum
tomatoes, polenta, black olives, virgin olive oil, peppers, red
onions and broccoli. The restaurant is very popular with
people who like vibrant and tasty food in a simpler style than
has prevailed in recent years. A three-course meal costs about
£40 per person. The river views are best from the eight outside
tables, which are used when the weather is fine. The Café can
cater for disabled visitors but there are no special facilities.

9. THE SHIP INN

🍺 ⌂ & ◇ ▭

41 Jews Row, London SW18 1TB   (Tel. 081-870 9667)
Open 11am–11pm Mon–Sat; noon–3pm, 7pm–10.30pm Sun

This pub, in the middle of an unattractive industrial area, still
manages to be extremely popular with the upwardly mobile
youngsters of Wandsworth, Battersea and Fulham, especially
since it added its conservatory. It has two pleasant bars,
although the river views are better from the large garden. The
food is inventive and popular, tending more towards the
imaginative bar snack rather than the formal meal. A three-
course meal would cost approximately £10 per person. They
also have barbecues in the summer, and in the winter they
serve Young's Winter Warmer beer, which lives up to its
name.

10. THE WATERFRONT RESTAURANT

IOI 🏠 🍷 🚫 💳

Harbour Yard, Chelsea Harbour, London SW10
(Tel. 071-352 4619)
Open 12.30pm–3pm, 7pm–11.30pm; closed Sun evenings in summer, and all day Sun in winter

Inside the new Chelsea Harbour complex, this chic restaurant seats 120, with six tables in the arched windows overlooking the smart yachts in the harbour pool below. They also have 10 tables on the outdoor terrace during the summer, which have excellent views. The restaurant is beautifully decorated, with paintings on the walls, as well as sculptures and plants in the corners, and the furniture is modern and pleasant. The bar is made out of grey marble and chrome, and is striking. The food is northern Italian, with emphasis on seafood and fresh vegetables, and a three-course meal costs between £20 and £30 per person. The restaurant is popular, so booking is advisable, especially for the window tables. There is a lavatory for disabled visitors.

11. THE BATTERSEA BARGE

IOI 🏠 🍴 🚫 💳

Nine Elms Lane, Battersea, London SW8
(Tel. 071-498 0004)
Open noon–3pm, 6pm–late; closed Sundays

This barge, tucked away on the south side of the river between Chelsea and Vauxhall Bridges is best located by looking for the Federal Express warehouse: the barge lie in its lee. The intrepid diner is likely to be well rewarded for his search. The Battersea Barge offers excellent English and French bistro-style food, at very reasonable prices. A three-course à la carte dinner costs around £15 per person, and table d'hôte is available for £11; both of which represent extremely good value for money, considering the quality of the food. The views are very good across the river to Pimlico and Chelsea, and the character of the restaurant is civilized without being pretentious. The eternally fascinating bulk of Battersea

Power Station looms large just along the river, and if you fancy a stroll after lunch or before dinner, Battersea Park is nearby.

N.B. The Barge was threatening to move to the northern bank of the Thames during 1992; call before visiting just to make sure of its location.

12. THE ELEPHANT ON THE RIVER

IOI ⚙ 𝄞 ⊘ ▭

129 Grosvenor Road, London SW1V 3SY
(Tel. 071-834 1621)
Open 7pm–1.30am; Closed Mon
This large restaurant, which provides dinner and dancing, also has tremendous river views from 40 of its tables. The cuisine is international and varied, and a three-course dinner costs in the region of £30 per person. They have an extensive wine list, which starts at £10 and goes up to an astonishing £550 per bottle, if you feel like splashing out. There is a five-piece dance band which plays every night, and the place is apparently popular with actors who come to relax after performances. The restaurant is also open for Sunday lunch, which is very family-oriented, with children being especially welcome. The staff are very friendly and helpful, but there are no facilities for the disabled.

13. THE TATTERSHALL CASTLE

⊡ ⚙ 𝄞 ⊘ ▭

Kings Reach, Victoria Embankment, London SW1A 2HR
(Tel. 071-497 3597)
Open noon–10.30pm. Restaurant open noon–3.30pm,
6.30pm–10.30pm
Boasting four bars, a nightclub and a restaurant, this large converted ship on the Embankment is a lively place to have a drink on the Thames, with pop music playing in all areas. The restaurant serves English food, roast lunches and salads (the three-course lunch costs approximately £8), although there are no water views from the restaurant. The large deck area provides good views along the river.

14. **RESTAURANT SHIP HISPANIOLA**

IOI 🛳 🍷 🚫 ▭

Victoria Embankment, London WC2   (Tel. 071-839 3011)
Open noon–2pm, 6pm–10pm; closed Sat lunch, all day Sun
This permanently moored ship, which was originally a
steamer on the Clyde, provides a pleasant, floating restaurant
which can accommodate 170 people. All of the tables have a
water view, and there is a promenade deck on the port side.
There is another entire deck which is used for private
functions. The cuisine is European with a bias towards French,
and there is an extensive wine list. A set three-course meal costs
£20.

15. **THE REVIEW RESTAURANT**

IOI 🛳 🍷 🚫 ▭

Level 3, Royal Festival Hall, The South Bank Centre,
London SE1   (Tel. 071-921 0800)
Open noon–2.30pm, 5pm–8pm
Closed Mon and Sat lunch
This enormous, airy restaurant, designed by the Conrans, has
impressive views across the Thames, especially from its eight
window tables. There are high ceilings, big pillars, huge floor-
to-ceiling windows, providing a feeling of quiet spaciousness
rare in London. The cuisine is international, with main courses
between £8.50 and £11.50, and vegetarian dishes always
available. The set, three-course lunch menu costs £9.95; the
set, four-course Sunday lunch is £12.95, and their two-course,
pre-concert supper is £10.95. It is ideally placed for concert-
goers and others using the extensive cultural facilities of the
South Bank Centre to relax and have a pleasant meal in elegantly
modern surroundings; the view at night with the lights of the
opposite bank, and the interesting new development at
Charing Cross station, shining on the water should be enough
to tempt anyone. Good access and facilities for the disabled.

16. THE SAVOY HOTEL AND RIVER RESTAURANT

🏨 36/202 🏘 ♨ ⚔ 🛏

The Strand, London WC2R 0EU   (Tel. 071-836 4343)
£175 (single) to £615 (double suite with river view) per room per day

This magnificent hotel, long the epitome of sophistication, offers marvellous river views from its Thames-side rooms, although the prices for double riverside rooms start at £260 per night. The decor throughout the hotel is stylish and varied, utilizing Art Deco and classicism to create a unique feel for each room, and no expense is spared to provide a feeling of traditional luxury. Although 70 yards from the water, the restaurant provides a fine view of the Thames, as long as you ask for a table with a view, and an ideal environment for power breakfasts (traditional English breakfast £15.75: 7am–10.30am Mon–Sat; 8am–10.30am Sun), sophisticated lunches and dinners (set lunch £24.20: 12.30pm–2.30pm; set dinner from £29.50 (£35–£40 at weekends): 7.30pm–11.30pm, until 10.30pm on Sundays). There is dancing every night except Sunday. These window tables also give lounge lizards a grandstand view of the London Marathon in April. Lounge suit or black tie evening.

17. THE WINE BARGE

🏠 🏘 ♨ ⚔ 🛏

The Wilfred Sailing Barge, Victoria Embankment,
London WC2R 2PP   (Tel. 071-379 5496)
Open noon–midnight, Mon–Fri

This pleasant wine bar/restaurant has been created on board a 1927 Thames sailing barge, whose mast, at 100 feet, is the highest on the river. It has been sensitively converted, panelled with wood throughout, and it has a friendly atmosphere; the South American theme on Saturdays and Sundays livens things up at the weekend. There is seating for 60 people downstairs but it is difficult to see the water, although on deck, where there are 20 tables, the river flows past close by on both sides. They have live piano music on Fridays. The menu is composed mainly of pasta, lasagne, hot-pots and salads, and a three-course meal costs about £13 per person. They also have a small bar menu. Pets allowed on deck but not in the main restaurant.

18. THE GOURMET PIZZA COMPANY
IOI 🏠 🎿 🐾 ▭

Gabriel's Wharf, 56 Upper Ground, London SE1 9PP
(Tel. 071-928 3188)
Open noon–10.45pm
This recently opened pizza restaurant is situated at the end of an interesting little market development, overlooking the Thames to the east of Waterloo Bridge. It serves pasta and pizzas that are less conventional than usual and combines the ease of pizza eating and serving with a rather more gastronomic approach. The results are exotic with cajun prawn and chicken, Camembert and Chinese duck, and so are the prices (between £5 and £7.50 for the pizzas). There is also a wide range of vegetarian dishes. The staff are young, enthusiastic and friendly. They especially welcome children, and have children's menus, high chairs, and a magician on Sundays. Ten tables have good views of the water.

19. DOGGETT'S COAT AND BADGE
🍺 🏠 🎿 🐾 ▭

1 Blackfriars Bridge, London SE1   (Tel. 071-633 9081)
Open 11am–11pm Mon–Sat; noon–3pm, 7pm–10.30pm Sun
Closed from 7pm Sat and 3pm Sun in winter
This pub was named after an 18th-century actor, Thomas Doggett, who made a celebrated river crossing and gave his coat and a badge to the ferryman in gratitude. Occupying four floors, it offers views of the Thames, although because of its position on Blackfriars Bridge it also offers views of London traffic. The restaurant has an à la carte menu and better views of the river and the city skyline. (A three-course lunch costs about

£13.50 per person; the restaurant is not open in the evenings). The bars serve cask-conditioned beers, and also do salads and quiches for around £4. Boardroom with conference facilities and riverside terrace, available for hire.

20. **LE QUAI**

1 Broken Wharf, London EC4V 3QQ   (Tel. 071-236 6480)
Open 7.30am–10.30am, noon–2pm, 6.30pm–9pm Mon–Fri; closed Sat and Sun
Located halfway between Southwark Bridge and Blackfriars Bridge on the riverside walk along the north bank, this elegant, modern French restaurant is popular with City workers. The decor is plush and tasteful, with scumbled walls and a black marble bar; a wall of windows facing the river provides good views. Main courses from the classic French menu cost about £20. Bar meals cost £9.95. Breakfast is popular – you need to book – and costs £7.50. The champagne bar is open all day. Lavatories for the disabled.

21. **THE FOUNDERS ARMS**

Bankside, 52 Hopton Street, London SE1
(Tel. 071-928 1899)
Open 11am–11pm Mon–Sat; noon–3pm, 7pm–10.30pm Sun
To the east of Blackfriars Bridge on the south bank, this narrow, modern and popular pub makes the most of its riverside position with huge floor-to-ceiling windows looking out towards St Paul's Cathedral on the far side. It also has 20 tables outside. They serve Young's cask-conditioned real ales, and the restaurant, which seats 35, does steaks, salads and seafood (a three-course meal costs between £10 and £15). Bar snacks are also available. Sunday lunch (£11.50) is popular, so it is worth booking. Just behind the pub is the Royal Academy's Watercolour Gallery, and the site of Shakespeare's Globe theatre, which is being rebuilt. The pub can cater for disabled visitors though there are no special facilities.

22. THE ANCHOR BANKSIDE

34 Park Street, London SE1   (Tel. 071-407 1577)
Open 11.30am–11pm Mon–Sat; noon–3pm, 7pm–10.30pm
Sun. Restaurant open noon–3pm, 6pm–10pm Mon–Sat;
noon–2pm, 7pm–10pm Sun
The original building perished in the Great Fire of London; the
present pub, situated to the east of Southwark Bridge, has
great character, and views of the river from the upstairs bar,
the restaurant (main courses £9–£20), and the terrace (which
seats 200).

23. THE OLD THAMESIDE INN

St Mary Overy Wharf, 1 Clink Street, London Bridge,
London SE1   (Tel. 071-403 4243)
Open 11am–11pm Mon–Fri; 11am–3pm, 6pm–11pm Sat;
noon–3pm, 7pm–10.30pm Sun
In the shadow of London Bridge and just behind Southwark
Cathedral, this pub, converted out of an old warehouse, has
timber beams, brick-arched windows and fine river views
from two of its three bars and the riverside terrace (which seats
about 80 people). Also in view are the new Lloyds building, St
Paul's Cathedral and the Monument. The restaurant, also with
terrace, serves lunch and dinner (main courses £11–£15.50, set
lunch £16). Only yards away a three-masted schooner, the
Kathleen and May, is permanently docked: it is tucked neatly
between buildings, with only a few feet to spare on either side
of its rigging. The Clink – an old ecclesiastical prison destroyed
in a poll-tax riot in 1381, and now a prison museum – is just
down the road.

24. THE REGALIAN

IOI ⚐ ⚡ ◁ ▭

Swan Pier, Swan Lane, London Bridge, London EC4R
(Tel. 071-623 1805)
Open 11.30am–3.30pm Mon–Fri; dinner-dances at weekends
(see below)
This large boat, permanently moored west of London Bridge
on the north bank, offers cuisine of a high standard which is
popular with people who work close by in the City. The
feeling of being on a boat is heightened by the fact that the
Thames Line river boat service docks at the same pier, and the
wash from these can cause the boat to rock as though in a gale.
All of the tables have a river view, and there is also a bar. The
menu – English and French cuisine – costs from £10 a head.
Dinner-dances are held on most Friday and Saturday nights.
These cost £40 per person (to include dinner, drinks, cabaret
and disco). Tickets must be booked in advance. The boat is also
available for private hire.

25. THE HORNIMAN AT HAY'S

🍺 ⚐ ⚡ ◁ ▭

Hay's Galleria, London Bridge, London SE1 2HD
(Tel. 071-407 3611)
Open 9am–11pm Mon–Fri; 9am–6pm winter weekends
Right on the river-terrace of Hay's Galleria, this large, multi-
level pub is filled with large fern trees, dark wood, tiles and
brass in an attempt to re-create the atmosphere of the 1830s
when the eponymous Frederick Horniman used to set out on
voyages of exploration from this wharf. It has a carvery
restaurant, open for lunch only (three-course lunch £16.50),
and a hot pantry which serves quiche, shepherd's pie, curries
and so on for about £5. They have a good selection of beer,
including Tetley's and Wadworth's 6X. The river views are
good, and there are seats outside as well. There is wheelchair
access to the pub, though no facilities for the disabled.

26. THE QUAYSIDE RESTAURANT

IOI 🏠 🚫 ▭

World Trade Centre, International House, 1 St Katherine's
Way, London E1 9UN   (Tel. 071-481 0972)
By Tower Bridge, on the slip road leading to the Tower Hotel
Open noon–2.30pm, 6pm–10pm; closed Sat lunch and Sun
dinner
A luxurious restaurant, with real trees (on coasters) in the hall.
A long set of rooms overlooks St Katherine's Yacht Haven,
and provides a romantic setting, with live music every
evening. Fifteen of the tables have a water view. There is also a
small terrace outside which can be used if weather permits.
Cuisine is modern English and French; set meals cost from £23,
à la carte also available. Dinner dances Friday and Saturday.
They also have functions facilities.

27. THE TOWER THISTLE HOTEL

🏨 750/808 🏠 🔥 🚫 ▭

St Katherine's Way, London E1 9LD   (Tel. 071-481 2575)
£118–£290 per room
This huge hotel, resolutely boxlike in appearance, and an
unattractive brown colour to boot, nevertheless boasts fine
views of Tower Bridge, St Katherine's Dock and the newly
refurbished warehouse frontage at Butlers Wharf on the other
side of the river. The hotel is of international standard, and has
a spectacular lobby with huge marble pillars and banks of
mirrors. It also has a coffee lounge, a bar with a nautical theme
and three restaurants of varying luxury. All the bedrooms have
televisions and trouser-presses, and the executive rooms have
mini-bars. Room service is 24-hour. Suitable for disabled
visitors.

28. **THE BLUEPRINT CAFÉ**

🍷 🏠 ♿ ⊘ 💳

Butlers Wharf, London SE1 2YD   (Tel. 071-378 7031)
Open noon–3.30pm, 7pm–11pm Tues–Sat; noon–3.30pm Sun
On the first floor of the fascinating Design Museum, this restaurant makes the most of its wonderful position with sliding glass windows that open out on to a long riverside terrace. The views, especially along the river to nearby Tower Bridge, are splendid. There are eight tables within the restaurant next to the windows, and ten on the terrace when the weather is suitable. The restaurant is chic and bright and cheerful, and the staff are friendly and helpful. The food is inventive and Mediterranean in influence. Main courses cost between £8 and £10. Access for the disabled, but no lavatories.

29. **THE ANGEL**

🍺 🏠 ♿ ⊘ 💳

101 Bermondsey Wall East, Rotherhithe, London SE16 4NB
(Tel. 071-237 3608)
Open 11am–3pm, 5.30pm–11pm (11am–11pm in summer)
Mon–Sat; noon–3pm, 7pm–10.30pm Sun
There has been a pub on this site since the monks of Bermondsey Priory first opened a tavern here in the 15th century. In the intervening centuries, it became the haunt of smugglers. Samuel Pepys, Captain Cook and Laurel and Hardy are all reputed to have frequented it, and the walls of the pub are covered with pictures and photographs illustrating the local history. As well as being steeped in Thames-side history, the pub also offers some of the most picturesque and classic views of Tower Bridge and the City. There is a balcony, built of wooden boards on pilings over the river, which is lit by lanterns at night and the water laps underneath at high tide. The restaurant is open for both lunch and dinner, has five window tables, and main courses cost about £13.50. The bar also serves food.

30. **THE MAYFLOWER**

🍺 🏠 🐕 🕰 ▭

117 Rotherhithe Street, London SE16 4NF
(Tel. 071-237 4088)
Open noon–3pm, 6pm–11pm Mon–Fri; noon–3pm, 6.30pm–
11pm Sat; noon–3pm, 7pm–10.30pm Sun
Another docklands pub steeped in history, the Mayflower is
named after the ship which took the first pilgrims to America
and which was moored nearby, and there are claims that some
of the ship has actually been incorporated into the structure of
the pub. There are many wooden beams and panels about the
place which might support this theory. Another interesting
and even less well-known fact about the pub is that it is the only
place in the British Isles, apart from the American Embassy,
which is licensed to sell American postage stamps. There is a
wooden jetty outside which holds 40 people, and affords
excellent views across the river to Wapping. Inside, there are
two bars which are dark and full of character, although the
small leaded windows make viewing the river difficult. The
spacious bars upstairs, which has good river views, offers
decent bar food (£2–£10). Closed on Sunday and Monday
evenings. Dogs must be kept on a leash.

31. **THE PROSPECT OF WHITBY**

🍺 🏠 🐕 🕰 ▭

57 Wapping Wall, London E1 9SP   (Tel. 071-481 1095)
Open 11.30am–3pm, 5.30pm–11pm Mon–Thurs; 11.30am–
11pm Fri and Sat; noon–3pm, 7pm–10.30pm Sun
This is London's oldest pub, dating back to 1520, when it was
known as the 'Devil's Tavern' because of the pirates and
smugglers who congregated here. Justly famous for its
history, it used to be frequented by Judge Jeffreys, of the
'Bloody Assizes' fame, who used to eat his dinner while
watching the hanging of convicts at the execution dock on the
other side of the river. The pub is very popular with tourists,
and it has an international reputation. The interior of the pub is
suitably authentic, with lots of old wood, panelling, flagstones

and a pewter-topped bar. It has two bars, one with good water views, a riverside terrace, a garden on the river wall and two restaurants upstairs. These serve a variety of food from an à la carte menu; a main course is between £7 and £20, and it is advisable to book. They also have live music on Thursday, Friday and Sunday nights.

32. THE BARLEY MOW

144 Narrow Street, Limehouse Basin, London E14 8DP
(Tel. 071-265 8931)
Open 11.30am–3pm, 5.30pm–11pm Mon–Sat; noon–3pm, 7pm–10.30pm Sun
This pub, recently converted out of the 200-year-old dock-master's house, commands panoramic views over a huge sweep of the river, from the Isle of Dogs to Bermondsey, due to its position at the entrance to the old Limehouse Basin dock. There are 20 tables outside, and good river views are also available from both of the bars. The house has been sensitively converted: palm trees and cane chairs contribute to its relaxed atmosphere. The restaurant seats 30, and offers good pub food. The new 'traditional English restaurant' upstairs overlooks the river and offers three-course meals for £14–£18. Small children should be kept under close supervision, as there is a frighteningly steep drop down the dock wall about five feet from the (fenced-in) beer garden. Lavatories and access for the disabled.

33. THE GRAPES

76 Narrow Street, London E14 8BP   (Tel. 071-987 4396)
Open 11.30am–2.30pm, 5pm–11pm Mon–Sat; noon–3pm, 7pm–10.30pm Sun
Restaurant open noon–2pm, 7pm–9pm; closed Sun, Sat lunch, Mon evening

Like many Docklands watering holes, this small, dimly lit pub has a long and colourful history. Dickens apparently used it as a model for the 'Six Jolly Fellowship Porters' in his novel *Our Mutual Friend*. The interior is cosy and pleasant, with a collection of prints and pictures adorning the walls and there is a small glassed-in snug above the river. The restaurant upstairs is good for seafood, and there are tremendous views of the Thames from the window tables.

34. BOOTY'S

92a Narrow Street, London E14   (Tel. 071-987 8343)
Open 11am–3pm, 5pm–11pm Mon–Fri; 7pm–midnight Sat; closed Sun
This popular wine bar enjoys extreme proximity to the river; it is not unknown for the local river policeman to drop by and enjoy a glass of wine on the river itself, on the deck of his launch. The bar is popular with local office workers, and can consequently be busy at lunchtimes. The views from the few window tables are worth the traffic jams in Narrow Street; make sure of your seat by booking in advance. Food is available at lunchtimes and in the evenings; baked potatoes and chilli, coq au vin and goulash, all home made.

35. THE HENRY ADDINGTON

Mackenzie Walk, Cubitt Steps, Canary Wharf, London E14
(Tel. 071-512 9022)
Out from the semi-inhabited shopping centre of Cabot Place West, and past the fountains of Cabot Square, the Henry Addington sits beside an impressive stretch of dockside terrace, looking south across the water to the building site that is Heron Quay. Inside, there is an impressively long bar, with a cosier, lounge-style seating area tucked away at the back. The design, as you would expect, is very modern, with woodwork and marble where, ten years ago, you would have found black

and chrome. For six months, the Henry Addington had the distinction of being the only pub in Canary Wharf, and consequently was packed out at lunchtimes; now it shares the trade with the Cat & Canary on the opposite side of Cabot Square, though it still gets the best of the sunshine on sunny days. A range of sandwiches and bar meals are available at lunchtime.

36. **THE TRAFALGAR TAVERN**

Park Row, Greenwich, London SE10   (Tel. 081–858 2437)
Open 11am–11pm Mon–Sat; noon–3pm, 7pm–10.30pm Sun.
Restaurant open noon–3pm, 6pm–10.30pm; closed Sunday evenings and Mondays
This large pub is situated so close to the Thames that the river laps against its brickwork, so the view from the large windows is impressively watery, as one looks across the river to Cumberland Mills. It is a very easy pub to find, because it is next door to the impressive Naval College. The pub has been open since 1827, and is famous for its annual whitebait dinners which were originally instituted by Gladstone in 1830. As pubs go, the Trafalgar Tavern is smart and comfortable, and has large and magnificent banqueting facilities for 250 people. The à la carte Whitebait restaurant specializes in seafood, and a three-course dinner would cost around £25, and they serve a range of guest beers which change regularly. Children allowed in restaurant, but not in the pub. There are lavatories on the ground floor, but no special facilities for disabled visitors.

37. **THE YACHT**

Crane Street, Greenwich, London SE10 9NP
(Tel. 081–858 0175)
Open 11am–11pm Mon–Sat (noon–3pm, 5.30pm–11pm in
winter); noon–2.30pm, 7pm–10.30pm Sun
Situated halfway down a somewhat insalubrious alleyway,
this pub nevertheless has good water views, especially from
the four window tables in the restaurant, and the small patio.
They offer traditional cask-conditioned ales, and the restaurant
has a range of meals, including scampi, ploughman's lunch and
baked potatoes, which are reasonably priced (last orders for
meals 2.20pm and 8.10pm). The bar is circular, in the centre of
the spacious room, and gives a pleasant impression of space.
Ramps and lavatories for the disabled.

38. **THE CUTTY SARK**

Ballast Quay, Greenwich, London SE10 9PD
(Tel. 081–858 3146)
Open 11am–11pm Mon–Sat; noon–3pm, 7pm–10.30pm Sun
This dark and cosy pub is in a listed warehouse dating back to
1695, and derives much of its character from its different levels
and its old feel. It's a friendly place, and there are good river
views over towards the Isle of Dogs and much of industrial east
London. There are four window tables in the pub, and eight
outside on the river bank. The restaurant offers good food,
with a three-course dinner costing £19 per person. No facilities
for the disabled.

39. THE GUN

27 Coldharbour, Isle of Dogs, London E14
(Tel. 071-987 1692)
Open 11am–3pm, 5pm–11pm Mon–Sat; noon–3pm,
7pm–10.30pm Sun

This small pub used to be popular with dockers, and still retains something of the unpretentiousness of the old days of heavy industry. In common with the other docklands pubs, it has had its fair share of history, including being the rendezvous point for assignations between Lord Nelson and Emma Hamilton. It has a fine balcony at the back of the pub which overhangs the river, and gives great views of the wharves and the Blackwall Power Station (dogs and children are allowed out here, but not in the bars). There are three bars, the best one being the middle bar which has the access to the deck. Bar snacks available. Access and lavatories for the disabled.

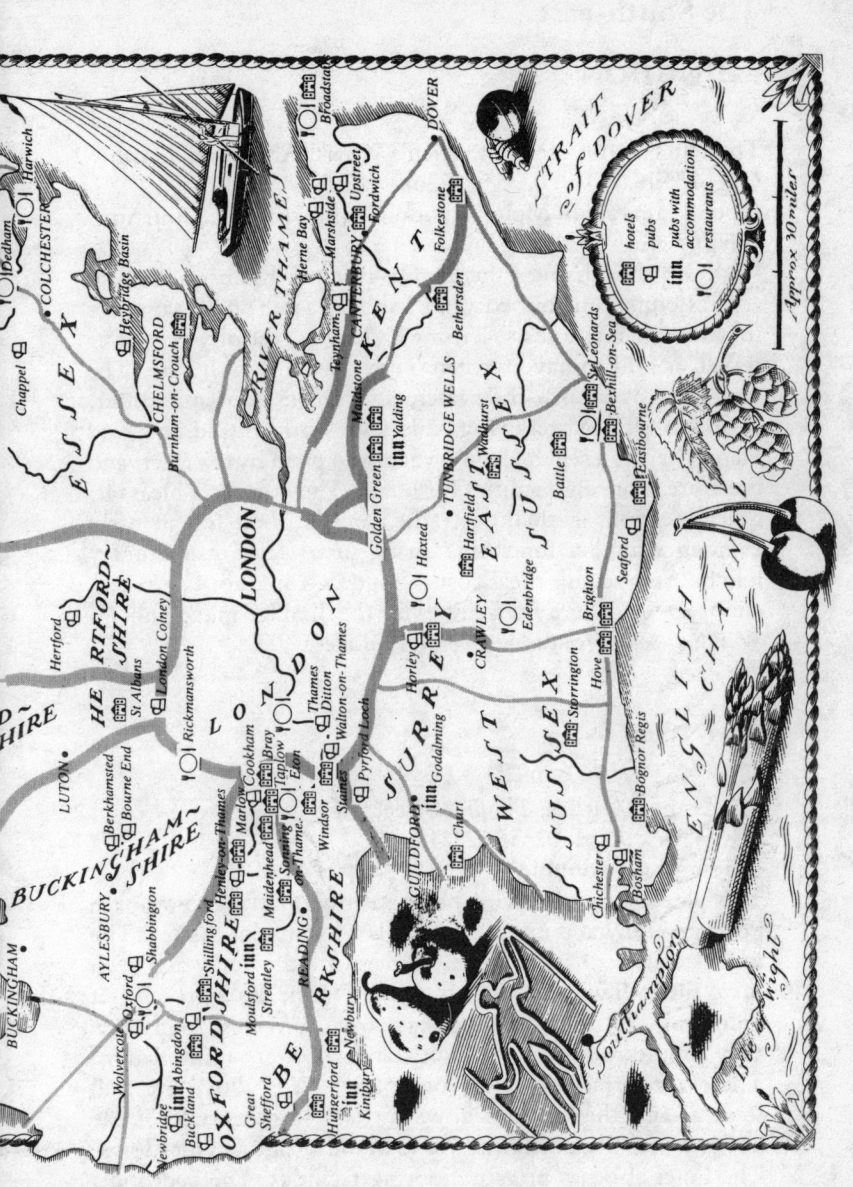

The South-east

ABINGDON

The Old Anchor Inn, 1 St Helen's Wharf, Abingdon, Oxon
OX14 5EN   (Tel. 0235 521726)
Open 11am–11pm Mon–Sat; noon–3pm, 7pm–10.30pm Sun
£25 pp b&b
Right on the Thames, this family-run pub has been recently
and tastefully refurbished: there has been a pub on the same site
for more than 100 years. Jerome K. Jerome, the doyen of river
travel, is said to have written *Three Men in a Boat* here. The
main bar overlooks the water, and serves Morland Bitter,
Morland Old Masters Dog Mild and Morland Old Speckled
Hen. There is a separate dining area and patio by the river, and
there are mooring facilities for boats. The pub has a pleasant,
quiet location, with little traffic, and is good for an early
evening drink, a lunchtime snack or a traditional Sunday
lunch. An evening meal costs about £7–£8; a hot bar snack,
about £3–£4. There are facilities for the disabled in the pub.
Walking; boat hire nearby; moorings outside

ABINGDON

The Upper Reaches, Thames Street, Abingdon, Oxon
OX14 3JA   (Tel. 0235 522311)
£75 single, £95 double
This pleasant, if somewhat bland member of the Trust House
Forte group, was until 1968 the mill for Abingdon Abbey. The
mill stream now actually runs underneath the hotel, and even
turns the mill wheel, which is situated in the dining room (set
dinner £14.95). The buildings have been converted to provide
cosy public rooms and a high standard of accommodation.
There are terraces outside, one of which is above the mill
stream, and the Thames flows by on the other side of the
hotel, where there are good views of the bridge and meadows.
The hotel also has private mooring facilities. The bedrooms

are cheerful and comfortable, with reproduction furniture and brass light fittings.

Walking; boat hire nearby; Unicorn Theatre in the old Abbey; fishing; swimming; roller skating; shooting and golf can be arranged

ALDEBURGH

🏨 19/30 ⌂ 🎻 ⬧ 💳

Wentworth Hotel, Wentworth Road, Aldeburgh, Suffolk IP15 5BD   (Tel. 0728 452312)
Closed first two weeks in January
£45–£60 pp dinner and b&b
A somewhat plain exterior belies the comfort, style and dignity of this hotel on the sea front, which has been run by the same family for 70 years. The owners pride themselves on the quality of the accommodation and service that they offer, and deservedly so. The atmosphere of the hotel is extremely welcoming. There is a sunken terrace garden facing the sea, log fires, framed prints and antiques in the lounges. Most of the tables in the dining room (which seats 80 people) have a view of the sea, and the food is good (three-course set dinner, £16.50). The staff would be very happy to explain about the nearby sporting facilities but should you just wish to relax and stroll along the beach, they will understand. There are two ground-floor rooms, though there are no special facilities for disabled visitors.

Sailing and sea fishing (no licence needed); Aldeburgh and Thorpeness golf courses nearby; beach; International Festival of Music at Snape Maltings every June; Havergate Island and Minsmere bird reserves (10 miles away)

ALDEBURGH

🏨 15/38 ⌂ 🎻 ⬧ 💳

The White Lion, Market Cross Place, Aldeburgh, Suffolk IP15 5BL   (Tel. 0728 452720)
£55–£65 single, £70–£95 double b&b
With its imposing whitewashed façade, in a prime position

throughout, and the rooms are light and airy. Some bedrooms have four-poster beds, and the rooms at the front have good sea views. There are two residents' lounges, one of which is non-smoking, a buttery bar for light meals and a restaurant which serves good fresh food, and is open to non-residents (set four-course evening meal, £15.25).

Sailing; fishing (licence necessary for river fishing); windsurfing; waterskiing; Aldeburgh and Thorpeness golf courses nearby; International Festival of Music at Snape Maltings every June; Havergate Island and Minsmere bird reserves (10 miles away)

BATTLE

7/12

Little Hemingfold Farmhouse Hotel, Telham, Battle, East Sussex TN33 O11   (Tel. 04246 4338)
From £65 double b&b

Little Hemingfold Farmhouse Hotel may not be smart but it's idyllic. To get there, you turn off the main Battle road and drive down a steep rutted lane overhung by trees. At journey's end you'll find a lake – on which you can fish for trout – simmering in the sun, a vista of fields and woods and a funny little 17th-century white-painted house that is larger than it looks, surrounded by 40 acres of its own land. Inside, there's a big sitting room with elegant windows and a Somerset Maugham atmosphere encouraged by rattan chairs. The tiny beamed bar is covered with straw matting, to match the general rustic effect, while in the dining room you'll eat at a large table with other guests unless you warn owners Alison and Paul Slater that you want to be alone. Food is homely and substantial, with the added bonus of Hemingfold-grown vegetables and fruit and a cheeseboard of several luscious varieties from which you can help yourself. Three of the bedrooms are in the main house, the others are in the adjoining inner courtyard – pets can be accommodated in the latter rooms, at the owners' discretion.

Fishing and boating on lake; swimming in lake; grass tennis court; boules

BECCLES

 4/13

Waveney House Hotel, Puddingmoor, Beccles, Suffolk
NR34 9PL (Tel. 0502 712270)
£43 single, £56.80 double, £63 four-poster
In a beautiful position on the banks of the River Waveney, this
grey stone hotel is only five minutes from the town centre.
Parts of the building date back to 1592. The rooms, though
well appointed and with modern facilities, are a little
unprepossessing, and lack style. Its attractive location on the
riverbank makes it a popular stopping place for boaters, who
like to use the bar – which overlooks the river – and the
moorings, especially in the summer. The public rooms are
furnished in a simple style, and the restaurant seats 60, and
serves English and French food – a set three-course meal costs
£12.
*Municipal swimming pool nearby; boat hire (in Puddingmoor);
fishing; golf course nearby*

BEDFORD

53/115

Bedford Swan, The Embankment, Bedford, Bedfordshire
MK40 1RW (Tel. 0234 346565)
£66 single, £76 double b&b
Conveniently located on the embankment near the town
centre, the hotel is elegant and spacious. It has recently been
refurbished inside, and offers a wide range of facilities for
guests, including a delightful indoor swimming pool and a spa
bath, and two banqueting halls in addition to the restaurant.
Most of the tables in the restaurant overlook the river. The
rooms are spacious and tastefully decorated, and many have
good views of the tranquil River Ouse running peacefully
outside.
*Walking; fishing (rod licences available); Woburn Abbey, Safari
Park and Althorp nearby; Shuttleworth Aircraft Collection at Old
Warden; river boat trips can be arranged; Cecil Higgins Trust
Museum; new sports complex nearby*

BERKHAMSTED

The Boat, Gravel Path, Berkhamsted, Hertfordshire
(Tel. 0442 877152)
Off the A41, on Ravens Lane, east side of town
Open 11am–3pm, 5.30pm–11pm Mon–Sat; noon–3pm, 7pm–10.30pm Sun
This tastefully decorated and well-maintained new pub is thankfully free from the menace of computerized games that often clutter up modern pubs. The Boat enjoys a good position by the canal, and there are moorings for people arriving by river. There is a friendly atmosphere, encouraged by the landlords, and the beer, which includes Fuller's London Pride, Chiswick and ESB, is very well kept. Outside, there are 10 tables overlooking the canal, and in the summer there are barbecues on Friday and Saturday evenings, and Sunday lunchtimes. There are also good-value lunchtime bar snacks to be had (Mon–Sat). The pub can cater for the disabled.
Fishing (rod licences available in town); walks along canal to Hemel Hempstead

BETHERSDEN

Little Hodgeham, Smarden Road, Bethersden, Kent
TN26 3HE   (Tel. 0233 850323)
Off the Bethersden–Smarden road
Open mid March to 1 October
£44.50 pp dinner and b&b (£39.50 pp dinner and b&b for stays in excess of four nights)
This picture-postcard Tudor cottage has roses tumbling round the door, ancient wooden beams, antiques and leaded windows, and is over 500 years old. It is set in rose gardens and surrounded by wooded farmland in the Weald of Kent. The water comes in the shape of a large pond, known as Hodgeham Water, and large water gardens. There is also a swimming pool. The real attraction is the atmosphere of gracious living which is due to the efforts of the proprietress, Erica Wallace.

She has set high standards, and guests can be sure of enjoying the very best in luxurious gentility. Silver cutlery, bone-china coffee cups and cut-glass and crystal bowls are the norm. Dinner is like a dinner party, with all guests eating at the same table. The food is chosen and prepared by Miss Wallace, and guests are asked their likes and dislikes when booking. If one is after a genteel house-party atmosphere, this is the perfect place – the level of attention and the warmth of the welcome guarantee that you will enjoy your stay.

Many stately homes, castles and gardens to visit nearby; walking; fishing; swimming; tennis; golf

BEXHILL-ON-SEA

25/41

The Cooden Resort, Cooden Sea Road, Cooden Beach, nr Bexhill-on-Sea, East Sussex TN39 4TT   (Tel. 04243 2281)
£65 single, £85 double b&b

The hotel is right on the seafront, and has marvellous views of Pevensey Bay, the English Channel and Beachy Head on the horizon. The bedrooms are decorated with lightwood furniture and floral fabrics. There are two bars, one of which has good sea views, and a smart restaurant which serves a wide range of international cuisine, with set lunches costing £12.25 and set dinners £17.25. Ten of its tables have good views of the water. The hotel also boasts a large health and leisure club, with swimming pools, spa bath and sauna, exercise equipment and massage. They also offer banqueting and conference facilities. Pets can be accommodated by prior arrangement. Facilities for disabled visitors include a bedroom in the annexe, ramps and lavatories.

Beach walks; health club; beauty salon; windsurfing; fishing; tennis; golf; squash; swimming pool

BLAKENEY

🏰 14/50 ♨ ♿ ⬦ ▭

Blakeney Hotel, The Quay, Blakeney, Holt, Norfolk
NR25 7NE   (Tel. 0263 740797)
Village on the B1156
£51–£78 pp dinner and b&b (minimum stay, two nights)
This 1920s red-brick hotel is located in enclosed gardens on the quayside, and has good views of Blakeney Point. Blakeney offers what many English seaside resorts no longer do – an unspoilt, traditional seaside setting, and the hotel complements this nicely. The emphasis of the hotel is on comfort and the staff make every effort to provide an efficient and professional service. The bedrooms vary in size and decor, but tend towards comfort and simplicity. The hotel's facilities include an indoor swimming pool, sauna, billiard room, beauty salon and games room. Twelve of the tables in the restaurant have sea views. It is idyllically peaceful in the winter. There is one ground-floor room for disabled guests.
Coastal path walks; sailing (tuition and boat hire can be arranged); fishing (trips with local boatmen, fly fishing nearby); tennis; beach; waterskiing and windsurfing (equipment not supplied); riding and golf courses nearby; bird watching

BOGNOR REGIS

🏰 23/51 ♨ ♿ ⬦ ▭

Royal Norfolk Hotel, The Esplanade, Bognor Regis, West Sussex PO21 2LH   (Tel. 0243 826222)
£55 single, £70 double b&b
Built in the 1840s by the Duke of Norfolk, this Trust House Forte hotel has in its time provided accommodation for Queen Victoria, Queen Alexandra and Napoleon III. The hotel is in a beautiful spot, has a fine Regency exterior, and enjoys lovely views across its gardens to the sea. The decor is smart, there is a good view of the water from both floors, and the staff are friendly and helpful. The rooms vary in size and comfort so make sure to ask for one of the better ones when booking. As well as the main swimming pool, there is a children's pool and

games area; a baby-listening service is available on request. The restaurant seats 125 people, with seven tables looking out to sea. A set lunch will cost you £10, the set dinner £14 for three courses. *Tennis courts at hotel; beach nearby; walks on Sussex Downs and along the waterfront; sea fishing can be arranged; sailing at Little-hampton; surfing, windsurfing and jetskiing equipment at Surf Shop opposite; golf at Goodwood; nature reserve at Selsey Bill; Goodwood Races; bowling green; riding on Sussex Downs*

BOSHAM

Anchor Bleu, High Street, Bosham, West Sussex PO18 8LS
(Tel. 0243 573956)
Open 11am–2.30pm, 6pm–11pm Mon–Sat; noon–3pm, 7pm–
10.30pm Sun
This 17th-century, white-painted pub (with a blue anchor) is right on the seafront: before it became an alehouse, it used to be the storehouse for the local manor. It has low ceilings and stone floors, and half of the bar looks towards the sea. The tide is a major factor in life here, and the sea views depend on it to some extent. More spectacularly, the parking is also dependent upon its caprices – photographs of the foreshore car park taken in December 1989 show vehicles floating away in high water. There is a waterside terrace and a rear garden each of which seats 30. Bar snacks are available from noon to 2pm and 7pm to 9.30pm, and Ruddles and Webster's beers are served.
Walking; bird watching; Chichester harbour and boats nearby; beach at Selsey and the Witterings (15-minute drive away); fishing at Selsey

BOURNE END

Three Horseshoes, Winkwell, Bourne End, Hertfordshire
(Tel. 0442 862585)
In Winkwell hamlet, off the A41
Open 11am–2.30pm, 6pm–11pm Mon–Sat; noon–3pm, 7pm–
10.30pm Sun; 11am–11pm Sat from May to October

Standing on a swing bridge in a quiet glade by the canal, the Three Horseshoes has been in business since 1535. Pretty and white painted outside, with baskets of hanging flowers, this is everyone's idea of 'Ye Olde Worlde Pub'. The atmosphere is highly traditional with dark wood-beamed ceilings, gleaming brass and inglenook fireplaces in both the Tack Room and the aptly named Snug bars. Nestling right on the water's edge, this appealing pub also offers plenty of seating on the canalside terraced courtyard. Both bars overlook the canal to some extent and serve tempting lunchtime snacks with a variety of sandwiches, cold meat or seafood platters and a choice of five hot dishes per day for around £4 (food is available at lunchtime every day, and Tues to Sat evenings). Children are welcome to visit the courtyard terrace. Several moorings are available beside the pub for those boating along the canal.

Walking; boating nearby; canoeing and fishing (rod licence necessary) in Hemel Hempstead; two sports centres nearby

BRANDON CREEK

The Ship, Brandon Creek, Downham Market, Norfolk
PE38 0PP   (Tel. 035376 228)
On the main A10 where the two rivers Great Ouse and Little Ouse meet
Open 11am–3pm, 6.30pm–11pm Mon–Sat; noon–3pm, 7pm–10.30pm Sun

This pub is unusually situated in that it occupies the point of confluence of the Great Ouse and the Little Ouse – the Great Ouse flows behind the pub, and the Little Ouse in front, so this pub is very definitely on the water – front and back. It is very convenient for people arriving by water, as there are extensive moorings for boats. There are tables outside, and a riverside patio which offers plenty of seating during warmer weather. The interior is extremely spacious – part of it used to be a forge, and the bar is over 100 feet long. The restaurant offers good-value food and river views, and bar snacks are also available.

This is a friendly and comfortable pub, with a nice warm atmosphere. They often change the range of ales, including Ruddles (Best and Country) and Webster's Yorkshire. Because of its location, the pub can get very busy. There are special disabled entrances and lavatory facilities.
Walking; fishing (rod licence needed)

BRAY

🍽 ⌂ 12 ♿ ✗ ▭

Waterside Inn, Ferry Road, Bray-on-Thames, Berkshire
SL6 2AT   (Tel. 0628 20691)
Open noon–2pm Wed–Sun; 7pm–10pm Tues–Sun.
Closed 26 December–8 February, Sun dinner October–Easter
This highly polished Thames-side restaurant is renowned for the quality of its cuisine, a well as the size of the bill at the end of the meal. It is beautifully situated on the river, and half the tables inside have excellent views; the floral arrangements are fabulous. There is a pretty terrace outside for pre-dinner drinks or after-dinner coffee and there is also a private dining room. The chef, Michel Roux, is so well known that booking is absolutely essential; if sheer quality of food is important to you then this is a very good place to come. The set lunch is excellent value for money (£25.50 on weekdays, £32.50 at weekends); the set dinner costs £52.50 for five courses. They have valet parking and a large and attentive staff. The Inn can cater for disabled visitors, but has no special facilities.
Walking; fishing; windsurfing at Bray marina (five minutes away); restaurant has one boat for hire, and there are plenty available locally; moorings can be arranged

BRAY

🏠 20/25 🏡 ⚓ 💳

Monkey Island Hotel, Bray-on-Thames, Maidenhead,
Berkshire SL6 2EE   (Tel. 0628 23400)
Exit 8/9 from the M4, take Old Mill Lane from Bray across the
M4
£105–£155 per room b&b
Originally an 18th-century hunting lodge, the hotel is set on a
pretty, small island in the Thames and is accessible only by
footbridge. The name originated not from any exotic pets kept
here, but because of the local monks who fished from the banks
of the island. These days, peacocks, swans and wildfowl
wander through the garden. Inside, the hotel is highly civilized
and elegant, and most of the rooms have lovely river views.
The Pavilion restaurant, perched on the narrowest tip of the
island, has seating for 80–100 and all tables look upstream;
gentlemen are required to wear a jacket and tie. The food, at
breakfast as well as dinner, has received high praise. The River
Room (a good place for weddings, dinners or seminars) is
actually suspended over the Thames.
*Plenty of walks; windsurfing in Bray marina; residents can fish from
island*

BRIGHTON (HOVE)

🏠 21/61 🏡 🚴 🐟 💳

The Alexandra Hotel, 42 Brunswick Terrace, Brighton,
Sussex BN3 1HA   (Tel. 0273 202722)
£29.50 single, £55 double b&b
This elegant Regency hotel has recently been restored, and its
Grade I listed façade looks out over Hove esplanade to the sea.
The interior decor continues the Regency feel, and the public
rooms are stylish and comfortable. The bedrooms are simply
decorated and well equipped, and some of the larger suites
have seafront balconies. The restaurant is on the lower ground
floor and consequently has no sea views, but serves good food,
with the set three-course dinner costing £12. The spacious
bar has good sea views. They also offer banqueting and

conference facilities. Pets can be accommodated by prior arrangement.

Beach; windsurfing; tennis; golf; Royal Pavilion; sports centre, with swimming pool, nearby

BRIGHTON

🏨 38/204 🏘 🍷 ⟨🍴⟩ 💳

The Hospitality Inn, King's Road, Brighton, Sussex
BN1 2GS   (Tel. 0273 206700)
£115–£135 single, £135–£155 double b&b

A monstrous five-star structure that defies description but is most striking to look at. The entrance atrium is so big and high it reduces the large restaurant at its front to insignificance. There is a luxurious variety of real plant life in this atrium, including full-grown trees, and there is a piano and acres of space for lounging. The whole effect is very agreeable and restful, even when there are dozens of people coming and going. Service is excellent – and friendly. The spacious rooms and huge suites are tastefully decorated (bedrooms with a sea view are more expensive than others). The Promenade restaurant seats 110 people, and offers tremendous views out to sea (set dinner, £16); there is another, smaller restaurant, the Noblesse, which can seat an additional 48 people (set dinner, £21). Babysitting can be arranged. There are good facilities – including four specially equipped rooms – for the disabled.

Indoor pool; gym; solarium; sauna; walks along the beach; watersports nearby; fishing by arrangement

BRIGHTON

🏨 77/200 🏘 🍷 ⟨🍴⟩ 💳

The Grand, King's Road, Brighton, East Sussex
BN1 2FW   (Tel. 0273 21188)
£123 single, £158 double b&b. Suites, from £460

Surely the best known of Brighton's grand old seafront hotels, The Grand, with its white-wedding-cake façade fringed with balconies, is for many the proper face of Old Brighton.

Completely refurbished after the bombing in 1984, it boasts the highest degree of period decor, though the service – which can verge on the patronizing – and the clientele are not always quite up to the image of elegant seaside nostalgia and five-star luxury that the hotel's image purveys. Creature-comforts are extensively catered for, from the impressive Kings Restaurant, via Hobden's Health Spa (with indoor pool, sauna, solarium etc.) to the Midnight Blues night club; a drink in the Victoria Bar will set you up nicely for an evening on the town. Disabled visitors are well provided for: there is a ramp at front of the hotel, and three rooms with specially adapted facilities.

Most activities, from clay pigeon shooting, via go-karting, to paragliding and archery, can be arranged by the hotel

BROADSTAIRS

IOI 🏠 🅧 ⬷ ▭

Mad Chef's Bistro, The Harbour, Broadstairs, Kent
CT10 1EU　(Tel. 0843 69304)
Open 11am–10pm in summer; in winter, 11am–2pm;
6pm–10pm all week (except 6pm–11pm Sat); closed Christmas and Boxing Days and when the sea floods the kitchen
With good views across Viking Bay, and Bleak House just behind, the surroundings alone deserve a visit, without the attractions of this interesting restaurant. Inside, the bistro has effective nautical decor: the odd anchor lying tastefully on the hearth, nets hung from the ceiling, and other seafaring knick-knacks. The three window tables have the best views, though the water is visible from most of the 70 places. The restaurant boasts extensive seafood and vegetarian menus: the set lunch costs £6.50. There is a bar at the back which has Warsteiner on tap and eight ciders. This year, the bistro is specializing in Kentish wines, from £4.50 a bottle. It is worth keeping an eye out for the genuinely eccentric, eponymous Mad Chef: do not be too surprised if he rushes up and begins to consume your food or wine during your meal.

Deep sea, harbour and beach fishing; Viking Bay beach (10 yards away); walks along coast to Ramsgate, Margate and Sandwich; jetski and canoe rental in Kingsgate; windsurfing in Kingsgate (no equipment supplied)

BROADSTAIRS

🏨 12/18 🕊 🔥 🐾 💳

The Royal Albion Hotel, Albion Street, Broadstairs, Kent
(Tel. 0843 68071)
£70 double b&b
A nice mix of small, family-run hotel with chintzy comfort and old-fashioned, slightly grandiose charm (somehow you can only ever find it at the seaside) in this pretty, spick and span resort. The rooms are cosy and those overlooking the sea are literally backing on to the prom; some with a rather majestic veranda, which is large enough to entertain guests for tea. The hotel restaurant is, curiously, two doors along the street. Founded in 1850 by a Swiss pastry cook and confectioner, Frederico Marchesi, it is run by two of his great grandsons and, like the hotel, overlooks the little bay. (Pets are welcome, at the manager's discretion.) Unlike in innumerable refurbished family hotels (but as in any good French establishment), here the skill is concentrated on the food, not the curtain drapes, and you are assured magnificent helpings of fresh seasonal vegetables. Unfortunately, access may be difficult for the disabled (the hotel is approached by steps front and back and there is no lift).
Coastal walks and many historical attractions for Charles Dickens fans, including Bleak House where the great man wrote David Copperfield

BROADSTAIRS

🍽 🕊 🔥 🐾 💳

Morelli's, 14 Victoria Parade, Broadstairs, Kent
(Tel. 0843 62500)
Open 9am–10pm every day
A proper ice-cream parlour right on the seafront, open all year

in the daytime and in summertime until 10.30pm. Restored in 1957 and practically untouched since, this large café/tearoom is resplendent in 1950s kitsch with original Lloyd Loom basket chairs, sunburst clocks telling you it's time for a Knicker-bocker Glory and fountains with tiny plastic dancers that whirl about in the bubbles. The walls are decorated with tempting pictures of Banana Gondolas and Meringue Glacés, which are magnificently served with all the requisite paper parasols and wafer trimmings. The staff are smartly turned out in red and white striped waistcoats or starched white headdresses, and whip up sundaes with foot-long teaspoons. Coffee comes in glass mugs and silver-mesh cradles and you can sit with a decent cappuccino and watch the gulls bobbing on the waves. Allow plenty of time to enjoy yourself here; the ice creams are huge and accordingly quite expensive (about £3) and a family bill can come as a bit of shock. No special facilities for the disabled, but access is easy and staff are very willing to help.

BUCKLAND

The Trout Inn, Tadpole Bridge, Buckland, Faringdon, Oxon (Tel. 036787 382)
On the Bampton to Buckland road, four miles north east of Faringdon
Open 11.30am–2.30pm, 6pm–11pm Mon–Sat; noon–3pm, 7pm–10.30pm Sun; 11am–11pm 1 May to end September
This Thames-side pub has been here, in this out of the way spot, since 1888. It exploits its river position by offering customers free mooring, and there is a mile and a half of fishing owned by the pub, for which day tickets are available. It has a pretty exterior, and the small bar has a flagstone floor and plants dotted around it. There is a variety of bar snacks and meals available, from steaks to sandwiches, at reasonable prices. Outside is a garden with nice, if not outstanding, views downstream. There is a hut that sells soft drinks and crisps, and in the summer they have barbecues. There is also a camp- and caravan-site on the waterfront. The pub is a free house, and

the beers available include Gibbs Mew Salisbury and Chudley, Wiltshire Keg, Archers, and several guest beers. Children are allowed into the eating areas and the garden.
Fishing; walking; moorings; music (e.g. barn dances) one night each week

BURNHAM-ON-CROUCH

Ye Olde White Harte Hotel, The Quay,
Burnham-on-Crouch, Essex CM0 8AS   (Tel. 0621 782106)
£19–£34 single, £33–£55 double b&b
This 400-year-old inn is very popular with the sailing fraternity; situated on the River Crouch, it has its own private jetty. The bars have a strong nautical feel, with wooden floors, high-beamed ceilings, collections of old brass and sea pictures, and good views of the yachts on the estuary outside. Beers on offer include Tolly Cobbold and Adnams ales, and the landlord eschews jukeboxes and video games. The bedrooms have recently been refurbished, and have pale-coloured soft furnishings contrasting with the original beamwork. The bedrooms are simple but very comfortable, and have character, and some have good water views. The restaurant seats 50; set lunch £9, set dinner £9.50.
Walking; yachting; golf and riding nearby

CAMBRIDGE

Arundel House Hotel, 53 Chesterton Road, Cambridge
CB4 3AN   (Tel. 0223 67701)
£28.50–£52 single, £40.50–£72 double b&b
Five minutes from the city centre, the hotel overlooks the River Cam and Jesus Green; in the summer, you can pick up a punt from just outside the front door. The building consists of a row of large, 19th-century terraced houses, and is decorated in soft colours. The bedrooms at the front have a view of the

river and the green. The overall atmosphere is pleasant, and the staff are welcoming. The restaurant, which has recently been refurbished, has a reputation for serving up some of the best food in the area, and offers children's and vegetarian menus, and a wide range of bar meals. As well as regularly winning prizes for the exemplary cleanliness of the kitchen, the hotel has also received the Heartbeat Award for its healthy food options. Prices are also extremely reasonable, with the three-course lunch costing £7.95. Unfortunately, none of the tables has a view of the river. The large hotel car park is a bonus, as parking in Cambridge can be difficult. There are 14 ground-floor rooms. The hotel can cater for disabled visitors, but there are no special facilities.

Walking; punting; fishing nearby (hotel has details); tennis court, outdoor swimming pool and gymnasium nearby

CAMBRIDGE

The Garden House Hotel, Granta Place, Cambridge
(Tel. 0223 63421)
Call for directions
Double b&b, from £115; single, £82

A modern hotel, a bit lacking in character but with a magnificent river frontage and many rooms (all twins or doubles) with balconies and river view. Although something of a Piccadilly Circus in terms of tourist traffic, this hotel is jollier than many of similar size and benefits from a busy cosmopolitan atmosphere and friendly staff. An award-winning three acres of grounds lead down to the river Cam and make for an excellent base for watery sightseeing. There are beautiful walks from back of hotel to Grantchester, via the tow-path. The hotel will arrange punting and prepare picnic hampers (it is famous for its 'weddings by punt'). The restaurant seats 130 with large windows overlooking gardens and river. The riverside lounge is a good hideaway to escape the serious overcrowding in many of city's lunch spots, serving light meals from 10am–10.30pm. An indulgent riverside cream tea watching the swans is a must, with gargantuan scones and clotted cream. Rooms are tastefully furnished, spacious and refreshingly equipped with a tea and coffee tray (which so often, these days, appear to be confined to b&bs). Rooms on ground floor are accessible for the disabled with a ramp to the lounge area, but there are no other specific facilities.

City centre and university colleges and grounds within easy walking distance; punting

CAMBRIDGE

The Boathouse, Chesterton Road, Cambridge CB4 3AX (Tel. 0223 460905)
Open 11am–11pm Mon–Sat; noon–3pm, 7pm–10.30pm Sun
With commanding views over the River Cam and Jesus Green, the pub gets very busy on fine summer days. A deck and waterside lawn provide ample outside seating for a drink or a bite in the sunshine. The bar has bookshelves, and rowing paraphernalia on the walls, and large windows giving good views over the garden and the river. The clientele is predominantly young. There is live jazz on Sunday evenings. A side counter serves good bar meals (from baked potatoes to steaks, including six daily specials); beers on offer include Greene King Abbot and Flowers IPA. There is a reasonably sized car park (always handy in Cambridge).

Walking; punting; boating; fishing nearby

CAMBRIDGE

The Anchor, Silver Street, Cambridge   (Tel. 0223 353554)
Open all year, every day; summer 10am–11pm
Café bar open every afternoon (no alcohol Sunday pm)
Very much the 'in' place to meet in this famous university city, this pub sits right on the edge of the Cam in what is known as the Mill Pond. The water laps over its narrow pavement,

which in summertime is crammed with students, tourists and tough-skinned regulars who don't mind a bit of rumbustious jostling. Chauffered or self-hire punts are available at the side of the pub which adds to the fun and jolly atmosphere. The inside sprawls over two floors, both with good river views. One entrance is via a rather quaint barless foyer with old leather armchairs (a rare treat if you are waiting for a friend and don't fancy standing idly at the bar). The café bar downstairs is an excellent idea – a pub setting with juke box and high-spirited students, where you can have pot of tea and deliciously long chocolate éclairs while watching the traditional Mill Pond river frolics, with as many overboard as punting. There is traditional pub food – lasagne, casseroles, ploughmans etc. – on offer, plus a daily vegetarian choice. Live jazz every Tuesday.
Punting

CAMBRIDGE
IOI ⌂ ♿ ⌧ ▭

Sweeney Todds, The Mill, Newnham Road, Cambridge
(Tel. 0223 67507)
In Newnham, off the ring road
Open noon–11pm, every day
An old water mill bordering the river Cam has been converted into this pizza restaurant. A big hit for family treats and sturdy lunches but a little too boisterous for an evening out unless you are in a celebratory mood (the restaurant can seat 150). There are excellent river views from two sides. The main dining area is set around the old waterwheel (fully operational) which juts up through the floor housed in a glass case. The largest tables have a central glass panel through which you can spy the river flowing underneath. The open brickwork interior and quarry-tiled floors can accommodate spilt ice-cream, and the atmosphere is noisy and friendly, and can easily cope with a five-year-old's birthday party. The food extends from the usual range of pizzas with tasty, complicated toppings, to

grills, hamburgers and generous salads (limited choice for vegetarians). The average cost per person, including drinks, is £9.50 (children £2.25). Private car park and good wheelchair access (no toilets for the disabled).
Punts for hire opposite the restaurant

CHAPPEL

The Swan, Wakes Colne, Chappel, Colchester, Essex
CO6 2DD   (Tel. 0787 222353)
Just off the A604, visible from road
Open 11am–3pm, 6pm–11pm Mon–Sat; noon–3pm, 7pm–10.30pm Sun
The Swan is conveniently located just off the main road, and set among rolling fields. There is plenty of seating outside, both in the courtyard, with its tubs of flowers and French street signs, and in the pretty garden, which has picnic tables going down to the River Colne. In contrast, the interior, with its oak timbers, low beams and huge open fireplace, gives one the impression of what the pub might have been like 500 years ago when it was originally built. The pub has a friendly and enjoyable atmosphere. The glass-sided restaurant serves a range of grills and fish dishes and so forth, and a three-course lunch costs around £16 per person. Bar snacks are also available. It is a free house, and serves Greene King ales, and Mauldon's bitter. Just below the garden is an extremely impressive Victorian viaduct.
Colne Valley Steam Railway Museum is 300 yards away; walking

CHICHESTER

Crown and Anchor, Dell Quay, Chichester, West Sussex
PO20 7EB   (Tel. 0243 781712)
Open 11am–2.30pm Mon–Thurs; 11am–3pm Fri and Sat;
noon–3pm Sun; and 7pm–11pm every evening

This former hostelry on Chichester harbour dates back to the reign of Henry VIII. The dark-beamed 'wet bar' has a big fireplace, a Ring-the-Bull game (a ring hangs down from the ceiling on a six-foot wire, which is swung from any direction to hook it on to the peg in the bull's nose on the wall), and a wood floor for wet yachtsmen and dogs. Ships' lanterns, old copper kettles and funnels hang on the walls. There is also a larger, carpeted dry bar, which is more couth but less attractive. The waterside garden has seating for 150 people. Beers include Ruddles, Webster's, Watney's, Holsten, Foster's, Carlsberg and a range of traditional ales, and bar snacks are available from noon to 2pm, and 7pm to 9.30pm, except on Sundays. The restaurant has a huge window overlooking Dell Quay and the sea, and an extensive range of fresh fish on the menu. Children are welcome in the restaurant, but not in the pub.

Four-mile walk from Chichester Yacht Basin to Fishbourne; boat launch at nearby yacht club; windsurfing at Chichester marina; beach (not sandy); fishing from quay; Roman palace; Chichester festival (late August)

CHURT

3/53

The Frensham Pond Hotel, Churt, Farnham, Surrey
GU10 2QB   (Tel. 025125 5161)
£76 single, £88 double b&b

The Frensham Pond Hotel, as its name implies, overlooks the beautiful man-made expanse of water known as Frensham Pond. This was built by local monks in 1770, and enhances this already beautiful area. During the Second World War it had to be drained because it presented too much of a landmark to passing German bombers. Now, however, peace and tranquillity are the hallmarks of this hotel. The bedrooms are modern, spacious and well appointed. The well-regarded restaurant has 12 tables with good water views, and the quality of the food is high (three-course meal, £15.75). The staff are young, friendly and helpful. The hotel has very good leisure facilities, including a plunge pool, spa bath, gymnasium, two squash courts, two saunas and solarium. There are ground-floor suites including one specially adapted room, and special lavatories for the disabled.

Walking (much National Trust land nearby); golf; tennis; riding; bird watching; clay pigeon shooting

CLEY-NEXT-THE-SEA

Cley Windmill Guesthouse, Cley-next-the-Sea, Holt, Norfolk NR25 7NN   (Tel. 0263 740209)
Once in Cley, follow the signs for the windmill
£22.50–£28 pp b&b

Charming and unusual, the Guesthouse, converted out of an 18th-century windmill, occupies an imposing position on the edge of the salt marshes. The sea is a little way off, but the views are nonetheless spectacular and panoramic. A fine balcony runs the whole way round the mill from one of the rooms, and gives superb views over the marshes and Blakeney harbour. At the top there are observation and information rooms, complete with telescope. The bedrooms are named after the role they used to serve when the mill was operational: the Stone Room, the Wheat Chamber and so forth. The delicious set dinner (for residents only) costs £14.50, and local fish is a speciality; bring your own wine. There are also two self-catering units available, created out of old mill warehouse buildings which cost from £70 for two per week (low season) to £240 for four to six people (high season). An idyllic venue for getting away from it all, but busy in summertime.

Walking; sailing; windsurfing; fishing; golf; pebble beach nearby

COLTISHALL

🏨 2/10 🏡₃ 🦯 🎣 ▭

Norfolk Mead Hotel, Church Street, Coltishall, Norfolk
NR12 7DN   (Tel. 0603 737531)
Six miles north of Norwich on the B1150
Closed at Christmas
£49–£59 single, £65–£85 double b&b

Norfolk has always seemed rather starved of good restaurants
and country hotels, but here is one of the exceptions. The
gravel drive leads up to the wisteria-covered hotel which
stands alone in 12 acres of beautiful grounds, well removed
from the main road. The accommodation and dining facilities
are elegant and tastefully decorated in coordinating pastel
colours and floral designs. The dining room is open for dinner
only (7pm to 9pm, set menu £21.50), except for lunch on
Sundays (noon to 2pm), and is open to non-residents. The
tables have good views over the lawns down to the River Bure.
The food is modern, enticing, and of an extremely high
standard and focuses strongly on local produce.
*Lake stocked with carp in the hotel grounds; swimming pool; 20
minutes from the coast; fishing for residents (no licence needed for lake,
rod licence required for river); interesting walks; antique shops in the
village; Norwich cathedral*

COOKHAM

🍺 🏡 🦯 ⬦ ▭

The Ferry Inn, Cookham, Berkshire SL6 9SN
(Tel. 0628 525 123)

Essentially a riverside pub, the Ferry has been developed over
the years, and now, under the banner of Harvester Inns, offers
quite sophisticated restaurant service, in addition to the usual
bar facilities. This is a particularly appealing stretch of river,
and the pub's great attraction, which lures the crowds on
summer weekends, is the outdoor terrace and lawn stretching
down to the edge of the Thames, close to a slipway for
launching small vessels. On the Berkshire side of the Thames,
the charming village of Cookham is probably best known for

its associations with the artist Sir Stanley Spencer. In a former chapel on the High Street, well worth visiting, the Stanley Spencer Gallery contains a number of his paintings and drawings (open Easter to October, 10.30am to 6pm; between November and Easter, open 11am to 5pm on weekends and public holidays only). Spencer's grave is in the churchyard of Holy Trinity, Cookham, and inside the handsome church hangs a copy of his painting, *The Last Supper*. Disabled visitors can gain access to the bar and patio, but not the restaurant, which is 'all stairs'.

Boat hire nearby; in summer, boat trips to Windsor and Maidenhead

CROMER

The Bathhouse, The Promenade, Cromer NR27 9HE
(Tel. 0263 514260)
Closed March 4–12
£24.50 per person, b&b (seaview rooms, £27 per person)
It is rare to find a hotel room that actually overhangs the beach but here you can sit in the large family room and imagine you are in a deckchair. Accommodation is spacious, comfortable and unfussy – so you won't feel guilty if you spill a little sand around the place. As the bars are busy with locals, there is a lively atmosphere even in winter (when many small hotels feel disturbingly quiet). Make sure you try out the Bathhouse's excellent Cromer crab salads and sandwiches. This stretch of coast is famed for its bird watching, and twitchers abound. The beaches at Holkham are magnificent for walking, with miles of clean sands and dunes, and there is a wonderful absence of seaside paraphernalia such as hot dog stalls and candyfloss. There are no specific facilities for disabled visitors, and the stepped entrance may make access difficult.

Bird watching; beaches

DEDHAM

🍽 ⚓ 🏃 🚫 ▭

Le Talbooth, Gun Hill, Dedham, Essex CO7 6HP
(Tel. 0206 323150)
Off the B1029 (call for specific directions)
Open noon–2.30pm, 7.30pm–9.30pm
This exclusive country restaurant is extremely well known for the quality of its food and the professionalism of its staff. Situated in the heart of John Constable country, it looks down over picturesque gardens to the River Stour – a view of great charm. The impressive, half-timbered Tudor building dates from 1520; inside, it is elegant and comfortable. There is seating for 75 people, and all of the tables have very good views of the river. The menu is firmly haute cuisine, and displays much culinary style and imagination. Gourmets on a budget should note the set lunch, which, at £19.50 for a three-course meal, represents good value for money. The wine list is also extremely good, and deserves investigation.
Fishing; tennis; country walks

DUNWICH

🍽 ⚓ 🍷 ◁ 🚭

The Flora Tearooms, Dunwich Beach, Suffolk
(Tel. 072873 433)
Open 10am–5pm every day from early March to late November
So well known for its fresh fish and chips it can be overrun with coachloads of hungry visitors unless you time your arrival properly. Abutting the beach, this restaurant grew from a tiny timber shack into a large and airy beamed restaurant which can seat 104 inside and 160 outside, and has cleverly kept itself unpretentiously devoted to serving a good fry up with all the trimmings. A meal here is a wonderful finale after the windy walk along the shingle to Walberswick (the next seaside village) and back, and is particularly tempting after a couple of pints of Adnams ale at the Ship Inn in the centre of Dunwich village. If it is fine, you can sit outside at long benches and

wooden tables. The fish is caught locally and the sole is particularly delicious; portions are always generous. What's more, you can really bump up your calorie-intake with one of their fresh cream cakes to follow. To escape the queues, avoid weekends and school holidays where possible, and take a very early or late lunch. It is well worth taking the time to visit the little village museum with a superb model of the major part of Dunwich which now, due to hundreds of years of erosion, lies under the sea. Good facilities for the disabled with adapted toilets and ramps.

Beach; Dunwich museum; walks

EASTBOURNE

🏚 79/114 ≈ 🏠 ♂ ◁ ▭

Cavendish Hotel, Grand Parade, Eastbourne, East Sussex BN21 4DH   (Tel. 0323 410222)
£70 single, £115 double, executive suite £220
A magnificent 19th-century hotel, even more splendid than its brochure's pictures suggest. The large and highly luxurious first-floor rooms, with their high ceilings and friezes, are as nothing compared to the suites, which are hugely vast and comfortable. A large reception hall leads into the Marine restaurant, the Coronet bar and sun lounge (which is slightly noisy, as traffic passes right in front). The mezzanine floor, overlooking the hall, has tables set for writing. The restaurant seats 350; 10 alcove window tables and many others have water views. The set dinner costs £17 for four courses; traditional Sunday lunch costs £10.50. Traditional afternoon teas are served in the sun lounge. There are lifts to all floors and ramps from the car park to the hotel, which may help disabled visitors, though there are no specially adapted rooms.

Beach; sea fishing can be arranged; speedboats from pier and waterskiing; sailing club; windsurfing nearby; golf; tennis holidays can be arranged; walks along South Downs; Beachy Head at the end of the seafront

EASTBOURNE

🏨 47/93 ⌂ ◁ ▭

Langham Hotel, Royal Parade, Eastbourne, East Sussex
BN22 7AH   (Tel. 0323 31451)
£29–£36 pp dinner and b&b

A two-star hotel in an ideal location, closer to the sea than most
of its big brothers in Eastbourne, with a sea-facing terrace
running the length of it that seats about 150. The Langham has
been a family hotel since 1913; the rooms are bright and
cheerful, and reasonably sized. The restaurant offers a good
choice of food at low prices – a three-course lunch costs £6.25,
the table d'hôte dinner costs about £9.50. There are eight tables
by the window, and a fair number of the 160 places have a sea
view. In the upstairs bar, there is live music one night a week,
and in the wine-cellar bar there are dances four nights a week
through the summer season (May to September).

Hotel has membership of the Ball Park where guests can use the
spa bath, sauna, snooker and gym for free, and pay court fees for other
activities; nearby Treasure Island children's activity centre; Blue Flag
beach, sandy at low tide; sailing club nearby (with tuition); fishing
(beach and deep-sea); windsurfing; jetskiing; tennis; bowling
packages; three golf courses in Eastbourne; Beachy Head and South
Downs Way walks

EASTBOURNE

🏨 58/108 ⌂ ♨ ◁ ▭

Queen's Hotel, Marine Parade, Eastbourne, East Sussex
BN21 3DY   (Tel. 0323 22822)
£80 single, £65 pp double

In a good position just east of the pier, the hotel was built in
1880 and still retains its original size and shape. The period
decor is tasteful, and the sea view from the sea-facing rooms
and the bar terrace is splendid. Rooms at the front on the first
and second floors have balconies which get the sun most of the
day. The dining room has no sea view, but is of an impressive
size (gentlemen are advised that they should wear a jacket and
tie for dinner); dinner dances are held here on Saturday nights

in the summer and on 'festive occasions'. There is a choice of basic hot dishes or cold buffet at lunch and dinner (four-course dinner £17). Vegetarians can choose from a separate menu that offers daily choices (though choices have to be made in the morning). No facilities for the disabled, but there are two lifts, large rooms and helpful staff.

Watersports; fishing; golf; riding (10 minutes' drive); the hotel has membership of the Ball Park (see Langham Hotel above for details)

EDENBRIDGE

IOI 🎒 🏃 🚫 ▭

Honour's Mill, 87 High Street, Edenbridge, Kent TN8 5AU (Tel. 0732 866757)

Easy to find, 15 minutes off the M25

Open 12.15pm–2pm, 7.15pm–10pm; closed lunchtime on Sat, evening on Sun, all day Mon

This mill, beside the River Eden, dates from 1750, and was grinding corn until it was flooded in 1968. The mill wheel is still in the centre of the building, in the area which is now the bar. Upstairs, the restaurant seats 38 people in a room with an attractive high ceiling and low beams, and looks east across the mill pond. The cooking is described as regional and modern French. The set lunch costs £19.95; the set dinner £31.75, and Sunday lunch is £22.50, all including service, coffee and petits fours. The menu changes twice a year but there are daily specials for each course. The wine list that accompanies the meal is equally impressive.

Walks around Hever Castle; watersports and fishing nearby; sailing and fishing (15 minutes' drive)

ETON

🍴 ⌂ ⚘ ⌀ ▭

The House on the Bridge Restaurant, 71 High Street, Eton,
Berkshire SL4 6AA　(Tel. 0753 866836)
At end of Eton High Street, on Windsor bridge
Open noon–2.30pm, 6pm–11pm Mon–Sat; noon–3pm,
6pm–10.30pm Sun
Closed 25–27 December
Situated on Windsor bridge, near Eton College's old boat
houses, the restaurant looks over the River Thames at the
towering ramparts of Windsor Castle. There is a good, multi-
level lounge for pre-meal drinks, and the restaurant, spread
over three levels, is tastefully decorated and seats 80 people,
with extensive river views from all tables. The riverside
gardens and verandas enhance the setting. Cuisine is international; a three-course table d'hôte meal costs £15.75, Mon–
Sat. There are no facilities for disabled visitors, who would be
better off at the Montmorency (Tel. 0753 854479), sister
restaurant to the House on the Bridge, which is on the opposite
side of the river and has wheelchair access. This is a modern
restaurant, specializing in fish, and featuring a vast, Dali-esque
mural. A two-course lunch here costs £10.50 Mon–Sat, and
£12.50 on Sundays.
*Walking; Windsor Castle and its parks; boat trips; rowing; fishing
nearby*

FOLKESTONE

🏨 ²⁰/₅₇ ⌂ ⚘ ✍ ▭

Burlington Hotel, Earl's Avenue, Folkestone, Kent
CT20 2HR　(Tel. 0303 55301)
£36 single, £33 pp double b&b
Built in the 1890s for the Earl of Radnor, this impressive
Victorian hotel has a comfortable and relaxed atmosphere, and
splendid views of Folkestone and the Channel from many
rooms, though a building in front of it obscures some of the
views. The rooms are light and airy, decorated with patterned
carpets and fitted cupboards, some with terraces looking out to

the Channel. The Bay Tree restaurant serves lunch (£8.50) and dinner (£14), and offers a typical hotel menu with an extensive list of 57 wines, and advice on which would go well with each type of dish. An attractive place to stay as a base to discover the coast and the cathedral city of Canterbury.

Walking; fishing; beach (two minutes away); watersports at Hythe Lake; boat hire in Folkestone; golf at four championship courses; sports centre nearby

FORDWICH

4/11

The George and Dragon Hotel, King Street, Fordwich,
Canterbury, Kent   (Tel. 0227 710661)
Off the A28, the Canterbury to Margate road
£33 single, £44 double b&b

First licensed to sell ales in 1562, the George and Dragon hotel was once little more than a riverside ale-house. It has, of course, undergone many changes and modernizations, yet it successfully retains an authentic and historic atmosphere. Nestling on the banks of the River Stour, the hotel offers adequate and well-equipped bedrooms and warm, traditional public areas. The Beefeater Steak House restaurant opens to non-residents and is decorated in cheerful, rustic style. Menus cover steak, fish, chicken, gammon and lamb dishes accompanied by crisp salads or vegetables with three-course meals in the region of £10 to £15 (open 6pm–10.30pm Mon–Thurs; 6pm–11pm Fri and Sat; noon–10.30pm Sun). In the bar area, the hotel also serves a good selection of bar food from £1.50 to £4 (6pm–10.30pm Mon–Sat; 11am–2.30pm, 7pm–10.30pm Sun) plus a range of beers, wines, spirits and liqueur coffees to suit every taste. Additional facilities include private parking for a maximum of 70 vehicles and riverview gardens with seating for over 40 guests during the summer.

Walking; fishing

GODALMING

inn 6/20 🏠 ⅃ ✎ ▭

The Inn on the Lake, Ockford Road, Godalming GU7 1RH
(Tel. 0483 415575)
On the A3100, just south of Godalming town
£80–£90 per room b&b

A Tudor inn, showing few signs of age save for the occasional
crooked floorboard, set in two acres of gardens overlooking
the lake. The bedrooms are comfortable and individually
furnished (all have double beds); one has a four-poster, and six
have private spa baths. There is a pleasant bar with Flowers,
Boddingtons, the occasional guest beer and bar meals on offer;
this opens on to a comfortable lounge. The restaurant seats 80
people; about eight of the tables have a view of the lake, and
within the restaurant there is a fish pond with exotic Japanese
koi carp. The set lunches and dinners cost £10.50 Sun–Fri, and
there is also an à la carte menu.
Walking; West Surrey golf course nearby; Winkworth Arboretum

GOLDEN GREEN

🏨 2/3 🏠 ⅃ ⌀ ▭

Goldhill Mill, Golden Green, Tonbridge, Kent TN11 0BA
(Tel. 0732 851626)
Call for directions
Open January to mid-July, and September to December
From £40 single; £50 double

Tucked away at the end of a private drive, this peaceful retreat,
beside the river and with a pair of resident swans, is set in its
own 20 acres of land. The Mill was mentioned in the
Domesday Book, and the working mill wheel and a large part
of the original mill machinery is on display in the kitchen/
breakfast room, though as the owners point out, the tone of the
house is luxurious rather than rustic. The bedrooms, done out
in pretty colours and with lavish soft furnishings, might
belong to a top-class hotel. One has a four-poster; two have
double whirlpool baths, and little extras such as fresh fruit,
flowers and mints are provided. Guests are asked not to smoke.

As well as the large, attractive garden, there is a floodlit tennis court for the amusement of guests. Next to the Mill is Ciderpress Cottage (open all year), which provides self-catering accommodation for up to six people.

GREAT SHEFFORD

The Swan, Great Shefford, nr Newbury, Berkshire RG16 7DS (Tel. 048839 271)
Two miles from the M4, on the A338 towards Wantage
Open 11am–3pm, 6pm–11pm Mon–Sat; noon–3pm, 7pm–10.30pm Sun
A large, roadside Courage pub with the river running alongside the lounge bar and patio area. One bar has a view of the river, if you get there early enough to get in. It's a popular and noisy pub, decorated with racing memorabilia and photographs, and tends to be full of racing folk from the Lambourn area all gossiping furiously – keep your ears open for tips. The large patio terrace/barbecue area overlooks the water, with a service bar. Together with the large garden room, the restaurant (open until midnight) seats about 70 people, and there is space for plenty more outside. The bar serves a good many spirits but only about three bitters and two real ales; a wide range of bar food is also available. Children are welcome in the eating areas only. Dogs are welcome on the patio. The doors are wide enough to admit wheelchairs, but there are no specific disabled facilities.

GREAT YARMOUTH

Carlton Hotel, Marine Parade, Great Yarmouth, Norfolk NR30 3JE   (Tel. 0493 855234)
On the sea front
£51 single, £71.50 double, £140 executive suite
To compensate for the amusement arcades and the garish seafront, the Carlton Hotel has gone up-market and has recently been gutted and re-vamped. Now, it offers comfort

and good facilities in very good taste. The decor is elegant and tasteful, and in keeping with the style of the Victorian building. It has always been the best hotel in Great Yarmouth, but this recent refurbishment certainly confirms its position at the top of ladder. Simpson's restaurant, within the hotel, is open to non-residents and seats 150 people, with six window tables. The food is traditional English, and the set dinner costs £16.25. Penny's bar and grill is open all day, serving coffees and snacks.

Walking; indoor/outdoor watersports across the road; sea and fresh water fishing can be arranged; beach nearby; winter season entertainment

HARTFIELD

🏨 ³/⁴ 🏠₇ 🛇 🐾 💳

Bolebroke Watermill, Edenbridge Road, Hartfield, nr East Grinstead, East Sussex TN7 4JP   (Tel. 0892 770425)
One mile north of Hartfield on the B2026
Open March–November
From £45 for two, b&b
The watermill merited a mention in the Domesday Book, and all possible original features have been retained and restored, including the steep, narrow stairs, the corn-bin bathrooms, the mill stones and the drive wheels in the sitting room (Note: this makes it unsuitable for small children and elderly or disabled people). There are two new rooms in the Millers Barn: the Honeymooners' Hayloft complete with a view of the pond, and a twin-bedded room downstairs. The atmosphere is delightfully rustic, and the surroundings are idyllic: there is a willow-fringed mill pond with Muscovy ducks, and six and a half acres of grounds in which guests can wander through streams, pasture and woodland. The residents-only dining room (reached by descending through a hatch) seats 12, with no water views. Mrs Cooper offers a 'Taste of Sussex' supper tray – a light, four-course supper of local produce served on a wicker tray (£10 per person), by arrangement. No smoking anywhere.

Walks in Ashdown Forest, including the three-hour Winnie-the-Pooh Trail; Wellie-walk from the Watermill (follow the wellies in the trees); fishing locally (five-minute drive); riding can be arranged

HARWICH

IOI 🏠 ♨ ⚡ 🞖

Pier at Harwich, The Quay, Harwich, Essex CO12 3HH
(Tel. 0255 241212)
Open noon–2pm, 6pm–9.30pm Sun–Fri; 6pm–10pm Sat
A well-known restaurant which caters for both simple and sophisticated tastes: dishes range from elaborate seafood to fish and chips. There is seating for 100 people; half the tables look out at the water. There is some accommodation: the six rooms (single from £45, double from £62.50 b&b) are attractively decorated with quality soft furnishings and offer a very good view over the quay, the sea and the Suffolk coast across the estuary.
Boat trips nearby

HAXTED

IOI 🏠 ♨ ⚡ 🞖

Haxted Mill Restaurant, Haxted Road, Haxted,
nr Edenbridge, Kent TN8 6PU   (Tel. 0732 862914)
Signposted from the B2029
Open noon–2pm, 7pm–11pm Tues–Sat; noon–2pm Sun.
Closed Sat lunchtimes, and from Christmas to the end of January
A relaxing and unpretentious restaurant, with a beamed ceiling, whitewashed walls and fresh flowers, recently converted from the mill barn. The creative menu focuses on seafood, and there is a good view of the mill stream from five first-floor window tables. The outdoor terrace has tables with cloths, flowers and candles, and makes a wonderfully romantic spot on a warm summer evening. There is water on three sides of the terrace; the stream rushing through the sluice makes a lovely sound. The mill itself, which is nothing to do with the

restaurant, is 400 years old, has an extensive museum and exhibition of old tools and opens at weekends (from noon to 5pm) and Wednesdays from Easter to 31 May, then daily (from noon to 5pm) from June to September. A five-course dinner and drinks costs about £40 to £45 per person; bistro lunch and drinks is about £10. No specific facilities for the disabled, though half the restaurant and the terrace and lavatories are all on the same level.

Walking; club fishing; Lingfield race course (one and a half miles away)

HEACHAM

IOI 🏠 ♿ ◇ 💳

Miller's Cottage Tea Room, Caley Mill, Heacham, Norfolk PE31 7JE   (Tel. 0485 70384)
On the A149
Open 10am–5pm

A sweet-smelling position for a morning coffee, light lunch or cream tea as Miller's Cottage is attached to the only working lavender farm in England. The building is an old 19th-century corn mill which still retains its rustic charm. Customers can sit on the patio or enjoy the sight of the river from tables in the well-kept garden. As well as the noted pastries, home-made scones and gateaux, home-made soups and sandwiches are on offer. The adjoining gift shop has a country theme, selling lavender products (including lavender marmalade and lavender honey) and plants, local crafts and other attractive presents. Children are only allowed into the gift shop. Concrete ramp and disabled lavatories are on site.

Walking; gift shop; guided tours of the lavender farm from late May to late September

HENLEY-ON-THAMES

Red Lion Hotel, Hart Street, Henley-on-Thames, Oxon
(Tel. 0491 572161)
Next to Henley bridge
£43–£70 single, £83–£95 double; breakfast £5.50–£7.50

The Red Lion has been a stopping point for travellers on the old London road since the 16th century. Historians believe that it was built in 1531 to accommodate the craftsmen and their apprentices who constructed the parish church of St Mary the Virgin. It is right next to the bridge over the Thames in the middle of the town. Most of the bedrooms are 17th century, and some afford views of the finish of the Henley Royal Regatta. One bedroom is 16th century, furnished in keeping with the period, and boasts a fine four-poster bed. The first guest of note whose visit was recorded was Charles I, who stayed in the hotel in 1632; the original coat of arms has been preserved in one of the rooms. The Regency-style restaurant has pretty striped high-backed chairs and a view of the water. The cuisine is of the traditional English style, and a three-course à la carte meal costs about £22.50.

Boating; rowing; fishing; walking; Henley Royal Regatta (first week of July)

HERNE BAY

Bun Penny, 46 Central Parade, Sea Front, Herne Bay, Kent
(Tel. 0227 374252)
Open 11am–11pm Mon–Sat; noon–3pm, 7pm–10.30pm Sun

The pub is named after the coin issued in the early years of Queen Victoria's reign which had the Queen's head wearing a bun rather than straight hair as figured on later mints. Recently renovated, this traditional pub boasts high ceilings, an airy atmosphere, and a selection of real ales including Shepherd Neame, Spitfinger and Master Brew. Two of the three bars overlook the water, as does the large garden, which is just across the road from the sea. A wide selection of bar meals –

sandwiches, sausage, egg and chips and steaks, all very good value – are available from noon to 2pm, and 8pm to 10pm. Wheelchair ramps are available, and there are helpful staff.
Beach walks; watersports (no equipment supplied)

HERTFORD

The Old Barge, 2 The Folly, Hertford, Hertfordshire
SG14 1QD   (Tel. 0992 581871)
Call for directions
Open 11am–4.30pm, 5.30pm–11pm Mon–Sat; noon–3pm, 7pm–10.30pm Sun
Situated on the edge of the canal, which is known as the River Lee, The Old Barge is a comfortably renovated traditional pub. It is close to the town centre and is popular with the locals. The interior is uncomplicated and typical of this kind of establishment with old beams and antiquities, though it has a slightly sombre air about it. The beers that are on offer include well kept Adnams, Burton ale, Tetley's and Abbot's. There is also a wide range of lagers, wines and cask-conditioned ciders. The restaurant has three tables overlooking the canal and serves lunch (from noon to 2pm), and dinner (from 6pm to 9.30 pm, no food on Sunday evenings) with an extensive menu, daily specials and a wide selection for vegetarians. A main course in the evening would cost approximately £6.25. Other appealing factors include the pub's fishing rights (licence obtained in the town), and mooring facilities. No disabled facilities, though the pub is all on one level.
Fishing; museums nearby; boating; county market in Hertford on Saturdays

HEYBRIDGE BASIN

Old Ship, Lock Hill, Heybridge Basin, Malden, Essex
CN9 7RX   (Tel. 0621 854150)
Follow signs from Heybridge to Heybridge Basin, then to the end of the track

Open 11am–11pm Mon–Sat in summer (11am–3pm, 6pm–11pm Mon–Sat in winter); noon–3pm, 7pm–10.30pm Sun
Built in 1798 as the lock-keeper's cottage, the Old Ship sits beside the lock gates where the Chelmer river and canal meet the Blackwater estuary. The basin is used to lock boats in that are travelling to and from the sea to stop them getting stuck in the mud when the tide goes out. A very popular pub with sailing enthusiasts, the Old Ship welcomes visitors with a choice of quality beers and bar snacks. Benskin's Best, Burton ale and Adnams are served by the new landlord. Food is available day and evening; warming, home-made soups and stews in the winter and light salads and cold meats in the summer. Children are not allowed in the pub but a new play area outside is being built.
Sailing (moorings in front of pub); walking

HOLYWELL

inn 🏊 🏠 ♿ 🐾 🛏

The Olde Ferry Boat Inn, Holywell, St Ives, Huntingdon, Cambridgeshire PE17 3TG   (Tel. 0480 63227)
Signposted off the main road through Needingworth
£39.99–£49.50 single, £49.50–£68 double b&b
Reputedly the oldest inn in Britain, dating back to AD 560, and featured in the *Guinness Book of Records*. The Inn is said to be haunted by a ghost called Juliet, though no one has seen her recently. The setting is rural and peaceful, on the banks of the River Ouse, with views a long way downriver. Under new management, the accommodation has recently been attractively and comfortably refurbished. The main pub areas have a cosy atmosphere, with three open fires, timber and panelled walls and welcoming sitting areas. The restaurant seats 50 and offers a range of classy bar snacks and daily specials. Meals are served every day, and throughout the year. These involve home-made specialities such as the 'Norfolk Sizzler' (a curried turkey pancake), Stilton pâté and smoked chicken in lemon mayonnaise. The clientele are a mixture of locals, business people and tourists. There are no facilities for the disabled,

though the main reception rooms have wide doors and are on one level.

Walking; fishing (with permission); St Ives market Mon and Fri; Cambridge (20 minutes away)

HORLEY

Langshott Manor, Langshott, Horley, Surrey RH6 9LN
(Tel. 0293 786680)
Closed Christmas Day
£98 double room
Here's a smart, family-run hotel, just eight minutes from Gatwick, which will clasp your BMW to their bosoms while you're away for no extra cost. The trick and, incidentally, treat, is that you must first spend a night at Langshott Manor, circa 1580, standing in three acres and with its own picturesque lake (or large pond, depending on which way you look at it) complete with a cherished pair of breeding swans, lots of ducks and a little bridge. The hotel is full of polished wood, antique furniture, lamps, pictures, flowers and a fat cat called Michael asleep outside a bedroom door. On the ancient staircase, candles burn in metal holders attached to newel posts. On a practical note, the food is excellent – owner Patricia Noble is an Elizabeth David aficionado – and everything is freshly cooked on a formidable old Esse stove: 'No microwaves for me', she says. A three-course dinner costs £22.50 per person.
Tennis and swimming nearby; croquet lawn; riding, clay pigeon shooting and golf nearby

HORLEY

Ye Olde Six Bells, Church Road, Horley, Surrey RH6 8AD
(Tel. 0293 782209)
Three miles from the M23, Junction 9
Open 11am–11pm, Mon–Sat; noon–3pm, 7pm–10.30pm Sun
Ye Olde Six Bells has been an inn since the 13th century, but its

history goes further back than that, to AD 827. A 1000-year-old beam still holds the building together. The garden runs down to the banks of the River Mole, and the pub enjoys good views of the water from the conservatory and the bench tables outside. The restaurant, on an upper level under the heavily beamed roof, is self service, offering home-cooked food at £4.60–£8.95 for a main course. Booking is advisable for the evening. The pub decoration is traditional with an open fire and tiled floor. Bass, Worthington's and Charrington IPA are on hand pump; fruit machine, darts and dominoes are to be found to entertain the customers who tend to be young. Children are allowed in the conservatory area but not in the bar.
Fishing; walking

HORNING

Petersfield House, Lower Street, Horning, Norfolk NR12 8PF
(Tel. 0692 630741)
Easy to locate alongside the River Bure
£58 single, £72 double b&b
Petersfield House is a 1920s building in two acres of landscaped gardens, in the village of Horning, on the banks of the River Bure. The accommodation is comfortable, with period decoration in peaceful colours. The restaurant does not overlook the water but has pretty views of the garden. The set dinner costs from £14.50 with a choice of six starters and main courses and three sweets that change daily. The cuisine is English and an à la carte menu is also available. The hotel is a popular retreat for business people, older guests and families in the summer. Those arriving by boat can take advantage of the hotel's private moorings. The landscaped gardens and picturesque river setting mean that you would never be short of a place to stroll. The main hotel areas are all on one floor, and there are three rooms on the ground floor which can be used by disabled guests although they are not especially equipped.
Walking; sailing; fishing; day launch hire (about £7 per hour/£40 a day, by prior arrangement)

HOVE

Sackville Hotel, 189 Kingsway, Hove, East Sussex BN3 4GU
(Tel. 0273 736292)
On the sea front
£60 single, £70–£90 double b&b
Built as four private houses in 1904 and turned into an hotel in
1930, the Sackville still retains many of its original features. Set
back from the seafront, the views are of the bowling greens and
the beaches. The bedrooms are individually designed with
both antique and modern furnishings, and some of the
balconies share the same sweeping sea views as the reception
areas. The Camelot suite features a four-poster bed and several
other rooms have seating areas. Oak panelling lines the walls of
the lounge and bar. The dining room seats 80, and 11 tables
enjoy a view of the sea. The menu is English with the accent on
local fresh produce, including seafood. The set price for the
table d'hôte is from £9.50 for two courses for both lunch and
dinner. Light meals and snacks are served in the sun lounge
which faces south and captures the best of the sun all year
round. The hotel's private parking is a useful added bonus in
this busy seaside resort. A babysitting facility allows parents
time off to enjoy their holiday.
*Watersports; fishing; walking; golf; cricket; tennis; bowling green;
swimming pool and health centre nearby; pebble beach*

HUNGERFORD

Marshgate Cottage, Marsh Lane, Hungerford, Berkshire
RG17 0QX   (Tel. 0488 682 307)
From High Street, down Church Street for half a mile, turn
right into Marsh Lane
Closed Christmas and New Year
£25–£35 single, £35–£50 double b&b
Set on the marshes of the Kennet and Avon canal and a regular
host to ornate barges, pleasure boats, swans and ducks,
Marshgate Cottage offers friendly family accommodation.

The buildings have been developed to form a south-facing courtyard around a 350-year-old thatched cottage. (This original building is older than the canal, and was used as a pest house in the 1640 plague.) Accommodation is tasteful and modern. Goats and ducks wander about, but you can't bring your own pets. The main road is far enough away not to be too noisy, ditto the railway behind. The family room has the best access to the garden. There is a dining room (serving snacks in the evening), which seats 22 residents, and most tables have a view of the canal. Hungerford is a paradise for anyone keen on antiques, with 20 shops and a market for browsing. Six ground-floor rooms are accessible to wheelchairs, though they have no special disabled facilities, and there is one step up into the reception area.

Many walks; cycling routes (bicycles can be hired in advance, £8–£10); canal trips (including horse-drawn); canal and trout fishing (permits can be arranged from local clubs); site of Special Scientific Interest next door, with rare plants and birds just outside windows; Newbury racecourse (nine miles away); small, beautiful and professional Watermill Theatre; Avebury stone circle and Silbury Hill (12 miles away)

HUNGERFORD

The Bear Hotel, Charnham Street, Hungerford, Berkshire
RG17 0GL   (Tel. 0488 682 512)
On the main A4 in Hungerford
Restaurant opens 7.30pm–9.30pm Sun–Thurs; 7.30pm–10pm Fri–Sat
£69.50–£77 single, £92–£120 double b&b
Established as long ago as 1297 and carefully restored over recent years, the Bear Hotel epitomizes all that is expected of a traditional English inn, while offering 20th-century modern conveniences. Timber beams and antique furnishings enhance both the public areas and the well-appointed bedrooms. Bedroom suites, four-poster and half-tester rooms are available as are courtyard rooms complete with a view of the River

Dunn. The richly decorated restaurant is highly regarded for its regional French wines. The weekly house menu offers set lunch for £13.95, and a set dinner for £19.95. If you want a more casual meal, try the Kennet room or the cocktail bar (bistro-style food and light snacks). The main bar is elegant and spacious, with large French windows that open on to the courtyard with its charming pergola. The hotel and restaurant are accessible for the disabled.

Walks on the Kennet and Avon canal; fishing on the canal and the River Dunn; golf; clay pigeon shooting

HUNTINGDON

🏨 6/26 ⛺ ☂ ◇ 💳

Old Bridge Hotel, Huntingdon, Cambridgeshire PE18 6TQ
(Tel. 0480 52681)
On the main Huntingdon inner ring road, off the A604
£71–£88 single, £96–£110 double b&b
The Old Bridge was built in the 18th century as a private bank, with lawns running down to the River Ouse. Comfortable rooms offer pleasant views over the river. Each is individually decorated with special attention paid to fabrics and pretty touches such as handmade bedspreads. The reception areas have recently been refurbished: one striking new feature is the mural in the terrace lounge. The à la carte restaurant seats 40, costs £19–£25 for three courses and regular favourites such as a large roast sirloin of beef and a fresh fish dish. For more seclusion but at no extra price, the Cromwell room seats 30 for private parties. The terrace lounge is a less formal setting for meals (stir fries and vegetarian dishes are a speciality here). Friendly and professional staff will help to arrange any sporting activity for you. The proximity of the main road makes access very easy, though it does take the edge off the otherwise peaceful setting. The hotel can cater for disabled guests, though there are no special facilities.

Walking; canoeing at local club; boat hire; fishing nearby; clay pigeon shooting and riding can be arranged

HUNTINGDON

IOI ⁴∕⁴ ♿ ♨ ⊘ ▭

The Olde Mill, Bromholme Lane, Brampton, Huntingdon, Cambs. PE18 8NE (Tel. 0480 459758)

Off the A604 between Huntingdon and Brampton

Bar food 11am–2.30pm and 5.30pm–11pm Mon–Fri, 11am–11pm Sat, noon–3pm and 7–10.30pm Sun; restaurant noon–2.30pm and 6–10.30pm Mon–Sat, 12–10.30pm Sun

Accommodation open all year

£25 per room b&b

It would be hard to find a better location than that of this 900-year-old former mill, mentioned in the Domesday Book. It's on an island on a wide stretch of the River Ouse, where anglers and boaters enjoy the river and its inlets. The mill wheel still turns and forms an almost mesmerizing attraction in one of the bars, while upstairs is an area for bar food, up more stairs a small restaurant area, and above that a larger dining area with wonderful views of the river. Owned by the Beefeater chain, the food leans towards the safety of steaks and scampi, but with a few more exciting offerings such as pork satay, vegetable stroganoff or salmon in a white wine and basil sauce. Four remarkably cheap en-suite rooms are also available, though access for the disabled is difficult. The only other drawback is the Mill's immense popularity, but you couldn't have such a lovely setting and not expect to share it with others.

Riverside walks, boating, fishing

IPSWICH

⊟ ♿ ♨ ⊘ ▭

Butt and Oyster Pub, Pin Mill, Ipswich, Suffolk IP9 1JW (Tel. 0473 780764)

Off the B1456, follow signs to Pin Mill; pub is at the bottom of the lane

Open 11am–11pm Mon–Sat in summer (11am–3pm, 7pm–11pm in winter); noon–3pm, 7pm–10.30pm Sun

An unspoilt traditional pub with good facilities and friendly service. The pub has a long history and is mentioned in travel writings of 1565. The views over the estuary are magnificent and the water laps the lower walls of the pub at high tide. Home-cooked food with daily specials on the board costs about £1.20 for a starter and £4 for a main course. Ipswich-brewed cask-conditioned beers are a speciality and the bar serves Tolly mild, bitter and original. There is seating outside at the water's edge and plenty of boating activity to contemplate: the pub is home to many of the old Thames sailing barges, and trips on the estuary can be arranged. An annual barge race takes place at the beginning of July, and the finishing line is just outside the pub. The location is popular with children as the shallow rivulets allow for hours of messing around. Beware of oncoming traffic, the lane to Pin Mill is narrow and parking is difficult.

Walking; watersports; fishing nearby; muddy foreshore of a beach

IPSWICH

Mortimer's on the Quay, Wherry Quay, Ipswich, Suffolk
IP4 1AS   (Tel. 0473 230225)
Call for directions
Open noon–2pm Mon–Fri; 7pm–8.15pm Mon; 7pm–9pm Tues–Sat. Closed Sun, bank holidays and the day after; 24 December–5 January and last two weeks in August

Although it is not easy to find, it is well worth the effort. Mortimer's is housed in a glass-roofed, 18th-century ware-house. It is simply furnished, lacks the ostentation of many inferior restaurants and offers high-quality service and food. Fish, seafood and shellfish are fresh daily, including a mixture of the local catch and a delivery down the coast from Grimsby. The menu depends on the fishermen's best offerings. A three-course meal with coffee costs about £14–£18. One of the specialities is fillet of lemon sole Dieppoise, which is steamed and served with mussels, prawns and mushrooms in a white wine and cream sauce. There is seating for 60; the 10 waterside tables offer impressive views over the docks, marina and the estuary. Note also that parking on the waterfront is difficult at

lunchtimes because of local offices. There is disabled access but no special facilities.
Interesting walks along the dock; fishing (rod licence needed); marina and sailing school next door

KING'S LYNN

IOI ⌂ ♿ ⊘ ▭

Riverside Restaurant, King's Lynn Arts Centre, 27 King Street, King's Lynn, Norfolk PE30 1HA   (Tel. 0553 773134)
Open noon–2.30pm, 7pm–11pm Mon–Sat
Located within the Arts Centre, the Riverside Restaurant is attractively set out and colour coordinated, with a good view of the River Ouse from the window tables and the terrace. The river is very active, dropping and rising 27 feet every day. At high tide the water is busy with shipping from the nearby docks. The restaurant is housed in a 500-year-old warehouse looked after by the National Trust – the natural brick is an integral part of the decoration. The à la carte menu is based on home-cooked English food; roast rack of lamb with accompanying vegetables costs £11.50. The Arts Centre gives visitors to the restaurant plenty to do and see before and after their meal as it has a gallery, artists' workshops and a theatre. No facilities for the disabled (though plans for an access ramp are in progress).
Arts centre

KINTBURY

inn ⚊⁵ᐟ⁵ ⌂ ♿ ⊲ ▭

The Dundas Arms, Station Road, Kintbury, Berkshire RG15 0UT   (Tel. 0488 58 263/559)
Off the A4, the Hungerford to Newbury road
Bar open 11am–2.30pm, 6pm–11pm Mon–Sat; noon–2.30pm, 7pm–10.30pm Sun
Closed at Christmas
£55 single, £65 double b&b
A pretty whitewashed inn located in a quiet little village,

opposite the station, with civilized accommodation, amicable staff, and the Kennet & Avon canal on both sides. The one bar overlooks the canalside garden and serves decent food from an extensive menu and Morland's bitter, Fuller's London Pride, Thomas Hardy and Adnams bitter. A large collection of blue and white china covers the wall, and the bar top is made out of shiny old penny pieces. The wine list received the Egon Ronay South of England Cellar of the Year 1990 accolade. The restaurant does not overlook the water but serves seriously good food at £25 for three courses. The chef uses fish from Cornwall and local game. Canalside tables in summer allow visitors to watch the highly painted barges go by and greet the friendly ducks. The pub gets busy at lunchtime, even out of season. Pets are accommodated by arrangement only. No facilities for the disabled, though there are ground-floor rooms and helpful staff.

Walking; fishing (need a permit from local club); ballooning nearby

LEATHERINGSETT

The King's Head, Leatheringsett, nr Holt, Norfolk
NR25 7AR   (Tel. 0263 712691)
Open 10.30am–3pm and 5.30–11pm Mon–Sat, noon–3pm and 5.30–10.30pm Sun

Twenty yards from the River Glaven, which runs behind the pub's large lawned garden and under an old hump-backed bridge, The King's Head was originally built as a beerhouse for the nearby Victorian brewery. Now its two bars and separate dining room serve local ales such as Adnams and Greene King, with coffee served in the mornings and food available at lunchtime and all evening. The food on offer includes home-made steak and kidney pies, home-cooked ham, crab salads, steaks and a traditional Sunday lunch. The King's Head is a friendly family-type pub, the same menu available whether you prefer to eat in the bar or the more comfortable dining room. There is easy access for wheelchairs, but no special toilet facilities for the disabled.

Riverside walks, gardens, working mill

LONDON COLNEY

The Green Dragon, Waterside, London Colney,
Hertfordshire AL2 1RB   (Tel. 0727 823214)
Village is off the M25; pub just off main street, by bridge
Open 11am–3pm, 5.30pm–11pm Mon–Sat; noon–3pm, 7pm–
10.30pm Sun
Close to a major road, yet in the midst of beautiful
countryside, this recently refurbished 16th-century pub enjoys
a lovely position at the start of several country footpaths. A
stream runs quietly by its garden tables, through weeping
willows and past the large green. The interior of the pub is
traditional and cosy, with open fires and a huge and
famous collection of brasses. The landlords have recently
added a kitchen and they offer a range of food, from bar snacks
to three-course dinners (a three-course meal costs about £9).
The atmosphere is relaxed and friendly.
Walks through fields, along the stream and up to some lakes; fishing
and bird sanctuary nearby

MAIDENHEAD

17/19

Boulters Lock Hotel, Boulters Island, Maidenhead,
Berkshire SL6 8PE   (Tel. 0628 21291)
Off Junction 7 of the M4
£79.50–£125 single, £100–£175 double b&b
Standing on a small island in the middle of the Thames, the
hotel was originally built as a mill house and cottages in 1726.
The mill race still flows underneath the restaurant. Close to
Boulters lock, the longest and deepest lock on the river, it used
to be a gathering place for high society during Victorian and
Edwardian days, when the area was often known as 'Mayfair
on Thames'. Nowadays the hotel provides comfortable
accommodation and good food. Many of the bedrooms have
water views, and are elegantly decorated and well equipped.
The restaurant, offering lunch at £18.50 and dinner at £26.50
(£30.50 on Saturday evenings for the hotel's own dinner

dance), looks downstream towards Maidenhead, and has excellent views from all of the tables (open 12.30pm–2.30pm, 7.30pm–9.30pm (1am on Saturdays) all week). There is a large patio terrace which is very pleasant in summer.

MAIDENHEAD

🏨 30/53 ⛲ 🎣 🚫 ▭

Thames Riviera Hotel, at the Bridge, Maidenhead, Berkshire SL6 8DW   (Tel. 0628 74057)
By Maidenhead bridge
£82.50 single, £93.50 double, suite £115; breakfast £7.95
This hotel is situated by the old bridge which originally helped to bring prosperity to Maidenhead. The building dates from the 1870s, and recent refurbishments have preserved the Edwardian feel. Close to the water, the views from the restaurant and the terrace are picturesque. Neither the coffee shop nor the bar, however, can lay claim to water views, and both have slightly gloomy atmospheres. The rooms are light and airy, and many of them have balconies and good water views. The bridal suite, complete with four-poster, has good views of Brunel bridge, which has the longest brick arch span in the world. The service is friendly and professional, and there are extensive conference and banqueting facilities.
Walking; boat hire nearby; Ascot racecourse and Windsor Safari Park both nearby

MAIDSTONE

🏨 18/40 ⛲ 🎣 ◁ ▭

Chilston Park, Sandway, Lenham, Kent ME17 2BE
(Tel. 0622 859803)
Lenham village off the A20, then follow signs to Boughton Malherbe
£72–£149 single, £94–£198 double b&b
Boasting 250 acres of parkland and a spring-fed lake, this beautiful Grade I listed building dates back to the 13th century. The hotel was remodelled in the 1700s and remains grandly

furnished: even the staff are turned out in traditional costume. The idea behind the hotel is to re-create an old-fashioned country-house party, and there are open fires, and at dusk hundreds of candles are lit, to give a very special atmosphere. The rooms are spacious and ornate, some with heavy four-poster beds. The hotel is owned by Judith and Martin Miller (authors of *Miller's Antiques Price Guide*), so the house is full of gorgeous antique pieces; depending on your attitude, you'll find it either grand or grotesque. The restaurant seats 80 and has 12 window tables, though seven others enjoy lake views. Set lunches, from £13 to £18.95, six-course dinner £33.50. Sunday lunch is £16.50, afternoon tea £8.50.

Walks along Pilgrims' Way; fishing (rods available); golf (three miles away); riding (Oathill, 20 minutes away); gliding (six miles away); windsurfing and waterskiing (Maidstone lakes); champagne, opera, antiques and 'Murder Mystery' weekends; hot-air ballooning by arrangement; archery, clay pigeon shooting; croquet; badminton; lawn bowls; golf driving range; putting green

MARLOW

36/64

The Compleat Angler, Bisham Road, Marlow Bridge, Marlow, Buckinghamshire SL7 1RG   (Tel. 0628 484444)
On the A404 between Maidenhead and Marlow
£120–£140 single, £140–£155 double
This famous hotel, occupying the spot on the Thames where Izaak Walton wrote his classic work on fishing in 1653, could not be much closer to the river. Beside the bridge and opposite the church, set in its own beautiful gardens, this hotel offers luxurious accommodation in lovely surroundings. There is plenty of space to enjoy the river from the gardens and from the waterside conservatory. The angling theme is continued throughout the hotel; bedrooms are all named after fishing flies and the best ones, which are slightly more expensive, have gorgeous river views. The large restaurant is also on the river, with the same superb views and extremely good, if unadventurous, cuisine. There is a helipad for guests arriving

by air. The hotel has wheelchair access, and one bedroom has been specially adapted for disabled visitors.

On-site fishing (equipment not supplied); boating; tennis; walking; clay pigeon shooting; flying and river cruises can be arranged

MARSHSIDE

The Gate Inn, Marshside, nr Canterbury, Kent
(Tel. 022786 498)
One mile north of Chislet, on Marshside Road
Open 11am–2.30pm, 6pm–11pm Mon–Fri; 11am–3pm, 6pm–11pm Sat; noon–3pm, 7pm–10.30pm Sun

This down-to-earth, genuine country pub is bordered by a stream on two sides, and the garden often has ducks, geese and pub resident Derek the one-eyed chicken wandering through it. The atmosphere inside the pub is entirely unpretentious – there are no carpets on the floor, no jukeboxes or fruit machines, and the beers are kept in the back room on tap; Shepherd Neame Old Ale, Master Brew and Bishop's Finger are the local brews. During Lent, the pub refuses to sell lager. Good bar food, such as soup and sandwiches, is available at lunchtime and in the evening, and is generous, healthy and reasonably priced. There are good water views from the bar. The pub is popular with those who prefer simple utilitarianism to frippery and who enjoy a traditional atmosphere. Access for the disabled.

Fishing (rods supplied); fly fishing nearby; walking

MILDENHALL

Riverside Hotel, Mill Street, Mildenhall, Suffolk IP28 7DP
(Tel. 0638 717274)
Off the A11, on the west side of town
£45–£66 per room b&b

This listed red-brick hotel has lovely landscaped gardens running down to the banks of the River Lark. It has recently undergone some refurbishments, and the restaurant is now in a delightful conservatory. Nearly all the seats have good river views, as do those on the outside terrace. The food is of a high standard – three courses from the table d'hôte menu cost £12, and a variety of bar snacks are on offer at lunchtime. During the summer they have barbecues in the garden. The bedrooms are very pretty, with floral prints and tasteful furnishings, and one of the rooms has a four-poster. The hotel has a famous Georgian staircase, which is worth inspecting.

Interesting walks; fishing (rod licence needed, the hotel has fishing rights); rowing boats for hire; bridge weekends; croquet; putting

MONK SOHAM

Abbey House, Monk Soham, nr Woodbridge, Suffolk
IP13 7EN   (Tel. 0728 685 225)
Off the A1120, the Stowmarket to Yoxford road
Closed Christmas and New Year
£18–£20 pp b&b

Formerly a Victorian rectory enjoying a quiet Suffolk countryside location, Abbey House's present owners have created a comfortable guest house set in 10 acres of secluded gardens complete with ponds, black swans, oaks and beeches. The genteel atmosphere is informal, warm and welcoming and enhanced by tasteful antique furnishings, soft colour schemes and a magnificently restored cast-iron fireplace in the dining area. Evening meals can be provided for residents and their guests by prior arrangement at £12 a head. Catering is in the traditional English style and features the house's own meat and vegetables (vegetarians should give advance notice). Guests are welcome to look at the Jersey cows, ducks, sheep, peafowl and other livestock in the grounds. The owners are delightful and most welcoming. A magnificent base for exploring many local attractions and places of interest such as the Norfolk Broads, historic Norwich, coastal bird reserves, and most of the 'Constable Country'.

Open-air swimming pool; countryside and coastal walks; sailing and windsurfing in Aldeburgh; pond fishing; nearby beaches

MOULSFORD

inn ⁸/¹³

Beetle and Wedge, Ferry Lane, Moulsford-on-Thames, Oxon
OX10 9JF   (Tel. 0491 651381)
Just off the A329 between Streatley and Wallingford
£65 single, £75 double b&b
This cosy Thames-side inn has lovely views and a relaxed
atmosphere. The bar has log fires, and serves Wadworth 6X,
Adnams best bitter and Tanglefoot. There is also an informal à
la carte restaurant, The Boat House, connected to the bar,
which has an open charcoal grill, and serves lunch and dinner.
In the main body of the inn, the more formal restaurant places
strong emphasis on the quality of the food, which could be
described as robust French cuisine with an English accent, and
is said to be extremely good. Specialities include terrines,
sorbets and brioches. The three-course dinner costs £25 per
person, and includes coffee and home-made chocolates. The
extensive and tranquil riverside gardens offer barbecues every
day in summer. Pets by arrangement only. There are ground-
floor rooms and lavatories for disabled visitors.
*Fishing by arrangement; rowing boats for hire (10 miles away); walks
along river and through water meadows; antique shops in Wallingford
(10 miles); golf nearby*

NEEDINGWORTH

inn ⁵/¹²

Pike and Eel, Overcote Lane, Needingworth, St Ives,
Cambridgeshire PE17 3TW   (Tel. 0480 63336)
Off the main road through Needingworth
Bar open 10.30am–3pm, 6pm–11pm Mon–Sat; noon–3pm,
7pm–11pm Sun
£32–£35 single, £48 double b&b
This popular pub, well off the beaten track, dates back to the
17th century. Set on the banks of the River Ouse, it has large
lawns running down to the water, where there is a marina.
Barbecues are held in the summer. There are two restaurants,
both with views of the river, although the glass-walled Garden

Room restaurant has the best of them, and a bar, also with fine views of the gardens and river. There is a good selection of food available, from ploughman's, via steaks, to full-blown à la carte meals. The bedrooms are comfortable and homely, with washbasins, televisions, and pleasant rural views. There are two peaceful lounges off the bar.

Golf; stables nearby; walking; watersports; fishing (with fishing rights)

NEWBRIDGE

The Maybush, Newbridge, nr Witney, Oxon OX8 7QD
(Tel. 0865 300624)
On the A415 exactly halfway between Abingdon and Witney
Open 11am–3pm, 5.30pm–11pm Mon–Sat; noon–2.30pm, 6pm–10.30pm Sun

This quiet pub is right on the Thames, and very close to where it joins the River Windrush – you can see the Windrush gently snaking through the fields in the near distance. There is a small terrace with tables and lovely views over the river and the meadows. During the summer barbecues are sometimes held here, and there is some mooring for boats. Inside, the decor of the single bar is simple, and there are several tables with good views. The pub serves Morland ales, and also does a wide range of bar grub, such as steaks, fish and pasta; there is also a selection of vegetarian dishes. All in all, a typical country pub in a beautiful position. The pub is accessible to disabled visitors, though there are no special facilities.

Walks along the Thames; fishing; small caravan park

NEWBRIDGE

The Rose Revived Inn and Restaurant, Newbridge, Witney, Oxon OX8 6QD   (Tel. 0865 300221)
On the A415 Abingdon to Witney, or float downstream and moor alongside the garden
£40–£45 single, £50–£55 double b&b

A pretty, large old riverside inn, on the upper reaches of the Thames. The à la carte restaurant, complete with impressive 16th-century fireplace, has tables outside on the terrace with good water views. The bar, again with good water views, has flagstone floors and open fires, and serves a range of bar meals. The beers on draught include Stella Artois, Morland's Revival and Original, and Old Speckled Hen. The rose theme is stressed, with rose-patterned wallpaper and pictures of roses decorating the walls. The extensive garden by the water seats 250, and is lit at night by old-fashioned street lights. The civilized, pleasant and well-appointed bedrooms all have good views overlooking the river. There is no charge for overnight mooring. It can become very busy during the summer.
Windsurfing and waterskiing nearby; fishing; walks

NEWBURY

24/32 12

Millwaters Hotel and Restaurant, London Road, Newbury, Berkshire RG13 2BY   (Tel. 0635 528 838)
Newbury signposted off the A4
£81–£140 per room
The tumbling rivers Kennet and Lambourn border the grounds of this pretty Georgian country house. Inside is extensively refurbished, with spa baths and mini-bars in some of the bedrooms; many of these overlook the rivers, and all are tastefully decorated, if a little bland. The spacious, to the point of being barn-like, restaurant seats 70; some tables inside and on the patio overlook the really lovely award-winning gardens, which are floodlit at night. The restaurant specializes in traditional English and French dishes, and the set, three-course meal costs £15. There is a summer house with waterside terraces for private parties. Despite being close to the industrial wasteland that surrounds Newbury these days, the hotel is an oasis of watery tranquillity, and the gardens are outstanding.
Walking; watersports; fishing in grounds on Kennet, Lambourn and lake; gliding by arrangement; special interest weekends include fishing, watercolour painting, music, riding and horse racing

NORWICH

The Ferry Inn, Reedham, Norwich, Norfolk NR13 3HA
(Tel. 0493 700429)
On the B1140, off the A47 Norwich–Great Yarmouth road
Open 11am–3pm, 6.30pm–11pm Mon–Sat; noon–3pm,
7pm–10.30pm Sun
Be warned that approaching this functional inn from the south
entails a short ferry crossing, as the establishment's name
suggests. The Ferry Inn enjoys a rural, tranquil location and
owns one of the last working vehicle ferries in East Anglia
which runs from 8am–10pm daily, transporting a maximum
of three cars. Across a quiet lane, the inn's garden-bench
seating overlooks the swans and moored boats of the River
Yale. Inside, the two bar areas (one with a sun lounge) offer a
certain amount of rustic character with their brass and copper
decorations, antique rifles and log fires coupled with modern
entertainments such as games and fruit machines. A fair
selection of generously portioned bar meals are on offer,
ranging from ploughman's at £3.50 to seasonal game at £6, and
beers include Adnams, Woodforde's and Beck's. The Inn can
cater for disabled visitors, but there are no special facilities.
Fishing rights (rod licence needed); camping nearby

NORWICH

Hotel Nelson, Prince of Wales Road, Norwich, Norfolk
NR1 1DX   (Tel. 0603 760260)
Opposite railway station on east side of town
£45 pp, dinner and b&b
Functional and modern, this purpose-built red-brick hotel has
been sensibly designed to maximize its riverside position.
There are large floor-to-ceiling windows in the lounge, and the
water views are also good from other areas of the hotel. It sits
on the banks of the River Wensum, and has nice waterside
gardens. The bedrooms are comfortable and airy, decorated in
restful colours, with thoughtful extras such as a fridge with

milk and fruit juice, mineral water and chocolates, and many of them have views of the Wensum. There are two restaurants, one on the ground floor, next to the river, and the other on the first floor, with a pleasant balcony looking over the river. The food is English and traditional, and the table d'hôte menu costs £12.50. The staff are refreshingly professional and most welcoming. There are lavatories, and there is a modified bedroom for the disabled.

Riverside walks; river cruises and boat trips can be arranged

OLD HUNSTANTON

🏠 ³¹/⁴² 🐾 🚫 ⬦ 💳

Le Strange Arms Hotel, Golf Course Road, Old
Hunstanton, Norfolk PE36 6JJ   (Tel. 0485 534411)
Off the A149 between Wells and Hunstanton
£50 single, £70 double b&b

In an impressive position right on the seafront, this Grade II listed hotel dates from 1600 and has fine lawns leading down to the beaches. The hotel's name comes from the local land-owning family, the Le Stranges, and the hotel occupies the more interesting and historical part of town. There are good facilities for families including a children's play area, children's menus and baby-listening, and there are spacious adjoining bedrooms. There is a snooker room, with a full-sized table. Half of the tables in the 50-cover restaurant look out to sea. There is a bar in the old stables, which also enjoys good sea views. The staff are helpful and friendly.

Walking; beach; watersports and fishing can be arranged by the hotel (rod licence available in Hunstanton, equipment not supplied); golf nearby

OTLEY

Otley House, Otley, Suffolk IP6 9NR   (Tel. 0473 890 253)
Village on the B1079
Open 1 March–1 November
£34–£38 single, £44–£50 double b&b

This charming, Grade II listed country manor house nestles in three acres of peaceful grounds complete with two smallish lakes, which used to be part of the moat round the house. French windows open on to smart lawns, wild ducks bob gently on the lake and the atmosphere is extremely tranquil. Inside the house, one tends to feel more like an invited guest than a passing traveller. The light and airy bedrooms are filled with antiques and freshly cut flowers. All guests eat around the same table in the dining room, equipped with crystal glasses and silver cutlery (set dinner £15.50). There is no choice of menu – let the owners know your pet hates when you book. After dinner there is a billiard room where guests gather for coffee, and this is the only room where smoking is permitted. For an elegant and civilized stay in beautiful countryside, Otley House would seem to to offer exceptional value.

Croquet lawn; fishing by arrangement; walking; riding; watersports at Woodbridge, Walderingfield and Orford; golf courses at Aldeburgh, Thorpeness and Woodbridge; beach at Aldeburgh (30 minutes' drive)

OXFORD

Cherwell Boat House, Bardwell Road, Oxford OX2 6SR
(Tel. 0865 52746)
Call for directions
Open noon–2pm, 7.30pm–10pm Tues–Sat; noon–2.30pm, 7pm–10pm Sun. Closed Mon all year, and Sun evenings in winter

This popular Oxford institution is on the River Cherwell, and the window tables look out over the ranks of moored punts and the meadows leading away towards Marston. The restaurant seats 50, and offers very good, simple food. The menu changes weekly, and there are only two or three choices per course, but the choices are well-balanced and often delicious. The price for the set dinner is £14.50. They also possess an outstanding wine list which is well worth investigating. The decor is plain and unspectacular, but it is compensated by the proximity of the Cherwell, and in the summer you can eat al fresco on the terrace. The Boat House as a whole can become very crowded in the summer with punters arriving and departing. The restaurant can cater for disabled visitors, but there are no special facilities.

Punting from boat house next door to restaurant (mid-March to mid-October); walks in the university parks

PETERBOROUGH

IOI ⌂ ⌦ ▭

The Grain Barge, The Quayside, Embankment Road,
Peterborough, Cambridgeshire PE1 1EG   (Tel. 0733 311967)
Near town centre, next to the Key Theatre
Open noon–2pm and 6–10.30pm, seven days
In a city singularly lacking in good eating places, the Grain Barge Peking Restaurant is worth knowing about. Moored on the River Nene, with swans drifting by, it has a reasonably pleasant outlook if you can ignore the DIY Supercentre on the opposite bank. Access is via a gentle ramp, and inside the decor is relaxing, and the service extremely friendly. Booking is recommended as its food is justifiably popular and, unusually for an ethnic restaurant, it can be found in several food guides. There are a couple of set-price menus, and a very wide à la carte choice, including delicious duck and fish specialities. The wine list circles the globe, from California to, yes, Chinese wines. Superior Oriental cuisine.

Peterborough Cathedral; Nene Valley Railway; Flag Fen Bronze-Age archaeological site

PYRFORD LOCK

The Anchor, Pyrford Lock, Ripley, Woking, Surrey
GU23 6QW   (Tel. 09323 42507)
Off the A3, pass Wisley Gardens, continue along same road to
pub
Open 11am–3pm, 6pm–11pm Mon–Fri; 11am–11pm Sat;
noon–3pm, 7pm–10.30pm Sun
This modern, open-plan country pub was built in 1936 and
extended six years ago. It has very good views of the canal, the
lock and a hump-backed bridge. There is a large canalside
terrace with tables, where teas are served in the summertime,
and a large waterside garden with seating for 50. Inside, in the
large bar, the picture windows look out over the canal, and one
can watch the narrow boats passing slowly by. There is a
parents' and children's room upstairs, which is decorated with
narrow-boat bric-a-brac. The bar serves Directors, Best, and
John Smith's bitters; and there are bar lunches and dinners.
*Canalside walks; Wisley Garden; boat hire at Guildford and
Farncombe; rowing-boat hire at Byfleet (one and a half miles)*

RAMSHOLT

inn ²′²

Ramsholt Arms, Dock Road, Ramsholt, Woodbridge, Suffolk
IP12 3AB   (Tel. 0394 411229)
Village signposted from the B1083 (call for detailed directions)
Bar open 11am–11pm Mon–Sat in summer (11am–2.30pm,
7pm–11pm Mon–Sat in winter); noon–3pm, 7pm–10.30pm
Sun
£25 pp b&b October to May only
Unless you know the area you may be tempted to give up
before you get there: the pub is on a private estate and has no
inn sign. Persevere. The setting and the view are stunning and
a far cry from city life. The pub is beside an old barge quay; the
River Deben flows quietly by to the sea. Local enthusiasts
would be more than happy to enlighten you on the wildlife of
the water and the vicinity. Two bars overlook the water, and

serve Adnams bitter and a selection of guest beers, and also food. The accommodation is modest, but clean and well maintained, and is able to boast royal visitors (the Duke of Edinburgh and the Prince of Wales), from the days when the pub was a shooting lodge. Bar meals are served at lunchtime and in the evening every day. Children are welcome in the dining room but not in the guest accommodation.

Interesting walks; sailing; beach nearby

RICKMANSWORTH

IOI ⌂ ♦ ⌀ ⇋

Black Jack's Mill, off Park Lane, Harefield, Middlesex
UB9 4HL   (Tel. 0895 823120)
Call for directions
Open 12.30pm–2pm, 7pm–10pm; closed Sun evening and all day Mon

A splendid watery setting, with the Grand Union Canal just behind the restaurant, the river in front of the garden and a lake beyond that. Part of the canal runs under the building and turns a cormetic wheel. Parts of the building are 900 years old, and are recorded in the Domesday Book. The food is Italian and English (set Sunday lunch £12.50) and there is seating for 45, with six tables having a water view. There are some tables outside in summer. Water views from inside can be slightly disappointing (some tables with canal view, others river and lake view), but one can take drinks outside in summer on to the patio. The mill used to be the haunt of film stars when Denham studios were open, and Rosemary Clooney, Bob Hope and Sir John Mills used to eat here often. There are some facilities for the disabled.

Fishing nearby; sailing club opposite; bird watching; walks along canal; boat rental in Uxbridge (four miles away)

The River House Restaurant, which overlooks the Exe estuary: Lympstone, Devon

The Royal Oak, on the harbour: Langstone, Hampshire

The Warehouse Oyster Bar and Restaurant, on the quayside: Poole, Dorset

Eddrachilles Hotel: Badcall Bay, Scourie

The Waterfront Wine Bar, on the new dockside: Leith

The Altnaharrie Inn, on its own island – the launch collects guests: Ullapool

The Green Park Hotel, seen across Loch Faskally: Pitlochry

St Michael's Manor House: St Albans, Hertfordshire

The Butt and Oyster Pub at Pin Mill: near Ipswich, Suffolk

The Trout Inn: Wolvercote, Oxfordshire

Black Jack's Mill − the canal runs under the restaurant: Rickmansworth, Middlesex

The Portmeirion Hotel, looking across the Traeth Bach estuary: Portmeirion, Gwynedd

New Hall Hotel, with lily-fringed moat: Sutton Coldfield, West Midlands

The Old Manse Hotel: Bourton-on-the-Water, Gloucestershire

The Pump House, in front of the magnificent Port of Liverpool building:
Albert Dock, Liverpool

Waterton Park Hotel, on its own island: Wakefield, West Yorkshire

Kirkby Fleetham Hall: Northallerton, North Yorkshire

The Watermill Coffee Shop, housed in a 17th-century mill: Caldbeck, Cumbria

ST ALBANS

🏨 9/22 ⛲12 🐕 ◁ ▭

St Michael's Manor House, Fishpool Street, St Albans,
Hertfordshire AL3 4RY   (Tel. 0727 864444)
Follow signposts towards cathedral
£74 single, £88 double b&b (four-poster-bedrooms and
special weekend rates also available)
In a very tranquil setting, yet only 10 minutes' walk from the
cathedral and the main town, the hotel offers the benefits of
both town and country location in one. The front façade faces
St Albans' historic cathedral, while the hotel's particularly
attractive rear conservatory backs on to five acres of award-
winning and charming garden, complete with a picturesque
lake. Also facing the green surrounds of the lake are 40 of the
100 seats in the restaurant, which serves a set lunch at £16.50,
dinner at £18.50 and also offers a comprehensive à la carte
menu averaging £22 for three courses. (Restaurant open
12.30pm–2pm Mon–Sun; 7pm–9pm Mon–Sat; 7pm–8pm Sun
evening buffet.) The comfortable bedrooms are pleasantly
decorated with pastel-coloured soft furnishings. Dogs are
accepted by prior arrangement with the hotel management.
With its adapted bathroom facilities and ramps, the restaurant
is suitable for the disabled, but an overnight stay is not
recommended.
*Golf; local sports centre with swimming pool; walking; many local
historical sites to visit; tennis (outdoor and indoor)*

ST IVES

🏨 0/22 ⛲ 🐕 ◁ ▭

The Dolphin Hotel, Bridge Foot, London Road, St Ives,
Cambridgeshire PE17 4EP   (Tel. 0480 66966)
In the town centre
£53 single, £63 double, £73 family room (sleeps 4) b&b
This purpose-built hotel with simple accommodation is
conveniently placed at the edge of an attractive and traditional
market town, right on the edge of the River Ouse. It is a
popular location with both fishermen and boating enthusiasts.

If the bedrooms do not boast a water view, the hotel's 'Waterside Restaurant' more than compensates with good views from virtually all of its 120 seats. The modern English/French-influenced cuisine includes table d'hôte lunch and dinner at £12.95, or à la carte meals in the region of £17.50 for three courses (restaurant open noon–2pm, 7pm–9.30pm every day). The Dolphin also has a bar, residents' lounge and night porter service and a functions suite. Pets are accepted by prior arrangement only. During 1992, another 25 bedrooms were being added, including two specially adapted for disabled visitors.

Walking; boat trips; fishing by arrangement (rod licences available nearby)

ST LEONARDS-ON-SEA

IOI 🏠 👌 🕸 ▭

Röser's, 64 Eversfield Place, St Leonards–on–Sea,
East Sussex TN37 6DB   (Tel. 0424 712218)
Open noon–2pm, 7pm–10pm; closed Sat lunch and all day Sun and Mon

Directly on the St Leonards seafront and just opposite the pier, this 35-seat restaurant set in a Victorian terraced residence offers reasonable sea views across the road and promenade from the three front tables. The food is inventive but some may consider it slightly pricey although owner/chef, Gerald Röser, clearly puts great thought and energy into it. He uses a wide range of leaves, including many Japanese ones that give a startling boost to the flavour of the salads. Sushi features on the menu when the supply of fresh fish permits; also tartare of scallops and oysters. Set lunch costs £15.95 and the three-course dinner à la carte averages £24 including VAT and service. The 400-strong, award-winning wine list (Egon Ronay, Wine List of the Year 1991) should appeal to all palates and is priced from a reasonable £7.95 to a frightening £395. Not a restaurant for the casual eater, but a real treat for the food connoisseur. Group catering for up to 40 guests is available in a first-floor function room with panoramic sea view. The restaurant can cater for the disabled but has no specific facilities.

Beach; watersports, including windsurfing; waterskiing in the harbour; fishing from pier; boat trips from harbour (Deep Sea Fishing Club nearby); walking

ST LEONARDS-ON-SEA

25/52

Royal Victoria Hotel, Marina, St Leonards-on-Sea, East Sussex TN38 0BD   (Tel. 0424 445544)

From £66 single, £83.50 double b&b

Built in 1828, the hotel was refurbished in suitably grand style for a visit by Queen Victoria. The first flight of the impressive staircase ends at an enormous wall mirror, creating such a successful illusion of space beyond that the management found a centrally placed plant necessary to protect guests from embarrassing self-injury. The bedroom suites are luxuriously appointed and the 25 sea-view suites feature old sash windows large enough to gain access to the roof. The first-floor restaurant seats 120 diners and is open to non-residents with excellent sea views from eight of the tables. The set dinner costs £18 and a separate seafood menu is always on offer. Elegant public rooms include an arched and columned lounge with fine sea views, plus an intimate cocktail bar. In the luxuriously appointed bedroom suites, children under 12 may share with parents free of charge. Small pets are only accepted by prior arrangement at a nominal fee.

Beach; river fishing nearby; sea fishing from Hastings can be arranged; windsurfing, sailing and waterskiing can be arranged; yacht hire; many walks; riding and golf nearby

SEAFORD

The Golden Galleon, Exceat Bridge, Seaford, East Sussex
BN25 4AB　(Tel. 0323 892247)
On the A259, the Seaford to Eastbourne road
Open 11am–3pm, 6pm–11pm
A traditional, tied pub just opposite the River Cuckmere,
featuring low oak beams, red Turkish carpeting and an open
log fire in winter. Bar meals range from soups (£2) to steaks
(£12), although the specialities are generally Italian. Both the
bar and the garden, with bench and patio seating, overlook the
river and the point where canoeing enthusiasts set off on an
Outward Bound course – a potentially entertaining event
for passive onlookers. Easily reached from Eastbourne or
Brighton, the pub serves Directors, Courage Best, Harvey's
Armada and John Smith's beers. Dogs must be kept on leads.
Children are admitted during the summer months. No
facilities for the disabled, though there are plans to change this
soon.
Walks in National Trust land; canoeing nearby; fishing; beach

SHABBINGTON

The Old Fisherman Pub, Shabbington, Buckinghamshire
HB18 9HJ　(Tel. 0844 201247)
Off the A329 at Thame, follow signs to Wheatley
Open 11am–3pm, 5.30pm–11pm Mon–Sat; noon–2.30pm,
7pm–10.30pm Sun
Enjoying a lovely, peaceful situation on the River Thame, this
simple but charming 17th-century pub is beautifully placed for
a quiet summer's drink. There is a garden, with tables, that
runs down to the river. The owner/landlord was born and bred
in the village of Shabbington, and the pub is equally popular
with locals and tourists. Bar snacks are available at prices up to
£3.50 and beers served include Morrell's of Oxford. A small
restaurant opened during 1992. Accessible to disabled visitors.
Walking

SHILLINGFORD

🏠 15/37 ⌂ 🍷 ⟨ ▭

Shillingford Bridge Hotel, Ferry Road, Shillingford,
Wallingford, Oxon OX10 8LZ   (Tel. 086732 8567)
£57.50 single, £77.50 double b&b
Restaurant open 12.30pm–2pm, 7.30pm–10pm (9.30pm Sun)
all week

The hotel has a truly beautiful riverside setting, with splendid
views of an attractive reach of the River Thames. In the
summer, there are seats out in the garden, where verdant lawns
descend to the river bank and moored boats line the water's
edge. Specializing as a venue for corporate or private events,
the hotel is well equipped for banquets for up to 150 guests;
ideal for small conferences or wedding receptions. From many
tables in the 150-seat dining room guests can enjoy a view of
the river while sampling the three-course meals, table d'hôte
(£13.50) or à la carte (£18.50) menus. The bedrooms have
recently been refurbished and all have private *en suite* facilities
and colour television. The hotel can cater for the disabled, but
has no special facilities.

*Outdoor pool and squash courts on site; golf, coarse fishing, river craft
hire and walks nearby*

SONNING-ON-THAMES

🏠 4/36 ⌂ 🍷 ⟨ ▭

The Great House at Sonning, Thames Street, Sonning-on-
Thames, Berkshire RG4 0UT   (Tel. 0734 692277)
£69 single, £89 double b&b; breakfast £6.50–£8.50

A sister hotel to Sir Christopher Wren's House (see under
Windsor), the Great House at Sonning overlooks a broad
meander in the River Thames which is frequented by
wildfowl. The hotel has four acres of beautiful grounds,
riverside gardens with seating on an extremely large summer
terrace and boasts two restaurants. The bedrooms are well
equipped, though lacking the appeal of the gardens. Table
d'hôte traditional English meals cost from £16.50 for lunch and
£18 for dinner in the 96-seat main restaurant, where all dining

tables overlook the river, and a full à la carte menu also offers three-course meals for approximately £17.50. Alternatively, the more casual 'Hideaway' restaurant in the beamed Elizabethan area of the hotel provides wholesome English meals in the £10–£12 price band. Pets are accepted but are not admitted to public rooms. The hotel is not adapted for the disabled although the restaurants may be accessible.

Walking; watersports; fishing (rods available at hotel); tennis courts on site

SOUTHWOLD

The Harbour Pub, Blackshore Quay, Southwold, Suffolk
IP18 6TA   (Tel. 0502 722381)
From the A1095 to Southwold, turn right at the King's Head and head for the water tower on the other side of the golf course
Open 11am–3pm, 6pm–11pm Mon–Sat in summer (11am–3pm, 7pm–10.30pm Mon–Sat in winter); noon–2.30pm, 7pm–10.30pm Sun
A quaint and refreshingly unpretentious pub on the quay. Its charm lies in simplicity and is enhanced by a sign that says 'Beware – ducks crossing'. The 400-year-old building has two bars: the lower one overlooks the River Blyth; the upper one faces the marsh. Mercifully, no chrome plating, no jukebox, and no one-armed bandits spoil the pub's old-fashioned atmosphere. A small scruffy garden with play area for children runs down to the water where ducks and geese wander freely. With no plates, knives or forks in sight, the food (fish, sausage or – topping the range – scampi and chips for £2.50) is largely fried and includes anything that can be served wrapped in a paper parcel. Food is available Friday and Saturday evenings in winter and all day, all week in summer. Children and pets are allowed in the garden only and dogs must be kept on leads.

Landlord Ron Westwood will give directions for interesting walks; children can go crabbing in the river just across from the pub; fishing in the river (no licence needed); beach (10 minutes' walk along the river)

STAINES

🏠 5/11 ⌂ 🦺 ⊘ 💳

The Swan Hotel, The Hythe, Staines TW18 3JB
(Tel. 0784 454471)
Take first left south of Staines bridge
£36 single, £55–£70 double b&b
Bar open 11am–11pm Mon–Sat; noon–3pm, 7pm–10.30pm
Sun (snacks noon–10pm)
This delightfully restored old inn was built in the 17th and 18th
centuries and enjoys a Thames-side setting with a sycamore-
shaded terrace beside the towpath. There are two bars serving
real ales including ESB and London Pride: both bars overlook
the river and are furnished with upholstered settles, armchairs
and original exposed fireplaces. Scattered horse brasses,
copper tankards and kettles add to their charm. Bedrooms are
comfortable and thoughtfully decked out with pine furniture
and peachy colour schemes. Catering ranges from a sandwich
in the bar to a full meal in the restaurant; all in all, there is
seating for 70 diners. A new restaurant overlooking the river
opened during 1992.
Walking; fishing; Windsor and Runnymede nearby

STORRINGTON

🏠 6/21 ⌂10 🦺 ⊘ 💳

Abingworth Hall, Thakeham Road, Storrington, West
Sussex RH20 3EF (Tel. 0798 813636)
Two miles west of the A24, on the B2139 between
Storrington and Coolham
£64 single, £87 double, £153 suite b&b
Set in ample, pretty gardens with its own one-acre lake and
islands, this gracious, elegant and historic old hall has a country-
house atmosphere. The estate dates back to the 14th century,
although the current house was built in 1910 after fire
destroyed its predecessor. The 50-seat restaurant, spanning
three interconnecting rooms of varied layouts, provides
French and traditional English cuisine (lunch £17, dinner

£27.50) with French, German, Italian, Spanish, New Zealand and Australian wines. The oak-panelled drawing room faces south and is shaded by a canopy of wisteria and its dark-wood decor contrasts severely with the lighter shades of the dining room and cocktail bar. A 20-seat conservatory overlooks the water. Rooms vary widely (the best is the double-lake-aspect suite) although all have a huge German stool bath, comfortable beds and plenty of space. Additional facilities include an on-site helipad. The hotel has eight ground-floor rooms but no special facilities for the disabled.

Heated outdoor swimming pool (May to September); tennis court; nine-hole pitch and putt course; walks to South Downs (maps available); beach and watersports (eight miles away); coarse fishing on lake (bring equipment)

STREATLEY

🏨 29/46 🏡 ♿ ⬦ ▭

The Swan Diplomat Hotel, Streatley-on-Thames, Berkshire RG8 9HR   (Tel. 0491 873737)
In Streatley, just off the A329
£82 single, £110 double, £187 suite b&b; breakfast £6.75–£8.75
A sunny, spick-and-span and extremely professional Scandin-avian-run hotel on the banks of the Thames, with good views of the old river bridge, and 23 acres of grounds. Giant carp swim beneath bridges in the grounds (no fishing here!). Inside the red-brick building, bedrooms are decorated in muted pastels with mahogany furniture; over half have a river view and some have riverside balconies. The restaurant seats 80 with many river-view tables and serves classical French cuisine with set lunch at £18.50, dinner £21.50 and à la carte meals for around £29.50. Light lunches and teas are available for non-residents. A Magdalen College barge moored alongside the hotel provides an excellent cocktail party venue. Both the barge and the hotel's function rooms contribute to its increasing success in the mini-conference trade. There are two ground-floor rooms adapted for the disabled and all public rooms and facilities are accessible.

Leisure club with gym and pool on site; watersports and fishing nearby; walking; clay pigeon shooting; golf; squash; tennis; rowing boats and bicycles may be rented

SUDBURY

The Mill Hotel, Walnut Tree Lane, Sudbury, Suffolk
CO10 6BD   (Tel. 0787 75544)
Off the A131 to Chelmsford
£50 single, £78 double b&b
Set on the River Stour with its own stretch of river for fishing, the 300-year-old mill features a restaurant and 'Meadow Bar' which are separated by the old mill wheel. Set in the old mill house, the restaurant seats 80 with seven water-view tables from which to enjoy a set lunch (£10.50), a set dinner (£17.50) or à la carte meals for £15–£25. The accommodation is in simple, individually styled bedrooms with views over the mill pond and surrounding acres of peaceful water meadows. On arrival at the reception lobby, guests may be fascinated (unnerved, even) by the presence of the mummified remains of a cat, which was supposed, in ancient times, to ward off evil spirits. The atmosphere of the mill is enhanced during the colder months by two roaring log fires in the day rooms. The hotel can cater for disabled visitors but there are no special facilities.
Many interesting walks; excellent coarse fishing (prior notice required); golf (two miles away); many antique shops

SURLINGHAM

Coldham Hall Tavern, Surlingham, nr Norwich, Norfolk
NR14 7AN   (Tel. 05088 591)
From Surlingham village follow signs for Coldham Hall
Open 11.30am–2.30pm and 6.30–11pm
No one knows the exact age of the Coldham Hall Tavern, but that matters little when you have a location as special as this.

The broad River Yare sweeps past the pub, between tree-lined banks, and from the pub's well-kept gardens and large patio there are impressive river views. There are also moorings, and inside the pub are open fires, a family room and a good standard of food. The bar meals range from simple sandwiches to Norfolk duck, while the newly opened restaurant mixes French cuisine with traditional English fish and steak dishes, and specialities such as the Spanish-based Lamb Segovia (food is available from noon–2pm, and 6.30–10.30pm, every day). Easy access for disabled visitors.

Riverside walks, bird sanctuary, nature reserve

SUTTON

The Anchor, Sutton, Ely, Cambridgeshire CB6 2BD
(Tel. 0353 778537)
Off the B1381
Open noon–2.30pm, 6.30pm–11pm Mon–Sat; noon–2.30pm, 7pm–10.30pm Sun

This 350-year-old inn is very much a winter pub, though well worth a visit in summer too. From the banks of the river at the Anchor, the views are exhilarating and it is an understandably popular spot with knowledgeable bird watchers as thousands of swans congregate in the surrounding flooded fens between November and February. The pub is spacious and simple yet traditional and homely, with log fires for cold, winter days. The landlord is most welcoming and enthusiastic about the locality, and very committed. There are no less than four bars, three of which are right on the water. There is an outdoor patio with seating and a very good bar menu offering fresh seafood, daily specialities and vegetarian meals. Three courses cost £11–£12. Beers include Tolly bitter. The Anchor has specially adapted disabled toilets and wide doorways to public areas.

Walking; ice skating in winter when shallow meadow waters freeze; fishing; very good bird watching (bird sanctuary nearby); Ely and Cambridge nearby

TAPLOW

Cliveden, Taplow, Maidenhead, Berkshire SL6 0JF
(Tel. 0628 668561)
On B476, two miles north of Taplow
Open all year
From £215 double or twin b&b
In a superb position above the Thames, set in 375 acres of garden and woodland, Cliveden qualifies as quite the grandest of grand hotels. The house, designed by Sir Charles Barry, dates from 1851, and was formerly the home of the Astors. Those with long memories will recall Cliveden's period of notoriety in the 1960s, and the startling reports of goings-on which filled our daily papers. After some years of service as the English outpost of California's Stanford University, Cliveden was converted into a luxurious hotel. There are two restaurants, both open to non-residents: the Terrace seats 70, all tables have a view of the river, lunch costs £21.50 (£31.50 at weekends), and dinner around £50 a head; Waldo's presents modern cuisine, boasts a Michelin star, and serves dinner only (£47 for four courses). The atmosphere is that of a country house, gracious and leisured, with palatial public rooms. A lift operates to bedrooms on the first floor, making them accessible for disabled visitors. The extensive grounds contain formal gardens, woodland walks within sight of the Thames, a water garden, masses of rhododendrons, pavilions, temples, statuary and a small grassy dell, once an open-air theatre where, on 1 August 1740, Thomas Arne's masque, *Alfred*, had its first performance, its finale introducing that patriotic number, 'Rule Britannia'.

Facilities include indoor and outdoor pools and tennis courts, saunas, steam rooms, treatment rooms, gymnasium, squash, badminton and snooker. Fishing (free for residents). Walking and riding on the estate, boating on the Thames

TEYNHAM

🍺 ⛺ 🔥 🍴 ▭

The Ship Inn and Smugglers Restaurant, Conyer Quay,
Teynham, Sittingbourne, Kent ME9 9HJ   (Tel. 0795 521404)
From Teynham, take signs to Conyer
Open 11am–3pm, 6pm–11pm Mon–Sat; noon–3pm, 7pm–
10.30pm Sun
A white-painted pub by a busy, working harbour with any
amount of history. The pub's interior, although somewhat
cramped, is convincingly decked out as a stone-walled
smugglers' tavern: strange dummies lurk silently in odd
corners; canvas-wrapped parcels are stacked on shelves;
silhouettes of furtive men and sailing ships stand poised against
the windows; and fishing nets hang from the ceiling. The
highly original nature of the pub's decor tends to obscure much
of the water view, but a small garden faces the boats on the
harbour water. The bar and restaurant bar have an extensive
snack menu including fresh oysters and fish daily. A full à la
carte restaurant meal costs in the region of £18 (open noon–
2.30pm, 7pm–10.30pm Mon–Sat; noon–3pm, 7pm–10pm
Sun). The pub's real speciality is the quantity of unusual drinks
on offer: there are nearly 160 wines, 250 whiskies (including
175 malts), 150 liqueurs and 50 brandies and rums. There is
also an extensive range of beers and lagers. Children are
admitted to the restaurant only; dogs to the bar only. The pub
can cater for the disabled but there are no special facilities.
*Saxon Shore Way walks; fishing; trout farm nearby; Sittingbourne
sports complex; on-site Ship's Library for purchase, exchange and
reference*

THAMES DITTON

🍺 ⛺ 🔥 🍴 ▭

The Albany Inn, Queens Road, Thames Ditton, Surrey
KP7 0QY   (Tel. 081-398 7031)
Open 11am–3pm, 5.30pm–11pm Mon–Thurs; 11am–11pm,
Fri and Sat; 7pm–10.30pm Sun
This large 1890s pub, originally built for the Duke of Albany's

paramour, has a spicy history and sits directly on the Thames riverbank with spacious car parking and extensive riverside terrace and garden seating. The roomy Victorian interior features a circular bar and predominantly dark-wood furnishings; there are excellent views across the Thames and to distant Hampton Court with its green expanse of grounds, river banks and boating. The pub lunches include a cold buffet and hot meals such as chicken in tarragon and mushroom, hot-pots and steak and kidney pie; price range £2.05 to £4.50. Real ales include Bass, Worthington's and Charrington's IPA.

Walking; boats for hire at Hampton Court; river trips to Kingston and London; skiff and punting club; fishing in Albany Reach

TITCHWELL

🏠 2/18 🏘 🔥 ♦ 🛏

Titchwell Manor, Titchwell, King's Lynn, Norfolk PE36 8BB (Tel. 0485 210221)
On the main A149 coast road
£31–£38 pp b&b

Formerly a manor house, this traditional hotel provides roaring log fires in winter and a warm and friendly family welcome. Set back from the main road and overlooking the Norfolk marshes and the sea beyond, the hotel has recently undergone a commendable facelift and now offers guests a comfortable, homely, Laura Ashley-style environment. Lunchtime bar snacks are available in the smaller dining area and the two restaurants (one of which has an attractive aspect over the salt marshes and sea) serve table d'hôte and à la carte meals with dinner priced at around £15.95. During the summer months, guests are invited to sit out in the pretty, walled rear garden adjoining one of the restaurants. The hotel has four ground-floor rooms and wide-access bathrooms which may be suitable for the disabled.

Walking; windsurfing (at Brancaster Staithe two miles away); sailing; fishing can be arranged by the hotel; boat trips; nearby beaches; golf courses; cycle hire; bird watching (Titchwen Bird Reserve opposite the hotel)

UPSTREET

The Grove Ferry Inn, Grove Ferry, Upstreet, nr Canterbury,
Kent CT3 4BP   (Tel. 022786 302)
Off the A28 east of Upstreet
Open 11am–11pm Mon–Sat; noon–9.30pm Sun May–
September (11am–3pm, 7pm–11pm Mon–Sat; noon–3pm,
7pm–10.30 pm Sun in winter)
The marvellously traditional and varied Grove Ferry Inn has
three bars and gardens and two of each enjoy an appealing
situation beside the River Stour. To the rear of the inn, a long
stretch of landscaped river frontage has outdoor summer
seating for at least 100 people, plus a beer garden shaded by a
canopy of trees. Tastefully and warmly illuminated both in and
out, the hotel is particularly attractive at night when the dozens
of copper bells, pots, kettles and even coal scuttles suspended
from the ceiling gleam amid the richly traditional decor. Beers
served include Director's and the pub's own label 'Ferryman's', and there is an extensive restaurant menu with many
daily specials. Food is substantial and English, with mixed
grills, steaks, fish, chicken and various hot and cold snacks
ranging from £3.95 to £10.95 per dish. Afternoon teas and
children's meals are also available. Additional facilities include
a 90-seat family room. The pub can cater for the disabled but
there are no special facilities.
*Walks through 11-acre picnic site nearby; Saxon Way (one-week
walk from Dover to Medway); Stodmarsh Nature Reserve (three
miles away); hourly river boat trips from pub; rowing; cabin cruising;
fishing (day tickets available from bailiff)*

WADHURST

Newbarn, Wards Lane, Wadhurst, East Sussex TN5 6HP
(Tel. 089288 2042)
Signposted from the B2099, the Wadhurst to Ticehurst road
£18–£20 pp b&b; self-catering cottages per week £81–£278
(sleeps two), £265–£408 (sleeps four–five)

A secluded, 17th-century farmhouse in a tremendous water-side setting. There is a pond to one side of the house, and in front of it 15 acres of landscaped gardens descend to the edge of Bewl Water – a vast man-made lake – which is the largest stretch of water in the south-east and has a good 17-mile walk round the circumference. The excellent views of the blue lake below and hills beyond can be enjoyed from both the ground and first floors of the hotel. The light decor in the bedrooms complements the old pine floors and low ceiling beams. An intimate dining room overlooks the water and seats six for breakfast only. 'Carter's Cottage' and 'The Hopper's Hut', two very attractive self-catering cottages, offer a good aspect over Bewl Water, and feature homely log-burning stoves and comfortable furnishings. Additional amenities include a games room with table tennis, pool and darts.

Walks around the circumference of Bewl Water; National Trust houses and gardens nearby; bicycles on loan; boat cruises; wind-surfing; canoeing; rowing from Bewl Water Visitors Centre (on the A21, 20 minutes away); trout fishery; riding can be arranged

WALBERSWICK

inn ⅝ 🏠 ♨ 🕊 🚗

The Bell Hotel, Ferry Road, Walberswick, Suffolk
IP18 6TN (Tel. 0502 723109)
Drive through village and turn left towards river
Closed during Christmas week
From £22 pp b&b

This 14th-century inn is on two waterfronts, and all its rooms look out on either the River Blyth or the sea. Walberswick is an intriguing mix of English village, fishing community and artists' retreat. The Bell has an inglenook with wood-burning stove, old flagstone floors, original timber beams and an unusual feature: a separate darts room. There is also a children's room, and more room for them to play on the large lawn outside. Food tends to be homely and hearty, and sugar-baked Suffolk ham in cider has long been a favourite, along

with fresh local fish, fisherman's pie, crab, scampi and just about anything else trawled from this delightful part of the Suffolk coast (food is available Monday–Saturday, from noon–2pm in the bar, and from 7–9pm in the restaurant). Two rooms are on the ground floor, with access for the disabled.
Boating, fishing, golf, beach, walks (nature reserve nearby)

WALTON-ON-THAMES

The Swan, 50 Manor Road, Walton-on-Thames, Surrey
KT12 2PF   (Tel. 0932 225964)
Open 11am–3pm, 5.30pm–11pm Mon–Fri; 11am–11pm Sat;
noon–3pm, 7pm–10.30pm Sun
This Victorian, white-painted pub boasts a spacious interior and a large attractive garden leading down to the road by the River Thames. Its peaceful and relaxing location offers views across the river to the facing houses and boats moored at the river bank. Summer barbecues take place in the illuminated garden (private barbecues can be arranged on request). The pub interior may seem a little bland as the copper ornaments and horse brasses are somewhat dwarfed by the enormous rooms, but it is worth a visit for the roast Sunday lunch, (reasonably priced at £6.95), or the considerable range of bar meals served daily (between noon and 3pm and 6pm and 9pm) at less than £10. The Swan serves Young's traditional beers. A separate cottage is available for private luncheons, meetings or seminars.
Walks along river; fishing (bring equipment); boat hire next door; two marinas nearby; public moorings for 10 boats

WANSFORD

The Haydock Hotel, Wansford, Peterborough PE8 6JA
(Tel. 0780 782223)
Signposted from the A1 and A47 near Peterborough
£70 single, £90–£99 double, £110–£125 four-poster b&b
Restaurant open noon–2.30pm, 7pm–10pm

A gracious, golden stone-built coaching inn, dating back to the 17th century, on the edge of the River Nene. Despite its proximity to the A1 and A47, Wansford remains a peaceful village and provides an idyllic setting for a relaxing stay. The flagstoned entry hall, with antique seats and longcase clock, sets the scene for the gracious and plush atmosphere of the hotel. The restaurant seats 95 people, is open to non-residents and offers mainly English cuisine, with dinner à la carte costing £18.50. The hotel counts two lounges (one of which is the setting for informal buffets at mealtimes), bar meals from 7.30pm to 10.30pm and a lovely, formal garden among its many other attractions. The new Orchard Room, where bar snacks are served all day, has recently opened. Bed and breakfast rates include early morning tea or coffee and morning papers. One *en suite* bedroom and a bathroom near the public areas are specially fitted for the disabled.

Walks; watersports at Ferry Meadows (five miles away); fishing (rod licence needed, available from the Anglian Water Authority in Oundle); pétanque courts; cricket field in hotel grounds; clay pigeon shooting can be arranged

WINDSOR

54/92

Oakley Court Hotel, Windsor Road, Water Oakley, Windsor, Berkshire SL4 5UR   (Tel. 0628 74141)
Off the A308 between Windsor and Maidenhead
£125 single, £145 double, £350 suite
With 35 acres of mature grounds reaching to the bank of the River Thames, this imposing Victorian Gothic mansion offers plush, though slightly characterless, rooms in keeping with the building's historic background. Day rooms include an original library, yellow and white river-view drawing room with ornate plasterwork, and billiards room complete with 300-year-old table. Primarily suited to private functions and corporate entertainment, the hotel boasts conference, banqueting and exhibition facilities for between four and 100 people, plus organized activity events for larger groups by prior arrangement. The 120-seat Oakleaf restaurant offers four

water-view tables and highly reputed modern French cuisine (set lunch £19, set dinner £29). Three-course lunches à la carte cost about £25 and a full vegetarian menu is available.

Walking; fishing (hotel has own rights on river); archery, clay pigeon shooting, rally driving, hot-air ballooning and other group activities by arrangement; croquet lawn; heliport; riding nearby; nine-hole golf course; jogging track; punting

WINDSOR

Sir Christopher Wren's House, Thames Street, Windsor, Berkshire SL4 1PX   (Tel. 0753 861354)
On riverside at Windsor–Eton bridge
£85–£90 single, £110 double; breakfast £6.50–£8.50
In keeping with its architectural appearance, this medium-sized hotel has tastefully decorated day rooms furnished with antiques, including a soothing lounge with a splendid marble fireplace. As its name suggests, the house was originally designed and inhabited by Sir Christopher Wren in 1676 during his period as Member of Parliament for Windsor and it has a fascinating historical background complete with resident ghost. The river is clearly visible from many bedrooms (three superior rooms have riverside balconies) and 30 window seats in the 75–120-cover restaurant. Guests can select from a reasonable range of meals à la carte or opt for the table d'hôte lunch and dinner at £16.50 and £21. During the summer months (from June until the weather becomes chilly) the hotel opens its additional river-view terrace restaurant. There is limited private parking and the hotel is not suitable for the disabled.

Walking; watersports; fishing; golf nearby; riding can be arranged

WOLVERCOTE

⊟ 🏠 ♨ ⬦ ▭

The Trout Inn, 195 Godstow Road, Wolvercote, Oxford
OX2 8PN   (Tel. 0865 54485)
Off the A40 north of Oxford (call for precise directions)
Open 11am–11pm Mon–Sat; noon–3pm, 7pm–10.30pm Sun.
Restaurant open noon–2pm Mon–Sun; 7pm–10pm
Mon–Sat
This very pretty and highly traditional Bass Charrington
'Vintage Inn' spurns jukeboxes and games machines to
preserve its idyllic and tranquil waterside setting beside the
River Thames: peacocks wander along the river terrace and
boats moor alongstream. There are no less than five bars, four
of which overlook the water, including the original 800-year-
old 'Stable Bar'. The restaurant offers tantalizing dishes such as
jugged venison braised with vegetables, bacon and red wine
(£12.65). Three-course meals average £20 and a variety of
salads and grills, plus vegetarian meals (on request), are
available. In the snack bar, prices range from £2.70–£6 with
barbecues and an outdoor Pimms and champagne bar at
evenings and weekends during summer. Drinks offered
include a good selection of wines, malt whiskies and real live
bitters; Bass Charrington's IPA. Additional attractions include
function rooms, Christmas meals and an annual firework
display on the inn's own river island. The inn is accessible to
the disabled and an advance telephone call assures personal
assistance from the helpful staff.
Walking; fish sanctuary

WROXHAM

🏠 8/18 🏠 ♨ ⬦ ▭

Hotel Wroxham, Broads Centre, Hoveton, Wroxham,
Norfolk NR12 8AJ   (Tel. 0603 782061)
£30–£45 single, £58–£72 double b&b
The town of Wroxham, considered to be at the centre of the
Norfolk Broads, is a busy, major crossing point for both roads

and waterways and this modern hotel, which forms part of a shopping centre, is right on the water's edge. From many bedrooms and the restaurant, the hotel overlooks a local gathering point for boats and boat enthusiasts. Welcoming non-resident bookings, the restaurant offers a wide selection of à la carte meals, a carvery lunch for £4.75 and three-course carvery dinner at £10.50. For £19.50 both residents and non-residents can dance the night away to popular live music at the hotel's Saturday dinner dances. The hotel may be accessible for the disabled: it has ground-floor bathroom facilities and wide doorways.

Walking; boating (self-drive launch, £10.50); fishing from the quay (rod licence available locally, £2)

YALDING

inn 8/8

The Anchor Inn, Twyford Bridge, Yalding, Kent ME18 6HG (Tel. 0622 814359)
Off the A26, the Maidstone to Tonbridge Road
Open 10.30am–11pm Mon–Sat; noon–3pm, 7pm–10.30pm Sun
£25–£35 single, £40–£55 double b&b

A coaching inn in distant times, the Anchor became a bargees' inn when the Hampstead canal was cut in 1744, and was extended into a hotel 200 years later. It is placed at the point where the canal joins the River Medway, and so benefits from a double water frontage. The long canalside garden borders two sides of the inn. The ancient, thatched part of the pub is highly atmospheric, with ceilings that are disconcertingly low for the taller visitor (hence the doorway sign reading 'Duck or Grouse'), old timbers, crooked walls and exceptionally solid, traditional furniture. Good bar meals are available until 10pm daily and three of the inn's bars overlook either the canal or the river, as do eight of the modern, airy bedrooms. The steakhouse restaurant seats 33 and offers three-course meals for around £15 (open from 8.30am–midnight). Drinks in the bars include real ales, Webster's, Ruddles and John Courage best bitter.

Walks in fields and along Medway; canoeing and boating (boatyards nearby); fishing in season on canal and River Medway (rod licence from tackle shops)

The Isle of Wight

BEMBRIDGE

inn ¹/₅ 🏕 🐾 🚭 ▭

Crab and Lobster, Forelands, Bembridge, Isle of Wight
PO35 5TR   (Tel. 0983 872244)
Open 10.30am–3pm, 6pm–11pm Mon–Sat in summer (11am–
3pm, 6.30pm–11pm Mon–Sat in winter); noon–3pm, 7pm–
10.30pm Sun. Closed November–Easter
£14–£16 pp b&b
This old country inn, dating from the early 19th century, is
situated in a unique clifftop position with panoramic views
over the Solent and the Channel. The two bars and restaurant
all sport the same nautical theme with an interesting array of
prints covering the walls. The timber and brick interiors of the
bar are complemented by pretty, cottage-style decor and
comfortable period furnishings. Low lighting creates a warm
atmosphere with a lively ambience, and a wide range of beers,

ciders, wines and spirits is available. There is also an excellent choice of bar snacks on offer. The leaded bay window in the dining room affords some spectacular views and it is here that one can take advantage of the fresh seafood on the evening à la carte menu; main courses cost from £7.50–£11. The comfortable bed and breakfast accommodation offers perhaps the best value for money on the island. Very friendly staff.
Walking; watersports; fishing; beach; riding; fishing trips; harbour

BONCHURCH

5/10

Peacock Vane, Bonchurch, Ventnor, Isle of Wight PO38 1RJ (Tel. 0983 852019)
£50 single, £85 double b&b
Peacock Vane is a charming house of outstanding character in a lush green setting, set among willow and beech trees and surrounded by beautifully landscaped gardens. While the style may not be to everyone's taste, the elegance found throughout the rooms is undeniable. The owners have completely refurbished and carefully restored the entire hotel; the decor and furnishings reflect the grandeur of the Victorian era. There is a conservatory, where tea, coffee and snacks are served. The formal Directors' dining room seats 16 people round the large oval table with a low-hung chandelier. The larger Ivory Room restaurant (open to non-residents) is elegant and the cuisine already has a good reputation (four-course set dinner £11.95). The individually designed bedrooms all sport period paintings and antique furniture, tasteful decor and fully equipped *en suite* facilities that offer the height of luxury. In the drawing room again antiques and plush furnishings abound but despite the rich elegance, an air of relaxed cosiness reigns. The charming staff work with dedication and pride, courtesy and attention. Dogs can be accommodated by arrangement.
Walks on Ventnor Downs; surfing; fishing; beach; golf can be arranged

BONCHURCH

🏨 12/19 🏠 ♨ 🌙 💳

Winterbourne Hotel, Bonchurch, Ventnor, Isle of Wight
PO38 1RQ   (Tel. 0983 852535)
Closed November–March
£45–£59 pp b&b

Winterbourne was home for Charles Dickens when writing
David Copperfield. In a letter to his wife, he described the house
and grounds as '. . . the prettiest place I ever saw in my life . . .'
It is a country house of considerable charm and character
combining an air of tranquillity with a good standard of
comfort. Set in beautiful grounds with extensive, well-tended
lawns and gardens, waterfalls, streams and a swimming pool,
it overlooks some remarkable coastline and the sea. The
spacious rooms are stylishly furnished and decorated, with all
conveniences provided and many concessions to comfort. The
romantic restaurant has an excellent reputation and uses fresh
local produce (three-course set meal, £19). A comprehensive
wine list is also available. These splendid surroundings create a
serene but informal atmosphere which is serviced by a genial
host and friendly staff. There is a ground-floor bedroom, but
no specific facilities for the disabled.
*Walking; watersports; beach; tennis; golf; riding and fishing can be
arranged*

CHALE

🏨 7/14 🏠 ♨ 🌙 💳

Clarendon Hotel and Wight Mouse Inn, Chale, Isle of Wight
PO38 2HA   (Tel. 0983 730431)
£30–£35 dinner and b&b

The Clarendon Hotel was once a coaching inn. Dating from
the 17th century, it maintains an air of antiquity, character and
charm and now provides excellent hospitality, with good
standards of comfort, a wide range of food and wine and a
selection of 365 whiskies. A five-course set meal costs about
£15, and there is a wide variety of bar snacks available. The
friendly, helpful and attentive staff are headed by the

proprietor, John Bradshaw, whose dedication and creativity won the establishment the award the Egon Ronay/Coca-Cola Best Family Pub of the Year in 1990. This was well deserved: there are good play areas and facilities for children both inside and out, and an impressive children's menu. The bedrooms are charmingly furnished with antique and period furniture. Home-from-home touches and fine paintings and prints set these rooms apart. The hotel dining room, with wonderful views of the sea, is comfortable and tasteful; a tremendous collection of English watercolours adorns the walls. The hotel and pub also offer a minibus service, available at special rates for ferry collection and island tours.

Walking; watersports on nearby beaches; fishing; trout farm nearby; beach; shooting and riding can be arranged

COWES

🍽 🏠 ♿ ⌖ 💳

Fastnet Restaurant, 124 High Street, Cowes, Isle of Wight PO31 7AY   (Tel. 0983 299251)
Open 10am–2.30pm, 7pm–10pm Mon–Sun

The Fastnet Restaurant is situated on Cowes High Street facing the working marina and with views of the Solent. It is a long, narrow space but the simple, bright white decor and furnishings make it airy and light. The large front windows give panoramic views and lead on to the summer terrace where many of the rich and famous have dined while watching the thriving activity and the yacht races. Main courses cost from £13–£15. Obviously, it gets very busy in and around Cowes Week, so booking is essential. The restaurant has an enviable reputation for serving fresh, local produce, cooked by the continentally trained chef. A comfortable and informal place with a convivial atmosphere generated by the friendly and good-natured staff. Accessible to wheelchairs, but no special facilities for the disabled.

Walking; watersports; fishing; beach

COWES

The Globe, The Parade, Cowes, Isle of Wight PO31 7QJ
(Tel 0983 293005)
Open 11am–11pm (10.30pm Sun) in summer; 11am–3pm,
6.30pm–11pm (10.30pm Sun) in winter
This attractive pub is located on the seafront of Cowes next to
the working marina. The decor and furnishings are simple,
stylish and elegant but with a relaxed, leisurely atmosphere
throughout. The extensive menu caters for all palates and
purses, from bar snacks through to full meals with much
fresh, local produce, and a good variety of vegetarian options.
The two bars are divided into eating and drinking areas and
there is a very agreeable conservatory (non-smoking). A
wrought-iron spiral staircase leads from the dining area to the
upper floor where private functions are held. The views across
the Solent to the mainland are really quite spectacular,
especially when the boat races are underway. Friendly and
helpful staff make for an enjoyable visit.
Walking; watersports; fishing; beach

COWES

The New Holmwood Hotel, Queens Road, Cowes, Isle of
Wight PO31 8BW   (Tel. 0983 292508)
Restaurant open 12.30pm–2pm, 7pm–9pm
£75–£85 double, £100 suite b&b
A unique and lovely location on the quieter side of Cowes,
right by the water's edge and Egypt Point, affords this
hotel some panoramic views of the Solent and a wonderful
vantage point for sunsets. The new proprietors have refurbished both the hotel and restaurant in elegant style using
comfortable furniture and some beautiful furnishings and
fabrics. The restaurant specializes in seafood; the set dinner
costs £13.50. They've managed to keep the hotel's charm and
character, and also the helpful and friendly staff. Bedrooms are

individually decorated, and the luxurious *en suite* bathrooms are something to write home about. The charming and relaxing restaurant is tastefully decorated in subdued pastel tones, and the views are magnificent. Following the completion of their extensive refurbishment programme, the hotel now has a sun terrace with heated pool and spa bath, three elegant lounges, a cocktail bar and conference facilities. Two rooms adapted for the disabled.

Walking; watersports; fishing; beach; private moorings; sailing; tennis court nearby

FRESHWATER BAY

Farringford Hotel, Freshwater Bay, Isle of Wight PO40 9PE (Tel. 0983 752500)
£25–£40 pp b&b

A gracious country house, once the home of Alfred Lord Tennyson, the Farringford is steeped in history. It stands in 33 acres of beautiful parklands and gardens, from which there are sweeping views of the bays and peninsulas of the island. With views of the sea on one side, the hotel adjoins approximately 100 acres of National Trust downland on the other. Each of the attractive and spacious rooms is traditionally furnished and decorated, with private bathroom, radio, television and direct-dial telephone. The large, elegant restaurant offers table d'hôte and à la carte menus making use of locally caught fish, island-grown vegetables and fresh farm produce (open 12.30pm to 2pm, and 7.30pm to 9.30pm; prices from £13.50 for a four-course meal). Candlelit dinner dances are very popular on Saturday nights. The views of the downs and golf course from the cocktail bar and the Tennyson drawing room are really quite spectacular. Mementoes of the famous poet are on display in the library.

Nine-hole golf course; tennis court; croquet lawn; bowling green; games room in hotel; walking; windsurfing; sea fishing at Yarmouth; beach

NITON

Buddle Inn, St Catherine's Road, Niton, Isle of Wight
(Tel. 0983 730243)
Open 11am–11pm Mon–Sat in summer (11am–3pm, 6pm–
11pm Mon–Thurs in winter); noon–2.30pm, 7pm–10.30pm
Sun
Situated on the southernmost point of the island, this old
smugglers' pub is a delightful collection of recently refurbished
16th-century buildings surrounding a central garden. It still
retains many of its original features including the flagstone
flooring and inglenook fireplace. Both the bars sport low-
beamed ceilings and rustic furniture; the atmosphere is cosy,
and locals and tourists can enjoy darts, pool and occasionally
live music. There is a good choice of food on offer including
ploughman's, salads and a variety of specials using the fresh
seafood. Morning coffee, afternoon tea, snacks and cakes are
available throughout the day during summer. There are good
parking facilities and coach parties are welcome.
*Walking; fishing; beach; watersports (four miles away); Morris
dancers on terrace on Wednesdays during the summer*

RYDE

18/75

Royal Esplanade Hotel, Esplanade, Ryde, Isle of Wight
PO33 2ED   (Tel. 0983 62549)
From £25 pp b&b
Built in 1837, the Royal Esplanade offers good, old-fashioned
sea-front grandeur. The ground floor has been refurbished,
with the slightly dated elegance replaced with new silk screens,
plush fabrics and stylish furnishings. However, thanks to the
dedicated staff, none of the comfortable and homely atmosphere has been lost. The hotel's amenities include a heated
outdoor swimming pool for the summer months, situated in a
lovely palmed terrace garden. Four-course meals in the
restaurant cost about £10.50. The bedrooms are spacious and

comfortable; those at the front of the hotel are particularly attractive. Local beers are on offer at the bar. The lounge and bar areas have plenty of quiet character, and comfortable furniture. Although a listed building of some historical and architectural interest, this hotel still attains the same high standards expected of modern-day establishments.

Outdoor swimming pool; windsurfing (and tuition) nearby; golf; squash; tennis courts; equestrian centre; steam railway; ice rink nearby

SEAVIEW

IOI 🏠 🍸 ⌀ 💳

The Old Fort, Esplanade, Seaview, Isle of Wight PO34 5HB (Tel. 0983 612363)
Restaurant open 7pm–10pm and Sunday lunchtime; closed Sun evenings and Mon in winter
Pub open 11am–11pm Mon–Sat; noon–3pm, 7pm–10.30pm Sun

Once a terrace of three cottages dating from the late 19th century, the Old Fort occupies a wonderful position right on the end of Seaview's esplanade, by the sea. Like many of the island's pubs, hotels and restaurants, the views are particularly impressive. This is a café, pub and restaurant, the latter on the upper floor; main courses in the restaurant cost from £7 to £14. The café and pub boast a large menu that offers a selection of meals including vegetarian, hot and cold dishes, with much of the emphasis being on the locally caught seafood. There is also a good children's menu available. The friendly staff generate a comfortable atmosphere that is enlivened by the occasional theme nights and the pianist on Friday nights. The restaurant upstairs has a more formal environment. The stylish furnishings, complementing the panoramic views of the sea, make a visit here something special. There is disabled access to the pub, but not to the restaurant.

Walking; watersports (just yards way); fishing; beach; sailing; golf nearby

SHORWELL

⊡ ⌂ ⚡ ◇ ▱

The Crown Inn, Walker's Lane, Shorwell, Isle of Wight
PO30 3JZ   (Tel. 0983 740293)
Open 10.30pm–3pm, 6pm–10pm Mon–Sat; noon–3pm, 7pm–
10.30pm Sun
In the exceptionally pretty village of Shorwell, this pub, dating
from the early 15th century, was once a staging post. It is
located in the heart of some truly historic sites with good access
to all the other facilities on the island. The trout stream running
through the charming, well-tended gardens plays host to a
variety of wildlife including a flock of ducks. There is also a
good play area for children. The intimate interior, with its
low-beamed bars and welcoming log fires, is comfortably
furnished with good facilities for families. A varied menu,
including vegetarian dishes, offers value for money with all
food made from fresh, local produce on the premises.
The staff pay attention to comfort and detail which helps to
make the Crown Inn a perfect pitstop.
Walking; fishing at trout farm down the road; beach 10 minutes away

ST LAWRENCE

▦ 25/37 ⌂ ⚡ ◇ ▭

Old Park Hotel, St Lawrence, Ventnor, Isle of Wight
PO38 1XS   (Tel. 0983 852583)
Closed November–March, though open over Christmas
£32.50–£48 pp dinner and b&b
Old Park was once a small farm dwelling but over the years it
has been enlarged and is now an imposing, Gothic-style grade
II listed house. Away from the main road, it is set in
magnificent woodland with extensive grounds that reach to
the sea. The decor and furnishings in the public areas reflect the
grandeur and status of the house with chandeliers, heavy oak
doors and gilt-edged mirrors in the comfortable lounge. The
beamed bar area is well stocked and there is also a coffee shop
open throughout the day serving light snacks. The spacious

restaurant is simply but comfortably decorated and the managers pride themselves on being able to cater for special diets. The family suites are one of the hotel's strongest points. The rooms in the west wing (more luxurious than those in the annexe) have recently been refurbished and many boast William Morris-design wallpaper and antique brass bedsteads. Some ground-floor rooms are suitable for disabled visitors.

Fully equipped leisure centre at hotel; popular tropical bird park; ornithology and murder mystery speciality weekends; walking; fishing; beach

TOTLAND

Waterfront Restaurant, The Promenade, Totland Bay, Isle of Wight PO39 0BQ   (Tel. 0983 754130)
Restaurant open noon–2pm, 6pm–10pm Mon–Sat;
12.30pm–10pm Sun. Café open 11am–10pm

Not the best-looking building on the island, but talk to anyone and they'll recommend the food. The Anglo-French specials created from the fresh, local produce have an outstanding reputation. The dining area is pretty if simple but it provides an excellent vantage point from which to watch the passing of the famous cruise liners and spectacular sunsets over this action-packed bay. It is a lively venue serviced by jovial staff and, due to its popularity, it really is essential to book in advance. The adjoining café serves coffee, tea, ice-cream and a selection of snacks. It also provides a take-away service. The restaurant is not accessible to disabled visitors.

Walking; jetskiing, waterskiing and surfing; fishing; safe beach

VENTNOR

The Spyglass Inn, Esplanade, Ventnor, Isle of Wight
PO38 1JX   (Tel. 0983 855338)
Open 11am–11pm Mon–Sat in summer (11am–3pm, 7pm–11pm Mon–Sat in winter); 11am–3pm, 7pm–10.30pm Sun

Ventnor is reputed to be the mildest and most protected resort on the island, and The Spyglass Inn sits at the end of this famous fishing cove with its own seawall and terraces. The building used to be the saltwater bathhouse and, with the aid of sympathetic refurbishment, the venue still boasts many of its original features. There is the obligatory nautical and sailing theme to its decor and furnishings, but take some time here. It is packed with fascinating pictures and wonderful antiques that set off the timbered interior perfectly. In summer, the terraces become a hive of activity as the live entertainment gets into swing with varied music – usually traditional jazz and blues, and a pianist plays every weekend. An extensive menu ranges from ploughman's and burgers to fresh, locally caught crab and lobster (which you can watch being brought up the seawall to the inn). The pub serves its own real ale and offers morning coffee and – at weekends – candlelit dinners, making everyone, young or old, most welcome. There is wheelchair access to the pub.
Walking; Victorian boats for hire; fishing; beach

WHIPPINGHAM

IOI 🏠 🍴 🐾 🛏

Barton Manor Vineyard and Gardens, Whippingham, Isle of Wight PO32 6LB   (Tel. 0983 292835)
Open 10.30am–5.30pm daily (1 May to second Sun in October); weekends in April; Easter holidays
Although the £2.50 entrance fee to this wine bar and café may seem a little steep – even if Princess Margaret has eaten there – the price of admission for Barton Manor is money well spent. Visitors gain access to the vineyards, the beautiful and extensive gardens and the award-winning restoration of Prince Albert's farm buildings that house the winery, and, of course, the wine bar. The wine bar offers a basic menu of excellent quality and sells English wine produced on the premises. The proprietor is keen to emphasize that their English wine is very different from 'British' wine. The lawns and gardens are beautiful and lovingly tended, boasting fabulous daffodil

displays in spring, an outstanding water garden, a scented garden and the NCCPG's National Collection of 'Red Hot Pokers'. And, lest we forget the manor's justification for being included in these listings, there is a delightful lily-covered lake, home to a variety of wildlife including some stunning black swans. Just a stone's throw from Osborne House, Barton Manor is well worth a visit.

WHIPPINGHAM

🍽 🏠 ♿ ◁ ▭

The Folly Inn, Folly Lane, Whippingham, Isle of Wight (Tel. 0983 297171)
Open 11am–3pm, 6pm–11pm every day (and longer in summer)
An extensive chalet-style building on the side of the Medina estuary, just south-east of Cowes. Simple, rustic furniture creates an atmosphere that is relaxed, informal and lively. The wood-panelled decor is teamed with cottage-style furnishings making the large areas more intimate and comfortable. Views of the boating and yachting fraternity on the estuary are fascinating: it's always a hive of activity down there. An excellent family room with games caters for children. The menu is kept simple but maintains a high quality and offers good value for money. The large terrace and garden provide ample seating to accommodate the summer crowds. The pub has its own moorings and pontoons with a water taxi service to and from the jetty adjoining the pub. There are 'music nights' five times a week in summer. Whippingham is a conservation area with a vast array of wildlife, all of which can be viewed from the pub itself. Good parking facilities are available. The Inn can cater for the disabled but has no special facilities.
Walks to Newport marina; sailing nearby; fishing

WHIPPINGHAM

Padmore House Hotel, Whippingham, East Cowes, Isle of Wight PO32 6LP   (Tel. 0983 293210)
Closed 24–30 December
£34–£45 single, £67–£69 double b&b
The hamlet of Whippingham is famous for its church, designed by Prince Albert. Padmore House is situated next to it, overlooking the river and Medina valley. It is a charming and elegant ivy-covered building with a Jacobean elevation to the rear and Queen Anne-style architecture at the front. The grounds extend to five acres and incorporate formal lawns, flowerbeds and paddocks. The house is decorated throughout in traditional, pretty, cottage-style fabrics and furnishings which create a relaxed environment. The wood panelling, period pieces and lace take you back to the more genteel ambience of days gone by. The restaurant is equally pretty and has a good reputation for the standard of its cuisine served by efficient and courteous staff: Sunday lunches are especially popular (£7.75 for three courses). The evidence on display in the lounge area of Queen Victoria's visits paints a fascinating picture.
Walking; sea fishing (two miles away); golf can be arranged

WOOTTON BRIDGE

The Sloop Inn, Wootton Bridge, Ryde, Isle of Wight PO33 4HS   (Tel. 0983 882544)
Open 11am–11pm Mon–Sat; noon–10.30pm Sun
The Sloop Inn is located very close to Fishbourne and the Portsmouth ferry. It combines eating and drinking areas served by friendly staff in a relaxed and informal atmosphere. The pub was converted from an old mill and is now one of Whitbread's Brewers Fayre chain. The large interior is attractively decorated and comfortably furnished with stylish fabrics and furnishings. Being part of a chain, the pub is able to

offer an extensive range of facilities including all those for the disabled, an excellent family room and also a mothers' room. The eating area looks out over the marina where there are public moorings and the development of extra facilities for the sailing set is in the pipeline. The menu is comprehensive, offering good value for money on their freshly prepared meals. There is wheelchair access and fully adapted lavatories for disabled visitors.

Walking; fishing nearby; beach

YARMOUTH

The Bugle Hotel, The Square, Yarmouth, Isle of Wight
(Tel. 0983 760272)
£40–£50 per room b&b

Once the distribution point for beer on the island, the Bugle boasts a 300-year history. Character and old-world charm are very much the key components to this simple but friendly hotel: nooks, crannies and winding corridors abound. The spacious bedrooms are simply but adequately furnished and decorated. All are comfortable. The beautiful, wood-panelled restaurant is elegant and intimate, serving food with an excellent reputation. The menu comprises seasonal dishes using fresh local produce and includes fish brought in daily. The two bar areas, with occasional live music, serve bar snacks and meals and offer good value for money. The wood-panelling and heavy beams create an intimate and cosy ambience with a lively atmosphere provided by the mix of tourists and locals. Much is made of the courtyard garden where barbecues are served daily throughout the summer. Also of note are the special spit roasts. Staff are charming, friendly and dedicated in the pursuit of improving standards and customer comfort.

Walking; fishing; beach; watersports

YARMOUTH

George Hotel, Quay Street, Yarmouth, Isle of Wight
PO41 0PE (Tel. 0983 760331)
Closed over Christmas (the bar stays open)
£22–£70 per room b&b
Situated directly on the seafront, this gracious 350-year-old house was once home to the governor of the Isle of Wight and boasts Charles II as one of its more famous guests. There are two bar areas that are elegant yet lively. The stylish pub is decorated and furnished with humour on a nautical theme. The dining areas are gracious and romantic, especially the conservatory. The food has a good reputation: menus are seasonal and varied, and specialize in fresh fish. The spacious rooms are full of character and charm with wood panelling, elegant antique furniture, tasteful decor, open fireplaces and home-from-home touches throughout. The pretty and well-tended garden looks out across the water and has the unusual features of its own lobster tank, from which one can choose supper, and an extensive barbecue area; the views are quite special too. A relaxed, informal atmosphere pervades this establishment, with its genial owner and helpful, friendly staff. In summer, a band plays on Friday and Saturday nights. The restaurant is accessible to disabled visitors, but not the accommodation.
Walking; fishing; watersports; beach

Wales and
the Heart of England

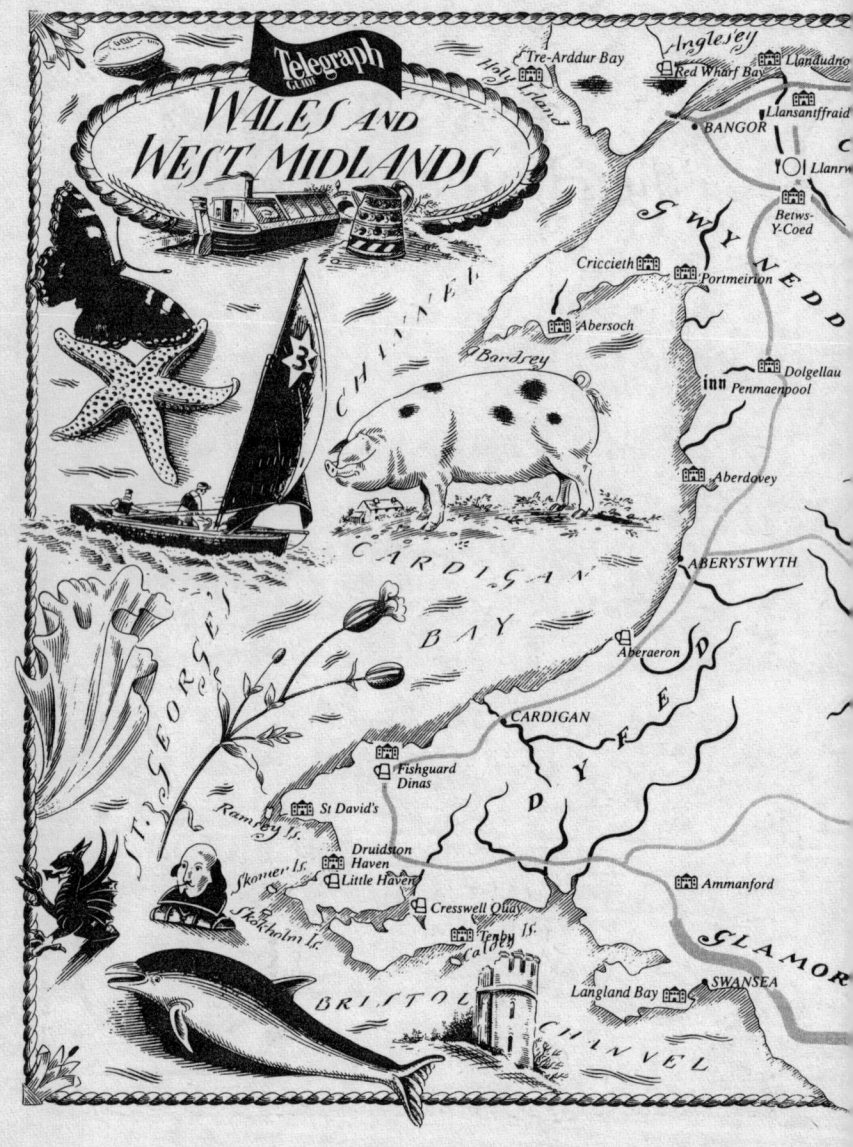

Telegraph GUIDE

WALES AND WEST MIDLANDS

Anglesey

Tre-Arddur Bay
Holy Island
Red Wharf Bay
Llandudno
Llansantffraid
BANGOR
Llanrw
Betws-Y-Coed
SWYNEDD
Criccieth
Portmeirion
Abersoch
Bardsey
Dolgellau
inn Penmaenpool
Aberdovey
CARDIGAN
ABERYSTWYTH
BAY
Aberaeron
CARDIGAN
DYFE
Fishguard
Dinas
Ramsey Is. St David's
Druidston
Haven
Skomer Is. Little Haven
Skokholm Is.
Cresswell Quay
Tenby Is.
Scalby
GLAMOR
Langland Bay SWANSEA
BRISTOL
CHANNEL

CHANNEL

St. GEORGE'S

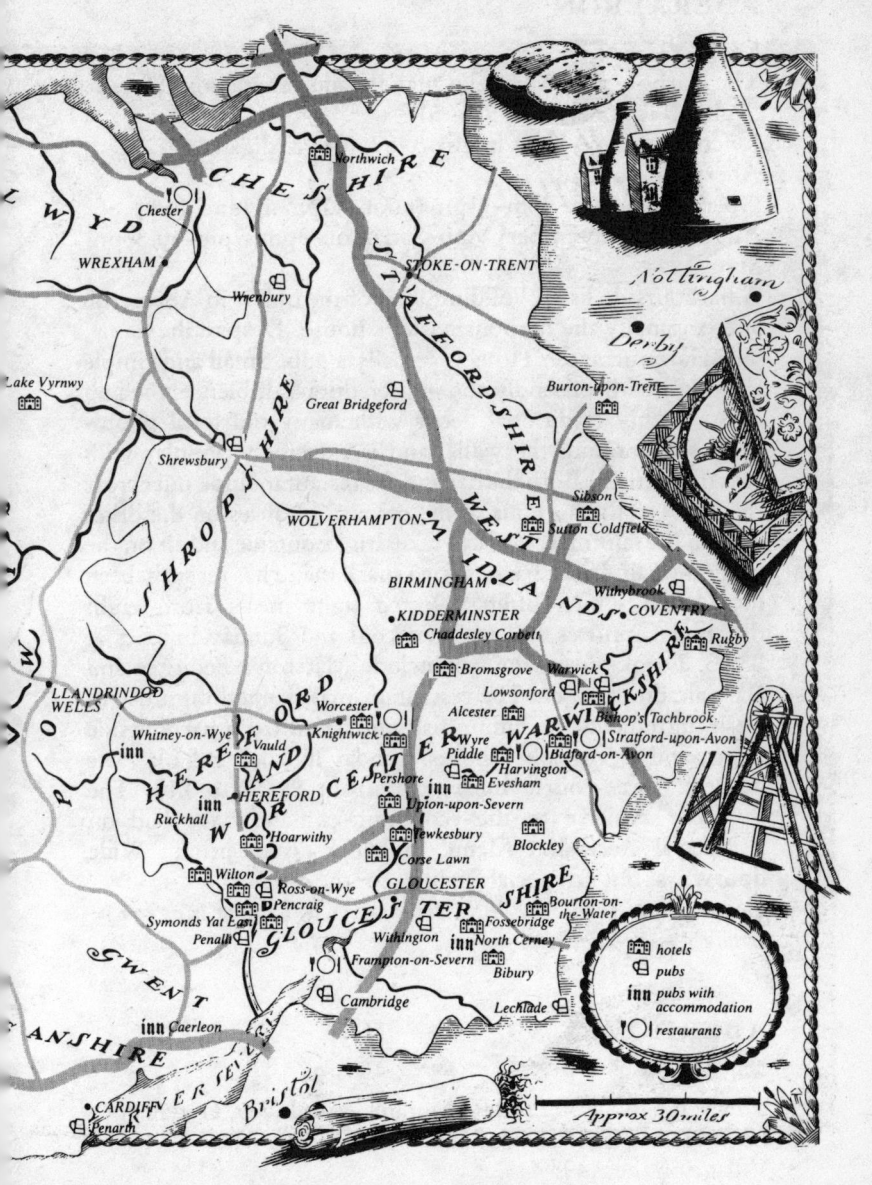

CHESHIRE

Northwich

Chester

WREXHAM

Wrenbury

LWYD

Lake Vyrnwy

SHROPSHIRE

Shrewsbury

Great Bridgeford

STAFFORDSHIRE

STOKE-ON-TRENT

Burton-upon-Trent

Nottingham

Derby

WOLVERHAMPTON

WEST MIDLANDS

Sibson

Sutton Coldfield

BIRMINGHAM

Withybrook

COVENTRY

KIDDERMINSTER

Chaddesley Corbett

Bromsgrove

Lowsonford

Warwick

Rugby

Alcester

WARWICKSHIRE

Worcester

Knightwick

Wyre
Piddle

Bishop's Tachbrook

Stratford-upon-Avon

Bidford-on-Avon

Whitney-on-Wye

Vauld

Harvington

HEREFORD AND

Pershore

Evesham

inn

inn

HEREFORD

WORCESTER

Upton-upon-Severn

Ruckhall

inn

Hoarwithy

Tewkesbury

Blockley

Wilton

Corse Lawn

Ross-on-Wye

Pencraig

GLOUCESTER

GLOUCESTERSHIRE

LLANDRINDOD
WELLS

POWYS

Symonds Yat East

Penallt

Withington

Bourton-on-
the-Water

Frampton-on-Severn

Fossebridge

North Cerney

inn

Bibury

Cambridge

Lechlade

SWENT

GLAMORGANSHIRE

inn Caerleon

CARDIFF

Penarth

RIVER SEVERN

Bristol

Approx 30 miles

🏨 hotels

🍺 pubs

inn pubs with
accommodation

🍴 restaurants

ABERAERON

🗔 🏨 🍸 🍽 ▭

The Harbourmaster Hotel, Quay Parade, Aberaeron, Dyfed
SA46 0BT   (Tel. 0545 570 351)
Junction of the A482 with the A487, the Cardigan to
Aberystwyth road
Open noon–3pm, 7pm–11pm (noon–11pm in June, July,
August and September) Mon–Sat; noon–3pm, 7pm–10.30pm
Sun
A harbourside listed building, one of the oldest in Aberaeron
and originally the harbourmaster's house. Despite the name,
The Harbourmaster Hotel is actually a pub. Small and simple
in design with a friendly and unpretentious ambience, the pub
offers highly traditional decor with many old local photographs decorating the walls, and is extremely popular with
local fishermen. Both the bar and the restaurant look out across
the boats in the harbour to the colourful houses on the other
side; in the summer, you can take drinks outside and sit on the
harbour wall. In the bar, a varied snack menu has recently been
introduced which offers selected light meals from eight
different countries and includes cold and Sunday lunches at
£3.95. Drinks from the bar include Marston's Pedigree and
Bass ale on draught. The restaurant makes maximum use of
fresh ingredients, including fish purchased from harbourside
boats, and serves cold lunches, Sunday lunches and à la carte
dinners: three-course meals cost from £9.75 to £18. The
owners, sensitive to the economic climate, have laid on
a 'Special Recession Menu' at knock-down prices. Wide
doorways, but no special facilities for the disabled.
*Games room; pebble beach; crabbing; deep-sea fishing trips can be
arranged from harbour*

ABERDOVEY

🏨 3/5 🏨 🍸 🏷 ▭

The Maybank Hotel and Restaurant, Aberdovey, Gwynedd
LL35 0PT   (Tel. 0654 767 500)
Village on the A493

Hotel and restaurant closed 9 January–10 February.
£21.45–£25.85 pp b&b; £33–£40 pp dinner and b&b

Set in the centre of a picturesque village perched between the hillside and the coast, the hotel offers beautiful, restful views over the village and the Dovey estuary from its large bay windows. Bright, clean and light inside, both the Victorian-style sitting room and the restaurant look out to pretty public gardens directly opposite the hotel, and the sea beyond. A three-course dinner from the à la carte menu costs about £17. Vegetarians are well catered for; the restaurant received a mention in the *Vegetarian Food Guide*. Non-residents must book in advance from 1 November to 15 February. Bedrooms are attractive and offer many little extras. Children under 10 stay at half price and under threes stay free if occupying their parents' room. Dogs are accepted at a charge of £1 per day and a small surcharge is applied to credit card payments.

Fishing in estuary; river fishing (licences available in village); sea fishing (trips can be arranged in village); sailing at Dovey Yacht Club; golf at village course; windsurfing (tuition available); Outward Bound Centre courses in canoeing, sailing, rock climbing and camping; RSPB sanctuary nearby; walking; beach

ABERDOVEY

The Penhelig Arms Hotel, Aberdovey, Gwynedd
LL35 0LT   (Tel. 0654 767 215)
Village on the A493
£26–£35 pp b&b

An outstanding restaurant and public bar are the focus of this warm and welcoming harbourside hotel. All tables in the restaurant overlook the sea and original three-course dinner menus feature fresh game and local seafood and cost £14.95. Local fishermen and dogs congregate in the bar, which may well be the only one in Wales with bidets in the loos. In summer, lunches from the varied bar menu can be eaten out of doors at harbourside tables. All bedrooms have private facilities with colour television, radio and tea-making equipment.

There is wheelchair access to the restaurant and the bar.
Walking; pony trekking; windsurfing (tuition available); fishing in estuary; river fishing (licences available in village); sea fishing (trips can be arranged in village); beach; golf on 18-hole links course with reduced fees for guests; Outward Bound Centre with courses in canoeing, sailing, rock climbing and camping

ABERDOVEY

8/11

Plas Penhelig Country House Hotel and Restaurant,
Aberdovey, Gwynedd LL35 0NA   (Tel. 0654 767 676)
Open mid March–December
£37.50–£40.50 pp b&b
A long, winding drive climbs up to this clifftop Edwardian country house with views south over the Dovey estuary and Cardigan Bay. Set in seven acres of beautiful listed gardens, with orchards, original Edwardian greenhouses and a unique walled kitchen garden, the hotel restaurant is almost completely self-supporting in organic fruit and vegetables. A pretty stone terrace with flowers and seating overlooks the water. Most of the tables in the restaurant (which seats 38 people) offer a water view while you dine; a three-course dinner costs from £14.95 and is sure to include locally raised meat and game or fish from nearby rivers. Traditional decor in public areas includes an oak-panelled entrance hall and beamed lounge with chintz-covered armchairs and open fire, stained-glass windows and fresh flowers. Bedrooms are modern and conventional; the most pleasant rooms are to be found in the turret. Local trains stop by request at the Penhelig Halt railway station at the bottom of the hotel drive.
Croquet green; putting green; walks in Snowdonia, Cader Idris; watersports; fishing can be arranged (bring equipment); golf; beach; bird watching; windsurfing; Outward Bound Centre nearby

ABERSOCH

 10/17

The Porth Tocyn Hotel, Abersoch, Pwllheli, Gwynedd
LL53 7BU   (Tel. 075881 3303)
Two and a half miles south of Abersoch; hotel right at the end
of the road
Open Easter–mid November
£40–£45 pp b&b

Converted from a row of miners' cottages and set in 25 acres of
its own farm land, this neat little hotel has been run by the
Fletcher-Brewer family for 40 years and both the atmosphere
and the proprietors, who have an exhaustive and highly
entertaining knowledge of local history, are wonderfully
unstuffy. The comfortable, chintzy sitting rooms with period
furniture, reading materials and plenty of fresh flowers, afford
excellent views from the Lleyn Peninsula over Cardigan Bay to
Snowdonia. There is a cosy, unobtrusive bar area. The
restaurant has a straightforward approach to good food and
much of the hotel's excellent reputation is based on the
successful mixture of conventional and adventurous cuisine:
choices range from a two-course meal with coffee at £16.50 to
the full-blown five-course menu with a wide selection of
dishes at a very reasonable £22. The wood-panelled, homely
dining room seats 50 and while most tables have a water view,
five are directly beside the window. There are three ground-
floor bedrooms available which would be suitable for the
disabled.

*Tennis court; outdoor pool; a good base from which to explore the
beautiful Heritage Coastline with 26 unspoilt beaches and many
beautiful vantage points; plenty of walks (hotel offers its own book of
walks); watersports in Abersoch; sea fishing; riding and clay pigeon
shooting can be arranged; nine-hole golf nearby*

ALCESTER

🏠 9/18 🏡 🔥 🖋 🟦

Arrow Mill, Arrow, Alcester, Warwickshire B49 5NL
(Tel. 0789 762419)
Closed for two weeks from Christmas Eve
£60 single, £68–£84 double b&b
An attractive 19th-century mill conversion with a history
dating back 900 years, Arrow Mill offers individually
decorated, spacious, pine-furnished bedrooms retaining
characteristic timber and brickwork. The public areas have
plenty of rustic charm with exposed beams and log fires which
provide a comfortable and intimate atmosphere; the original
water wheel, still driven by the mill stream, is displayed in the
Gun Room bar. The restaurant, which enjoys an excellent
reputation and offers three-course meals for around £13.50, is
manned by friendly and helpful staff and seats 72 with 11
water-view tables. The restaurant and the Gun Room and
Miller's bars are open to non-residents. There is wheelchair
access to the ground floor (bars and restaurant), but no special
facilities for disabled visitors.
Walks; fly fishing for trout on site; clay pigeon shooting; archery;
coarse fishing; gliding and hot-air ballooning nearby

AMMANFORD

🏠 0/11 🏡 11 🚴 🖋 🟦

The Mill at Glynhir, Llandybie, Ammanford, Dyfed
SA18 2TE   (Tel. 0269 850 672)
Off the A483, on the Llandeilo road; (call for full
directions)
Closed at Christmas
£29.50 pp b&b, £33.50–£47 pp dinner and b&b
A modern conversion of a 17th-century water mill, built on the
steep side of a valley overlooking the Black Mountains of the
Brecon Beacons National Park and within walking distance
of the ruins of Carreg Cennen Castle, perched on the edge of a
330-foot-high cliff. A pretty stretch of the River Longhar runs

through the garden and provides a mile of trout fishing. Bedrooms are modern and individually named after the many local castles and include the luxury Glynhir suite which incorporates the original stone wall of the mill. The noise of rushing water is clearly audible from all bedroom windows. Because of the steepness of the hill, the hotel is built on several levels with access to the front door and reception via a small footbridge. Both the 30-seat dining room and the sitting room are decorated in modern style but retain the 3-foot-thick walls of the old mill. Three-course meals with coffee cost from around £13.50. Additional attractions include a subterranean indoor pool with underwater jet stream, and views out on to the valley and the remains of an ancient steel foundry in the hotel grounds. £1 a day charge for dogs.

Walking (Brecon Beacons National Park); trout fishing at hotel, sea trout and salmon fishing locally; 18-hole golf (free to residents, equipment hire organized in advance on request); riding nearby

BETWS-Y-COED

7/13

Ty Gwyn Hotel, Betws-y-Coed, Gwynedd LL24 0SG (Tel. 0690 710 787)
On the A5, 100 yards south of Waterloo bridge before entering village
£17–£36 pp b&b, some four-poster beds
Charming and cheerful 'olde-worlde' 17th-century coaching inn, furnished with lovely antiques and situated in the Vale of Conwy town known locally as the 'Gateway to Snowdonia'. The hotel offers cosy and comfortable accommodation, with traditional public areas including an ancient beamed bar area complete with inglenook, log fires, oak settles and deep window seats overlooking the River Conwy. The chintzy restaurant offers a good selection of reasonably priced dishes using many local ingredients, including a set three-course meal at £13.95. Light meals are also available from the extensive bar menu. Four-poster and half-tester bedrooms are available. All rooms are tastefully furnished and come complete with the

sound of rushing water – light sleepers be warned! Topping the range is the Alpine suite, offering a private lounge, balcony and health spa tub. A small patio at the rear of the hotel overlooks the valley. The Bunkhouse behind the inn is well-suited to group bookings and provides accommodation for 24 at £8 pp b&b. One ground-floor room is AA approved as suitable for the disabled.

Golf; climbing; walking; watersports (seven miles away); fishing (salmon, sea trout and trout)

BIBURY

🏚 14/20 🐎 🏊 💷

Bibury Court Hotel, Bibury, Cirencester, Gloucestershire
GL7 5NT   (Tel. 028574 337/324)
Bibury on the A433 between Burford and Cirencester; hotel stands behind the church
£50–£55 single, £68–£74 double b&b
Once a family residence, this beautiful Jacobean mansion of outstanding dimensions enjoys a glorious setting in six acres of private grounds bordered by the River Coln. Reputedly visited by Charles II and the Prince Regent, the hotel's history includes a celebrated period of litigation which is said to have inspired Charles Dickens's *Bleak House*. A true reminder of the age of gracious living, Bibury Court is elegant, tasteful and spacious throughout with panelled rooms, four-posters and much fine antique furniture. Additional facilities include a cocktail bar, television salon, pool room and conference rooms. A relaxed atmosphere is created by the charming and informal proprietors who run the establishment as a country house rather than a hotel. Restaurant prices average £20 for a three-course meal. Short-break rates are available on request.

Interesting walks; tennis; squash; golf; sailing, windsurfing, waterskiing, jetskiing and more at nearby Cotswold Water Park; riding and shooting (by arrangement); racing; croquet, putting and fishing on site

BIBURY

🏨 ≈10/20 ⚐ 🕯 ◁ 💳

The Swan Hotel, Bibury, Cirencester, Gloucestershire
GL7 5NW   (Tel. 028574 204)
On the B4425 (A433) between Burford and Cirencester
From £70 single, £100 double b&b

A picturesque, 18th-century, creeper-clad, Cotswold-stone coaching inn enjoying a central location in the village of Bibury. Set in immensely pretty gardens from which a natural spring descends to the River Coln, the hotel has been completely refurbished. The decor is on country-house lines, with occasional references to the 1930s deco. A lift has been installed; stables have been converted into a brasserie called Jankowski's, and a courtyard and a fountain have been added. There are fewer bedrooms, but these are larger, with capacious bathrooms. All of the beds are antique; some are four-posters. Afternoon teas will be served both in the main restaurant – which is decorated in grand, 1930s style – and the brasserie. Lunch or dinner in the restaurant costs about £25 per person; a three-course meal in the brasserie, about £15–£20. Non-residents are welcome. The bar, panelled in bleached oak, has comfortable leather armchairs and a proper fireplace, and links the main body of the hotel to the brasserie (soups, sandwiches and ploughman's lunches are available from the bar). Dogs can be accommodated by prior arrangement. There are no ground-floor bedrooms, but the lift is a good size and should make many first-floor rooms accessible to disabled visitors.

Interesting walks; trout fishing (for hotel residents); sailing, waterskiing, jetskiing, windsurfing and more at nearby Cotswold Water Park; tennis, squash and golf nearby; shooting can be arranged; the hotel offers packages for Cheltenham races (including transport by helicopter)

BIDFORD-ON-AVON

|O| 🚴 👤 ⌦ ▭

White Lion Hotel, High Street, Bidford-on-Avon,
Warwickshire B50 4BQ   (Tel. 0789 773309)
By the bridge in the centre of the village
Open 7pm–9pm Mon–Sat; noon–2pm Sun
Visitors to this half-timbered and whitewashed house situated
on the banks of the Avon are sure to appreciate the quiet,
waterside location with views across to Bidford's picturesque
eight-arched bridge and the rolling Cotswolds. The recently
refurbished, intimate bar exudes a comfortable and relaxed
atmosphere and the pretty, informal 40-seat restaurant, with a
river-view balcony, has started to build a good reputation with
visitors. Specializing in fresh fish dishes but also offering
vegetarian meals, the restaurant has a good à la carte menu with
three-course meals in the region of £18 per person, while the
bar menu concentrates on lighter meals for £2.95–£5.75. The
welcoming atmosphere is enhanced by friendly and helpful
staff but the restaurant is not suitable for the disabled.
*Gliding club with micro-lighting nearby; boat; children's play area;
fishing and mooring rights on River Avon; hot-air ballooning nearby*

BISHOP'S TATCHBROOK

🏨 ≈$^{4/10}$ 🚴 9 👤 ⌦ ▭

Mallory Court Hotel, Harbury Lane, Bishop's Tatchbrook,
Leamington Spa, Warwickshire CV33 9QB
(Tel. 0926 330214)
Off the A452 out of Leamington Spa, follow signs to Harbury
£120–£200 double, £330 double suite b&b
This large country-house hotel, a member of the prestigious
Relais et Chateaux group, is set in the heart of rural Britain, in
10 acres of private grounds encompassing extensive lawns,
formal rose garden and water and herb gardens. Converted in
1913 from a private residence, Mallory Court has 10
individually decorated and named rooms of the very highest
standard, and benefits from lovely views across the beautiful

rolling countryside of the northern edge of the Cotswolds. The Blenheim suite is particularly splendid with an art deco bath and trompe-l'oeil painted ceiling. The attractive panelled restaurant, open to non-residents, seats 50 with six water-view tables and offers modern French classical cuisine with menus which are light and innovative, created using fresh herbs and vegetables from the estate gardens. The set lunch costs £22.50; set dinner £38–£45. The hotel features an elegantly presented pink lounge and drawing room for reading or relaxation and is well placed for exploring Warwick, Leamington Spa and Stratford-on-Avon.

Tennis court; croquet; outdoor pool; squash court

BOURTON-ON-THE-WATER

The Old Manse Hotel, Victoria Street, Bourton-on-the-Water, Gloucestershire GL54 2BX   (Tel. 0451 20642)
£37.50 single, £60 double b&b

A lovely country hotel at the centre of what must be one of the quaintest Cotswold villages. Accommodation is in individually decorated rooms with pretty furnishings, including a honeymoon suite with *en suite* double spa bath and one room with a half-tester bed. The spacious bar – with an open fireplace which is lit in winter – serves a variety of basket meals, seafood, meat and pasta dishes at lunchtime as well as offering a cold-buffet counter. Two- and three-course lunches or four-course dinners in the warm and attractive restaurant cost £7.95, £8.75 or £14.75 respectively, and a varied vegetarian menu is on offer, given advance notice. The table d'hôte set dinner costs £15.75. Special two-day breaks are available from £80 per person per two nights including breakfast and dinner. The ground floor is adapted with ramps and specially fitted bathroom facilities for the disabled, making the restaurant easily accessible although an overnight stay is not recommended.

Walking; fishing can be arranged through hotel; motor museum; model railway museum; perfumery; Birdland; model village

BROMSGROVE

Grafton Manor, Grafton Lane, Bromsgrove, Worcestershire
B61 7HA   (Tel. 0527 579007)
In Bromsgrove, off the A438 and Worcester Road
£80–£150 per room b&b
Commissioned in 1567 and rebuilt in the early 18th century,
this beautiful Grade II listed manor house in stone and pink
brick is surrounded by 30 acres of lovely grounds bordering a
lake. The hotel has been painstakingly restored and is carefully
tended by a charming family who offer gracious dining and
accommodation in rooms of individual character equipped
with all modern conveniences. The dining room seats 48 and
offers a set three-course lunch at between £15.50 and £21.50
and a four-course dinner at £28.50. The lake in the hotel's
grounds is preserved as a swan sanctuary and the only tiny blot
on the landscape is the sight of the motorway. Recent
improvements include the planting of a natural screen of 1500
trees to mask the motorway view. Pets are not accepted in the
hotel although kennels are available in the grounds. The manor
is accessible to wheelchairs and there is one ground-floor
bedroom which may be suitable for disabled guests.
Walking; golf nearby

BURTON-UPON-TRENT

Riverside Inn Hotel, Riverside Drive, Branston, Burton-
upon-Trent, Staffordshire DE14 3EP   (Tel. 0283 511234)
Off the A5121 to Burton-upon-Trent
£28–£58 single, £50–£68 double b&b
The focus of this light, airy and formal hotel set in an original
but much-modernized inn is its large and highly reputed
riverside Garden Room restaurant, which seats 180 diners and
caters for both private and business clients. Seven water-view
tables are available from which to enjoy international and
traditional English cuisine. Prices for the three-course lunch
menu start at £9.95; the table d'hôte dinner costs from £14.95.

River views are extremely pleasant and a neat garden extends from the hotel to the river bank. Decor is straightforward and largely pink and the bedrooms, although sometimes limited in space, are well maintained and equipped and set in a separate wing of the building. The hotel has a largely commercial clientele and it is therefore less expensive to visit at the weekend than midweek. Additional facilities include a bar, lounge, three banqueting rooms (seating a total of 150) and hotel golf course. The restaurant is accessible to wheelchairs although an overnight stay is not recommended for the disabled.

Walking; watersports; coarse fishing on River Trent; fly fishing nearby; three local golf courses; race meetings at Uttoxeter and Nottingham (40 minutes away); nearby Meadowside sports complex offers swimming, squash and saunas

CAERLEON

inn ²/⁴ 🏠 🕎 🚫 ▭

The Hanbury Arms, Uskside, Caerleon, Gwent
(Tel. 0633 420361)
On the A4236, just before Caerleon bridge
Open noon–3pm, 6pm–11pm Mon–Sat; noon–3pm, 7pm–10.30pm Sun
£15–£20 pp b&b

Ancient and basic, the Hanbury Arms is an original 16th-century inn located in an area of great historical interest; not only does the fortress of Isca (AD 75) mark Caerleon as one of the most important Roman military sites and the third principal Roman garrison in the UK, but it is also considered to be one of the possible locations of Camelot. Tennyson and Arthur Machen have been numbered among its patrons. There is a lounge bar and a public bar overlooking the River Usk, which produces exceptionally high tides. In the bar, beers served include Hancock's HB and draught Bass and snacks are available. In summer, a large beer garden on the water's edge seats 100 for outdoor drinking.

Roman amphitheatre; Roman baths and exercise halls; legionary museum (Tel. 0633 423134)

CAMBRIDGE

🛏 🏠 🐕 🚫 💳

The George Inn, Bristol Road, Cambridge, Gloucestershire
GL2 7AL   (Tel. 0453 890270)
On the A38, the Bristol to Gloucester road
Open 11am–2.30pm, 6.30pm–11pm Mon–Sat; noon–3pm,
7pm–10.30pm Sun. Closed 25 and 26 December
A pretty garden on the banks of the River Cam offers riverside
seating for patrons of this comfortable, well-maintained pub
which runs regular special events and theme evenings
providing different bar dishes from around the world. Large,
relaxing and set in an idyllic rural area, The George Inn offers
cosy, cottage-style surroundings, lively staff and an excellent
location for family excursions to many places of historic
interest. During the summer months the pub operates a garden
barbecue and grill beside the river. Overlooking the river, the
traditional bar/restaurant seats 146 people in five areas and
offers an extensive à la carte menu costing about £8 for a three-
course meal. Specialities include a variety of fresh fish dishes
and unusual regional recipes such as 'Kromskies' (otherwise
known as deep-fried, diced and breadcrumbed gammon, beef
and lamb). Beers served include Boddington's.
Many interesting walks including the late Sir Peter Scott's
Wildfowl Sanctuary at Slimbridge, one mile's walk away; salmon
fishing in the River Cam and the Gloucester–Sharpness canal

CHADDESLEY CORBETT

🏨 ≈ 2/8 🏠 🐕 🚫 💳

Brockencote Hall, Chaddesley Corbett, nr Kidderminster,
Worcestershire DY10 4PY   (Tel. 0562 777876)
On the A448, the Bromsgrove to Kidderminster road
Closed 26 December–mid January
£57–£115 per room b&b
An impressive Georgian house set in 70–acre grounds
encompassing a lake which is home to Canada geese, ducks,
herons and occasionally swans. Public areas are light and
airy with stripped pine and maple doors and handsome

panelling, and include a small but bright reception lounge with marble fireplace. The individually decorated bed-rooms boast every convenience and are elegantly styled and furnished with quality dark wood. *En suite* bathrooms are mainly modern although a few retain period pre-war fittings. The hotel offers a comfortable relaxed atmosphere with friendly and helpful service. Seating 45, the dining room provides a set lunch for £16.50 and a three-course dinner for £19.50–£33.50. An excellent location both for conferences and country visits, with on-site secretarial and laundry facilities, but not suitable for disabled visitors.

Walks in grounds and Wyre Forest; Warwick Castle, crystal factories, and safari park nearby

CHESTER

IOI 🏠 🚴 ⊘ ▭

Telfords Warehouse, Tower Wharf, Raymond Street, Chester (Tel. 0244 390090)

Call for directions

Bar open 11am–11pm Mon–Sat; noon–3pm, 7pm–10.30pm Sun

Restaurant open 7pm–10pm Mon–Thurs; 7pm–10.30pm Fri and Sat; noon–2.15pm and 7pm–10pm Sun

Named after the builder, Thomas Telford, this converted 250-year-old brick-built warehouse spans the canal and is decorated with many canal pieces, including the original crane which is still found in the beamed building. Formerly a storage house for coal, flour and grain, in 1987 the warehouse was converted to a friendly and cheerful 92-seat restaurant specializing in good, cheap Italian cuisine but also offering a traditional English à la carte menu. Three-course Italian pizza or pasta-based meals are available for approximately £7; three-course English à la carte meals for around £10. Four water-view tables are available in the restaurant; the open and spacious pub, with full glass frontage affording an excellent canal view, serves real ales including Theakston's bitter. Quite difficult to find if you are approaching by road but a good stopping-off point if you are on the canal. Live jazz during Sunday lunch and on Tuesday evenings.

CORSE LAWN

🏨 ≈ 5/19 🏠 🍴 🐦 💳

Corse Lawn House Hotel, Corse Lawn, Gloucestershire
GL19 4LZ   (Tel. 045 278 479)
Off the A417, the Gloucestershire to Ledbury road, on the A4211
£65 single, £95 double b&b
An elegant two-storey Grade II listed red-brick Queen Anne house decorated and furnished with exquisite taste and style throughout. The hotel is situated on a long and graceful common complete with fringed trees, hedges and scattered houses. A new bedroom wing has been erected and tones sympathetically with the original building. The hotel's calm and attractive front lawn sports a large duck pond and pretty garden seating. The bar area offers light meals and snacks and the restaurant provides provincial French cuisine and an extensive wine list, with weekday lunches at £15.50; Sunday lunch at £17.50 and dinner at £23.50 every day. Lunch is served from noon to 2pm, dinner from 7pm–10pm, and non-residents are welcome. Two private dining rooms, seating a total of 55 diners, are available for private functions. The hotel enjoys a good reputation for quality food and service in a relaxed and comfortable atmosphere and has five ground-floor rooms with specially fitted *en suite* facilities for the disabled.
Walking; fishing; croquet; tennis; swimming pool (open air); riding

CRESSWELL QUAY

The Cresselly Arms, Cresswell Quay, Dyfed SA68 0TH
(Tel. 0646 651210)
Village signposted off the A4075
Open 11am–3pm, 5pm–11pm Mon–Sat; noon–3pm and 7pm–
10.30pm Sun
The delightful old stone creeper-clad pub in the Pembrokeshire Coast National Park is frequented by both car and boat
traffic, though the boaters have to leave with the tide. The
interior is traditional, with a high beam and plank ceiling, wall
benches, red and black flooring tiles and simple furnishings.
The pub has two bars with open fireplace or working Aga, one
of which overlooks Cresswell Quay Creek. Beers served
include Hancock's HB, tapped from barrels behind the bar,
and a local brew nicknamed 'Firewater'. Light meals on offer
are fairly limited but keenly priced and include sandwiches for
50p and ploughman's lunch at £1.50; the sides of Welsh bacon
hanging above the Aga have been known to yield slices to
peckish locals. Picnic tables are situated on the quay with a
view over the creek. The pub is accessible for the disabled but
does not offer adapted facilities.
Fishing from quay; walking

CRICCIETH

The Moelwyn Restaurant, 27/29 Mona Terrace, Criccieth,
Gwynedd LL52 0HG   (Tel. 0766 522500)
On the seafront at Criccieth
Open Easter to November
From £19.50 pp b&b
Just 80 yards from Criccieth's pebbly beach, this creeper-clad
Victorian building modestly announces itself as a 'restaurant
with rooms'. It offers a more sophisticated alternative to the
nearby Beach Café and the Blue China Tearooms. Pink is the
prevailing colour in the pretty dining room, which seats 30,
with four tables by windows looking out over Cardigan Bay.

Swathed curtains, plants and flowers in alcoves and on tables, and attentive service combine to create an atmosphere of charm and comfort. Touches of style are continued in the menu, which contains such offerings as fillet of sea bass with scallops, prawns and Muscadet (£9.50), lobster thermidor (£16.95), and fruit sorbet to punctuate the meal. Sunday lunch comes as a set three-course meal for £8.75, and the main course offers a choice from Welsh lamb, Scottish beef and local salmon. All six bedrooms have *en suite* bathrooms and colour television. There are no facilities for the disabled, and while the restaurant is not difficult of access, there are no ground-floor toilets. Criccieth itself is a not unattractive little town, very largely unchanged since Victorian times, with an impressive castle dominating the seafront. It makes an ideal base for exploration of Snowdonia and the coast of North Wales.

Fishing in the River Dwyfor (licence obtainable locally), and in the sea for anyone with a boat. Watersports, climbing, walking, shooting, bird watching, tennis, riding, museums all in the area. Criccieth Golf Club is 1 km from the town centre, and the Criccieth Festival takes place in June. Trains on the famous Ffestiniog Railway run from nearby Porthmadog, and the Snowdon Mountain Railway is at Llanberis, less than an hour away.

DINAS

The Sailors Safety Inn, Pwll Gwaelod, Dinas Cross, Dyfed SA42 0SE   (Tel. 03486 207)

Bar and restaurant open 11am–11pm seven·days a week

Situated right at the end of the isolated cove of Pwll Gwaelod, below windswept Dinas Head on the famous Pembrokeshire coastal path, this wonderful 16th-century pub, once a smugglers' haunt, has all the right ingredients: a bottomless pool, the ghost of Black Bart, and the original wrecker's light illuminating the entrance to the bar. Decor is refreshingly simple, with a warm, relaxed atmosphere enhanced by a fine old stone fireplace, whisky-keg seats and fishing nets that lend a nautical air. The magnificent oak bar was originally a ship's dresser, brought back from Calcutta in 1922. The pub is renowned for its food (bar snacks and lunch) and for its range of real ales. In the summer, there are seats outside overlooking the bottomless pool. Fairly easily accessible for the disabled.

Small private beach below pub; rod and line fishing from cove

DOLGELLAU

Borthwnog Hall Country House Hotel and Restaurant, Bontddu, Dolgellau, Gwynedd LL40 2TT   (Tel. 0341 49271)
On the A496, the Dolgellau to Barmouth road, by the toll bridge across the Mawddach estuary
Closed Christmas Day and Boxing Day
£38 pp b&b, £50 pp dinner and b&b
A perfect example of a Regency country house, which looks out over the estuary to the Aran mountains to the east, and Cader Idris to the south. The hotel stands in beautiful grounds adjoining the RSPB nature reserve of Garth Gell and is centrally placed for walking or touring the Snowdonia National Park. Bedrooms are decorated with individual character and public areas are homely and welcoming with open fires during the winter months. Drinks may be taken in the hotel's garden or on the 600-foot promenade-style waterside terrace. The dining room, seating 28, offers set dinner for £13.75 and a three-course à la carte meal set at around £18 per person. The hotel may well be unique in that it has its own art gallery, set up by owner Vicki Hawes, which shows original paintings, sculptures and pottery by Welsh artists. The gallery is open daily from 10am to 5pm and prices start at £20.

Canoeing and windsurfing on estuary; golf at Dolgellau and Harlech; Snowdonia National Park

DRUIDSTON HAVEN

🏨 ⁵/₉ 🐾 🍸 ⦻ 🚬

The Druidston, Druidston Haven, nr Haverfordwest,
Dyfed SA62 3NE   (Tel. 0437 781 221)
Two miles north of Broad Haven, on the cliff above
Druidston Haven
£19.50–£24.50 pp b&b; four cottages, two with water view,
each sleeps five–eight people £178–£363 per week; party
bookings only from September to February
Perched directly above the quiet and unspoilt Druidston beach,
this is a delightfully unconventional hotel with few rules or
formalities. There is homespun decor and simple accommodation and it is a haven for those who love the outdoors or
informal artistic, music, craft and theatre evenings. The
restaurant and flagstoned cellar bar open out on to a terrace with
spectacular views of St Bride's Bay. The inventive home
cooking, presented with flair, uses many fresh local ingredients
and ranges from Mexican, through Indonesian and Indian, to
Italian and Welsh. Dinner costs between £13 and £16, including
wine, and can be prepared for almost any special dietary needs if
advance notification is given. Accommodation is in simple,
spacious bedrooms which are comfortable but do not feature the
usual hotel gadgetry. There is not only accommodation for the
disabled but also activities with instruction for disabled group
bookings.
*Beach; climbing, sea-canoeing and field archery instruction on the
premises; riding on beach; walks on Pembrokeshire Coast National
Park footpath; windsurfing courses locally; scuba diving; beach
fishing below house (river and reservoir fishing seven to 10 miles
away, trout pool one mile away)*

EVESHAM

🏨 ≈⁷/₇ 🐾 🍸 ⦸ 🚬

Riverside Hotel and Restaurant, The Parks, Offenham Road,
Evesham, Worcestershire WR11 5JP   (Tel. 0386 446200)
Off the B4510, the Offenham road
£51 single, £71.50 double b&b

Set in three acres of grounds by the River Avon, this comfortable country-house hotel enjoys a scenic location in a former 15th-century deer park once belonging to Evesham Abbey. The hotel is prettily decorated with attractive furnishing in the thematically designed bedrooms, all of which have *en suite* bathrooms and a view of the garden sloping to the river and vale beyond. A garden terrace, seating 50, with river view, is used for light meals or drinks when the weather permits. The elegant dining room, with large bay windows looking out to the river, specializes in English and French cuisine, and makes maximum use of local ingredients; the set lunch costs £14.50, the set dinner £17.95. Lunchtime snacks are also available in the downstairs bar from Monday to Saturday. *Fishing (equipment provided); private moorings; hire boats available at the hotel*

FISHGUARD

24/62

Fishguard Bay Hotel, Quay Road, Goodwick, Pembrokeshire, Dyfed SA64 0BT   (Tel. 0348 873571)
Near the end of A40, at Goodwick, overlooking Fishguard Harbour
From £55 per room (£27.50 pp b&b sharing double or twin room)
Set amid woodland high above Cardigan Bay, this was originally a mansion house called Wyncliffe. Early in the century, it was extended, and became the Fishguard Bay Hotel, managed by the Great Western Railway, providing accommodation for passengers on the newly-opened sea route to Ireland. In those far-off days, a single room could be had for five shillings, and dinner was three shillings and sixpence. In 1979, the hotel was designated a Building of Historic and Architectural Interest. The seashore and Goodwick Beach are within a few hundred yards. Tea is served on the terrace in good weather, and the dining room, seating 50, with six tables overlooking the water, offers a table d'hote menu for £12, with house wine at £5.95 a bottle. There is also an à la carte menu,

and bar meals are available. The hotel features in the 1992 *Good Beer Guide*, and offers a large range of beers, lagers and, thanks to the Irish connection, Guinness. For all its outward grandeur, this is a curiously old-fashioned place. Guests arriving off the ferry in the small hours may lament the absence of tea- or coffee-making facilities in the bedrooms, although there is a cheerful welcome from the night-porter. For the disabled, there are three ground-floor bedrooms with their own bathrooms, a lift to the upper floors, and level approaches, with no steps to negotiate. And for the weary voyager, fresh from tossing on the Irish Sea, this solid mansion is a most welcome sight.

Fishing in sea and river. Water sports, golf, tennis, riding, bird watching, walking, climbing in vicinity

FISHGUARD

Hotel Plas Glyn-y-Mel, Lower Town, Fishguard,
Pembrokeshire SA65 9LY   (Tel. 0348 872296)
Hotel signposted from Lower Town
Open March–October
£40 single, £34 pp twin b&b

Situated two minutes from Fishguard Harbour, this sheltered Georgian country house overlooks the River Gwaun, which runs through the hotel's 20 acres of secluded grounds, complete with a hermit's cave and well. The atmosphere of the hotel is very much that of a private house, with antique furniture and open fires in public rooms. All bedrooms have tea- and coffee-making facilities and the two double-bed suites afford excellent family accommodation. The restaurant offers interesting modern cuisine (set dinner £17.50) with the emphasis on seafood and local produce, plus a balanced selection of wines. Dogs can be accommodated by prior arrangement at a cost of £2 per day. Additional attractions include a cosy, river-view lounge, a bar with an unusual period fireplace and a

conservatory, with an indoor heated pool, overlooking the gardens.
Hotel has quarter-mile of salmon and trout fishing on the River Gwaun (bring own equipment); beach nearby, and Newport Sands (nine miles away); sea fishing, riding and boating can be arranged

FOSSEBRIDGE

The Fossebridge, Fossebridge, nr Cheltenham,
Gloucestershire GL54 3JS   (Tel. 0285 720721)
Bar open noon–2pm, 6pm–9.30pm Mon–Thurs; noon–2pm,
6pm–10pm Fri and Sat; noon–2pm, 7pm–9.30pm Sun
£75 double b&b
A delightful Georgian house that is tastefully decorated throughout and sports some really exquisite fabrics. A Tudor coaching inn attached to the house contains the Bridge bar and the Bridge bar restaurant, for informal meals, with main courses costing from £5.50 to £12.50: there are exposed beams and an inglenook fireplace that creates a warm cosy atmosphere. The main hotel restaurant is situated on the first floor, seats 60 people and overlooks the River Coln (open noon to 2pm and 6pm–9.30pm; the table d'hôte menu costs about £18 for three courses). The hotel is surrounded by four acres of grounds, which include a trout lake. No facilities for the disabled, though there are no stairs into the bar.
Fishing (for residents, on trout lake); golf at Cirencester (six miles away); walking; riding nearby

FRAMPTON-ON-SEVERN

Savery's Restaurant, The Green, Frampton-on-Severn,
Gloucestershire GL2 7EA   (Tel. 0452 740077)
Off the A38 at the end of Frampton Green
7pm–9.15pm (last orders); closed Sun and Mon
Set in one of the most beautiful villages in the area, and on the longest village green in the country, the restaurant can seat 24 people. On warm evenings, customers often wander, glass in

hand, to look at the swans on the nearby pond. The small, intimate cottage-style restaurant is attractively furnished in pink with prints, plants and ruched curtains and offers a blackboard menu that in the main is straightforward and British, including salmon from the Wye or Severn rivers. The set dinner, with a choice of five dishes per course, is priced at £19.95. Run by friendly proprietors who have a wide reputation for quality and excellent service, the restaurant is situated in an area offering many river views and walks, although there is no direct view of water from the tables. There is wheelchair access to the restaurant, but not to the lavatories. *Interesting walks; watersports; riding; fishing (information provided at the hotel); rivers in all directions within a quarter of a mile*

GREAT BRIDGEFORD

The Mill at Worston, Great Bridgeford, Staffordshire
ST18 9QA   (Tel. 0785 282710)
Off the A5013 from Eccleshall
Open noon–3pm, 6.30pm–11pm Mon–Sat; noon–2pm, 7pm–10.30pm Sun
This well-converted water mill is now a pub, though it is still in working order, and you can drink among the old machinery. There is a museum next door; a comprehensive information booklet gives details of the hoists and gears and the wheel (the museum is open all the time). There has been a mill on this site since 1279; this particular building, of red brick and tile, with symmetrically placed iron-framed windows, came into being in 1814. Inside, the building is spacious, and attractive. Beers on offer at the bar include Marston's Pedigree, and there is an extensive bar menu; meals are available all day, and the top price is £6. A good place to take children: there is a family area in the pub, and a play area with swings outside in the garden. The new owners are planning many changes and improvements. There is also a pretty stream in the garden; it is worth putting up with the London–Birmingham trains which

rush past on the opposite bank every five minutes. The pub has access and a lavatory for disabled visitors.
Nature trail for children; museum; a bird watch; walk to Izaak Walton's Cottage; coarse fishing

HARVINGTON

🏛️ 15/15 🏠 👃 🚫 ▭

The Mill at Harvington, Anchor Lane, Harvington, Evesham, Worcestershire WR11 5NR   (Tel. 0386 870688)
Signposted from Evesham–Stratford road
Closed at Christmas
£54 single, £85 double b&b
Set back from the main road in a peaceful part of the historic village of Harvington, which is recorded in the Domesday Book, this recently opened hotel and restaurant has been tastefully decorated throughout. A Georgian house and former maltings and baking mill retaining many original features, such as beams and open fires, it is set in eight acres of wooded parkland with excellent views of the River Avon across a beautifully laid lawn that is abundant with wildlife. A relaxed and comfortable atmosphere prevails and friendly staff assure efficient service. The restaurant has 50 seats between two rooms; all tables look out on the 200-yard stretch of willow-shaded water frontage. Snack lunches cost from £3.95, the set dinner from £19.75. Special weekend breaks cost from £89 per person for two nights, including breakfast and dinner. There are three ground-floor bedrooms with disabled access.
The river is popular with leisure boats doing 'The Avon Ring'; river fishing; moorings; secluded heated outdoor swimming pool; tennis court; in-season windsurfing nearby (book through hotel); rowing club (four miles away); gliding (five miles away); walking

HOARWITHY

Upper Orchard, Hoarwithy, Ross-on-Wye,
Herefordshire HR2 6QR   (Tel. 0432 840649)
Open February–December
Wine-tasting weekends: beginner's £120 pp, fine £150 pp,
classic £220 pp. Two-day 'Walking with Wine' breaks, £80 pp
b&b (includes wine-tasting, Wye Valley talk and extensive
country walks)

The Hurleys are a charming, friendly couple whose knowledge and love of wines and walking is infectious. They open
their comfortable, 18th-century house to the public and serve
home and locally produced food for the duration of a relaxed
but informative wine-tasting weekend. Forty of these are held
each year between February and December, and all stages are
catered for: beginners, fine and classic. These weekends
include two tutored wine-tastings, two full breakfasts and two
four-course dinners with a good selection of wines. Guests are
welcome to browse around the well-stocked wine cellar or set
off on any of the many recommended country walks varying
from a distance of three to 16 miles. The owners, authors
of five books on local pedestrian routes, are happy to
lend their expertise or even wellies and walking sticks
from the hotel's central supply. A homely and comfortable
residence with traditional, cosy sitting room with armchairs
grouped around a log fire. Bedrooms are decorated in soft
pinks and greens with pine or mahogany furniture. Beamed
dining room offers home cooking with emphasis on organic
produce.
Walking; cycling

KNIGHTWICK

The Talbot Hotel, Knightsford Bridge, Knightwick,
Worcestershire WR6 5PH   (Tel. 0886 21235)
On the B4197, off the main A44 Worcester–Leominster road
£25–£32 single, £42–£58 double b&b

Nestling in the Worcestershire countryside just yards from the River Teme, The Talbot Hotel first became prominent as an inn during the late 14th century. It is now a fully licensed free house and residential inn providing home cooking and adequately furnished and decorated rooms with good facilities. The heavily beamed, attractive lounge bar with its carved or leatherette armchairs is dominated by a huge open fireplace and the informal 20-seat Edwardian dining area serves a varied menu based on local produce with a bias towards meat and poultry dishes. Vegetarian meals are always available on the frequently changing menu, which provides à la carte three-course meals for around £15. This is a family-run hotel with a friendly ambience which also offers a function room for weddings and parties plus seating on the garden lawn for drinks during the summer season.

Fishing (hotel has rights), squash courts and sauna on site; walking and hunting nearby; pheasant and clay pigeon shooting for groups, and canoeing, can be organized by prior arrangement

LAKE VYRNWY

The Lake Vyrnwy Hotel, Lake Vyrnwy, Llanwddyn, Montgomeryshire SY10 0LY   (Tel. 069 173 692)
Off the B4393 from Llanfyllin; well signposted
£60–£110 per room b&b (lake-view rooms from £72.50)
Cradled in the Berwyn mountains, on the edge of Dyfnant Forest and the Snowdonia National Park, Lake Vyrnwy is a spectacularly beautiful place – complete with a romantic, turreted 'Wagnerian' tower and hidden, drowned village. This country-house hotel and sporting estate enjoys breathtaking views over the water, sole sporting rights over 24,000 acres of woodland plus sole fishing rights on the 1100-acre lake. A display of fishing flies, deep armchairs and roaring fires create a warm atmosphere that appeals to both sport enthusiasts and those simply seeking a peaceful and relaxing country break. The simple, pretty bedrooms have been tastefully refurbished; a newspaper and pot of tea magically appear on the bedside

table each morning. The lake is visible to all diners in the 80-seat restaurant, but the seven tables in the new conservatory offer a truly spectacular aspect. Lunch costs £9.75, dinner £19.75 and Sunday lunch £10.75. The restaurant and tavern are accessible to the disabled, but the bedrooms have no special facilities.

Bicycles and two sailboats for guests; fly fishing (day ticket £9.25, boat hire £9.75); walking trails; game shooting; tennis; bird watching in RSPB wildlife reserve; ballooning; four-wheel driving and white-water rafting can be arranged; beaches (no swimming)

LANGLAND BAY

🏨 19/36 ⌂ ♨ ◁ ▭

Osborne Hotel, Rotherslade Road, Langland, Swansea
SA3 4QL   (Tel. 0792 366274)
From Swansea, follow signs for Mumbles, right at mini-roundabout and follow signs for Langland and Caswell
From £71 single b&b, from £85 twin b&b
A magnificent location – on the southern approach to the Gower Peninsula and, quite literally, a pebble's throw from the sea – endows the hotel with a panoramic view of the Bristol Channel and, on clear days, Devon and Somerset. Although it stands but a few miles from the M4 and Swansea Airport, Langland Bay seems to belong to another world, a splendid place to get away from it all and enjoy a really relaxing weekend. The restaurant has a capacity of 76, and 11 tables command a direct view of the sea, with partial view from another nine tables. The menu offers wide choice: the three-course table d'hote meal costs £14.95. Beers on draught include Tetleys and Burton. Bar meals, afternoon teas and mid-morning coffee are also available. A lift operates to all floors and, for the disabled, there are some rooms with wide doors to the bathrooms.

Fishing (enquire at hotel about charges). Watersports, golf, tennis, walking, riding, bird watching; in Swansea, theatre, museums, concerts

LECHLADE

The Trout Inn, St John's Bridge, nr Lechlade,
Gloucestershire GL7 3HA   (Tel. 0367 52313)
On the A417 (call for directions)
Pub open 11am–3pm, 6pm–11pm Mon–Sat; noon–3pm,
7pm–10.30pm Sun. Restaurant open 7pm–10pm Thurs–Sat
A Grade II listed old English pub, with flagstone floors and
low-beamed bar partly panelled and decorated with stuffed
trout and pike, in a rural setting by an old weir pool and the
first lock on the River Thames. The Trout Inn boasts two
water-view bar areas, one of which opens on to the large public
beer garden where visitors are welcome to participate in the
summertime outdoor games of *pétanque* and 'Aunt Sally' (a
famous Oxfordshire game). The spacious bar offers an
impressive range of bar snacks and light meals for approximately £3–£10 (available every day until 10pm) and the
restaurant, which lists local trout as a speciality, provides
three-course meals for about £15. The pub has excellent family
facilities both indoors and in the garden, where there is a
marquee throughout the summer for private functions. There
is no jukebox, but with the aid of live jazz every Tuesday
evening a fun atmosphere prevails. Although not specially
adapted for the disabled, the pub is easily accessible, and there
is an outdoor lavatory with a wide doorway.
*Riverside walks; boating from the nearby marina; coarse fishing;
nearby trout farm (fly fishing); pub sells day tickets for fishing on the
weir pool; private moorings*

LITTLE HAVEN

The Swan Inn, Little Haven, Pembrokeshire SA62 3UL
(Tel. 0437 781256)
Village on the A4341, near Broad Haven; pub on sea wall
Pub open 11am–3pm, 6.30pm–11pm Mon–Sat; noon–3pm,
7pm–10.30pm Sun. Restaurant open 7pm–10pm Wed–Sat
Perched on one side of the broad, sandy cove, so close to the

beach that water comes right up to the windows, The Swan enjoys a sublime position in one of the prettiest villages on the Pembrokeshire coast. In the comfortable bar, large bay windows look out to sea, and the decor is comfortable and unpretentious with traditional high-backed settles, exposed stonework, and old prints. Llanelli-brewed beers, real ales and imaginative snacks (which cost from £1.50 to £5.50) are served from the solid wood bar while the menu in the 20-seat restaurant focuses on seafood and offers main courses for about £11–£15.50. The low sea wall provides waterside seating in summer in lieu of chairs outside. Access to the pub is via several steps.

Pembrokeshire coastal walks; watersports (bring own equipment) at Broad Haven; sandy beach

LLANDUDNO

🏨 9/17 ⛵ 🎿 🐟 ▭

The Bellevue Hotel, 26 North Parade, Llandudno LL30 2LP (Tel. 0492 879547)
Closed during the week from November to March
£33.50–£37.50 pp dinner and b & b; self-catering holiday flats sleeping 4–6 people, £120–£280 per week
Facing south-east from the foot of the limestone headland of Great Orme, just opposite the old Victorian pier house and opera house, the simple, friendly and sparkling-clean Bellevue is excellent value. Both the sitting room, with its large bay window, and the fishing-net-strewn Fisherman's Bar have a marvellous view of the beach and the bay beyond. Light lunchtime meals are available in the bar for approximately £4. A pretty 35-seat evening restaurant, offering set dinner for £9, opens out on to a paved sun terrace and beach views. The bedrooms are comfortable and well equipped and all are *en suite* with colour television and video. Next door, Bellevue House offers four fully equipped self-catering holiday flats with access to all hotel facilities including the snooker and games room.

Walking; watersports with own equipment; fishing; beach; ski slope; toboggan run

LLANDUDNO

8/21

St Tudno Hotel, North Parade, Llandudno, Gwynedd
LL30 2LP   (Tel. 0492 874411)
On the promenade near the Great Orme, opposite the
Victorian pier
£36–£53 pp b&b

Situated in the centre of the town of Llandudno, a pretty, tree-lined Victorian seaside resort, this attractively decorated and very well maintained hotel overlooks the pier and north-shore beach. Facilities at the St Tudno include two lounges, one of which is reserved for non-smokers, an attractive reception/ coffee lounge for morning coffee and afternoon tea and a Garden Room restaurant seating 60 people. Decorated with hand-painted floral scenes, hanging baskets and an abundance of flowers, the restaurant offers many 'Taste of Wales' specialities with set lunch at £9.50 or £11.50, and set dinners costing up to £22.50 for the full six courses. The hotel's numerous awards include one for the 'Best Hotel Loos in Britain' and the 21 lavishly ruched, draped and colour-coordinated bedrooms are well equipped, though some are rather small. One ground-floor room is suitable for disabled guests.

Heated covered swimming pool; nearby golf; ski slope; walking; nearby waterskiing and windsurfing in bay; boat trips from pier; fishing; sandy beach

LLANSANTFFRAID

2/4 10

The Old Rectory, Llanrwst Road, Llansantffraid, Glan
Conwy, Clwyd LL28 5LF   (Tel. 0492 580611)
Signposted on the A470
Closed 7 December–1 February
£61–£67.50 pp dinner and b&b

A delightful Georgian rectory set in two and a half acres of pretty gardens with superb views over the Conwy estuary, Snowdonia mountains and the soaring towers of Conwy

Castle. The country-house decor is unfussy and relaxed: guests dine together around a large antique table, and bedrooms are comfortably furnished with hardwood half-tester beds. Wendy Vaughan's cooking reflects a French influence, has received many awards and is based on the freshest local produce, including salmon, turbot, Welsh lamb and Welsh black beef. A four-course dinner costs £24.50 for non-residents. A harpist sometimes plays before dinner on summer evenings. The Vaughans are only too willing to provide assistance and recommendations for walking tours from their extensive local knowledge. A non-smoking hotel.

Walks in Snowdonia National Park; sailing (three miles away); sea and river fishing (within five miles); beach (three miles away); Bodnant Gardens (two miles away)

LLANRWST

IOI 🏠 ♨ ◇ 💳

Tu Hwnt I'r Bont, Llanrwst, Gwynedd, North Wales
(Tel. 0492 640138)
Attached to the west end of Llanrwst bridge, close to town centre
Open 10.30am–5.30pm Tues–Sun, Easter to first Sunday in October, and all bank holidays

This National Trust cottage was built in 1480 as Llanrwst's original courthouse. Now a tea room, the aptly named 'Beyond the Bridge' sits so close to the River Conwy that it floods several times each year; a fact illustrated by the marks on one wall recording the highest flood levels since 1978. The low oak-beamed ceilings which allow only shorter customers to walk fully upright justify the presence of 'Mind your head' warnings in no less than 26 languages. The tea rooms are decorated with original antique furniture and bric-a-brac and are recommended for the hot scones with jam and fresh cream (£1.80) and barabrith (Welsh speckled bread). The light lunch menu includes meat salads for £4 or ploughman's with hot granary rolls and Welsh cheese for £3. Home-made mustard, scones and specially blended tea are sold on the premises and the upstairs gift shop sells Welsh craftwork. The tea rooms are accessible for the disabled but there are no lavatories at all on site.

Waterskiing, jetskiing and canoeing on nearby lakes; many lakes within walking distance; salmon fishing on river, trout fishing on Lake Crafnant nearby; children's swings in park; miniature golf; bowls; cricket; football; walks by River Conwy and signposted walks in Gwydir Forest (half a mile away)

LOWSONFORD

Fleur de Lys, Lowsonford, nr Henley-in-Arden, Warwickshire B95 5HJ   (Tel. 0564 782431)
Open 11.30am–11pm Mon–Sat; noon–3pm, 7pm–10.30pm Sun

A heavily beamed and attractively furnished 17th-century pub with extensive bar areas including an excellent family room. The varied and changing bar menu boasts a reputation for quality, offers up to 16 choices of dish per course and is reasonably priced at between £1.50 and £3.95 for starters; £4.50 to £8.50 for main dishes and £1.85 for dessert. A children's menu at £1.95 and vegetarian meals are always available. Outside the pub, the extensive and pleasant beer garden offers plenty of seating, ample parking for clients and a good rustic play area for young children. The Birmingham–Stratford canal runs along the foot of the garden and provides six boat moorings, making the pub an ideal stop-off point for those exploring the waterways. The pub's old-fashioned layout means that it is not suitable for disabled access.

Boating; walking; fishing

NORTH CERNEY

inn 6/6 🏠 🍴 ✒️ 💳

The Bathurst Arms, North Cerney, nr Gloucester,
Gloucestershire   (Tel. 028 583281)
On the A435
Open 11am–3pm, 6pm–11pm Mon–Sat; noon–3pm, 7pm–
10.30pm Sun
£26–£42 pp b&b

The six individually decorated rooms in this rosewashed 17th-century pub are each named after a flower, attractively furnished and have a light, pretty decor. Set in very rural surroundings (though just off the main road) with a comfortable rustic atmosphere, this freehouse is an ideal pitstop, especially during the summer months when the barbecue meals are available. Run by an enthusiastic and hospitable couple who are passionately dedicated to providing quality food and drink, the inn has a separate room with an open fire which seats parties of up to 50: an interesting venue for a private function or conference. In summer, barbecues take place in the large riverside beer garden which is bordered by flowers and floodlit during the evening. A small family room is available for young children. The pub is accessible to the disabled although it has not been specially adapted.
Cotswold Water Park (waterskiing, windsurfing, horse riding and jetskiing); golf; Roman villa; fishing; walking

NORTHWICH

🏨 30/60 🏠 🍴 ✒️ 💳

Friendly Floatel, Northwich, Cheshire CW9 5HD
(Tel. 0606 44443)
Off the A556 north-east of Chester
£46.25 single, £52.25 double, breakfast £3.75–£5.75

This hotel is literally on the water: you will find it floating at the confluence of the River Weaver and the River Dane, right in the centre of Northwich. Although the situation is not picturesque, the place has fascinating novelty value. One of the UK's few floating hotels, it is smartly decked out in black and white, to blend with the other buildings in the town centre. Two swing bridges either side of the floatel are the only examples of their kind in the country, and still open up occasionally to admit passing craft. All of the cabins (bedrooms to landlubbers) have balconies; those that do not look out on to the water have views of the landscaped gardens. The Waterside restaurant, aboard the floatel, seats 65 people and overlooks the floating garden, a fountain and the floodlit water court. The table d'hôte menu costs £12; the à la carte menu from £15 (non-residents are welcome). There is a ramp up to the floatel, and three of the cabins on the lower deck are specially designed for disabled visitors, with large bathrooms (and rails), low-level light switches and so on.

Walks, watersports and fishing nearby; sauna and sunbed for residents only

PENALLT

The Boat Inn, Lone Lane, Penallt, Monmouth, Gwent
NP5 4AJ   (Tel. 0600 712615)
Approach via railway footbridge across Wye, from Redbrook, Gloucestershire (on the Monmouth–Chepstow road). Parking in Redbrook Rovers car park
Open 11am–3pm, 6pm–11pm Mon–Sat; noon–3pm, 7pm–10.30pm Sun

As if its idyllic riverside location weren't enough, this pretty Welsh sandstone pub also offers a wide range of immaculately kept real ales. A list of 'Today's Real Ales', 12 to 14 beers long, and the 'original gravity number' for each are chalked up on a blackboard menu. Tapped from a gleaming row of barrels behind the bar, beer is kept cool by a bare stone wall cut into the hillside. The simple interior decor features quarry tile and flagstone floors, and warm wood panelling. Pan Haggerty, Rogan Josh and smoked Wye salmon (during summer months) are among the local bar menu specialities: prices range from £1.20 to £4.20. Streams and a small waterfall trickle down grassy hillside terraces, where the natural, green, terraced garden provides plenty of seating in summer from

which to spot the occasional passing badger, deer or rabbit.
Canoes can tie up below the pub.
Wye Valley walks and Offa's Dyke path; canoeing; salmon and coarse fishing

PENARTH

The Captain's Wife, Beach Road, Swanbridge, nr Penarth,
South Glamorgan CF6 2UG   (Tel. 0222 530066)
Off the A4267, three miles from Penarth
Pub open 11.30am–3.30pm, 5.30pm–11pm Mon–Fri; all day
Saturday (in summer 11am–11pm); noon–3pm, 7pm–
10.30pm Sun. Restaurants open noon–2.30pm, 7pm–10.30pm
(Smuggler's Haunt restaurant is closed Sun evening, Mon and
Tues morning)
A delightful old pub, with two restaurants and a resident
ghost, looking over a pebbly beach, Sully Island and beyond to
the Bristol Channel. Low tide allows walkers to cross to the
island, though some have been stranded by the incoming tide.
The large traditional bar, with exposed stone walls and wood
floorboards with scattered rugs and Liberty prints, is split into
several areas, one of which is enhanced by a rustic high-backed
settle surround. In the Smuggler's Haunt grill above the bar,
diners can enjoy charcoal-grilled steaks and chicken, served
with a make-your-own salad and potatoes, while gazing upon
the bar's vast stone fireplace from the balcony. Mariner's à la
carte restaurant, serving fish and steak grills, opens on to the
pub's pretty flagstoned courtyard with a rose trellis, dovecote
and white doves. Prices in the two restaurants range from
£3.95 to £10.50 per main dish.
Walking; beach; watersports and deep sea fishing trips from Penarth

PENCRAIG

Pencraig Court Hotel, Pencraig, Ross-on-Wye, Herefordshire
HR9 6HR   (Tel. 098 984306)
On the A40 just out of Ross-on-Wye
Open April–October
£30–£45 pp b&b

Situated on the top of a hill, this elegant, Grade II listed
Georgian house has spectacular views across the beautiful Wye
Valley and River Wye and affords easy access to the Forest of
Dean and Raglan, Goodrich and Chepstow castles. Well
decorated and furnished and refreshingly spacious inside, the
hotel is light and airy with comfortable public rooms including
a television salon and sitting room. The range of bedrooms is
located on first and second floors and includes a four-poster
honeymoon suite. Despite the hotel's close proximity to the
A40, there is a tranquil atmosphere, enhanced by the three and
a half acres of extensive lawns, gardens and woodland, around
which guests can stroll. The elegant restaurant seats 25 to 30
people and opens for dinner only (£14 for a four-course meal).
The hotel has a large private car park set well away from the
road.
Salmon and trout fishing can be arranged; walking

PENMAENPOOL

The George III Hotel, Penmaenpool, Dolgellau, Gwynedd
LL40 1YD   (Tel. 0341 422525)
Off the A493, two miles west of Dolgellau
Closed Christmas and New Year
£31–£56.60 single, £85–£95 double b&b

At high tide, boats moor alongside this delightful 17th-century
inn, situated on a magnificent headland in the Mawddach
estuary amid the inspiring scenery of Snowdonia National
Park. The hotel has two bars, both of which overlook the
estuary; the Cellar, only open in summer, is a flagstoned,
black-beamed bar with nautical decor which opens out to

tables by the water and offers toasted sandwiches and a self-serve cold buffet from £3.95, while the Dresser bar, with its excellent estuary views, produces an imaginative selection of food such as smoked trout, Dublin Bay prawns and roast spare rib of pork. In the hotel's restaurant (which seats 45 people, with three water-view tables) the menu features game and fresh seafood with a three-course dinner costing from £15. Six bedrooms are in the creatively restored shoreside railway building and although each room has a slightly different charm, all 12 have wonderful views over the estuary.
Precipice Walk; New Precipice, Cader Idris and Torrent walks nearby; sea and river fishing; beach; golf; riding (one mile away); pony trekking; gold and slate mines

PERSHORE

The Angel Inn and Posting House, 9 High Street, Pershore, Worcestershire WR10 1AF   (Tel. 0386 552046)
Closed Christmas Day
Bar open 10am–11pm Mon–Sat; noon–3pm, 7pm–11pm Sun
£40–£64 double room b&b (two four-poster rooms available)
Set in the heart of Pershore, a thriving market town which dates back to AD 972 and displays many buildings of great character and historic interest, this tempting coach inn enjoys period decor in all the public areas and an especially attractive and relaxing oak-panelled restaurant with room for 50. Set lunch is priced at £13.95 and dinner à la carte ranges from £7.50 to £13.50 per main dish. Alternatively, light meals and bar snacks (from £1.75 to £4.50) may be taken throughout the day in the lounge area, where guests and passers-by are also invited to take coffee or Pershore cream teas. The Inn assures helpful and efficient service with accommodation in individually decorated rooms kitted out with all modern conveniences. A spacious garden behind the hotel leads down to private moorings along the river bank. The hotel may be accessible to the disabled but does not have special facilities.
Walks and fishing nearby

PORTMEIRION

The Portmeirion Hotel, Portmeirion, Gwynedd LL48 6ET
(Tel. 0766 770228)
£68–£150 per room/suite b&b

Set at the water's edge on the little, wooded peninsula of Portmeirion, with sweeping views across the Traeth Bach estuary to the mountains beyond, the Portmeirion Hotel's position alone is sublime. It stands near an 18th-century colonnade, a medieval town hall, a glorious jumble of colour-washed cottages, a pantheon and a campanile which together make up the Mediterranean-flavoured fantasy village built by Sir Clough Williams-Ellis between 1925 and 1973. The hotel interior is luxurious with a typically 'Portmeirion' theatrical flavour. From the 'Italian', 'Indian', 'Peacock' or indeed any of the individually decorated and named bedrooms, guests enjoy superbly clear views of the estuary and with the columns in the curved restaurant coming from a wrecked ketch, at high tide it's like dining in a 1930s ocean-going liner. Lunch costs £13.50, dinner £25 (non-residents are welcome). Seasonally priced self-catering cottages nearby are available from £213 to £635 per week for two to eight people, but be sure to book well in advance. The hotel facilities include disabled toilets, but the rocky, sloping terrain of Portmeirion may be off putting to the disabled. There is an admission charge to the village for day visitors.

Heated outdoor pool open from May to September; tennis court; walking; pony trekking; watersports; fishing; several sandy beaches

RED WHARF BAY

The Ship Inn, Red Wharf Bay, Anglesey   (Tel. 0248 85 2568)
Off the A5025
11am–11pm Mon–Sat; noon–3pm, 7pm–10.30pm Sun

An extremely pretty, crooked, whitewashed 16th-century inn directly on the waterside in Red Wharf Bay. The welcomingly traditional interior and the three bars in this inn are decorated

with old clocks, fishing paraphernalia, ships' wheels and ropes, Toby jugs, and have old fox-hunting cartoons adorning the walls. All bars and the 34-seat upstairs restaurant (generally available for private functions only) overlook the bay and the 10 square miles of Cockle Sands where scores of boats are moored in summer. The large lawn of the beer garden stretches to the beach and provides outdoor picnic-table seating for up to 120 customers during the warmer season. The Ship Inn is well known and highly popular for its delicious and unusual bar food, such as parsnip cobbler and venison sausages, averaging £4.80–£5.10 in price, though specialities such as home-cured gammon steaks cost £7.75. The menu is revamped daily and all dishes come with garnish, potatoes and accompanying vegetables. There are plenty of vegetarian dishes on the menu. Beers served include the landlord's eponymous Kenneally's bitter. The inn has a specially widened door and may be suitable for the disabled.
Walking; windsurfing and canoeing in bay; fishing; beach

ROSS-ON-WYE

Hope and Anchor, Riverside, Ross-on-Wye, Herefordshire
(Tel. 0989 630030)
From the A40/A49 roundabout, follow signs to Ross
Open 11am–11pm Mon–Sat (mid June to end of August);
11am–2.30pm, 5pm–11pm Mon–Sat (Sept to mid June);
noon–3pm, 7pm–10.30pm Sun
The lively bar area overlooking the River Wye is divided by arches, and has a strong boating theme, amplified by all the boating bric-a-brac. The upstairs parlour bar is cosy, with Victorian prints on the walls, and armchairs, and opens into the Victorian-style dining room. Pretty and well-tended gardens lead directly to the river bank and the extensive river frontage, from which an Edwardian pleasure boat belonging to the pub is launched in the summer months. Local cider, Guinness, Murphy's, Flowers Original and Bass are on draught at the bar. Bar snacks are available at lunch and dinner, priced from £1.95 to £4.50, and there are riverside barbecues in

the summer. The pub no longer offers bed and breakfast accommodation, but does have a four-bedroom house for rent in the holidays (£150–£250 per week, two rooms have river views). This is 40 yards behind the pub, and is called River View. There is wheelchair access to the pub.

Walking; canoeing (PGL); fishing by the pub; Silver Band concerts on summer Sundays (May–August, 7.30pm–9.30pm on lawn)

ROSS-ON-WYE

Wye Lodge, 24 Wye Street, Ross-on-Wye, Herefordshire
HR9 7BT   (Tel. 0989 66599)
Off the main Hereford–Monmouth road (call for directions)
£19.50 pp b&b
A comfortable 'home from home' atmosphere is offered at this attractive and fully restored Victorian house, which has a garden descending to the bank of the River Wye. Although generally a bed and breakfast guesthouse, providing the full four-course English breakfast, there is a residents-only river-view restaurant seating six for dinner on request (from £10). The sympathetic conversion of the basement and cellar provides good amenities and accommodation for families. Just yards from the lodge, a garden gateway leads to the river bank and the hotel has the added bonus of being next door to the excellent 'Hope and Anchor' pub (see above). Pets are generally accepted, subject to prior notification and the owners' agreement. There are two ground-floor rooms for disabled visitors.

Many interesting walks; fishing; canoeing nearby

ROSS-ON-WYE

Pengethley Manor Hotel, Harewood End, Ross-on-Wye,
Herefordshire HR9 6LL (Tel. 0989 87211)
Call for directions
£50–£77 pp b&b

Set in 15 acres of beautiful countryside, overlooking a trout lake in the heart of Herefordshire, Pengethley Manor is surrounded by attractive lawns, gardens and wooded walks. The hotel's history dates back to the reign of Henry VIII. The fine oak-panelled library has an open log fire in winter. Individually decorated rooms are tasteful and boast very elegant furnishings; some have beamed ceilings. The Georgian restaurant seats 50, with three water-view tables, serves much home produce and has an excellent reputation: cuisine includes Wye salmon, Welsh lamb, and local beef, cooked with fresh herbs from the garden. Vegetarians do not have to make do with 'alternatives': they have their own complete menu. Lunch costs £15, the table d'hôte dinner £21. The staff are friendly and obliging. One of the ground-floor rooms has facilities for disabled visitors. There is a helipad.

Nine-hole pitch and putt; outdoor heated swimming pool; trout lake; snooker room; croquet lawn; interesting walks in Forest of Dean and Symonds Yat; sailing; on-site or river fishing can be arranged

RUCKHALL

inn 2/5

The Ancient Camp Inn, Ruckhall, nr Eaton Bishop, Herefordshire HR2 9QX   (Tel. 0981 250449)
Off the A465 just outside Hereford (call for directions)
Bar open noon–2.30pm, 6pm–11pm Mon–Sat; noon–2.30pm, 7pm–10.30pm Sun
£58 double room b&b (without view £35 single, £48 double)
Perched 80 feet above the River Wye on the site of an important Iron Age settlement, the inn has beautiful views over the river. It is a very secluded spot – you are not likely to find it by accident. Airy, modern rooms offer the convenience of *en suite* facilities but blend sympathetically with the intimate and informal surroundings of the 19th-century restaurant and bar areas, where hand-made wooden furniture and the stone-walled bars make for a rustic atmosphere. The bar overlooks the river and serves Woods Parish bitter. Bar meals can be served on the terrace. The restaurant seats 30 and opens in the evenings only; bar meals are available at both lunch and supper

(Note that there is no food available on Sunday or Monday nights). There is disabled access to the pub, restaurant and lavatories, but not to the accommodation.
Walks in beautiful countryside; 400 yards of river frontage available for fishing; golf nearby

RUGBY

 7/31

Brownsover Hall Hotel, Brownsover Lane, Old Brownsover, Rugby, Warwickshire CV21 1HU   (Tel. 0788 546100)
Off the A426 between Rugby and Junction 1 of the M6
£40–£100 per room b&b
An imposing mock-Gothic hall, rebuilt by Sir Gilbert Scott in the 18th century for the Broughton-Leigh family and set in seven acres of woodland with attractive lawns that lead to the banks of the river. The interior boasts some impressive architecture with stone archways and a timbered gallery. The restaurant seats 60 people: the set lunch costs £9.95, the set dinner £16.95. The whole hotel has been recently refurbished with elegant yet comfortable furnishings and decor. More developments are in the pipeline and will add 60 more bedrooms, a banqueting hall and leisure centre. There are already impressive conference facilities.
Walking; sailing; waterskiing; fishing organized through hotel

ST DAVID'S

14/25

The Warpool Court Hotel, St David's, Pembrokeshire SA62 6BN   (Tel. 0437 720300)
West of St David's (call for directions)
Bar open noon–2pm Mon–Sun; restaurant open noon–2pm, 7pm–9.15pm Mon–Sun
£38–£55 pp b&b
The Warpool Court Hotel, built in the 1860s as St David's Cathedral Choir School, adjoins National Trust land in the Pembrokeshire Coast National Park and is worth visiting for

its superb coastal location overlooking St Bride's Bay,
Skokholm and Skomer islands. The building itself houses a
unique collection of antique ceramic wall tiles and has a 70-seat
restaurant and a bar, both of which enjoy stunning views of the
bay and welcome non-residents. Traditional lunch and dinner,
at around £12 and £22 respectively, are served in the restaurant,
although at midday guests and visitors may prefer to sample
the bar meals (from £3 to £10). The hotel assures a choice of at
least two vegetarian meals at each serving. Extra facilities
include two sitting rooms (one with clear water view), cot
loan, baby-listening service, plus a large garden with summer
seating facing the bay. Pets are only admitted to certain
bedrooms and a charge of £4 per day is applied. The ground
floor and restaurant are all on one level but there are no special
facilities for the disabled.

*Covered heated swimming pool (Easter to end of October); all-
weather tennis court; sauna; gym; children's play area including table
tennis and pool at hotel; free coastal trips in hotel's boat about three
times a week, weather permitting; Pembrokeshire coastal path walks;
watersports at nearby Whitesands Bay and Newgale beach; sea
fishing; beaches within short drive; recently added attractions include
satellite movies and free golf*

SHREWSBURY

The Boathouse Inn, Port Hill Road, Shrewsbury, Shropshire
(Tel. 0743 362965)
On the B488 just south west of Shrewsbury
Open 11am–11pm Mon–Sat; noon–3pm, 7pm–10.30pm Sun
Comfortable, quiet and quite cosy with two bars, the Inn
caters for teachers at lunch and early evening and yuppies at
night, according to the staff. It is in a lovely spot, particularly
nice on a summer evening, though a little tricky to find if you
are coming through the town. The long lounge bar looks
across the river to the 'quarry', an extensive park, which can be
reached by an attractive iron bridge that crosses the river just
beyond the pub. There is a patio area outside the pub, and also a

good beer garden. Bar food – for example, ploughman's or lasagne – is available beween noon and 2pm, and 5pm and 7.30pm; beers on offer include Boddington's, Wadworth's and Flowers (IPA and Original). Pets can be accommodated by request.

Walking; quarry park; watersports; fishing

SIBSON

Miller's Hotel and Restaurant, Main Road, Sibson, Nuneaton, Warwickshire CV13 6LB   (Tel. 0827 880223)
On the A444, the Nuneaton–Burton-on-Trent road
Bar open for meals noon–2.15pm, 7pm–10.15pm Mon–Sun; restaurant open 12.15pm–2.15pm, 7pm–9.45pm all week except Mon and Sat lunch
£51–£71 per room b&b
Miller's Hotel and Restaurant is set in a stylish mill and bakery conversion that is adequately furnished and decorated with reasonably sized rooms. Decorative fountains are to be found both in and outside the hotel and a small stream, turning a large waterwheel, runs through the bar area. For residents and non-residents alike there is a stone-walled, beamed dining area which serves a traditional roast lunch on Sundays for £7.95 (£4 for children) and à la carte midday and evening meals at approximately £17. A large selection of hot and cold meals are also served in the bar lounge and are priced in the region of £1.95 to £4.95. The range of accommodation in double, twin and single rooms includes colour and satellite television, tea- and coffee-making facilities and *en suite* bathrooms. A simple four-poster bridal suite is available, as are conference facilities for a maximum of 80 people. The hotel is well placed for access to Bosworth battlefield, Twycross zoo and Kingsbury water gardens and is suitable for the disabled with ramps and ground-floor rooms.

Walking; Bosworth Field; Twycross zoo; coarse fishing locally

STRATFORD-UPON-AVON

🏨 ≈4/63 👪 🏌 🕭 ▭

Arden Hotel, 44 Waterside, Stratford-upon-Avon,
Warwickshire CV37 6BA   (Tel. 0789 294949)
Opposite entrance to Swan Theatre (call for directions)
Bar open 12.30pm–2pm all week; restaurant open 12.30pm–
2pm, 6pm–9pm all week
£54–£68 single, £79–£100 double b&b
The Arden Hotel occupies a very central position overlooking
the Swan Theatre, the River Avon and the surrounding
green, where a summer marquee is erected providing a good
venue for weddings and private receptions. Shakespeare's
father is believed to have been buried here. The hotel is
actually two very attractive annexed houses, dating from the
17th century and Regency period, but until the intended
interior refurbishment is completed, furnishings may seem
slightly disappointing. In recognition of its key location in
such a theatrically important town, the hotel's 70-seat
restaurant offers not only carved buffet lunch (from £9.95)
and dinner à la carte from 7pm–9pm, but also a special pre-
theatre set dinner for around £13.50 from 6pm to 9pm. The
bar, which is regularly patronized by theatre and television
actors, is open for snacks and light lunches from £1.40 to
£4.50. The dining areas accommodate non-residents for all
meals, morning coffee and afternoon tea. A very pretty,
terraced garden with seating looks out over the theatres,
green and river. Ten de luxe bedrooms and meeting facilities
are available.
Walking; windsurfing and fishing can be arranged

STRATFORD-UPON-AVON

🏨 70/247 🏘 🔥 ◁ ▭

Moat House International, Bridgefoot, Stratford-upon-Avon,
Warwickshire CV37 6YR (Tel. 0789 414411)
Central Stratford
£62.50–£175 per room b&b
Restaurant open noon–2.30pm, 6pm–11pm Mon–Sat;
12.30pm–2.30pm, 6pm–11pm Sun. Warwick grill open
7pm–11pm Mon–Sun, 12.30pm–2.30pm Sun
A large, modern, low-rise building with extensive facilities for
conferences and business functions. The huge flagstoned lobby
with open fireplace is a concession to character; otherwise the
decor and furnishings, although stylish, are rather uniform.
The bedrooms with contemporary furnishings are well
equipped with all modern conveniences, including 20 with up-
to-date child-minding systems. Attractive lawns and terraces
overlook the river and the Royal Shakespeare Theatre as do the
new riverside carvery restaurant and the on-site leisure centre.
Lunch in the 230-seat riverside carvery costs £11.50, dinner
£14.50, and a three-course dinner in the à la carte Warwick grill
costs about £25. There are two lively bars, one of which
adjoins the in-house Monday-to-Saturday nightclub. Non-
smoking bedrooms are available to guests. The hotel's dining
facilities are open to non-residents and it is well adapted for
the disabled, with two purpose-built bedrooms, lifts, ramps
and converted bathroom facilities.
The hotel has its own leisure centre with swimming pool, spa bath,
steam room and solarium, gymnasium, sauna, beautician, chiropodist
and masseur (open 7am–10pm Mon–Fri, 9am–8pm Sat–Sun);
nearby, guests can find an all-weather football pitch and tennis courts,
fitness centre, squash, walking and rowing; fishing, watersports and
boating can be arranged

STRATFORD-UPON-AVON

IOI 🏠 🚴 🐾 🟦

The Box Tree (Royal Shakespeare Restaurant), Waterside,
Stratford-upon-Avon, Warwickshire CV37 6BB
(Tel. 0789 293226)
Inside the Royal Shakespeare Theatre
Open: 12pm–1.30pm, 5.45pm–11pm
Here, at the very nerve-centre of the Shakespeare industry, the
Royal Shakespeare Theatre enjoys an incomparable position,
with picturesque views of willows along the Avon, occasional
processions of narrow-boats and other pleasure-craft lazily
cruising by, swans and waterfowl in constant profusion, and
the spire of Holy Trinity Church, where William Shakespeare
was baptized and buried. The Box Tree (echoes of *Twelfth
Night*), overlooking the river, seats 120, with 15 tables by the
window looking down on the water. A three-course meal
costs £21.70, and there is an extensive menu with a distinctly
continental flavour. For theatre-goers, meals are served before
and after evening performances, but the restaurant is also open
to the public. There are no facilities for the disabled, and a flight
of stairs has to be negotiated. On the floor below, a self-service
restaurant offers hot and cold dishes.
*Fishing (fee payable), golf, tennis, swimming nearby and three RSC
theatres (Royal Shakespeare Theatre, Swan and The Other Place).
Sightseeing in Stratford includes visits to the five properties of the
Shakespeare Trust, including Shakespeare's birthplace, and river
trips.*

SUTTON COLDFIELD

🏨 50/60 🏠 🐾 🟦

New Hall Hotel, Walmley Road, Sutton Coldfield, West
Midlands B76 8QX   (Tel. 021 378 2442)
£92 pp b&b, £250 per suite
Run by a charming and friendly couple, this rather exclusive
hotel and restaurant is an oasis set in 26 acres of beautiful
grounds and surrounded by a lily-fringed moat just six miles
from Birmingham. It is a 12th-century, Grade I listed building,

reputedly the oldest inhabited moated manor house in England. The Elizabethan oak-panelled dining room and parlour are wonderful; a new drawing room has just been built. Stained-glass and leaded windows add to the unique character of the individually decorated rooms. Most of the bedrooms are in the new wing. There is a very peaceful and relaxed atmosphere to the whole place. The restaurant (decreed Restaurant of the Year by the *Good Food Guide* in 1990) is open to non-residents (set lunch £13.50; set dinner £24.95), and the cuisine is described as modern English and creative. There is one specially adapted bedroom for disabled visitors.

Croquet lawn; putting green; golf driving net; archery; two floodlit, all-weather tennis courts; clay pigeon shooting can be arranged for parties of guests; walks in the 3500-acre Sutton Park nearby; eight miles to Kingsbury water park; riding nearby; golf course (five miles away)

SYMONDS YAT EAST

18/20 ⌂12

Royal Hotel, Symonds Yat East, Ross-on-Wye, Herefordshire HR9 6JL (Tel. 0600 890238)
Village signposted off the A40 (call for directions)
Closed in January
£29.50–£34.50 pp b&b

Being at the end of the lane, this hotel – a converted 19th-century hunting lodge – boasts the nicest situation on the Symonds Yat East river front. There is a charming, if slightly dated feel about the opulent decor and furnishings, but the atmosphere is comfortable and relaxed. The hall boasts columns and arches, a galleried stairwell, and hand-carved wooden friezes. The huge lounge, with a log fire, overlooks the River Wye. Extensive and very attractive rose gardens slope gently to the banks of the river. The staff are notably friendly and helpful. There are two restaurants which seat 80 people between them. There is a Finnish garden sauna cabin and a solarium, which guests can use for a small charge.

Billiards room in hotel; walking; fishing, golf and riding can be arranged

SYMONDS YAT EAST

Saracens Head Hotel, Symonds Yat East, Ross-on-Wye,
Herefordshire HR9 6JL   (Tel. 0600 890435)
Off the A40 near Monmouth, south of Ross-on-Wye, follow
signs to Symonds Yat East
Closed in January
Bar open noon–2pm, 7pm–10pm Mon–Sun
£18.50–£22.50 pp b&b

The Saracens Head Hotel, once a cider mill and stopping place
for barges using the river, stands near an ancient river ferry
crossing in the idyllic and picturesque Wye Valley and offers
wonderful river views from all public areas. A lively
atmosphere pervades the establishment from the bar, with its
central open fireplace and cocktail area, to the large and
extremely popular Riverside restaurant. Both bar and
restaurant are open to non-residents at all sittings. The midday
and evening bar menu (in the £1.50 to £5 price range) includes
soups, salads, ploughman's, and plenty of fresh river fish; table
d'hôte lunch is also provided for £11.95. For those preferring
to dine à la carte, three-course meals in the Riverside restaurant
cost about £16 (restaurant open 7pm–10pm). Beers available at
the bar include Bass real ale, Grolsch and Newcastle Brown.
Between the hotel and the river bank, an attractive terraced
garden offers extensive open-air seating. The compact but
nicely decorated rooms are equipped with all modern
conveniences and guests are invited to enjoy 30-channel
satellite television in the lounge. The bar and restaurant are
accessible to disabled visitors, but not the accommodation.
*River trips on hotel's 'Kingfisher' boat with bar and buffet; good
walking; swimming and fishing with hotel permission*

TENBY

🏰 ≈ 4/9 🏠 🦢 🚫

Goscar Rock Hotel, The Norton, Tenby, Pembrokeshire
SA70 5AA (Tel. 0834 2177)
Facing North Beach in Tenby. Note that in summer, no cars
are allowed through town between 11am and 4pm, 2 July–
September. Use free buses instead
£28 pp b&b, £41–£43.50 pp dinner and b&b
The pretty Georgian house that is Goscar Rock Hotel has an
excellent view along the North Beach to the dramatic Goscar
Rock and the curve of the sea front. The dining room and
lounge share this view, and there is also a light and modern
conservatory. Decor and furnishings throughout are in
keeping with the style of the house, and seven of the bedrooms
are *en suite*. The food is described by owner and chef Bill
Campbell as 'New English and definitely not nouvelle' (dinner
only, not on Sunday evenings; a four-course table d'hôte meal
costs £17.20). Fourteen seats in the dining room have a sea
view, and there is a family bedroom with connecting children's
room.
Blue Flag beach opposite hotel; fishing trips from harbour; lots of
castles in the area; golfing (18-hole course in Tenby); tall ships race in
Milford Haven (20 minutes by car) in July

TEWKESBURY

🏰 ≈ 4/29 🏠 🌡 🐦

The Royal Hop Pole Hotel, Church Street, Tewkesbury,
Gloucestershire GL20 5RT (Tel. 0684 293236)
£45 pp b&b
A fine, half-timbered hotel in the town centre, attractively
decorated and furnished. The hotel has a cosy feel and is full of
character; the drawing room is better described as elegant.
There are log fires in the timbered restaurant, which work to
create a wonderfully intimate atmosphere. Regional and
seasonal dishes can be found on the menu; beef and Guinness
pie is a house speciality. The set lunch costs £7.95, the set
dinner £14.95. There are some four-poster beds, and several

'feature' rooms. At the back of the hotel, well-laid lawns and pretty gardens stretch down to the banks of the River Avon; in summer, guests can bring their drinks out here from the bar. The hotel has private moorings on the river, which visitors can use. There are some ground-floor rooms, but none of these is specially adapted for disabled visitors.
Walking

TRE-ARDDUR BAY

Tre-Arddur Bay Hotel, Holyhead, Anglesey, North Wales
LL65 2UN   (Tel. 0407 860301)
3 miles from Holyhead on B4545
From £39 to £55 pp b&b
Three hundred yards from sea, on the edge of a rocky bay with sandy beaches, the Tre-Arddur Bay Hotel is only five minutes by car from the car ferry at Holyhead. At the hotel, an agreeably informal atmosphere prevails, but service is prompt, courteous and unaffectedly friendly. A three-course dinner costs £15.95, and the menu features (naturally) Welsh lamb, leeks and chicken in a sauce of Welsh liqueur whose ingredients are not disclosed. Bar meals are served in a lovely, airy conservatory, which conveys something of a tropical feeling on a bright summer's day. The decor is attractive, but artificial flowers on the tables slightly mar the effect. Prawns in Marie Rose sauce, tucked into a fresh brown roll (£3.95) are among the excellent 'lighter bites', while serious eaters may turn to steak in Guinness pie (£4.60). Vegetarian specials are available. The hotel has recently undergone renovation, and the large bedrooms, some containing four-posters, are beautifully decorated, with matching floral patterns on curtains and wallpaper. Lees Traditional Ale, drawn from the wood, is as good a pint as any. For disabled customers, an access ramp leads to the reception area, and there is a ground-floor toilet, but no lift to upper floors. Visitors in wheelchairs can be accommodated in the restaurant and bar area, but not in bedrooms.
Fishing, free from the shoreline, and the hotel can arrange boat-hire;

watersports on the spot, and a sub-aqua club; bowling green and tennis courts free to residents; walking and riding in the area, and shooting in season; golf course ¼ mile away; for bird watchers, the RSPB nature reserve at South Stack is two miles distant

UPTON-UPON-SEVERN

Pool House, Hanley Road, Upton-upon-Severn,
Worcestershire WR8 0PA   (Tel. 0684 592151)
On the A449 (off the A4104 from Pershore)
Closed at Christmas
£18.50–£27 pp b&b
A charming Queen Anne period house with direct river frontage and lovely views across the meadow. The spacious rooms are tastefully decorated – the flower arrangements are splendid – and offer excellent facilities for families (cots and high chairs can be provided, for example). There is a television room as well as a sitting room. The beautifully laid lawn is screened from the road by a wall and is plenty large enough to accommodate a marquee. Private dinner parties and functions can be catered for. Most of the tables in the dining room look out to the river.
Interesting walks; fishing; marina for watersports in Upton (book through hotel)

UPTON-UPON-SEVERN

The Swan Hotel, Riverside, Upton-upon-Severn,
Worcestershire   (Tel. 0684 592601)
Bar open 11am–11pm Mon–Sat (summer); noon–3pm,
7pm–10.30pm Sun
£37.50 single, £55 double b&b
The hotel dates from 1540, and the bedrooms are decorated in keeping with the character of the hotel, with traditional furnishings. The attractive beamed lounge overlooks the river, and serves bar lunches from a menu that changes daily. The

restaurant, cosy and beamed, is decorated in cottage style and offers a more extensive menu; there is seating for 50 people. The proprietors, Peter and Sue Davies, have established a widespread reputation for excellent food and draught beer during their 30 years in residence. There is a small garden overlooking the river. The restaurant, bar and lavatories have wheelchair access, but not the hotel.

Fishing and walks nearby; marina opposite the inn for watersports

VAULD

Vauld Farmhouse, Vauld, Marden, Herefordshire HR1 3HA
(Tel. 056884 898)
Off the A49, the Hereford–Leominster road (call for directions)
£30–£60 per room b&b

A beautiful, Grade II listed, 16th-century farmhouse that is well and truly off the beaten track. This fine half-timbered building lies in a quiet country lane in the hamlet of Vauld, known locally as 'sleepy hollow'. The accommodation is excellent, decorated with comfort, charm and period style in mind: there are many heavy beams and whitewashed walls. It would be hard to find a more relaxed, away-from-it-all atmosphere. There are three duck ponds next to the house, and a 17th-century cider mill barn stands opposite, offering four more bedrooms and a guest lounge. A four-course dinner can be provided, by arrangement, for residents only, and costs £12.50 (no lunch); guests are welcome to bring their own wine. The dining room has a large open fireplace, and a flagstone floor. Pets can be accommodated, by prior arrangement.

Good walking; canoeing; fishing on Wye, Lugg and Arrow rivers can be arranged; riding and golf nearby

WARWICK

Saxon Mill, The Coventry Road, Guys Cliffe, Warwickshire
CV34 5YN   (Tel. 0926 492255)
On the A429 Warwick–Coventry road
Open 11am–11pm Mon–Sat (11am–2.30pm, 5.30pm–11pm
October–April); noon–2.30pm, 7pm–10.30pm Sun
This Grade I listed, fully functional watermill that dates from
as far back as 1061, is set in a beautiful location, overlooking
the ancient weir pool and the historic ruins of Guys Cliffe
House. A public pathway passes the restaurant entrance beside
the river, which is visible to bar drinkers via a glass panel in the
pub's flooring. The timbered and whitewashed interior of the
bars and 98-seat 'Harvester' dining area create a warm and
inviting atmosphere. Both the dining room and restaurant bar
have excellent river views, as does the summer garden area
with bench seating and children's play area. Prices in the à la
carte restaurant average £14 for a three-course meal while the
bar menu offers a fairly wide range of lighter meals and snacks.
Saxon Mill is an ideal setting for family visits but it is not
suitable for disabled visitors.
Walking; fishing.

WHITNEY-ON-WYE

Rhydspence Inn, Whitney-on-Wye, Herefordshire
HR3 6EU   (Tel. 04973 262)
At junction of the A438 and A470 between Hereford and
Brecon
Open 11am–2.30pm, 7pm–11pm Mon–Sat; noon–2.30pm,
7pm–10.30pm Sun
£25–£30 pp b&b
A lovely 16th-century timbered drovers' inn, with a warm and
cosy atmosphere, 'complete with genuine creaks, groans and
draughts', add the charming and informative proprietors. The
inn is a short distance from a tributary stream of the River Wye
(which marks the England–Wales border), and is surrounded

by attractive gardens and beautiful countryside. The individually decorated bedrooms are tastefully in keeping with the character of the inn, as are the three dining rooms (these provide seating for 72 people in all. The food has a good reputation, and a three-course meal from the à la carte menu costs between £12 and £20). The bar serves Robinson and Marston real ales, local Dunkerton cider, and bar snacks such as steak and kidney pie (£6.25). The dining rooms are accessible to wheelchairs, but not the accommodation.

Walking; canoeing; coarse and trout fishing; golf; riding and gliding can be arranged

WILTON

Bridge House Hotel, Wilton, Ross-on-Wye, Herefordshire HR9 6AA   (Tel. 0989 62655)
£53 double b&b
A lovely situation that boasts the best river views in Ross, with no sign of the A40. The 250-year-old hotel stands in one and a half acres of land running down to the river, and is efficiently run by a very friendly staff. The spacious rooms are adequately decorated, and the dining room has just been renovated, to give a more intimate atmosphere. There is much emphasis on quality and value for money, especially in the restaurant where much on the menu is home grown. The dining room seats 20 people (set dinner £11.50), and non-residents are strongly advised to book in advance.

Walks in forests and mountains around Wye Valley; watersports; fishing can be organized through hotel; canoeing

WITHINGTON

The Mill Inn, Withington, Cheltenham, Gloucestershire
(Tel. 024289 204)
Signposted from the A436 and A40
Open 11am–2.30pm (3pm on Sat), 6.30pm–11pm Mon–Sat; noon–3pm, 7pm–10.30pm Sun

A heavily beamed, attractive Cotswold house with cottage-style furnishings and the obligatory inglenook fireplace. The original 16th-century flooring adds to the authentic atmosphere of the pub, which has a good reputation for food such as trout and chicken Kiev. The staff are lively and friendly, and the clientele is a blend of locals and tourists. A pretty garden beside the stream is excellent for families and for anyone who wants to appreciate this secluded spot fully: there are no buildings in sight across the valley. Several rooms of varying size are available for private functions for 25 to 40 people. There are four rooms for bed and breakfast accommodation (£24.50 to £38 per room; none of them has a view of the river). The inn is accessible for wheelchairs, but there are no special facilities for disabled visitors.
Walking; riding nearby; Roman villa (ask at pub)

WITHYBROOK

The Pheasant, Main Street, Withybrook, nr Coventry, Warwickshire CV7 9LT   (Tel. 0455 220 480)
On the B4112 between Nuneaton and Rugby
Open 11am–3pm, 6pm–11pm Mon–Sat; noon–2.30pm, 7pm–10.30pm Sun
Closed Christmas Day and Boxing Day
This 17th-century pub enjoys a delightfully rural situation beside the brook from which the village takes its name, and has a lively atmosphere and friendly staff. The two beamed bar areas, filled with artefacts, seat up to 75 people and offer an extensive bar menu including many vegetarian selections with prices ranging from £1.50 to £11.50 per dish. Beers served include draught Guinness and cider, Courage, Directors and John Smith's. Sunday lunch in the slightly more formal 28-seat à la carte restaurant costs around £10 per person with a wide choice of dishes per course (meals available from noon to 2pm, and 6.30pm to 9.45pm). A large outdoor terrace overlooking the brook provides summer seating for 150 for drinks, light snacks or lunches in the pretty, rustic gardens. The pub is not

specially adapted for the disabled but it is fairly easily accessible.
Walking; fishing

WORCESTER

IOI ⚐₁₀ ♿ ✗ ▭

Brown's Restaurant, 24 Quay Street, Worcester WR1 2JN
(Tel. 0905 26263)
Open 12.30pm–2pm, 7.30pm–9.45pm; closed Sat lunchtime and Sun evening
Closed at Christmas
Architecturally interesting, this corn mill has been elegantly converted and furnished in modern style. The very comfortable lounge/café seating both in the gallery and ground floor overlook the river and bridge. The restaurant seats about 100 in all; 10 tables have a direct view of the water. The food (described as New English and French, and organic where possible) maintains an excellent reputation; the menu changes every two or three weeks. Char-grilled meat and fish dishes are a speciality. The set lunch costs £15, Sunday lunch £20, and set dinner £30. The restaurant is accessible to wheelchairs, and so are the lavatories.
River sailing; rowing; salmon and trout fishing; walks in Malvern hills, Wyre Forest and Bringsty Common (ask at pub)

WORCESTER

▦▦ ¹²/₁₅ ⚐ ♿ ◁ ▭

The Diglis Hotel, Severn Street, Riverside, Worcester
WR1 2NF   (Tel. 0905 353518)
On a side street leading to the river, adjacent to Worcester Cathedral
£32.50–£43.50 single, £65.50–£76.50 double b&b
In an attractive, listed brick house next to the River Severn, this is a comfortable and relaxed hotel serviced by a friendly and informal staff. It is close to Worcester Cathedral and has a terrace overlooking the river and county cricket ground which

is perfect for wedding receptions and private functions. The decor is slightly old fashioned. The restaurant, which is now run separately, seats 46 people, and has five tables which look out on to the river. Bar snacks are available at lunchtime (more substantial meals can be provided, if you have booked in advance, and non-residents are welcome at dinner). The bar is accessible to wheelchairs, but not the accommodation.

Walks along river; Cathedral; Royal Worcester Porcelain factory; river trips available at Worcester Steamer Co.

WRENBURY

Dusty Miller, Wrenbury, Cheshire CW5 8HG
(Tel. 0270 780537)
Open 11am–11pm Mon–Sat (March–September); noon–3pm, 6pm–11pm Mon–Sat (October–February); noon–3pm, 7pm–10pm Sun

A popular spot, especially if you are on a boat; the Llangollen canal passes the pub, and the lock right outside is one of its best features. The pub was originally a working mill that dates back to the 16th century. The present pub is a conversion of the 19th-century mill building, whose wheel was worked by the adjacent River Weaver. The bars have the original heavy beams, and are adorned with old milling and farm equipment. There is seating for 60 people outside in the canalside rose garden. The first-floor restaurant seats 38 people and looks out on to the canal; à la carte dinners cost between £13 and £15. One of the two bars also has a view of the canal, and there is an extensive bar menu, providing food between noon and 3pm, and 7pm and 9.30pm every day. The resident proprietor Robert Lloyd-Jones, who carried out the conversions, is extremely knowledgeable about the area, and has twice won the Innkeeper of the Year award. He can also boast that his was one of the first pubs in the country to receive a hygiene certificate.

Walking; watersports; fishing; yacht club at Bridgemoor Winsford Flashes; English Country Cruises next door

WYRE PIDDLE

The Anchor Inn, Main Road, Wyre Piddle, Pershore,
Evesham, Worcestershire   (Tel. 0386 552799)
On the B4084, the Pinvin–Evesham road
Open 11am–2.30pm, 6pm–11pm Mon–Sat; noon–3pm, 7pm–
10.30pm Sun
A quaint but lively 17th-century pub with traditional beams
and inglenooks. There are beautiful views from the dining area
and the very pretty garden sloping down towards the River
Avon. The staff are delightfully friendly and serve food with
an excellent reputation (there is a restaurant, where main
courses cost about £8; bar snacks are also available) in a
wonderfully homely atmosphere. The bar has Flowers
Original and Hooknorton on hand pump. The pub has private
moorings on the river, which can be used by customers. The
pub has wheelchair access and staff are more than willing to
help disabled visitors.
*Walks nearby (Bredon Hill, Malvern hills, Cotswolds); boating and
canoeing on river; golf nearby*

Central England
and the North

NORTH AND CENTRAL ENGLAND

Telegraph

SCOTLAND

NORTH SEA

NORTHUMBERLAND

Cornhill-on-Tweed

Bellingham

Seahouses

Alnmouth

Cullercoats
Tyenmouth
Chollerford
Haydon Bridge
Bardon Mill
Greenhead

NEWCASTLE

TYNE & WEAR

DURHAM

DURHAM

CARLISLE

Brampton

CUMBRIA

Caldbeck

Penrith
Ullswater
Bampton

Keswick
Grasmere
Skelwith Bridge
Watermillock-on-Ullswater
Hawkshead
Ambleside
Windermere
Bowness
KENDAL
Newby Bridge
Spark Bridge
Ulverston
Morecambe

LANCASTER
Milnthorpe
Arnside
Heaton with Oxcliffe

Richmond

Hubberholme
Burnsall

CLEVELAND

MIDDLESBOROUGH
Saltburn
Easington

Piercebridge

Northallerton

Lealholm

Whitby

Scarborough

Bridlington

Stamford Bridge
North Dalton

YORK

Acaster
Malbis

HUMBERSIDE

NORTH YORKSHIRE

Newton-on-Ouse
Knaresborough
Linton

IRISH SEA

NORTH

LYTHAM

Hambleton
little
Singleton
Blackpool
Lytham St Annes
Preston

WEST YORKSHIRE

Helmshore
Sowerby Bridge
Bury
Manchester
GREATER MANCHESTER

MERSEYSIDE
Liverpool

Chester

Stoke-on-Trent

Birmingham

SOUTH YORKSHIRE

Strouborough
Walton
SHEFFIELD

DERBYSHIRE

Ashford-in-the-Water
Rowsley

Castle Donington

Shardlow

NOTTINGHAM~SHIRE

NOTTINGHAM
Rutland

Barrow-upon-Soar
Barkby
Stapleford
LEICESTER~
LEICESTER SHIRE
Medbourne
Hambleton

LINCOLNSHIRE

Grimsby
Brandy Wharf
LINCOLN
Bourne

NORTHAMPTON~
SHIRE

Northampton

Bedford

A Pleasant Some ROADS

hotels
pubs
inn pubs with
accommodation
restaurants

Approx 30 miles

ACASTER MALBIS

inn 6/8

The Ship Inn, Acaster Malbis, York YO2 1XE
(Tel. 0904 705 609/703 888)
South of Bishopthorpe on the B1222, just to the east of Acaster
Malbis
£35 single, £50 double b&b
A cosy, traditional inn, The Ship dates from the 17th century;
in those days, it was frequented by Cromwell's army and
assorted river pirates. The inn is separated from the River Ouse
by the pub car park. This slightly mars what could be a perfect
site, but you can see the river from one of the two bars, and
from the three window tables in the restaurant as well as from
the garden (which overlooks the river). The bars offer hand-
pulled beers and bar meals; the restaurant seats 40 people and
has more elaborate food on offer; steaks and fresh fish are
specialities, and a set meal costs £10.95. Downstairs, there is an
open fire in winter; upstairs, the bedrooms are pretty and
simply furnished. There are extensive mooring facilities for
visitors who are passing on the river. In the summer, a
marquee springs up on the lawn.
*Walking; boating (inn has private moorings); coarse fishing (£3 a
day), tickets available from the pub; York racecourse five minutes
away; mini cruiser (£35 a day), barges and yachts can be hired nearby;
ferry runs twice a day to York (£4.50)*

ALNMOUTH

10/10

The Marine House Private Hotel, 1 Marine Road, Alnmouth,
Alnwick, Northumberland NE66 2RW   (Tel. 0665 830 349)
Off the A1068
£33–£37 dinner and b&b
Alnmouth is a sleepy, unspoilt and beautiful seaside village. In
medieval times it was an important sea port, and in the 18th
century was famous for its smugglers. Originally a granary,
then a vicarage, this charming, unsophisticated seaside guest
house was converted by its present owners 15 years ago. The

golf links is just across from the hotel and the beach runs from the links to the sea. Room 1 is the best, with a bay window and window seat looking out to sea, but all of the rooms have sea views and mod cons. A terraced garden rises behind the house to the churchyard and also has fine, sheltered sea views. There are two self-catering cottages, and one newly built studio for two (£74–£386 and £35–£256 per week). The dining room seats 30, and all tables look out to sea. Dinner is at 7pm, for residents only. The owners also rent out Begonia House, an 18th-century sea-captain's house that sleeps four to seven people, and has fine views of the bay and the beach from its drawing room, for between £193 and £400 per week, depending on season.

Games room; football; cricket; horse riding; golf; walking; wind-surfing; sailing; canoeing; fishing; beach

AMBLESIDE

Wateredge Hotel, Waterhead Bay, Ambleside, Cumbria
LA22 0EP   (Tel. 05394 32332)
Closed December to February
£43.50–£75.25 pp dinner and b&b
Converted from two 17th-century fishermen's cottages, the hotel is set at the heart of Lake Windermere's bustling tourist centre. There are low-beamed ceilings and farmhouse dressers in the lounge and bars, where nooks and crannies offer private, cosy seating. The windows offer good views of the length of the lake and the swans on the jetty. Bedrooms are bright and decorated with floral prints and cottage-style decor. The dining room seats 48, serving a sumptuous six-course dinner (£21.50), including dishes such as paupiettes of plaice with spinach farcies served on a shellfish sauce followed by fresh mango and raspberry crème brûlée. In summer, morning coffees, lunches and teas are served on the patio and lawns leading down to the lake's edge.

Watersports; walking; trout fishing (equipment not supplied); private jetty (launch fee from £3.50); lake cruises from £3.75

ARNSIDE

Stonegate Guest House, The Promenade, Arnside, Cumbria LA5 0AA   (Tel. 0524 761171)
£15 pp b&b

The guest house, built in 1884, is right on the water and pretty promenade in a quiet, unspoilt village, which boasts spectacular views of the Kent Estuary and Lakeland hills. It is situated at the start of one of the week-long Lakeland walks and would be an ideal base for people who want to be close to the famous beauty spot but want to escape the commercialism. The bedrooms are pretty and still have original fireplaces. The dining room seats 20, with six tables overlooking the sea. The set dinner is £8.50, and involves home-made food such as soups, pâtés, chicken, fish and vegetarian dishes. There is room for 12 on the sea-facing patio, where teas and dinner are served in summer; non-residents are welcome here at weekends. It is a non-smoking hotel.

On Cumbrian Cycle Way; walking; watersports; windsurfing; fishing; grass and pebble beach; sailing club on estuary; bird watching

ASHFORD-IN-THE-WATER

Riverside Country House, Ashford-in-the-Water, Bakewell, Derbyshire DE4 1QF   (Tel. 062981 4275)
Off the A6, between Bakewell and Matlock
£80–£92.50 per room b&b

A Georgian country-house hotel with a warm atmosphere and a walled garden that leads down to the River Wye. There is an oak-panelled lounge with an open fire for drinks before and after dinner. Rooms are individually decorated, with many floral prints, and with four-poster and half-tester beds. The restaurant is open to non-residents for afternoon teas and Sunday lunch. A four-course dinner is £28.50 and offers a mouth-watering range of nouvelle cuisine such as pigeon and quail eggs salad followed by freshly caught brown trout served with a champagne and dill sauce. However, if you have a particular favourite dish the chef will prepare it for you, given 24-hours' notice. There is an impressive list of 89 wines. There are four ground-floor rooms suitable for disabled visitors, all with *en suite* facilities.

Local stately homes worth visiting include Chatsworth, Haddon Hall and Hardwick Hall; walks along River Wye in the Peak District National Park; golf can be arranged; hang gliding and rock climbing nearby; mine visits; croquet on the lawn; fishing

BAMPTON

🏠 16/18 🐾 ♿ 🔖 💳

Haweswater Hotel, Lakeside Road, Bampton by Penrith CA10 2RP   (Tel. 0931 3235)
On minor road, southwards from Bampton, about halfway along the length of Haweswater
£25 pp b&b single, £23 pp double
Here, the traveller will find himself a little off the beaten track, though the area attracts visitors in plenty during the season. A dam deepened and extended the lake of Haweswater to turn it into a reservoir supplying water to Manchester, but it is none the worse for that. Its eponymous hotel, a solid building of 1930s vintage, is the only habitation for miles around. The hotel stands by the road which skirts the eastern side of Haweswater, and makes an ideal base for excursions. Do not expect grandeur or sophistication here: the hotel caters conscientiously to the basic needs of walkers and bird watchers. Pets are accommodated at the management's discretion. Home cooking means generous portions, and afternoon teas are memorably sustaining. The area is an RSPB reserve, and a short distance away, at Riggindale, can be found England's only resident pair of golden eagles.

Marvellous walks on the surrounding fells; boating and canoeing on Ullswater, bird watching; painting; fishing

BARDON MILL

Eldochan Hall, Willimoteswyke, Bardon Mill, Hexham,
Northumberland NE47 7DB   (Tel. 0434 344 465)
Off the A69, through Bellingham
£16–£17.50 pp b&b

A small stone-built family house, at least 200 years old,
converted from two derelict one-up-one-down cottages. It is
in a rural position close to the ancient Reiver castle of
Willimoteswyke. There are two double rooms for guests and a
very attractive residents' lounge with open fire, television and
games. Dinner is for residents only and is a good value three-
course meal at £9. Vegetarians and special diets can be catered
for. Down one side of the garden runs the babbling
Blackclough Burn, and there is a small terrace by the stream.
Hadrian's Wall, the Roman Fort at Housesteads and the
Roman settlement at Vindolanda are all close by. Guests
without transport can be collected from Bardon Mill station
half a mile away. Added extras include babysitting and laundry
services. In many ways the ideal country retreat, very tranquil,
very pretty. Four-legged friends can be accommodated by
prior arrangement.
*Walking; fishing (by arrangement only); swimming; windsurfing;
canoeing; tennis; riding; golf all nearby*

BARKBY

The Brookside, Barkby, Leicestershire   (Tel. 0533 692757)
Off the A47, east of Leicester; call for detailed directions
Open 11am–3pm; 7pm–11pm Mon–Sat; noon–3pm, 7pm–
10.30pm Sun

A 300-year-old pub, in an attractive, popular setting five miles
away from Leicester. A small, quietly burbling brook runs
outside the front door. The interior is decorated with
paintings, brasses and naval memorabilia. The publican's
Toby jug collection, started over 30 years ago, now numbers
upwards of 200. The pub is tied to Allied Breweries and serves

Tetley's bitter, draught Burton Ale and Ansells Traditional Mild on hand pump. Both bars overlook the water and serve bolstering lunches to businessmen and tourists alike. Main courses cost from £3.50 and the favourite speciality is the beef ruff – a hearty sandwich made with a long French stick. Worth the effort of finding it.

Walking; fishing

BARROW-UPON-SOAR

The Navigation Inn, 87 Mill Lane, Barrow-upon-Soar, Leicestershire   (Tel. 0509 412842)
Take the A6 to Loughborough, then the A675
Open 11am–2.30pm, 6pm–11pm Mon–Fri; noon–3pm, 7pm–10.30pm Sun
The pub is well situated in a secluded area by a picturesque arched bridge and lovely stretch of river where the River Soar joins the Grand Union Canal. There has been a building on this site since the days of the Domesday Book; the pub was formerly a resting place for buyers visiting the gravel mine, and then for the navvies who dug the canal. The lounge overlooks the water, and the decor is tasteful and relaxed. There are four real ales on offer at the bar, and good home cooking; the atmosphere is friendly. Outside, there is open-air seating in the garden for when the weather is good, moorings and a good, long, well-worn skittles alley. There is wheelchair access to the ground floor and the garden.

Fishing; walks across fields to Quorndon and Mountsorrel villages

BELLINGHAM

The Riverdale Hall Hotel, Bellingham, Hexham, Northumberland NE48 2JT   (Tel. 0434 220 254)
Take the B6320 to Bellingham, turn west towards Charlton
£35.50 single, £29.50 double/twin pp b&b
A mid-19th-century villa and stables with a modern extension,

which was recently voted the best hotel in Northumberland. The surrounding area was fought over for centuries as it lies 10 miles from Hadrian's Wall and the Scottish border. The hotel sits above its own cricket ground on a terrace above the North Tyne. The bar, games room, indoor swimming pool and extremely fine restaurant all have river views and there is not a single house or farm in sight across the valley. The bedrooms are light and airy and some have four-poster beds. Fifteen garden bedrooms with river views were added in 1992. The restaurant seats 70 and serves award-winning meals for lunch and dinner. Residents can fish for salmon from the hotel's grounds and the management plays host to about 20 touring cricket teams each year. An annual golf tournament is held on the Bellingham course opposite the hotel. A peaceful, relaxed and comfortable place to stay. There are bedrooms on the ground floor, but the bathrooms are not wide enough to admit wheelchairs.

Indoor heated swimming pool; sauna; cricket; golf; putting greens; walking; fishing; watersports (motor boats, windsurfers and sailing boats can be hired on Kielder Water)

BLACKPOOL

The Clifton Hotel, Talbot Square, Blackpool FY1 1ND
(Tel. 0253 21481)
On the promenade, opposite north pier
£55 single, £85 double b&b
One of the more classical old promenade hotels. Thoughtful decoration blends in well with the magnificent staircase and stained-glass windows. The hotel has recently been renovated, giving the main bar, cocktail bar and residents' lounge good sea views. Newly refurbished bedrooms have high ceilings and mouldings. The restaurant seats 150 people, and serves lunch, high tea and dinner. The table d'hôte menu for £9.50 (£5 for lunch) is a mixture of English, French and Italian cuisine of basic fish and steak choices. The hotel has very good value weekend breaks especially in the low season: £35 per person

for dinner, bed and breakfast. Other packages include the theatre, dinner dances, racing, bowling and the Blackpool illuminations. Babysitting facilities available. Two rooms have disabled facilities and hotel has disabled access.

Walking; watersports; fishing; theatre; fun fairs

BLACKPOOL

204/273

The Pembroke Hotel, North Promenade, Blackpool
FY1 2JQ   (Tel. 0253 23434)
On the promenade
£97 single, £122 double b&b

A hideous new building, but cunningly built so that 75 per cent of its rooms have a sea view. Recent refurbishments have added more rooms and a new marble reception area. Inside, the hotel is extremely comfortable as its four-star status suggests, with good service. There are very impressive conference facilities, and a big swimming pool and disco area. There is one à la carte restaurant, the Crystal Room, where 10 tables have a view of the sea, and also a carvery, the Promenade Restaurant, offering good-looking food (£14.25 for a main course). Pets can be accommodated by request (they're not allowed into the public rooms). There are three rooms that may suit disabled visitors (the bathrooms have doors that open outwards, but there are no handrails), and the hotel has disabled access.

Fishing; beach

BLACKPOOL

28/44

Revill's Hotel, 190–4 North Promenade, Blackpool FY1 1RJ
(Tel. 0253 25768)
£18–£25 pp double b&b, single-room supplement, £3 per night

A simple, family-run hotel on the promenade with old-fashioned decor. The sun room runs the length of the hotel and its large windows overlook the sea. The bedrooms facing out to sea are also light and sunny, though the decoration is fairly

basic. The lounge bar offers cabaret and other entertainment in the high season and on special occasions in the winter (such as Christmas). The dining room (dinner only) seats 90 people, with six water-view tables: food is straightforward and good value (fruit cocktail, roast, and sweet costs £6.50 to non-residents). A newly opened café/bar serves food all day. The hotel would suit those on a family holiday or anyone wanting a break in Blackpool for very reasonable prices.
Golf; walking; fishing; beach; theatre

BLACKPOOL

The Warwick Hotel, 603–9 New South Promenade,
Blackpool FY1 1NG   (Tel. 0253 42192)
£28–£48 pp b&b
A 1930s hotel, composed from four adjacent hotels along the promenade. The large swimming pool, with seven surrounding tables overlooking the sea, is particularly pleasant. The decor in the bedrooms is modern, and there are family rooms with bunk beds and large bay windows. The hotel has a large bar with a friendly atmosphere: bar lunches available. The restaurant seats 120, with 12 sea-view tables. Disabled access to ground floor only; no lifts to rooms.
Blackpool pleasure beach; indoor swimming pool; sun bed; The Sandcastle – an indoor water fun centre

BLACKPOOL

The River House Hotel, Skippool Creek, Thornton-le-Fylde,
nr Blackpool FY5 5LF   (Tel. 0253 883497)
10 minutes from Blackpool: call for specific directions
£65 single, £100 double b&b
There isn't yet a blue plaque that says Edward Heath, Sir Robin Day et al are habitués here, but in fact this hotel is famous for being crammed with politicians and journalist at conference times. Owner Mr Scott is buddies with them all. 'One evening

I had *nine* Cabinet ministers at dinner . . .' he'll tell you proudly. Although extemely watery when the tide is in – Mr Heseltine is reputed to have arrived by taxi and got his feet wet – at other times, The River House has a distinctly muddy outlook, though it has to be said mine host makes up for this with endless jolly conversation. The rooms, if you like antique furniture of the over-the-top variety, are a dream. Bathrooms are not *en suite* but compensate by being wildly eccentric – one has a vast bath with wooden 'hooded' shower and a flower-decorated loo and washbasin. Food is good and substantial – about £35 per person – and after dinner you can take your coffee and relax in the conservatory. Well-behaved children and pets are welcome.

Popular with bird watchers and painters; at least a dozen golf courses nearby, including Royal Lytham; clay pigeon shooting can be arranged

BLACKPOOL

IOI 🏠 🍷 🕊 ▭

The White Tower Restaurant, Blackpool Pleasure Beach, Balmoral Road, Blackpool FY4 1EZ   (Tel. 0253 46710)
Open 7pm–10.45pm Tues–Sat; noon–4pm Sun

The restaurant is situated on the second floor of the Wonderful World building; a fine example of 1930s sea-front architecture. Due to its elevation and curving façade the restaurant boasts panoramic views of the sea, the South Pier and the Promenade. It is next to all the lights and sights, rides and excitement of the pleasure beach. Acclaimed as one of the Fylde's top eating establishments, it offers main courses for between £10 and £15, and Sunday lunch from £7.95. There is seating for 70, and all tables look out over the beach. Coasters American Diner on the Promenade is run by the same management and would be a good place to have a drink before eating at the restaurant. It is a new establishment but the design is based on the 1914 casino building which was on the same site. There are facilities for disabled visitors.

Walking; watersports; fishing; pleasure beach

BOURNE

Bourne Eau House, Bourne, Stamford, Lincolnshire
PE10 9LY   (Tel. 0778 423621)
On the A15 north of Stamford
Closed at Christmas and Easter
£28–£30 pp b&b
This listed country house looks over the little Bourne Eau river
to the 12th-century abbey on the opposite bank, which can be
reached by a small wrought-iron footbridge. The architecture
is a mixture of Jacobean and Georgian, which contrives to give
the house the air of a gentleman's town residence. The lovely
Jacobean- and Elizabethan-style rooms are well furnished with
matching period antiques. Exposed beams, woodwork and
fireplaces are offset by white walls and tiles. One of the sitting
rooms has a finely carved 17th-century mantelpiece and a
concert piano. The flagstone-floored dining room seats eight;
dinner is for residents only. The set menu costs £18, and
offers generous portions of home-cooked food using local
Lincolnshire produce. Well-tended gardens run down to the
pretty stretch of water.
*Walks in Bourne Woods (two miles away); Lincoln and Ely
cathedrals; golf (two miles away); fishing, waterskiing and sailing on
Rutland Water nearby; Abbey Lawns across road with tennis courts
(hard and grass); cricket, football, bowls, outdoor and indoor heated
swimming pools in local leisure centre*

BOWNESS-ON-WINDERMERE

The Old England Hotel, Bowness-on-Windermere, Cumbria
LA23 3DF   (Tel. 0539 442 444)
£115 per room (breakfast £7.95)
This Georgian mansion, now a Trust House Forte hotel, is in
an excellent spot on Lake Windermere. The hotel is next to the
Royal Windermere Yacht Club and has views across to Belle
Isle and the Cumbrian hills. The decoration is fairly typical of
the chain; comfortable, with reproduction furniture, bright

chintzes and added touches such as the local author Wainwright's books in the bedrooms. Rooms with the best views cost £10 extra. The bar leads out to a terrace with sweeping lake and garden views. The dining room seats 120, serves 'classic English dishes' including fish, duck and rabbit. Most tables look on to the water, and a three-course dinner with coffee and sweetmeats costs about £16.95. Special diets catered for. Popular with business clientele. Other services include baby-listening, laundry, hairdressing salon and children's play area and high teas. Some ground-floor rooms, though no specific facilities for the disabled.

Walking; snooker; fishing; heated outdoor pool (May to October); watersports; private jetty; lake cruises

BRAMPTON

inn

Abbey Bridge Inn, Lanercost, Brampton, Cumbria CA8 2HG (Tel. 06977 2224)
Off the A69
Open noon–2.30pm, 7pm–11.30pm Mon–Sat; noon–2.30pm, 7pm–10.30pm Sun
£19.50 single b&b, £38 double, £44 double with private bathroom

The Abbey Bridge Inn sits on the banks of the River Irving next to a red sandstone humped-backed bridge built in the reign of James II. Within walking distance is the part-ruined Lanercost Priory (dating back to 1166). A very friendly and comfortable establishment with simple bedrooms, four with private bathrooms and three without. 'The Blacksmith's' bar/restaurant was converted from the 17th-century forge, and the dining tables are on a gallery up a wrought-iron staircase. The home-made food (such as deep-fried Brie, chicken satay, and crispy duck) looks very tasty and a main course costs around £5–£8. Summer days can be spent sitting in the garden next to the river. The hotel would make a good base from which to explore Hadrian's Wall, the Lake District and the Solway Firth area. The downstairs rooms could be used by disabled visitors, though these are not specially adapted. There is trained nursing staff on site. Meals can be taken at the bar.

Trout fishing (£5 a day); watersports and golf nearby; walking; Naworth Castle (one mile away)

BRAMPTON

Tarn End Hotel, Talkin, Brampton, nr Carlisle, Cumbria CA8 1LS   (Tel. 06977 2340)
Closed February
£40 single, £62 double b&b
A 19th-century farmhouse, with old barns, in a beautiful spot on the banks of Talkin Tarn, in the Talkin Tarn Country Park. The friendly, family hotel is right on the edge of the lake, with picturesque jetty and rowing boat. A leisurely walk around the circumference of the lake takes about 20 minutes. The rooms have good views and are prettily decorated, in a cottage style with Laura Ashley furnishings, antiques and patchwork quilts. The dining room seats 30 people, with six lake-view tables and serves French haute cuisine with main courses costing between £10 and £15. There are vegetarian choices on the à la carte menu and an extensive wine list. Non-residents are welcome. Bar lunches are available from noon to 2pm, and afternoon tea is served from 3pm to 4.30pm. There is one ground-floor room, but no specific disabled facilities.

Walking; Hadrian's Wall; watersports; coarse fishing; shooting; row boat rentals; golf course 200 yards away, £12 a day

BRANDY WHARF

Cider Centre, Brandy Wharf, Waddingham, Gainsborough, Lincolnshire DN21 4RU   (Tel. 0652 678 364)
Halfway between Waddingham and South Kelsey on the B1205 (the Grimsby to Gainsborough road)
Open noon–3pm, 7pm–11pm Mon–Sat; noon–3pm, 7pm–10.30pm Sun

Right beside the New River Ancholme, the Cider Centre pub has two bars, one of which overlooks the river. Up to 60 varieties of cider are on offer, 18 of them on draught. Some of these have an alcoholic content of over 7 per cent, and so are sold only in half-pints; visitors are advised to drink them slowly, and with respect. Good cheap bar food is available to punctuate the drinks. There is an orchard and 'Sydre Shoppe' museum next door. The Cider Centre offers visitors' berths for river cruisers, and they also have a caravan site that can accommodate five vans. There is access for disabled visitors, and specially adapted lavatories.
Walking; watersports; fishing

BRIDLINGTON

17/40

The Monarch Hotel, South Marine Drive, Bridlington, Humberside YO15 3JJ   (Tel. 0262 674 447)
On the seafront next to lifeboat station
Closed three weeks over Christmas
£37–£40 single, £25–£30 double pp b&b
Bridlington is a charming seaside resort, especially tranquil out of high season. There is a good balance between the modern bright lights and the original Regency architecture. The Monarch Hotel is typical of a seafront establishment that is comfortable but not luxurious; the public rooms are smartly attractive and the bedrooms well fitted. Good for families and those who want an accommodating, reasonably priced seaside break. (For a two- to four-night break, dinner, bed and breakfast costs £33–£40 per person per night.) The dining room seats 100, with six sea-view tables. The set menu of three courses is very good value at around £12 and includes fresh fish off the local trawlers such as Bridlington Bay fillet of ling; there are also exciting-sounding vegetarian dishes. There is a lift that can be used by disabled guests, but no special facilities.
Walking; watersports; hire boats; fishing (from pier, licence needed); beach; pleasure boats from harbour along coast; fun fair

BURNSALL

🏠 8/12 ⌂ 🏃 🚫 ▭

The Red Lion Hotel, Burnsall, Skipton, Yorks BD23 6BU
(Tel. 075672 204)
On the B6160, two miles from Grassington
£18–£23 b&b
Deep in the dales, the Red Lion is beautifully situated on the right bank of the River Wharfe just across from the village green. The only place from which it is easy to see the water is from the hotel garden where guests can take drinks and food from the bar. The hotel has a separate restaurant, which seats 50. They offer home-cooked food and the set three-course dinner (including coffee) costs £12. There is also a table d'hôte menu and one of the specialities of the house is roast duckling at £12.75. Decor is plain and traditional and the bedrooms are well furnished and comfortable.
Walking; swimming (half a mile away); fishing nearby (trout £16.50 a day, grayling £7 a day); river beach

BURY

🏠 17/47 ⌂ 🏃 ◁ ▭

The Boholt Hotel, Walshaw Road, Bury BL8 1PU
(Tel. 061 764 5239)
£48 single, £59 double b&b
This modern hotel has been built on the site of the birthplace of Henry Dunster (1609–59), the first president of Harvard University. It is in its own peaceful, 50-acre grounds on the outskirts of a busy town, overlooking a small, man-made lake with ducks, and next to two larger lakes. The hotel has been commendably involved in the 'greening' of the area, turning factory ruins into meadows and protecting wildlife. A 19-bedroom extension is underway as well as the addition of a squash court and indoor swimming pool with a sliding glass roof. The decor is an odd mixture of pine and red leather in the reception areas. There are two bridal rooms with four-posters. The restaurant is open from 7pm to 9pm and seats 60 people.

There is disabled access and ground-floor rooms, but bathrooms are not specially adapted.
Walking; watersports; fishing; picturesque gardens; tennis courts; leisure facilities (including spa bath, sauna and gym)

CALDBECK

Watermill Coffee Shop, Priests Mill, Caldbeck, Wigton, Cumbria CA7 8DR   (Tel. 06998 369)
Open 10am–5pm March–September; 10am–5pm Thurs–Sun in October; 10am–4pm Thurs–Sun in November
The café is part of a restored 17th-century watermill, in an extremely pretty complex with shops and a museum. It was originally built by the rector of the neighbouring 800-year-old church. The idea when restoring the building and grounds was to keep it all looking natural: 'Nothing garden-y'. In this successfully natural environment you can eat your picnic or the café food, listen to the bubbling river and watch cricket in the field beyond. The water wheel works by putting 10p in a slot. Dippers and wagtails live on the river banks among the daffodils and cherry trees. There is a tempting gift shop, with wares ranging from scented candles to framed locally taken photographs. The wholesome food from the coffee shop includes nutty cheese bake and lemon surprise pudding, all for reasonable prices. Other attractions within the complex include craft workshops, a bookshop and a mining museum. Bed and breakfast accommodation is available locally. There is wheelchair access to the café.
Walking

CASTLE DONINGTON

The Priest House Hotel, Kings Mills, Castle Donington, Derby DE7 2RR   (Tel. 033281 0649)
Off the A6, south east of Derby
£57.50 single, £67.50 double b&b

A low-beamed, attractive inn with a medieval tower and large grounds in a pretty spot by the River Trent. In the bar, you can find the wheels which used to drive the Chain Ferry across the river; there is also a games room and fruit machines. A good stretch of running water and woodland can be seen from the pub and garden. The restaurant seats 60 people, and serves a table d'hôte menu from £15.50 and à la carte from £18 to £20. One of the chef's specialities is half a sugar-roast duck with orange sauce. Hearty bar snacks are also available. The hotel is convenient for the East Midlands airport. Dogs can be accommodated by prior arrangement. One of the bedrooms is suitable for disabled visitors.

Walking; fishing (trout-permit £3 per day); riding; canoeing outside the hotel (bring own equipment); Donington Racing Museum; Alton Towers nearby

CHOLLERFORD

19/50

The George Hotel, Chollerford, Hexham, Northumberland NE46 4EW   (Tel. 0434 681 611)
From the A69, take the B6318 at Chollerford
£70 single, £90 double b&b
Once a small 17th-century coaching inn and farm, on the main military road between Carlisle and Newcastle, The George has been extended since the war to form a 50-bedroom hotel, and another 25 bedrooms are under construction. The hotel is set right on the banks of the North Tyne next to the five graceful arches of the 18th-century Chollerford Bridge. A very well-kept and peaceful formal garden leads down to the river; a larger informal garden stretches away upstream. In late August and September the salmon can be seen leaping the weir 100 yards from the hotel. A new restaurant has just been completed on the river side of the hotel (set four-course dinner £16.50). Rooms in the modern extensions have the best river views; furnishings throughout are in traditional country-house style. Pets can be accommodated by arrangement only. Two of the bedrooms are easily accessible for wheelchairs.

Hotel has fishing rights for salmon; swimming pool; sauna; spa bath; sunbed; putting; walking

CORNHILL-ON-TWEED

🏘 ⌇ 4/13 🏠 🚵 🐦 ▭

Tillmouth Park Hotel, Cornhill-on-Tweed, Northumberland TD12 4UU   (Tel. 0890 2255)
On the A698, one mile north of Cornhill-on-Tweed
£58 single, £86 double.
The perfect country-house hotel, built in 1882, using stones from nearby Twizle Castle, by the architect Charles Barry (son of the designer of the Houses of Parliament). It is lovingly maintained, and furnished in the Jacobean style, with an impressive gallery, stained-glass windows, and period four-posters in the bedrooms. There are several acres of garden, and five miles of high-quality salmon fishing on the Tweed. A ghillie will guide and advise if necessary. In winter, the River Till, which runs into the Tweed, can be seen from the dining room (which seats 70), drawing room and many of the splendid, enormous bedrooms. Trees block the views in summer. The restaurant serves traditional English food in season and a five-course meal costs £16.50. The guests can enjoy several miles of walking along Twill and Tweed within the 1000-acre estate.
Walking; fishing; beach (15 miles away); National Trust properties

CULLERCOATS

🏘 ⌇ 17/22 🏠 🚵 🐦 ▭

The Bay Hotel, Front Street, Cullercoats, Tyne and Wear NE30 4QB   (Tel. 091 252 3150)
Off the A193, opposite Cullercoats harbour
£18–£25 single, £33–£48 double b&b
Previously the local manor house, this is a modest, family-run hotel. It stands above the small harbour of Cullercoats, with a stunning view across the cliffs and the bay to the ruins of Tynemouth Priory. The American artist Winslow Homer

painted his seascapes from here in 1882–84. The beach remains unspoilt, and has recently been awarded a Blue Flag. The lifeboat is launched from the harbour, and small fishing boats operate from here too. The cocktail bar (very 1970s chrome), dining room (seats 60) and residents' lounge are on the first floor to make the most of the views. Three local bars are downstairs. Some bedrooms have been renovated, but some are still rather basic. For those who want to explore the city, one great advantage is that Newcastle is only 20 minutes away by Metro.

Walking; watersports; sea fishing can be arranged; beach

EASINGTON

Grinkle Park Hotel, Easington, Saltburn, Cleveland
TS13 4UB   (Tel. 0287 640515)
Signposted turning off A171 Guisborough to Whitby road
Open all year
Single room, £65 b&b, twin/double, £80 b&b

Although it lies only 10 miles from the industrial complex of Teesside, Grinkle Park somehow conveys an impression of remoteness, with prospects of rolling, green landscape. Originally the home of the Palmer family, once the world's largest shipbuilders, it became a hotel in 1947, but has happily managed to retain the atmosphere of a country residence, set in 35 acres of ancient woodland, ablaze with rich hues in autumn. In early summer, rhododendrons and azaleas make a dazzling show along the entire length of the impressive drive, and the large duck-pond provides another attractive feature at the end of the croquet lawn. The restaurant, seating 80, offers fresh local produce, including game, and Whitby cod. A three-course table d'hote meal costs £15.50. Bar meals are served in a conservatory extension, whose agreeable ambience is enhanced by a large camellia. There are no ground-floor bedrooms but, for disabled visitors, there is easy access to the restaurant and all public rooms. Bass, Stones and Tennents are available on draught. Recently the Tees Valley Tourist Board

named Grinkle Park the most romantic place to spend a weekend.
Tennis, walking and shooting in the imemdiate vicinity; riding, swimming, sailing within ten miles

FLEETWOOD

🏨 39/57 🛖 🍴 🚫 ▭

The North Euston Hotel, The Esplanade, Fleetwood
FY7 6BN   (Tel. 0253 876525)
£40.50 single, £58 double b&b
A semicircular hotel on the promenade, dating from 1841, with an unspoilt façade. Inside, there is a huge sea-view bar, and photographs of local history on the walls. There are very light bedrooms and suites, with large windows and balconies; some have views of the River Wyre, and some look out over the bay. The restaurant seats 85 and has good watery views from all tables. Lunch is £8.50, and a three-course dinner is £12.75. The famed speciality of the house is fish and chips. One hundred large portions of fresh haddock from the dock are served every day in the high season. The Chatterbox café and a family area in the pub make it a suitable hotel for children. There are disabled lavatories and ramps on the ground floor for lounge, bar and restaurant. The lift is not wide enough for wheelchairs but would help infirm visitors.
Walking; watersports; fishing; beach; golf; games room

GRASMERE

🏨 3/5 🛖 12 🍴 🦆 ▭

Lake View Guest House, Lake View Drive, Grasmere,
Cumbria LA22 9TD   (Tel. 0539 435384)
Open March–November
£21 pp b&b, £31 dinner and b&b (£3 extra for private facilities)
In a good location and off the beaten tourist track through Grasmere, this friendly bed and breakfast would make a good base for touring the Lakes. It is about 500 yards away from a pretty lake and a private footpath winds its way down the

garden to the water's edge where guests can sit and enjoy the tranquillity of Wordsworth country. The house has a sunny television lounge. Pictures by local artists decorate the walls, and are for sale. The dining room seats 12 and dinner is served at 6.30pm for residents only. Bring your own wine. Vegetarians and those with special diets can be catered for. Three self-catering flats are available which sleep two to five people and cost between £105 and £269 per week depending on the season. Two of these have water views. There is one ground-floor room suitable for disabled visitors.

Walks; row boats and windsurfers can be hired nearby; small pebble beach

GREENHEAD

🏠 2/4 🏡 ♿ 🚫 🛏

Holmhead Farm Licensed Guest House and Holiday Cottage, Greenhead, Haltwhistle, Northumberland CA6 7HY
(Tel. 069774 7402)
Off the B6318 (call for directions)
Closed at Christmas and New Year
£19.50 b&b; holiday cottage for four £150–£275 a week
This 150-year-old farmhouse lies directly in the line of Hadrian's Wall beside the upper reaches of the River Tibalt and just below the mound of the ruined 13th-century Thirlwall Castle. It was built with stones from the Wall, with Roman-style arches and a candle-lit, beamed dining room, and modern furnishings. Guests dine together round a large, oak table. The friendly owners offer good, clean, farmhouse accommodation. A large residents' lounge is equipped with television, radio, records, tapes and board games for the use of the guests. A converted garage harbours tables for snooker and table-tennis. A solarium, sunbed and foot massage machine are available to soothe tired limbs and sore feet after walking Hadrian's Wall or the Pennine Way. Mrs Staff is a very knowledgeable guide to the area. The river runs down one side of the small garden. In November, exhausted salmon, nearing their spawning ground, can be seen struggling upstream.

The ground floor of the cottage is specially adapted for the disabled.

Golf; riding; swimming; tennis; bowls; cycling; walking; windsurfing; canoeing; sailboarding; fishing; Roman army museum

GRIMSBY

IOI 🏠 ♿ 🐾 💳

Leon's Fish Restaurant, Riverside, 1 Alexandra Road, Grimsby, South Humberside DM31 1RD   (Tel. 0472 356282)
Closed for two weeks at Christmas
Not the most picturesque location, beside the canalized River Freshney, on a busy corner opposite the shopping precinct, but Grimsby is a working port, and this is a tremendously popular town-centre eatery. Pizzeria-style, the fish is fried in full view, in the central corner of the L-shaped restaurant, and customers seated at oak tables and chairs are served by waitresses in traditional black and white. The fish is purchased from the owner's brother each morning, so it could not be fresher: there is no cod on the menu as Grimsby folk consider it inferior to their favourite haddock. Main dishes cost from £5–£7. If you are in Grimsby and hungry, Leon's is the place for you. If you want a romantic meal by the water, go elsewhere.
Watersports; fishing

HAMBLETON

🍺 🏠 ♿ 🐾 💳

The Shard Bridge Inn, Shard Lane, Hambleton, Lancashire
(Tel. 0253 700208)
11am–3.30pm, 6pm–11pm Mon–Sat; noon–3pm, 7pm–
10.30pm Sun
The Shard Bridge is set in a very peaceful part of Lancashire, worth discovering along the little country roads, and is reached by a tiny toll bridge which costs the princely sum of 8p per crossing. It is a roomy pub with two bars overlooking the River Wyre. In summer you can sit out on the river bank and

admire the pretty view. Bar food is available (including soup, filled rolls, lasagne and steak). Bed and breakfast accommodation is available locally. There is disabled access and the pub is all on one level but there are no special facilities.
Walking; bird watching; waterskiing; jetskiing; boat racing and windsurfing nearby

HAMBLETON

Hambleton Hall, Hambleton, Oakham, Rutland,
Leicestershire LE15 8TH   (Tel. 0572 756991)
£110–£240 b&b
A first-class country-house hotel in a picturesque village, on a peninsula by the vast, quiet expanse of Rutland Water. Built as a hunting lodge in 1881, Hambleton Hall is an example of English luxury at its best. Guests are welcomed on arrival by delightful staff, into a formidable reception room with large comfortable armchairs, old paintings and an open fire. The decoration is very impressive throughout, with airy rooms that afford tremendous views of the lake. There are large amounts of fresh flowers and linen in evidence. The dining room, judged County Restaurant of the Year for 1990 by the *Good Food Guide*, seats 40 to 50 (set dinner £38.50); all tables have a view of the water. The chef's specialities include char-grilled loin of lamb with a tumblet (layers of potato, aubergine, courgette and tomato baked in olive oil and lamb juice) in a sauce of basil and tomato. To follow, try the hot sabayon soufflé of wild strawberries with its own ice and coconut tuile. Services offered by the hotel include secretarial, laundry and babysitting. There is disabled access to the hotel, a lift, and six rooms that would be suitable for the infirm but not for the severely disabled.
Walking; trout and pike fishing can be arranged; sailing club Whitwell (two miles); windsurfing; beach; helipad; golf (six miles away); tennis court; outdoor heated pool; riding; cycling; local market towns to visit; National Trust properties nearby

HAWKSHEAD

🏨 ²/₃ 🛶 🚴 🚭 🚂

Walker Ground Manor, Hawkshead, Cumbria LA22 0PD
(Tel. 09666 219)
On B5286
£25–£35 pp b&b

A 16th-century house of Lakeland stone, where one feels more a private guest than a paying customer. Wendy and Dennis Chandler and their son Peter are very chatty and friendly, and dine with their guests in the candle-lit dining room or conservatory, which is full of the heady smell of flowers. The house has its original panelling and a priest hole. Upstairs are beautiful old bedrooms, with four-poster beds and individual, personalized decoration. Two of these have private bathrooms and the other has use of two other bathrooms in the house. At the bottom of the wild, cottage-style garden is a small, pretty, tumbling stream which rises and falls depending on the weather. Dinner costs £12–£15 and may include fresh trout from Esthwaite Water or salmon from Scotland served with fresh vegetables from the garden, lightly baked in the Aga, followed by a good selection of cheese, fresh fruit salad or rich mousse. Lunch and teas can be made by arrangement. The Manor is a non-smoking hotel.

Walking and climbing nearby; fishing and rowing on Esthwaite Water; sailing and steamers on Windermere and Coniston; lake beaches nearby

HAYDON BRIDGE

🍺 🏠 🚴 🚭 🚂

The General Havelock Inn, Radcliffe Road, Haydon Bridge, Northumberland NE47 6ER (Tel. 0434 684 376)
Open 11am–2.30pm, 7pm–11pm Wed–Sat; noon–2pm, 7pm–10.30pm Sun. Closed all day Mon and Tues, and for three weeks in January

Opened as a private house in 1840, the inn obtained an ale licence in 1890 to quench the thirst of the local lead miners. The stable and hayloft have been converted into an airy restaurant

with river views. The self-taught chef provides well-flavoured home-made food using North Sea fish and local game. A three-course lunch costs £9.50 and a four-course dinner costs £16. A mouth-watering example of a main course could be chicken tarragon, cooked with pan-fried onions, lemon, garlic and cracked black pepper in a ginger and tarragon cream sauce. Bar snacks are also available. There is a tidy garden, with fine views of early 19th-century Haydon Bridge, now closed to traffic, and a terrace where diners can eat on fine days.
Fishing; walking; golf; Hadrian's Wall (four miles away); Roman museums

HEATON WITH OXCLIFFE

The Golden Ball (Snatchems), Lancaster Road, Heaton with Oxcliffe, Morecambe, Lancashire LA3 3ER
(Tel. 0524 63317)
Open 11am–11pm Mon–Sat; noon–3pm, 7pm–10.30pm Sun
Originally called Snatchems, this charming old pub is set in an area where reeds were cut to thatch the roofs of Lancashire. It is steeped in history: the name Snatchems evolved in the days when press gangs from ships on the River Lune would come to the inn and snatch their next crew from among the clientele. Tankards on the wall tell the story of the 'Queen's Shilling'; if this was dropped in your drink you would automatically be hauled off to work at sea. This practice led to the introduction of glass-bottomed tankards so that locals could have some forewarning of any impending curtailment of their liberty. The decor includes the original beams and low doors, and high-backed leather chairs. Real coal fires in the bar and restaurant and a hospitable landlord make the pub warm and friendly. The restaurant menu changes weekly. Choices include 16-inch pizzas served in the tops of barrels. Bar food is also available. The tide cuts off the road every day (the pub prints a booklet of tide times for customers). Outside seats on a raised terrace look over the river. Disabled access but no special facilities.

*Walking; bird watching; yachting (moorings available); salmon
fishing (need permit from Duchy of Lancaster); waterskiing arranged
by pub*

HELMSHORE

The Robin Hood Inn, 280 Holcombe Road, Helmshore,
Lancashire BB4 4NP   (Tel. 0706 213180)
By the textile museum, one mile off the M66
Open noon–11pm Thurs–Sat; noon–3pm, 7pm–10.30pm Sun.
Closed lunchtime Mon–Wed
A charming old pub, looking out over the River Ogden, with
views of the viaduct and two mill ponds from the back
windows. A beer garden and patio enable customers to enjoy
the scenery in the summer months. The interior is small, cosy
and totally unspoilt. There have been no attempts to make it
look genuine olde-worlde – it just is. The pub boasts hand-
pulled beer, open fires and a ghost called Wilf. Toast your own
crumpets over two open fires, or treat yourself to a Bury black
pudding. One of the rooms has pinball and old football
machines. The main theme of the pub, related to being on the
water, is the landlord's love of ducks, which adorn the walls
and corners in many shapes and forms. An added attraction is
live jazz and blues on Wednesdays and Saturdays. Bed and
breakfast accommodation is available locally.
*Walking; trout fishing (£8 for three hours, £15 for the day); textile
museum next door*

HUBBERHOLME

inn ¹/³

The George Inn, Hubberholme, Kirk Gill, nr Skipton, North
Yorkshire   (Tel. 075 676 223)
Off the B6160 at Buckden
Open 11.30am–3pm, 7pm–11pm Mon–Sat; noon–3pm, 7pm–
10.30pm Sun
£36 double b&b
Separated from the River Wharfe by a country road, the

George satisfies one's image of a truly rural pub, picturesque in its site and its buildings. The mighty fells rise either side of the tiny hamlet, culminating in Buckden Pike 2302 feet up. The 16th-century, Grade II listed, white-washed stone inn sits in this valley to the side of a stone bridge, opposite the 700-year-old churchyard. Inside are original oak beams, stone-flagged floors and open fires. Apparently the pub was a favourite of J. B. Priestley. Bar food and hand-pulled beers are on offer. The bedrooms are plain and simple; the breakfast room has pews (the building used to belong to the church) and shares the same view of the river as the bar. The inn is popular with artists who are inspired by the scenery. Dogs can be accommodated, for a charge of £2 per night.
Walking; fishing (permit needed)

HULL

!OI ⚏ ⚒ ⌦ ▭

Cerutti's, 10 Nelson Street, Hull, Humberside HU1 1XE
(Tel. 0482 28501)
Near the marina
Open noon–2pm, 7pm–9.30pm; closed Sat lunch, all day Sun, bank holidays
Closed for one week at Christmas
Housed in Hull's 17th-century stationmaster's house, next to the old ticket office for the Humber Ferry, Cerutti's has the atmosphere of a provincial gentleman's club. There is a comfortable bar downstairs and two dining rooms upstairs, the nicer of which is bright and well proportioned, overlooking the estuary. From here you look down on what was once the bustling pier of the Ferry, but is now a quiet, traffic-free piazza. The service is formal but friendly with clientele being served little eats with their apéritifs before being guided to their tables. There is seating for 36 people, with six water-view tables. The menu has a mainly French influence and focuses on fresh fish and seafood in different sauces: for example, Halibut Giuseppe (poached halibut with smoked salmon and avocado on a hollandaise sauce). Main course prices start at around £12.50.
Walks; watersports nearby; museums; art gallery; marina

HULL

49/99

Forte Crest Hotel, Castle Street, Hull,
Humberside HU1 2BX   (Tel. 0482 225 221)
Signposted 'New Hotel' from the A63; overlooks marina
£49.50–£110 per room (breakfast £8.50)

A modern hotel on Hull's new marina, designed and furnished
in a traditional style, with a nautical theme in the reception
areas. A good weekend base by the waterfront in a buzzing
town. The restaurant, bar and lounge overlook the marina, the
old dock warehouses and the new docklands residential
developments. The food is described as English, cooked with
plenty of fresh herbs in a light, modern way. A three-course
meal with coffee costs £15.50. The docklands are well worth
exploring, as there is a surprising amount of activity – not least
the building of the new Princes Quay shopping centre on stilts
above one of the old docks. The hotel runs special activity
weekends with themes such as murder and mystery, maritime
and heritage. The fitness club is equipped with an indoor
swimming pool, sauna and solarium. There are disabled
facilities on the ground floor, and one specially equipped
bedroom.

*Golf; ice-skating; sailing and sea fishing can be arranged; mega-
bowling; railway, maritime and William Wilberforce museums*

KENDAL

2/5

Millers Beck Country Guest House, Stainton, nr Kendal,
Cumbria LA8 0DU   (Tel. 05395 60877)
On A65, halfway between Kendal (3½ miles) and M6 (Jct 36)
Do not turn into Stainton
Closed in January and February
£16 pp b&b

Removed from the worst congestion of the Lake District,
Millers Beck provides a delightful refuge for the jaded
traveller, with pleasantly undemanding walks in the immediate neighbourhood. Parts of this converted corn-mill date

back to the early 17th century, but the accommodation is completely modernized. A free-running beck flows at various levels through the garden, but the waterwheel, sadly, disappeared long ago. Two galleried sitting areas overlook the mill-race, surrounding hills and rolling farmland. A conservatory has recently been built between the mill and the beck-wall, to serve as the residents' dining room, with seating for 12, and all tables affording a view of the water. For once, home cooking means exactly that, and the three-course dinner is excellent value at £8. The establishment is unlicensed, but guests are welcome to bring their own wine. A self-contained flat is also available at £160 per week. The only drawback of this admirable guesthouse is a certain amount of traffic noise from the main road.

Fishing. Watersports, golf, tennis, shooting, riding, bird watching, all within a ten-mile radius. Kendal's museums are immensely rewarding

KESWICK

Armathwaite Hall, Bassenthwaite Lake, Keswick, Cumbria
CA12 4RE   (Tel. 07687 76551)
From Keswick roundabout, take the A591 signposted Carlisle, 8 miles to Castle Inn Junction, turn left, then 300 yards ahead
Open all year
From £100 for twin/double room
Formerly a residence for Benedictine nuns, this is now a grand hotel in the best baronial tradition, providing an opportunity to sample gracious living, with breathtaking views of Bassenthwaite Lake just 400 yards away, and across the water to the massive lump of Skiddaw. There is even a helicopter pad for those in a hurry to go places. A house has stood on this site since the 11th century. In 1881, a local mine-owner converted Armathwaite Hall into a 'Victorian Country Gentleman's Residence' and this, in its essentials, is the same building guests see today, with modern improvements from more recent times. Every comfort is provided for residents, including an indoor pool, sauna, gymnasium, pitch-and-putt, tennis and

snooker. 'A house of perfect and irresistible charm', was how Sir Hugh Walpole described it, and there is no need to quarrel with that verdict today. The menu offers a wide range of traditional English food, classical French cooking, local game and vegetarian dishes. A six-course table d'hote meal costs £29.95: imaginative dishes served in the elegant dining room may include water-melon slices garnished with fresh figs wrapped in Parma ham, fillet of veal flamed in brandy, and dark chocolate mousse with white chocolate sauce and cointreau. The restaurant seats 90, 12 tables overlook the water, and there is also a leisure club grill room. The hotel has facilities for disabled visitors, including one bedroom with grab-handles, some ground-floor bedrooms, a lift which will accommodate wheelchairs, and easy access to public rooms.
Fishing (free); riding from hotel's stables, watersports, golf, hunting, walking, bird watching (over 40 species nesting on the estate)

KNARESBOROUGH

Mother Shipton's Inn, Low Bridge, Knaresborough
HG5 8HZ   (Tel. 0423 862157)
On the right, as you leave Knaresborough by the B6163
Open 11.30am–3pm, 5.30–11pm Mon-Sat; noon–2.30pm, 7pm–10.30pm Sun
This typical friendly Yorkshire pub has been here for over 300 years. A beer garden behind looks along the River Nidd to Knaresborough's impressive viaduct, and up to the imposing ruins of Knaresborough Castle above. This is a delightful place to sit in summer, while inside the bars are cosy, full of nooks and alcoves, with a lively mix of local people and visitors emerging from Mother Shipton's Cave, next door, where the 16th-century Yorkshire prophetess was allegedly born. Beer includes the Yorkshire ale that tastes as good as it sounds, Theakston's Old Peculiar, and the pub also provides good-value, tasty, home-cooked bar food, such as steak pies, soups, roast beef and a 'giant Yorkshire pudding'. (Food available daily from noon–2pm, and 7pm–9.30pm.) On the left as you

enter is a family room, and a ramp provides access for the disabled, with willing Yorkshire arms prepared to carry wheelchairs down the couple of steps to the beer garden. Dogs are allowed in if well-behaved, but not while food is being served.

Boating; race-going; riverside walks; castles

KNARESBOROUGH

inn ≋ 3/6 🏠 👃 🚫 ▭

The Yorkshire Lass, High Bridge, Harrogate Road,
Knaresborough HG5 8DA   (Tel. 0423 862962)
On the right as you leave Knaresborough on the Harrogate Road
Accommodation open all year. £35 single, £45 for two per room, b&b

The Yorkshire Lass is easy to find in spring and summer: just look for the floral displays and hanging baskets that almost hide the front of this riverside inn. The river is the Nidd, and overlooking it behind the pub is a terrace for sitting outside and weekly summer barbecues. Inside, one large bar offers simple lunchtime bar meals – soup, sandwiches, pies and quiches – while the evening menu includes steak, chicken, duck, fresh fish and specialities such as beef in ale and roast haunch of venison. The Scottish landlord, Derek Speirs, takes great pride in his range of real ales and sizeable collection of fine malt whiskies. Upstairs, the large bedrooms are all *en suite* and the old-fashioned furniture gives them a homely touch but all have modern facilities. Accommodation is not accessible for the disabled, but ramps lead into the bar, restaurant and out on to the terrace.

Boating; race-going; riverside walks; castles

LANCASTER

🛏 🏠 ✗ ◊ 🚲

The Water Witch Inn, Canal Side, Lancaster
(Tel. 0524 638238)
Open 11am–11pm Mon–Sat; noon–3pm, 7pm–10.30pm Sun
A simply-furnished canalside pub, decorated in a Victorian
Romany style in the heart of the old city of Lancaster. The stone
walls have narrowboat pictures and canal memorabilia. The
pub has a roomy feel, and overlooks a clean canal with barges,
swans and ducks. A wrought-iron staircase leads up to a secluded
eating area with pine benches and dresser. The hot platters
include lasagne, scampi, pizzas, steaks and vegetable stroganoff
at reasonable prices. A pool table, television and jukebox provide the entertainment downstairs. In summer, food is served
at bench tables beside the canal. Cars can be parked on the
other side of the water and the pub is reached by a small
footbridge.
*Walking; watersports at Morecambe; freshwater and sea fishing;
beach; canal cruises*

LEALHOLM

🏨 3/4 🏠 ✗ ◊ 🚲

The Board Hotel, Village Green, Lealholm, Whitby
YO21 2AJ   (Tel. 0947 87279)
Off the A171, the Guisborough to Whitby road
£10 pp b&b
This plain stone house is in the picturesque village of Lealholm,
deep in the Yorkshire Dales. Set on a bend in the River Esk, the
hotel overlooks the village green and its grazing sheep. A
modest, traditional establishment, with two bars downstairs, and pretty, plainly furnished bedrooms upstairs. The
residents' lounge has views of the river. Food is available in one
bar where the locals play dominoes. In summer drinkers can sit
in the hotel gardens overlooking the river. The hotel has
fishing rights on the Esk so guests bringing their own tackle
can fish for salmon there free.
Walking; watersports; fishing

LINTON

🏠 8/22 ⚘ ♨ ✍ 💳

Wood Hall, Linton, Wetherby LS22 4JA (Tel. 0937 587271)
Off the A661, three miles south of Wetherby
£98–£245 per room
A beautiful Georgian mansion with a Jacobean addition and a
new six-bedroom courtyard wing set on a hill overlooking
the River Wharfe. There are good river views from the
bedrooms. The interior decoration befits the exterior: the
original plasterwork has been preserved, while high-quality
restoration furniture fills the rooms and re-creates a country-
house atmosphere. Drinks in the bar are served on a grand
piano and the lounge is full of books, paintings and comfy
armchairs, and looks on to the River Wharfe. Bedrooms are
individually furnished with decoratively painted furniture and
modern conveniences. In the restaurant the chef Simon Wood
uses fresh produce, and presents his Anglo-French creations
with care and simplicity. The à la carte menu offers dishes
such as mousse scallopes and red mullet served with a hot
watercress, salmon, caviar and butter sauce. There is one
specially equipped room for disabled visitors on the ground
floor (on the same level as the restaurant, bar, lavatories and
access from car park).
*One hundred acres of grounds provide fine scope for walks along the
Wharfe valley; salmon, trout and barbel fishing (bring equipment);
snooker; archery, clay pigeon shooting and hot-air ballooning by
arrangement; National Trust properties; bird sanctuary; Leeds,
Harrogate and York nearby*

LITTLE SINGLETON

🏠 5/10 ⚘ ♨ ✍ 💳

Mains Hall Country House Hotel, Mains Lane, Little
Singleton, Lancashire (Tel. 0253 885130)
Off the A585
£38–£98 per room
Built in 1537 by an order of monks, Mains Hall is the oldest
building in West Lancashire, originally used by travellers

on their way to Cockersand Abbey. It is found at the top of a long private drive, in a fine, woodland setting overlooking the River Wyre. The interior reflects its impressive history with secret hiding-places used by Cardinal Allen of Rossall during the Papist persecutions. An extravagant wood carving decorates the panelled hall and the staircase. Some of the modernization is slightly at odds with the house (electric fires in lovely old fireplaces). One of the rooms has an impressive four-poster bed. The dining room seats 35; all tables overlook the river (dinner £17.50 to £27.50), and visitors to the restaurant are reputed to travel from as far away as London to sample the excellent beef, veal, pheasant and grouse. Two ground-floor rooms (with bathrooms) are suitable for disabled visitors.

Walking; fishing; beach (Blackpool); sailing; golf; bird watching; fishing lessons

LIVERPOOL

The Pump House, Albert Dock, Liverpool L3 4AA
(Tel. 051 709 2367)
Open 11.30am–11pm Mon–Sat; noon–3pm, 7pm–10.30pm Sun

An early 19th-century pump house renovated to a high standard, in a wonderful situation overlooking the water, the square ship *Zebu*, and the Port of Liverpool building. The conversion of the Albert Dock has been extremely successful, housing shops and exhibitions, and has now become the third most popular tourist attraction in Great Britain. The pub is very roomy, with lots of dark wood, a marble counter, and architectural prints on the wall. Tall ships visit the dock in summer (a very popular attraction). The pub is frequented by Granada celebrities, business people and tourists, who are all welcomed by the friendly staff and invited to enjoy a drink on the dockside and sample the bar food which is available from noon to 2.30pm. This involves generous helpings of a choice of 15 cheeses and four pâtés served on granary bread and garnished with pickles. There is a ramp into the pub, and a lavatory for disabled visitors.

Shopping galleries; Tate gallery; Maritime museum; the 'Beatles Story' in the Albert Dock

LIVERPOOL

🏠 74/226 🔼 🌡 ⟲ 💳

The Atlantic Tower Hotel, Chapel Street, Liverpool L3 9RE
(Tel. 051 227 4444)
At the head of the pier
£78 single, £86 double b&b

A modern hotel, somewhat startling in appearance, situated at the head of the pier, with good views of Liverpool's old buildings, Princes Dock and the Mersey. Bedrooms are light and airy, and there is one entire floor that is kept specifically for female guests, and another for non-smokers. One bar is in the style of a Pullman carriage; another is styled like a ship. The dining room seats 150 people, and 10 of the tables have a view of the water. There is a baby-minding service. The staff are friendly despite the vast size of the hotel. There are comprehensive conference and banqueting facilities. Limited disabled facilities (such as lavatories in some areas, and lifts for access between floors).

Albert Dock and its many attractions (see previous entry); walks at Sefton Park (one and a half miles away); fishing can be arranged; beach (three miles away)

LYTHAM ST ANNE'S

🏠 18/72 🔼 🌡 ⓧ 💳

The Chadwick Hotel, South Promenade, Lytham St Anne's
FY8 1NP   (Tel. 0253 720 061)
£32.50 single, £44 double

This modernized hotel has light and airy bedrooms, with white walls and brass beds; all the rooms have bathrooms, and some even have spa baths. The lounge has a large expanse of windows, which gives the impression that the seats have been

set out for an airport over the sea. The dining room, behind the lounge, seats 150 people, and 10 tables have a view of the sea. There is a cosmopolitan range of dishes on the menu, with the emphasis on seafood; the set lunch costs £6.40; the set dinner, £11.50. The Bugatti bar has a classic car theme, but no sea view. There are two ground-floor bedrooms with facilities for disabled visitors, and the hotel has wheelchair access.
Walking; watersports; fishing; beach; health club with indoor pool; spa bath; sauna; solarium; games room

LYTHAM ST ANNE'S

15/41

The Clifton Arms Hotel, West Beach, Lytham St Anne's
FY8 5QJ   (Tel. 0253 739 898)
£75–£130 per room
Originally a small inn on the Clifton estate, this attractive 150-year-old building is in the quiet part of St Anne's, overlooking the sea front. The bedrooms are massive with large windows and light-coloured furnishings. The lounge, cocktail bar, and most of the tables in the restaurant look over the Ribble estuary (lunch £9.75; dinner £15.50–£23). The menus offer fancy dishes such as 'Duet by Moonlight' which is slices of beef and veal, grilled and served with a pink peppercorn sauce. A good place to stay for peace and quiet, though only 15 minutes away from the bright lights of Blackpool. Pets can be accommodated by request. There is wheelchair access to the restaurant, and some rooms in the hotel are suitable for disabled visitors.
Walking; watersports; fishing; beach; golf; tennis; whirlpool bath; free in-house films; spa baths, sauna and solarium

LYTHAM ST ANNE'S

🏨 25/104 🏠 👃 🐟 💳

The Dalmeny Hotel, 19–33 South Promenade, Lytham St
Anne's FY8 1LX   (Tel. 0253 712 236)
Closed at Christmas
£25–£105 per room b&b
The Dalmeny Hotel is situated on the promenade overlooking
the sea and promenade gardens. The outside is rather ugly
and modern, but inside it is very comfortable. The rooms
are good value, especially the apartments (£35–£150, with
kitchenette and some with balcony). A good place for a family
holiday as the hotel offers an organized crèche, outside play
area, special children's tea menu and half portions, family
entertainments and a games room. All children can stay free in
the month of June. There are four different eating establishments to choose from: The C'est La Vie (lunch £12.50, dinner
£19.50), The Carvery (recommended for excellent value and
good food), The Barbecue, and The Buttery bar (salads and
teas). Other facilities include a non-smoking lounge, ballroom, beauty salon, large indoor swimming pool, squash
court, multi-gym; saunas and solariums. Six of the bedrooms
have disabled facilities.
*Beach; Blackpool illuminations; tennis and four championship golf
courses nearby*

MANCHESTER

🏨 81/166 🏠 👃 🐟 💳

The Copthorne Hotel, Clippers Quay, Salford Quays,
Greater Manchester M5 3DL   (Tel. 061 873 7321)
Three minutes from the Salford turning off the M62/M63
£87–£98 single, £97–£108 double
A smart, modern hotel on Salford Quay, catering mainly for
businessmen. There is a sunny and spacious reception area,
and comfortable, well-equipped bedrooms. There are two
restaurants, which have nine tables with views of the quay and
the marina between them: guests are required to wear formal
dress in Chandlers, the à la carte restaurant. The Quayside

Restaurant has a more informal atmosphere. There is a health and leisure centre within the hotel, comprising multigym, sauna, solarium and swimming pool. Moorings for visitors can be found at Salford Quay. The hotel has disabled access, and one bedroom which may be suitable for disabled guests. *Granada Television studios, Castlefield Urban Heritage Park and Manchester's Chinatown are all within range for visits*

MANCHESTER

The Mark Addy, Stanley Street, Salford, Manchester 3
(Tel. 061 832 4080)
Open 11.30am–11pm Mon–Sat; noon–3pm, 7pm–10.30pm Sun

Overlooking a now cleaner River Irwell, the pub is named after the 19th-century hero who rescued 50 people from drowning in the filthy water. Mark Addy was the only civilian to receive the Royal Albert Medal (otherwise known as the Victoria Cross) from Queen Victoria. The river (which looks more like a canal) marks the border between Manchester and Salford, and the pub was originally the waiting room for boat passengers. Mark Addy's story and the history of the quay, the prison, and the landing stage are well documented on the pub walls. All seats in the roomy bar overlook the water. Boddingtons Bitter and Marston's Pedigree serve to quench the thirst. The food on offer is somewhat of a novelty in that the range is so huge. Customers can choose from 70 cheeses from around Europe (and be advised on the best wines to accompany them), and eight meat and vegetarian pâtés, all served with freshly baked granary bread, and a doggy bag for those whose eyes are bigger than their stomachs. On the riverside is a pretty, terraced garden with a magnolia tree and private moorings. No disabled facilities but helpful staff. *Granada Studios tours; Castlefield Roman fort; shopping centre; walking*

MEDBOURNE

inn <u>0/3</u> ⌂ 🕯 ⌘ 🖶

The Nevill Arms, 12 Waterfall Way, Medbourne,
Leicestershire   (Tel. 085883 288)
Village on the B664, pub in centre of the village green
Open noon–2.30pm, 6pm–11pm Mon–Sat; noon–3pm, 7pm–
10.30pm Sun
£40 single, £50 double b&b
This picturesque inn enjoys an extremely quiet setting by the
River Welland. An open fire and lots of brass fittings create a
relaxed atmosphere. Fifty ducks have made their home on the
water, and have become the main theme of the pub; to be
found on the beer mats and flying – in effigy – up the wall.
Three newly converted bedrooms in an adjoining cottage are
decorated with pretty furnishings. Full English breakfasts are
served in the conservatory overlooking the terraced garden.
Two bars offer food such as beef stroganoff, steak and kidney
pie, treacle tart and bread and butter pudding. Indoor pursuits
include skittles, carpet bowls, darts, Connect 4, shove
ha'penny, dominoes and cards. There are riverside tables in the
garden and a dovecote over the water. Barbecues are held in the
summer months. One ground-floor room is suitable for
disabled visitors.
Walking; watersports (three miles away); fishing on river and Eye
Brook Reservoir; Rutland Water; cycle track

MILNTHORPE

inn <u>6/6</u> ⌂⌐14 🕯 ⌘ 🖶

The Ship Inn, Sandside, Milnthorpe, Cumbria LA7 7HW
(Tel. 05395 63113)
Open 11am–3pm, 6pm–11pm Mon–Sat (11am–11pm Mon–
Sat Easter to October); noon–3pm, 7pm–10.30pm Sun
Accommodation closed Christmas and New Year
£16.50 single, £38.50 double b&b
A pretty, white 17th-century inn overlooking Morecambe
Estuary and the mountains beyond. Original beams, ship
pictures and nautical maps adorn the inside, with good water

views from four windows. The pub is tied to Scottish and Newcastle and serves Theakston's ale, Younger's and Beck's. The food is reasonably priced and includes hot platters such as Cumberland sausage with traditional apple sauce. Several vegetarian items are on offer every day. Pool and darts are played in the pub. The bedrooms are attractive and light with pine furniture, and all overlook the estuary. A popular spot for bird watchers (heron can be spotted) and painters. Approach with care: at high tide water covers the road. The pub has disabled access but no special facilities.

Playground; walking; sailing in Arnside; sea fishing in Sandside; salmon fishing in Belar; bird watching in sanctuary; riding in Beatnam; summer guided walks from Arnside to Grange (takes four and a half hours); National Trust properties

MORECAMBE

The Clarendon Hotel, The Promenade, West End,
Morecambe, Lancashire LA4 4EP   (Tel. 0524 410 180)
Closed at Christmas
£29 single, £45 twin or double b&b
In a seaside town full of old-fashioned character, the Clarendon has good sea views and plenty of space. Morecambe is presently undergoing major improvements with the creation of a large sandy beach, and a new tourism centre in the old railway station. The hotel decoration is fairly average but the 'Davey Jones Locker' pub in the basement has a nautical flavour, with ships' clocks, big barrels supporting the bar and picture portholes. It is popular with locals and visitors alike. The dining room seats 70 people, with seven tables overlooking the water. The three-course set dinner for £9.25 is good value for typical old-fashioned hotel food – garlic mushrooms, roast lamb and a sweet trolley. The menu changes nightly and offers four or five choices for each course. Vegetarian meals can be prepared on request. The bedrooms are comfortable, spacious and well equipped. No facilities for the disabled, though there is a lift.

Walking; watersports; fishing; beach; golf; sea fishing

NEWBY BRIDGE

🏨 15/35 🏕 🔥 ⚔ 💳

Whitewater Hotel, The Lakeland Village, Newby Bridge,
Ulverston, Cumbria LA12 8PX　(Tel. 05395 31133)
On the A590 between the motorway and Barrow-in-Furness
£60 single, £85–£100 double b&b
Built around an old mill, from characteristic Lakeland stone
and slate, the hotel is right on the River Leven, and is an ideal
place to be pampered by day and fed to the gunwales at night.
You can indulge in a total health treatment: facilities within
the hotel include a swimming pool, a whirlpool, a gym,
sunbeds, squash courts, and two floodlit tennis courts. The
bedrooms are comfortable, and those facing the water have
one original stone wall. The dining room seats 70 people, and
four of the tables overlook the water. Bar lunches are available;
a set dinner in the restaurant costs £16–£18. Timeshare cottages
and apartments can be rented for between £400 and £750 per
week. There are no steps into the hotel, and there is a lift to the
restaurant that is large enough to accommodate a wheelchair.
Walking; fishing; shingle beach; watersports nearby; riding; archery;
clay pigeon shooting

NEWBY BRIDGE

🏨 30/70 🏕 🔥 ⚓ 💳

Lakeside Hotel, Newby Bridge, Cumbria LA12 8AT
(Tel. 05395 31207; reservations, Mon–Fri, 9am–5pm, on
05395 30001)
From M6, Junction 36, take A590 Newby Bridge, then follow
Hawkshead road and tourist signs to Lakeside Steamers
Open all year except 10 days in early January
From £45 pp b&b (some suites are available)
On the very edge of Windermere, yet far enough away from
the madding crowds, this must rank among the best locations
in the Lake District, just the spot for a carefree weekend.
Originally a 17th-century post-house, the hotel is now
luxuriously appointed and much careful thought has obviously
gone into creating its agreeable decor. Bedrooms are spacious

and most pleasingly furnished, with tasteful use of the Designers Guild materials. The restaurant and conservatory overlooking Lake Windermere serve fresh produce, including Cumbrian specialities, and provide seating for 120, with 18 tables giving a direct view of the water. A four-course table d'hote meal costs £20. There is also a brasserie, £12.50 per head, and bar meals are available for around £6.50. A wide range of beers, lagers and stout includes Theakston's XB and Theakston's Best. Excellent cream teas are served in the elegant conservatory, and staff are conspicuously friendly and helpful. For disabled visitors, there are six spacious rooms with some grab-rails. A few yards away, ferry boats run every twenty minutes in season from the Lakeside Pier to Fell Foot Park, just across the water. Nearby Lakeside Station is the terminus for steam trains from Haverthwaite, timed to connect with boats to and from Windermere/Bowness.

Fishing for trout on three tarns, free. Boat-trips on Windermere all day, golf fifteen minutes away, nature reserve for bird watching half an hour distant. Most other leisure activities are within easy reach and can be organized by the hotel

NEWCASTLE

🍴 👥₉ 🎿 ⊗ 💳

Fisherman's Lodge, Jesmond Dene, Newcastle-upon-Tyne NE7 7BQ   (Tel. 091 281 3281)
Off the A1058, about three and a half miles east of central Newcastle, in Jesmond Dene Park
Open noon–2pm, 7pm–11pm Mon–Fri; 7pm–11pm Sat.
Closed Sun and bank holidays

An extremely smart restaurant, sitting in a beautiful wooded dell which has the Ouse burn running through it. The building is a Victorian conversion, which is in earshot but unfortunately not in view of the babbling water. Nevertheless, this is a wonderfully picturesque setting and it is hard to believe you are so close to the centre of Newcastle. The staff are friendly and there is plenty of parking. The restaurant offers innovative dishes built around fresh, local seafood. Other gastronomic possibilities include oriental-style duck breast, veal, partridge and Northumbrian lamb. The set lunch is £15, and à la carte main courses start at £16.50. There are 65 covers in the comfortable and nicely decorated dining area. Customers can enjoy a pre-meal walk in the spacious park to see the Ouse waterfall and old mill. Booking is an absolute necessity. The restaurant is accessible to wheelchairs, but there are no lavatories downstairs.

Walking; Newcastle (three and a half miles away)

NEWTON-ON-OUSE

inn 2/5 🏠 🎷 ◇ ▭

The Dawnay Arms, Newton-on-Ouse, York YO6 2BR
(Tel. 034 74 345)
Well signposted from the A19, seven miles north-west of York
Open 11.30am–2.30pm, 6.30pm–11pm Mon–Sat; noon–3pm, 7pm–10.30pm Sun. Closed Mon lunchtimes in winter
From £19.50 pp b&b
A pretty 18th-century whitewashed pub with black shutters on the banks of the River Ouse. The pub stands near to Newton parish church and you can reach the National Trust's Beningbrough Hall from the village. Two traditional oak-beamed bars are decorated with red carpets, copper tables and a log fire. Tetley's Yorkshire Bitter, Theakston's hand-pulled beer and Dawnay wine are the specialities of the house. The dining room seats 50 people, overlooks the river and offers a candlelit dinner of home-made duck pâté, Highland salmon, steaks and vegetarian dishes. The traditional roast beef and Yorkshire pudding served at Sunday lunchtime is very popular. A sunny patio in the riverside garden is good for enjoying a drink and a bite on warm days. The inn has fishing rights (mostly trout) for its stretch of river and charges £1 per day. Private moorings, a large car park and local bed and breakfast all add up to make this an enjoyable place to visit. No facilities for the disabled, though the restaurant is accessible to wheelchairs.

Children's play house; North Yorkshire moor walks; fishing; boat hire (Linton Lock half a mile away); Beningbrough Hall nearby

NORTHALLERTON

🏛️ 12/22 🏕️ ⚡ 🦆 💳

Kirkby Fleetham Hall, Northallerton, Kirkby Fleetham
DL7 0SU   (Tel. 0609 748 711)
Two miles from the A1, signposted
£102–£175 per room b&b
This grand Georgian mansion, in its own 30-acre estate, nestles
in a valley between the North Yorkshire moors and the Dales.
There are no buildings in sight apart from a twelfth-century
church. A private lake offers fishing and a place to watch
wildfowl. A huge staircase dominates the reception area,
creating from the start a gracious, country-house atmosphere.
The public rooms and bedrooms, many of which still have
their original decoration, are very traditional and beautifully
furnished. The dining room seats 40 people, and all tables
overlook the lake. The sumptuous four-course dinner menu
(£25) offers dishes such as 'A *delice* of sea bass baked with Welsh
onions and fine celery on a rich port wine sauce'. The tranquil
spot and discreet service make this a wonderfully peaceful
retreat.
Walking; fishing; clay pigeon shooting; National Trust properties;
York and Harrogate nearby

NORTH DALTON

inn 3/7 🛏️ ⚡ 🚫 💳

The Star Inn, North Dalton, Driffield, Humberside
YO25 9UX   (Tel. 037 781 688)
Village on the B1246, between Pocklington and Great
Driffield
Open 11.30am–11pm Mon–Sat; noon–3pm, 7pm–10.30pm
Sun
£39 single, £55 double/twin b&b
Right next to the village pond and opposite the Norman village
church, this brick building has been an inn since Georgian
times. The Star was originally a mail coach stop between York
and Beverley minsters and lies on the famous Minster walk.
All around are the unspoilt, undulating Yorkshire Wolds. The

snug ground-floor bar is the village pub, where welcoming staff serve Tetley's Bitter and John Smith's traditional ales. The bar is full of curiosities such as old sewing machines, a wooden till and Victorian family photographs. The restaurant has its own bar area where guests can enjoy an apéritif before dining. Interesting choices might include rabbit pie followed by hot sticky toffee pudding. All drinking and eating areas overlook the pond. The pretty bedrooms are well equipped with books, cassettes, and even bath toys.

Walking; gliding (Pocklington gliding club); clay pigeon shooting (48-hours notice); watersports; fishing and beach within 20 miles; special 'murder' dinners can be arranged for group visits

PENRITH

6/10

The Old Church Hotel, Watermillock, Penrith, Cumbria
CA11 0JN   (Tel. 07684 86204)
15 minutes from the M6, just off the A592
Closed November to February inc.
From £50 per person b&b; from £75 double b&b
Here's a stately white house built in 1745 with lawns sloping down to the shores of Ullswater where a rowing boat is at the ready for guests. Owner Maureeen Whitemore runs soft furnishings courses throughout the year and her taste is reflected throughout the house. The hall is painted a confident red, with floral arrangements in huge vases. In one sitting room, bookcases and ceilings are deep pink with matching floral curtains. Flamboyant? Yes, but it looks terrific. In the restaurant, overlooking the lake, the food is classy, with plenty of interesting alcoholic touches: Cumberland ham with cider; roast duckling with port wine sauce. More alcohol at breakfast – try their Creamy Porridge oats with Whisky and Demarara! An immaculate, well-run hotel. Visitors with babies can be provided with backpacks and other useful pieces of equipment such as bottle sterilizers.

Fishing from shore or row boat; sailing boats for hire (there are moorings at the hotel); guided fell walking, cycling and pony trekking can be arranged

PIERCEBRIDGE

inn 8/40

The George Inn, Piercebridge, County Durham
(Tel. 0325 374 576)
On the B6275
£40 single, £50 double, £60 twin b&b

A lovely ancient coaching inn nestling on the banks of the River Tees and looking across to the graceful arches of Pierce Bridge. The area, once inhabited by the Romans, is steeped in history and archaeologists believe that the river here formed a basin where goods were transshipped from Dere Street to barges. The pub has four bars, one of which is reputed to have been a hiding place for Dick Turpin. Other features include a large, well-lit dining room with river views, a splendid 1920s function room with French windows to the river and a good-sized riverside garden for sitting out in fine weather. In the summer a ball is held in a marquee on the island. Bar meals are served all day, and the full dining menu is appropriately called 'The Feast' with a wide vegetarian choice, steaks and chicken dishes (a main course costing between £6 and £9), accompanied by a good wine list. The hotel rents two rods on the Tees for trout fishing. No disabled facilities but helpful staff.
Walking; fishing; Yorkshire Dales, Highforce and Aysgarth waterfalls nearby; Beamish Museum (working farm)

PRESTON

58/72

The Tickled Trout, Preston New Road, Samlesbury, Preston PR5 0UJ (Tel. 0772 877 671)
Near Exit 31 of the M6 (call for precise directions)
£74 single, £89 twin/double

A modern hotel, with standard decoration and piped music, which would make a good stopping off point on a north–south journey. You can just see the motorway, though more importantly there is a good view of the River Ribble. Bedrooms are large and well equipped, if a little characterless. Both of the bars overlook the river. Pets can be accommodated by request. There are good leisure facilities – a jet pool and exercise machines – for anyone needing a stretch after too many hours behind the wheel, and also a sauna and a solarium. The Kingfisher Restaurant, with the old beams of the original building, offers a variety of enticing dishes, and hosts a dinner dance on Friday and Saturday nights.

Walking; golf; riding; exercise machines; jet pool; sauna, solarium, and steam room

RICHMOND

Howe Villa, Whitcliffe Mill, Richmond DL10 4TJ
(Tel. 0748 85 00 55)
Off the A6108, half a mile out of Richmond
Open March to late November
£40–£45 pp dinner and b&b

Don't be put off by the less than tidy approach: the villa is an exquisite Georgian house tucked into a hollow and overlooking the River Swale. Lovingly restored by the owners, the public rooms and bedrooms are well proportioned and all are elegantly decorated. The first-floor sitting room and dining room command magnificent river views, though the bedrooms are on the ground floor, allowing only tall people to see the water. With just four bedrooms and 10 places in the dining room, Howe Villa feels more like a private house than a hotel. A four-course dinner costs £18. The menu changes every night; there is a choice of starters and sweets, and a hearty main course in between. Guests are offered a drink and canapés before their meal, but are asked to bring their own wine, which will be served without a corkage charge.

Walking; fishing (day licence in town); golf course in Richmond; riding

ROWSLEY

🏠 6/14 🛖 🐴 ⟨🐟⟩ 💳

The Peacock, Rowsley, Matlock, Derbyshire DE4 2EB
(Tel. 0629 733518)
On the A6 between Matlock and Bakewell
Bar open 11am–3pm, 6pm–11pm Mon–Sat; noon–3pm, 7pm–
10.30pm Sun; drinks service available in lounge from 11am–
11pm
£95 single, £125 double b&b
Built in 1652 as a dower house for Haddon Hall, The Peacock
became an inn in 1828. The small cosy bar has oak beams, a
copper bar and stone walls; the atmosphere strikes a balance
between traditional character and modern smartness. The
bedrooms are pretty, decorated in a relaxed style with friezes
and matching bedcovers. More rooms have river views when
the leaves drop in autumn. The restaurant has space for 45
diners, who can enjoy gazing at the garden and eating at tables
carved by the famous Mousey Thompson. A cold buffet (£8)
and other snacks are available at lunchtime; dinner (from
£23.50) is a three-course affair offering an English menu with a
wide selection of wines. The garden, which grows herbs,
reaches down to the River Derwent, with views of two
bridges. No facilities for the disabled, although the restaurant
is accessible to wheelchairs.
*Walking; fishing (hotel has 12 rods on a seven-mile stretch of the
River Wye, fishing for brown and rainbow trout from 1 April to 31
October); Chatsworth and Haddon Hall nearby*

RUTLAND

🏠 12/24 🛖 🐴 ⟨🐟⟩ 💳

Normanton Park Hotel, Rutland Water, South Shore,
Rutland, Leicestershire LE15 8RP   (Tel. 0780 720315)
Open all year
£52.50 single b&b; £72.50 double b&b
The conversion, six years ago, of Normanton Park on Rutland
Water from a derelict listed 17th-century stableblock won a
Sunday Times Country House award – it is now an attractive

L-shaped building of honey-coloured stone complete with clock and bell-tower. The formal Peacock restaurant, where some tables have a view across Rutland Water, can seat up to 90 people (à la carte, £20–£25), while in the jolly Sailing Bar you can eat for around £15. In the smart pinky-green sitting room, furnished with lots of comfy sofas, a collection of bellows adorns the fireplace. Some of the bedrooms lead directly on to the courtyard car park, making them accessible for the disabled.

Bicycles can be hired from the nearby cycle hire shop for a ride around Rutland Water, and canoeing, fishing and windsurfing are also available; riding and shooting nearby

SALTBURN

The Ship Inn, Saltburn, Cleveland TS12 1HF
(Tel. 0287 622361)
On the A174 as you come out of Saltburn
Open 11am–11pm Mon–Sat, noon–10.30pm Sun (summer);
11am–3pm, 6pm–11pm Mon–Sat, noon–3pm, 7pm–10.30pm Sun (winter)

Saltburn seems still to belong to another age, more gracious and leisured than ours, though some of the buildings now seem a little down-at-heel, and seafront entertainments have a faded air. The station buildings have been converted to house attractive boutiques, though there is still a regular pay-train to Middlesbrough, Stockton and Darlingon. Right on the seashore, this characterful pub has changed with the times, though its exterior still presents a defiant northern bleakness. From the furnishing of basic necessities in earlier days, standards have been raised to provide a varied and tempting range of hot and cold dishes, with several unusual items from oriental recipes. In addition to the restaurant, there are several bars, and tables are placed on the outdoor terrace in constant expectation of fine weather, and there is a children's room too. The beach, literally on the doorstep, is a mixture of pebble and sand, and close to the inn tower steep cliffs, with good walking

on the tops. Easy access to bar from back car park, but no specific disabled facilities.
Fishing from the end of Saltburn's truncated pier. Watersports, walking, golf are readily available. Saltburn's Victorian Carnival, an important event for the locals, attracts large numbers of summer visitors

SCARBOROUGH

🏨 ≋ 53/73 🏠 🕭 ⬦ ▭

The Esplanade Hotel, Belmont Road, Scarborough
YO11 2AA   (Tel. 0723 360 382)
£36–£65 b&b
Conjure up in your mind the image of a typical English seaside hotel, and there you have the Esplanade. An early Victorian building dating from 1830, it stands on a cliff, overlooking Scarborough harbour and the sea. The views from the restaurant, the terrace and the majority of the bedrooms are superb. The decor is very English, with lots of patterned wallpaper and reproduction furniture, though the restaurant, with 20 sea-view tables, is modern. The bedrooms are well furnished though the corridors have a slightly shabby feel. The hotel caters well for families with family suites and laundry facilities. Bar meals are available at lunchtimes in the Parlour bar, which overlooks the sea, and there is also a terrace with sea views. Scarborough beach is five minutes' walk away. Guests can fish from the town harbour. Pets can be accommodated by arrangement. The hotel can make arrangements for guests who want to visit the Stephen Joseph Theatre in the Round.
Walking; watersports; fishing; beach (five minutes' walk away)

SCARBOROUGH

🏨 ≋ 16/30 🏠 🕭 🍽 ▭

The Holbeck Hall Hotel, Sea Cliff Road, Scarborough
YO11 2XX   (Tel. 0723 374 374)
£53–£65 pp b&b
Once a fine 1880s Victorian mansion, now a luxury hotel,

Holbeck Hall is set high on the south cliff overlooking the sea in three acres of lawns, gardens and woodland. The most striking feature is a magnificent baronial hall complete with an enormous stone fireplace, original painted frieze, and minstrels' gallery. Many of the bedrooms overlook the sea, as do the dining room, the Rose Lounge and adjacent conservatory. Bedrooms are fitted out to a high standard. The original sumptuous decor makes this a good place for those who seek a top-class hotel on the coast with a slightly unusual country-house character. The restaurant serves good English food.

Walking; watersports; yachting; boating by arrangement; fishing (two rods on River Derwent, 25 minutes' drive away); beaches (20 minutes' walk, five minutes by car)

SEAHOUSES

The Beach House Hotel, Sea Front, Seahouses,
Northumberland NE68 7SR   (Tel. 0665 720 337)
Open April–October
£24–£29.50 pp b&b

In an enlarged and altered 1920s bungalow villa, this quiet and comfortable guest house has ravishing views of the Farne Islands. Downstairs there are two comfortable lounges and a dining room with huge picture windows making the most of the views. The bedrooms are individually decorated; only three of them face the sea. There is a large back garden, and from the green in front of the house you can see Bamburgh Castle to the north and Seahouses harbour to the south. There are regular boat trips from the harbour to the Farne Islands (and visits to Lindisfarne Priory) during the summer season. The owners say that they try to create a dignified yet laid-back atmosphere, but cannot control the dining-room stampede every evening. The food is imaginative and English, with home-baked bread, and fish dishes are a speciality. Dogs can be accommodated by prior arrangement. There is a large ground-floor room, with bathroom and ramps, that is suitable for disabled visitors.

Walking; beach; watersports (two miles away)

SEAHOUSES

🏨 8/12 🏠 👍 ✍ 🛏

The Olde Ship, Seahouses, Northumberland NE68 7RD
(Tel. 0665 720 200)
Village on the B1340
Closed December, January and part of February
£27–£32 single b&b, £38–£44 pp dinner and b&b
A stone's throw from the harbour, this 18th-century hotel,
originally built as a farmhouse, is not quite on the waterfront,
but has a nautical character all its own. There is a fantastic
collection of maritime memorabilia, collected over three
generations, which fills every spare corner of the building;
upstairs, the long gallery has a collection of model ships. Of the
public rooms, only the first-floor residents' lounge, with a fine
bay window, has harbour views. Three of the bedrooms are in
an annexe to the pub. The terraced garden, with a small putting
green, and the summer house, overlook the harbour. The
restaurant (no sea view) serves good home cooking; dinner
costs £12.50. Bar meals are also served.
Walking; fishing; beach; visits to Farne Islands bird sanctuary

SHARDLOW

🍺 🏠 👍 ✍ 🛏

Hoskins Wharf, London Road, Shardlow, Derbyshire
DE7 2GL   (Tel. 0332 792844)
On the A6, south-east of Derby
11am–11pm Mon–Sat in summer (11am–2.30pm, 6.30pm–
11pm Mon–Sat in winter); noon–3pm, 7pm–10.30pm Sun
A well-converted mill, with thick walls and original timbers,
in an attractive setting by the Trent and Mersey canal: water
actually runs underneath the restaurant. Large windows give
the clientele good views of the canal from the two bars. There
are moorings on the canal for those passing by boat who want
to stop for a drink. Meals are available in the grill room
restaurant at lunchtimes and in the evenings (main courses cost
between £6.55 and £11.75). Children are allowed into the

restaurant, but not into the bars. A motel is being built alongside the pub, which will add 28 bedrooms.

Walking along towpaths; watersports at Shardlow Marina; fishing on canal; barges can be hired next to the pub

SHARDLOW

The Old Crown, Cavendish Bridge, Shardlow, Derbyshire DE7 2HG   (Tel. 0332 792392)
Off the A6
Open 11.30am–3pm, 5.30pm–11pm Mon–Sat; noon–3pm, 7pm–10.30pm Sun
A comfortable, cosy and traditional English pub dating from the 17th century and overlooking the River Trent. The building is interesting inside, with beamed ceilings and old advertising prints on the walls. Good bar food is available at lunchtimes: as well as the standard menu, there are daily specials such as game pies (£3.75) and Mediterranean chicken in lobster sauce (£5.50). The pub offers a good range of malt whiskies and traditional beers. There is a large beer garden at the back, and plenty of car-parking space.

Walking; coarse fishing; Donnington Racing Museum

SKELWITH BRIDGE

Chesters Coffee Shop, Skelwith Bridge, nr Ambleside, Cumbria LA22 9NN   (Tel. 05394 32553)
Open 10am–5.30pm all week in summer; 10am–4.45pm all week in winter. Closed five days at the end of January
This friendly coffee shop is set in a gallery of shops by the River Brathay (which is just across the car park). There are wood-panelled walls, pine tables, a cosy wood-burning stove and burgundy festoon blinds, and a licensed restaurant is attached. It is well worth visiting for the mouth-watering cakes alone, if not for the pretty location. Hot lunches, teas and cappuccinos are also on offer. The lunchtime menu changes daily with

temptations such as chicken and asparagus sesame pie, and walnut and stilton profiteroles followed by banana toffee flan and lemon double layer cake, all at reasonable prices. You can sit outside in summer, though the tables are not directly over the water. After eating, visitors can easily spend all their money in the gift shop and the slate showroom. Tends to heave with people in the high season.

Walking; fishing

SOWERBY BRIDGE

The Moorings Inn, (Bolton Brow), Sowerby Bridge, West Yorkshire HX6 2AG   (Tel. 0422 833940)
Off the A58
Open 11.30am–3pm, 5.30pm–11pm Tues–Sat; noon–3pm, 7pm–10.30pm Sun and Mon
An unusual place, in that the surroundings smack of industry rather than leisure. The Victorian industrial buildings seem to be black with soot even now. The Moorings is a converted 1790 canalside warehouse at the canal basin between the westbound Rochdale canal and the eastbound Calder and Hebble Navigation canal. The inn was chosen as the setting for ITV's 'Stay Lucky'. Inside is a restaurant, which seats 60, and a bar. The canal is visible from both; food ranges from simple snacks through to steaks, with the daily special costing about £2.50–£8. From the bar you can see a collection of painted barges (you can also see a used–car dump, but only in the distance). You cannot hire barges from the Moorings itself but a boathouse nearby hires out barges by the week. There is wheelchair access to the inn, though the lavatory is up two steps.

Walking; fishing; barge hire nearby

SPARK BRIDGE

🏠 ⤳ ⁴ᐟ⁵ 🏘 ♿ ⬦ ▭

Bridgefield House, Spark Bridge, nr Ulverston, Cumbria
LA12 8DA   (Tel. 022985 239)
£42 pp b&b; £63 pp dinner and b&b

An elegant, 19th-century house in a pretty situation with lawns
stretching down to fields and the River Crake. The hotel has
three acres of wooded grounds and a vegetable garden which
supplies the restaurant. The decoration is comfortable but
not ostentatious, with log fires and armchairs to revive the
weary walker. The bedrooms are simply furnished and are
particularly peaceful as they do not house televisions. Mr and
Mrs Glister are very welcoming and friendly: she has been
named as one of the top five female chefs in England. Four
tables in the dining room (which seats 30) have river views.
Non-residents are welcome at dinner, which will cost them
£25. The emphasis is on local dishes, and the daily menu runs
to six mouth-watering courses, including sorbet and savouries,
followed by coffee and Kendal mint cake.

*Salmon and sea trout fishing available through hotel; windsurfing,
sailing and canoeing (bring equipment); shore beach (two miles
away); sandy beach (nine miles away)*

SPROTBOROUGH

🍺 🏘 ♨ 🍴 ▭

The Boat Inn, Sprotborough, Doncaster, West Yorkshire
DM5 7NB   (Tel. 0302 857 188)
By the bridge over the River Don at the south end of
Sprotborough village
Open 11am–3pm, 6pm–11pm Mon–Sat; noon–2.30pm, 7pm–
10.30pm Sun

The Boat Inn is situated in a secluded spot by the river, though
it is quite difficult to see the river from the inn thanks to the
high embankment. The attractive stone building was once a
farmhouse, and has its own courtyard, with tables where
guests can drink in summer. Inside there is a bar where food is

served and a separate restaurant. The bar has open stone fireplaces, and stools and wheelback chairs clustered round tables: very much the traditional country pub save for the odd garish touch which spoils the total effect. In the restaurant, main courses from the à la carte menu cost about £10 each. Barges and a water bus plough down the Don in summer. Literary sleuths may like to know that Walter Scott is said to have written *Ivanhoe* here. There is wheelchair access to the pub, and a lavatory for the disabled.

Walking; boating; fishing; Conisbrough Castle

STAMFORD BRIDGE

The Corn Mill, Main Street, Stamford Bridge YO4 1AE
(Tel. 0759 71274)
In the centre of Stamford Bridge, north-east of York on the A166
A very handsome, 18th-century industrial building on the River Derwent. Built on rock foundations, it was one of few mills to have sufficient current to drive the wheel without having to store up the water in a mill pond. Inside, one can see the original wheel and gears, grindstone and millrace. There are two bars and a restaurant, all overlooking the water. The car park looks directly on to the weir, with hundreds of ducks and pigeons. There is a good atmosphere, since so much of the original building and its oak beams remain; touches such as the coloured lights on the wheel, for example, seem a little naff by contrast. The carvery and steak bar offer food from noon to 2pm, and 7pm–10pm; the small Kiln bar has a rounded stone ceiling, completely covered with a mural of various faces and scenes. Live Country and Western music on Sundays, and a disco on Saturday nights are additional attractions. There is wheelchair access to the bars only.

Fishing (licence available from the local Post Office); pleasure boats for hire nearby

STAPLEFORD

🏨 ^{13/35} 🏠 ⚫ 🐕 ▭

Stapleford Park Hotel, Stapleford, Melton Mowbray, Leicestershire LE14 2EF　(Tel. 057 284522)
Off the B676, three miles south-east of Melton Mowbray
£126–£300 per room b&b

A Grade I listed, 16th-century building in 500 acres of parkland and woods, with fine views out over the lake. This country-house hotel is on a scale grand enough to put most of its rivals to shame, with young, extremely friendly staff. The atmosphere is surprisingly warm for such an exclusive place. There are 'signature' bedrooms, each decorated by a famous-name designer, from Turnbull and Asser to David Hicks. The bathrooms are palatial affairs in marble and mahogany with thick white towelling robes to wrap up in. The dining room seats 70 people, and the cuisine is described as 'Post Foodie', which perhaps translates best as 'a combination of styles from around the world'. Vegetables for the kitchen are grown in the walled garden. Breakfast is presented on Peter Rabbit china and is an unusually generous meal involving stilton and red Leicester soufflé and apple and raisin pancakes. Among other amusing luxuries are wellies and dogs on loan for walks in the woodland, and there is a helipad. No disabled facilities but helpful staff.
Clay pigeon shooting; stables; walking; watersports; tennis courts; croquet; mini-golf; riding can be arranged

TYNEMOUTH

🏨 ^{44/49} 🏠 ⚫ 🐕 ▭

The Park Hotel, Grand Parade, Tynemouth, Tyne and Wear NE30 4JQ　(Tel. 091 257 1406)
On the A193 sea front between Tynemouth and Cullercoats
£49.50 pp b&b; £68 executive suite

Standing proud on the clifftop above a beautiful sandy bay, this hotel retains much of its original 1930s *joie de vivre*, and boasts the finest sea-front position in Tynemouth. There are no bay views from the restaurant, though this does have a tropical aquarium, but the bar, with its curved metal windows, has a fine view. The whole hotel has recently been upgraded, so that many rooms share this view from the first and second floors. It is a popular local spot, particularly for weekend weddings, so come for the Tyneside experience, rather than for peace and quiet. Pets can be accommodated at the manager's discretion. One bedroom has a ramp and widened doors, and may suit disabled visitors.

Walking; watersports; fishing; beach; sea fishing and yachting can be arranged

ULLSWATER

Sharrow Bay Country House Hotel, Ullswater, Penrith, Cumbria CA10 2LZ   (Tel. 07684 86301)
Off the A66 (call for specific directions)
Closed December–February
£76–£140 pp dinner and b&b
Reputed to be the first country-house hotel in England, Sharrow Bay is now celebrating its 43rd year in business. The original managers still work alongside dedicated staff with a policy to 'nurture, nourish, cosset and care for' their welcomed customers. The hotel is a 17th-century converted farmhouse with grounds leading to the lake shore. The views from the main reception room look like a perfect picture, framed in the window. There is plenty to look at within the rooms apart from the views; chandeliers, old prints, dolls in dolls' chairs, a pretty conservatory, and a fireplace bought from Warwick Castle. Rooms in the Lodge and Bankhouse are more spacious with sitting areas to relax in. In the baroque-style breakfast room, converted from the old barn, guests sit at long tables on high-backed tapestry chairs. The dining room seats 65 people, with 15 tables overlooking the water. Non-residents are welcome at dinner (from £38.50), which is a lavish six courses, with a good selection for a set menu. There are no special disabled facilities but there is a downstairs bedroom.

Walking; watersports; fishing; lake beach

ULVERSTON

inn ~~~ 5/6 🛶 🍴 ⬦ 💳

Bay Horse Inn and Bistro, Canal Foot, Ulverston, Cumbria
LA12 9EL   (Tel. 0229 53972)
Follow signs to Canal Foot off the A590, the Barrow to
Greenodd road
Pub open 11am–11pm Mon–Sat; noon–3pm, 7pm–10.30pm
Sun. Restaurant closed Sun, and Mon lunch
Closed January and February
£60–£70 pp dinner and b&b

The approach to this wonderful inn on Morecambe Bay is
unpromising – through a chemical industrial estate – but
persevere. You will find a cosy pub with coal fires, old horse
brasses, and plates and dried flowers on the walls. Two
hundred years old, the building was originally a row of
fishermen's cottages with a small brewery and pub attached.
The new bedrooms all have their own patio and French
windows. The Bistro has a different atmosphere; most of it is
in a light conservatory overlooking the estuary. Chef Robert
Lyons used to work at the Miller Howe and people travel from
far afield to sample his cuisine and his general *joie de vivre*. His
policy is to produce quality English food using as much local
produce as possible. Children over 12 are allowed in the
restaurant, which seats 50 people. The set lunch costs £12.50;
dinner main courses cost £15 to £18. There is just one dinner
sitting: 7.30pm for 8pm. The clientele is half business from the
chemical works and half visitors who have come to check out
the good reputation of the inn for themselves. Intrepid
adventurers can test their nerves as there are guided tours over
the quicksands when the tide is out. There is wheelchair access
and a lavatory for disabled visitors.

*Walking; sea trout and salmon fishing (bring equipment); visits to
famous crystal factory in Ulverston which supplies all the British
embassies around the world*

WALTON

🏠 31/31 🏊 🚴 🚫 ▭

The Waterton Park Hotel, Walton Hall, Walton, Wakefield
WF2 6PW   (Tel. 0924 257 911)
Off the A61, the Wakefield to Barnsley road
£75 single, £97 double b&b
The hotel is a beautiful 1764 building, situated on a small island
in the middle of a lake surrounded by fine countryside, though
slightly spoiled by a range of modern squash courts built
opposite the entrance, and a modern leisure centre attached to
the back of the hotel. However, it is a very comfortable place to
stay with all modern conveniences and wonderful views over
the lake from all the public rooms. Inside the decor is fairly
anonymous, although some of the original plasterwork
survives. The restaurant seats 60; most tables have lake views.
Two menus are on offer, one at £15 for five courses including a
choice of a roast, fish, steak and a vegetarian dish, or a larger
selection of courses for £22. The coffee shop serves sandwiches, spaghetti and snacks which can be consumed on the
waterside patio next to the barbecue.
Indoor swimming pool, sauna, spa bath, solarium, gymnasium and
steam room; squash; fly fishing on lake (equipment can be hired);
walking; watersports with tuition on reservoir nearby (windsurfing,
sailing and canoeing) – advance booking available

WATERMILLOCK-ON-ULLSWATER

🏠 15/19 🏊 🚴 🐾 ▭

Rampsbeck Country House Hotel, Watermillock-on-
Ullswater, Cumbria CA11 0LP   (Tel. 07684 86442)
Fifteen minutes from Junction 40 of the M6 (call for precise
directions)
Closed January–February
£35–£45 pp b&b, £58–£70 pp dinner and b&b
A very pretty, comfortable, early 18th-century country-house
hotel, standing in 18 acres of parkland and gardens on the shore
of Lake Ullswater, with its own meadow running down to the
lake. There is a beautiful, well-kept garden: in summer, the

French windows of the drawing room open on to it for evening strolls. The main reception rooms are decorated in warm floral prints, while the bedrooms continue the flowery theme but in a lighter tone. Some of these rooms have magnificent views of garden, marina and lake together, and three rooms have balconies overlooking the lake. The dining room seats 40; non-residents are welcome at dinner (set dinner £27), which is based on award-winning modern classical English and French cookery, with ideas such as a 'Symphony of Seafood' followed by hot mango soufflé. Packed lunches can be made up for guests (£6), and special diets can be catered for. Children can be accommodated by arrangement. The management need prior warning if you are to be accompanied by four-legged friends – and they will be charged £2 per night.

Walking; fishing; watersports (hotel has its own marina; bring own equipment, no waterskiing); yacht tuition and charter £50 a day; beach; lake trips available

WHITBY

inn ³/³ 🏠 ✗ ◁ ▱

The Duke of York Inn, 124 Church Street, Whitby
YO22 4DE   (Tel. 0947 600 324)
Open 11am–11pm Mon–Sat May–October (11am–3pm,
7pm–11pm Mon–Sat November–April); noon–3pm, 7pm–
10.30pm Sun
£24 double (room only, no breakfast available)
The Esk Estuary is an area that is swimming in history and curious tales of bygone times. Captain James Cook sailed from the harbour on his voyage to the South Pacific; Bram Stoker wrote the original Dracula story here; and Church Street in the past has been the haunt of smugglers, whalers and press gangs. The Duke of York Inn is at the foot of a Norman abbey, and overlooks the picturesque harbour, with some of the best views in Whitby. A traditional pub, and apparently a favourite haunt of local fishermen, it is well known for its excellent beers; John Smith's cask-conditioned Yorkshire Bitter, Courage, Directors and Magnet Ale among others. The bar

food features plenty of local fish and crabs, fresh from the market opposite. The rooms are unsophisticated but pretty, but be warned, guests have to venture outside to find their own breakfast in one of the nearby cafés.

Walking; watersports; jetskiing; waterskiing; boating; fishing at the end of the pier (parties of fishermen can be taken out to sea very early in the morning, £20 pp); beach just below hotel

WHITBY

🍽 ♿ 🚭 🐾 💳

The Magpie Café, 14 Pier Road, Whitby YO21 3JN
(Tel. 0947 602 058)
Distinctive black and white building by the harbour
Open 11.30am–6.30pm mid March–November

A delightful restaurant, not unlike a country teashop inside and out. The Magpie is a simple, modestly furnished establishment with excellent, good-value food and seating for 100. It was built in 1750 as a private home, converted into a restaurant in 1937, and has been run by three generations of the same family since 1950. The menu is dominated by all varieties of fish (fresh off the boats) and chips, with plenty of options for weight-watchers. A three-course meal costs from £6.50. An ideal place for a family outing as there are children's menus, high chairs, baby-changing facilities and toy boxes. Sit upstairs by the window for the picturesque sea view with fishing boats chugging in and out of the harbour. No disabled facilities but helpful staff.

Boat hire from harbour; fishing parties in mid-summer; marina and yachting club; fishing; fossil and jet hunting; 'Dracula' trails; swimming; sunbathing; walking; waterskiing in harbour; sandy beach (two minutes' walk)

WHITEWELL

inn ~5/10~ 🏠 🍴 ◁ ▭

The Inn at Whitewell, Forest of Bowland, nr Clitheroe,
Lancashire BB7 3AT   (Tel. 02008 222)
Village in the Forest of Bowland
Bar open 11am–3pm, 6pm–11pm Mon–Sat; noon–3pm, 7pm–
10.30pm Sun
£43–£49 single, £57–£63 double b&b
An ancient inn, dating from 1380, with lawns stretching down
to the River Hodder, deep in the country but close to main
cities. The sport of orienteering was devised and originated in
the surrounding forest. The atmosphere is unpretentious, the
staff are friendly and the overall feeling is of a comfortable
country home. The superb, newly refurbished rooms have
beautiful views, and seriously good (Bang & Olufsen) sound
systems, and local artists' work is displayed on the walls. The
large dining room has river views, specializes in local game and
lamb (dinner costs about £20), and offers an extensive wine list.
Hearty bar meals are also served, rounded off with home-made
puddings or 'a confusing selection of little-known British
cheeses'. The Tap Room bar overlooks the water and houses
pub games. The owner, Mr Bowman, has set up something of
a cottage industry, producing wine, shoes, shirts, and shooting
stockings which are all sold on the premises, alongside other
quality goods. No facilities for the disabled, though there is
access to the restaurant, bar and garden areas.
*Walking; fishing nearby (hotel has six miles of fishing rights: sea
trout, £11 a day; salmon, £25 a day; equipment available), and
fishing tuition can be arranged; clay pigeon shooting, pheasant and
grouse shooting arranged for parties (bring equipment)*

WINDERMERE

🏨 ~25/31~ 🏠 🍴 ◁ ▭
Langdale Chase Hotel, Windermere, Cumbria
LA23 1LW   (Tel. 05394 32201/32604)
Off the A591, the Windermere to Ambleside road
£44–£56.50 pp b&b

A Victorian country house, built in 1896 by a Manchester cotton merchant, and turned into a hotel in 1933. It is a beautiful building, set in four acres of landscaped gardens on the edge of Lake Windermere, though unfortunately spoilt on the outside by modernizing of the windows. The interior feels very Victorian, with a grand imitation of a panelled medieval hall–gallery, and a real log fire in the reception hall. Two of the rooms have four-poster beds, and in addition to the hotel rooms there is a garden bungalow available. The dining room seats 60 people, with 12 tables overlooking the lake (set lunch £9.50, Sunday lunch £10.50, set dinner £19.95). Bar lunches are available, and cost from £2. Guests have the use of a leisure club nearby, where there is a swimming pool, spa bath, gym, squash courts and table tennis. Single room on ground level for disabled use.

Croquet; two grass tennis courts; two rowing boats for residents' use; two jetties and boathouse; walking; watersports; fishing

WINDERMERE

Miller Howe Hotel, Rayrigg Road, Windermere, Cumbria
LA23 1EY   (Tel. 05394 42536)
Off the A592
Open March–December
£81–£136 pp dinner and b&b

A very comfortable and well-thought-out hotel, built in 1916, with a fine terrace, three lounges and a conservatory all overlooking the lake. The decor is interesting, with collections of plates on the walls, and flying golden cherubs above the stairs. The rooms have good stereos with classical music, rather than televisions, and puzzles and books: room prices vary with view, and bookings need to be made two months in advance. The dining room, with an attractive mural, seats 70 people. Sixteen tables have a lake view (most of these tables go to residents). John Tovey's English country cooking is widely renowned; dinner is at 8pm for 8.30pm (from £30), and the menu changes daily. There is now a new conservatory-lounge

overlooking the lake, where teas and coffee are served. No direct access to lake from hotel grounds. Packed lunches can be made for guests, and special diets can be catered for.
Walking; watersports and fishing nearby; cookery courses

YORK

🍽 🏠 ♿ ◇ ▭

The Bonding Warehouse, Skeldergate, York YO1 1DH
(Tel. 0904 622527)
On the west side of Skeldergate bridge
Open 11am–11pm, Easter–October; closed 2.30pm–6pm, October–Easter
The Bonding Warehouse was originally just that – a place of storage for cargo brought up the Ouse and for produce of York to be transported out via the river. The original cargo chutes used to get the sacks from floor to floor are still in the building. Inside are a restaurant, tastefully styled allowing one to see the original features like columns and brickwork, and three bars, with great views of the river and Cliffords Tower opposite. In summer guests can eat and drink on the balcony overlooking the river. The Bonding Warehouse's speciality is live jazz – always at weekends and sometimes throughout the week too – in the Riverside Bar and restaurant, so you can eat your dinner on the balcony overlooking the river while the voice of a female jazz singer wafts out from the restaurant. The reasonably priced bistro food costs from £5 to £15.

YORK

🏨 73/138 🏠 ♿ ◇ ▭

The Viking Hotel, North Street, York YO1 1JF
(Tel. 0904 659822)
By Ouse bridge
£85 single, £105 double b&b
The Viking Hotel is a perfectly good hotel of its kind: modern, big, efficient with all the facilities you could need. But as with other hotels of this kind it does lack personality. However, it is

right on the River Ouse and many of the bedrooms, the Regatta restaurant (à la carte) and the Garden Court restaurant (set dinner £13.50) all look over the water; the lounge enjoys views of York. The hotel has its own moorings on the water below and can arrange for large parties of people to take boat rides down the Ouse from the hotel. A comfortable modern hotel to use as a base to discover York, but don't expect it to reflect York's history. There is a gym, sauna and solarium for guests' use, and themed evenings are a speciality.

Health and leisure club; walking; fishing; own moorings just below hotel, can arrange for large parties

Index

Europe by Train 1993

Katie Wood and George McDonald

The bestselling classic, recommended by *EUROTRAIN*

Europe by Train is still the best value and most comprehensive book on the market for eurorailers. It contains all the essential, practical information required by students and those on a tight budget:

- Maximizing the benefits of rail passes
- Train networks and station facilities
- The best routes
- Local transport
- What to see
- Where to sleep
- What to eat
- Where the nightlife is

In addition to being fully revised and updated for 1993, this year's new edition of *Europe by Train* includes even more information on eastern Europe, plus details of all new passes and tickets.

'Excellent . . . a reliable guide to the systems of all European countries' *Independent*

Fontana

On the Waterfront in France 1993

Telegraph Magazine Guide to Hotels,
Restaurants and Cafés

Edited by Gill Charlton

On the Waterfront in France is the definitive guide to eating, drinking and sleeping beside the sea and on the banks of lakes, rivers and canals throughout France. It contains detailed descriptions of over 600 waterside hotels, guesthouses, restaurants and cafés, each one personally inspected by our team of researchers.

- More than 350 family-run hotels and restaurants, including many converted watermills, and over 30 château-hotels and private châteaux
- Good value, seaside hotels, perfect for family holidays, from Brittany to the French Riviera
- Special emphasis on places to stay and eat in the Loire Valley and along the Dordogne and Lot rivers
- Seductive waterside restaurants off the autoroutes, with directions on how to reach them

This guide also contains useful information on sightseeing, good sandy beaches, boat trips and many sporting opportunities including fishing, cycling, canoeing and riding. With maps to help you on your way, *On the Waterfront in France* will prove an invaluable travelling companion – whatever your budget.

Fontana